The Oprah Affect

The Oprah Affect

Critical Essays on
Oprah's Book Club

Edited by
Cecilia Konchar Farr
and
Jaime Harker

STATE UNIVERSITY OF NEW YORK PRESS

Published by
State University of New York Press, Albany

© 2008 State University of New York

For information, contact State University of New York Press, Albany, NY
www.sunypress.edu

Production by Kelli W. LeRoux
Marketing by Anne M. Valentine

Library of Congress Cataloging in Publication Data

The Oprah affect : critical essays on Oprah's book club / edited by
Cecilia Konchar Farr and Jaime Harker.
    p. cm.
  Includes bibliographical references and index.
  ISBN 978-0-7914-7615-4 (hardcover : alk. paper)
  ISBN 978-0-7914-7616-1 (pbk. : alk. paper) 1. Book clubs (Discussion
groups)—United States. 2. Books and reading—United States.
3. Literature and society—United States. 4. Winfrey, Oprah—Influence.
5. Oprah Winfrey show. I. Farr, Cecilia Konchar, 1958– II. Harker, Jaime.

LC6651.O67 2008
374'.22—dc22

                                                              2008000120

10 9 8 7 6 5 4 3 2 1

For Gloria Cronin,
who first invited us to become professors,
and for Feminist Home Evening,
where we invited one another to be scholars and activists.

CONTENTS

ACKNOWLEDGMENTS

Cecilia wishes to thank the students at College of St. Catherine. They goaded me into reading with Oprah and continue to push me to think differently and better. Others at St. Kate's deserve my thanks as well—President Andrea Lee and Senior Vice-President Colleen Hegranes, who funded the trip that brought this collection together, my colleagues in Women's Studies and English, and the Corps de Catherine, who keep me going—and going. I also want to thank Jane Bunker, Fran Keneston, Kelli Williams LeRoux, and Larin McLaughlin of SUNY Press who have been delightful to work with over the past five years. As always, I thank Mum, the ever-growing Konchar clan, and the Konchar-Farrs, puppies included, for keeping me firmly planted in the wonderful messiness of life. And finally, thanks to Jaime, who embodies the best of colleague and friend.

Jaime wishes to thank her colleagues in the English department at the University of Mississippi, the College of Liberal Arts for funding research trips to Minnesota, and the former chair of the English department, Joseph Urgo, for his support of this project. I am grateful to my parents for their continued interest and support, and, as always, to my family: Alida, Grace, William, and Jack. Finally, thanks to Cecilia, for inviting me to apply my interest in interwar middlebrow culture to the contemporary work.

We both wish to thank the presses of University of Arkansas ("Everything Old Is New Again") and State University of New York ("Talking Readers"), as well as *Modern Fiction Studies* ("Beware the Furrow of the Middlebrow") and *The International Journal of Popular Culture* ("Oprah's Book Club and the Politics of Cross-Racial Empathy") for permission to reprint chapters previously published with them. Finally, we want to thank our contributors, whose ideas and insights brought this collection together.

INTRODUCTION

JAIME HARKER AND
CECILIA KONCHAR FARR

Oprah's Book Club has officially crossed over; it is now an academic, as well as a cultural, phenomenon. In the last five years, a small but significant number of essays on Oprah's Book Club have appeared in academic journals, including the *African-American Review, International Journal of Cultural Studies, College English,* and *Modern Fiction Studies.* The first book-length study, by Cecilia Konchar Farr, *Reading Oprah: How Oprah's Book Club Changed the Way America Reads,* was published in 2004 (SUNY), followed closely by *Reading with Oprah: The Book Club That Changed America* by Kathleen Rooney (Arkansas 2005). The recent *The Oprah Phenomenon* (Kentucky 2007) has a section dedicated to study of the Book Club. And here you are reading *The Oprah Affect.*

This growing academic attention is heartening. It certainly took literary scholars and critics a while to notice what publishers, writers, librarians, and readers began, as early as 1997, to call the most important influence on literacy in the past fifty years. Unfortunately, when we turn our attention to Oprah, literary scholars tend to identify the Book Club as a media phenomenon rather than a literary one, or as an unprecedented merger of literature and commercialism. It is much more.

Oprah's Book Club is, in fact, the latest in a series of reading events that highlight a long-standing debate about the definition and purpose of literature in American culture. This debate pits readers who want books that engage them emotionally or socially against those who seek books grounded in shared aesthetic or national values. Over the last two hundred years, the tension has grown between the sentimental and the formal, the passionate

1

and the dispassionate, the commercially successful and the underappreciated. Early on, novels became rich fodder for the debate because they could provide access to both the affective and the aesthetic, an emotional connection and an experience of individual delight. While underappreciated novels are well represented in most formulations of the American literary canon, other novels, often lost to today's readers, represent a shadow tradition, always present in those formulations but not frequently acknowledged except as foils. In this shadow tradition, readers are drawn to literature's affect. They value novels they can take personally, novels that can speak to, challenge or transform their lives, novels that entertain them with lively stories or call them into political or social awareness, even action.

Though these conflicting literary desires certainly cross national boundaries, they are particularly striking in an American context. The surprising success of Susanna Rowson's *Charlotte Temple*, often cited as the first American novel, is illustrative. Here was a seduction novel so real to its readers that they had to invent a gravesite at which to grieve their cherished fictional heroine (Davidson xiii). By the mid-nineteenth century, enthusiasm for this kind of affective novel-reading had become so pervasive in the United States that Abraham Lincoln is said to have teasingly given the novelist Harriet Beecher Stowe credit for starting the Civil War.[1] But *Uncle Tom's Cabin* is only the most famous of a host of politically charged sentimental novels, including slave narratives and captivity tales, which have inspired readers, especially women readers, over the last two centuries.[2]

In the first half of the twentieth century, for example, the *Woman's Home Companion* became the most successful women's magazine of its day, with a circulation of about one million, because its editor, Gertrude Lane, was a particularly avid patron of popular writers like Dorothy Canfield, Pearl Buck, Edna Ferber, Kathleen Norris, and Willa Cather.[3] These women novelists tended to operate outside the cutting-edge modernist milieu that has come to define that age in literary studies. They freely used mainstream institutions, like women's magazines and the Book-of-the-Month Club, to connect with their readers. And it worked; existing fan letters demonstrate the devotion readers had for such novelists.[4]

Feminist consciousness-raising novels of the 1970s represent another manifestation of this affective tradition; writers such as Marge Piercy, Alice Walker, Audre Lorde, Rita Mae Brown, and Marilyn French encouraged their women readers to rethink their lives and reframe their politics, and their readers took up the challenge in informal "CR" groups. The politics of these novels became more radical than those of the novels of the early twentieth century, but the central faith that fiction could challenge, transform, and change one's life remained.[5]

Indeed, as long as there has been a novel in the United States, critics and authors have railed against what they characterized as the effeminate influence of women's reading and writing communities, a group Nathaniel Hawthorne, in an 1855 letter, famously dubbed "that damned mob of scribbling women." Jane Tompkins's formulation of the debate, in her landmark essay "Sentimental Power," resonates across two centuries; canonical literary study, she writes, has taught "generations of students to equate popularity with debasement, emotionality with ineffectiveness, religiosity with fakery, domesticity with triviality, and all of these, implicitly, with womanly inferiority" (123). Even when men were the readers or the writers (as many have been all along), they suffered from association with this tradition.[6]

Observers of Oprah's Book Club will certainly find this feminized shadow tradition familiar—the enthusiastic embracing of novels, the passionate identification with characters and social causes, and the sense of connection readers feel with their favorite writers.[7] They will also recognize the critical disdain for all things popular and feminine.[8] Oprah, in other words, is a landmark literary influence in contemporary society, but she is not an unprecedented one. In the context of American literary history, Oprah's Book Club stands, not as an egregious undermining of who we are and what we represent, but as the latest manifestation of a long tradition that deploys affect, affinity, accessibility, and activism in the symbiotic relationships of readers and texts. Powered by women writers and readers, it attracts crowds, sells well, and makes unabashed appeals to emotion.

This characteristic in particular, the appeal to emotion, has been a flashpoint in discussions of the aesthetic value of novels. Immersed in the human condition as a generic imperative, the novel must count strong emotional response as a generic hazard. When readers were reduced to tears reading Stowe or Dickens, that was, for them, a sign of a good novel. For the critics, it was a mark of inferiority—in Dickens's case, a minor misstep for an otherwise competent novelist, in Stowe's, the manifestation of her failure as an artist. It was much smarter to avoid emotional responses altogether, with the stoicism of the naturalists or the modernists. Yet Oprah's insistence on the value of emotion to reading has been characteristic of her Book Club from its first meeting in November 1996, when readers encountered what Oprah called a "mother's worst nightmare," a child abduction, in Jacqueline Mitchard's *Deep End of the Ocean*. While critics have suggested that focusing on emotional (or, in Farr's formulation, empathic) response is to be immersed in a therapeutic, as opposed to a literary, environment, Oprah's Book Club regularly uses novels as a way to link emotion and intellect. Indeed, the very notion that these are two mutually exclusive modes is part of an Enlightenment inheritance that feminists have long critiqued for its gendered assumptions. Similarly, the critical rejection of emotion as sentimental has been a defining characteristic of the "literary" since that category was applied to novels, but especially since the modernist movement.

If the move toward emotion is specious, Oprah's next characteristic move, to reshape individual emotions into communal experiences, is even more suspect. The experience of Oprah's Book Club—its emphasis on affinity with other readers and with Oprah—has been a stumbling block for critics, who traditionally tend to think of reading as a private expression of personal taste. To consider reading a communal experience inspires suspicion; Orwellian groupthink, inspired by consumer capitalism, may erase individuality, replacing it with a repressive, unitary mode of reading. Sales of books through big box retailers and bookstore chains had already raised this specter when millions of readers began reading the same book because Oprah said to.

But social reading is also a defining characteristic of the shadow tradition of literature, beginning in earnest with the nineteenth-century women's club movement and coming to flower with the recent phenomenal popularity of book clubs across the United States. These communities of readers have been distinguished by women's passion around books, as sociologist Elizabeth Long demonstrated in her recent study, *Book Clubs*. She notes that "by looking at women's reading groups . . . one can see people in the process of creating new connections, new meanings, and new relationships—to the characters in the books or their authors, to themselves, to the other members of the group, to the society and culture in which they live" (22). Oprah's Book Club carefully followed its book club predecessors in format. Not only did it insist on connection through sisterly bonding and shared personal insights for all of its readers, but the smaller meetings of Oprah and the author with four or five chosen readers were regularly filmed in a studio that resembled a living room, with large comfortable chairs and couches and the remains of a shared dinner off to the side.

Long's book and several studies of reading practices before it have dramatically reshaped how literary scholars think about reading. Beginning with Janice Radway's *Reading the Romance*, reception historians have shown how reading is defined by cultural mores. The meaning of texts, in other words, is defined not by the words themselves but by the community of readers who construct that text—and this is as true of self-consciously literary communities like college classrooms as of book clubs in neighborhoods, at churches, or in gay and lesbian community centers. Reading, these critics argue, has always been social and communal, and the cultural work of fiction, to borrow Jane Tompkins's phrase, has engaged readers in larger social questions. The tenet that novels are an act of communication as well as of artistic creation is central to reception theory. Perhaps even more than poetry or short stories, a novel's structure is embedded in a larger culture. To emphasize the social and communal aspects of novel, then, is not to corrupt it, but to honor its tradition and history.

With their emphasis on what occupies "the general reader," reception studies also lead to questions about access. The legacy of the myth of the Romantic artist, the assumption that true art is by and for the privileged few and not the philistine masses, was reinvigorated by influential factions of modernists and postmodernists in the twentieth century. The critical stance that "if too many people like it, it can't be good" is, in many ways, a response to the rise of consumer culture and anxiety around that culture's effect on literature.[9] Though Oprah's Book Club tangled with literary value, moving to an all-classics format for several years (2003–2005) before returning to contemporary best sellers, it clearly grows out of a tradition that values art as a meaningful, indeed essential, part of many people's lives. A best-selling novel is, in this formulation, a best-*loved* novel, one that speaks to a wide audience and constructs a communal experience. We propose here that there may, indeed, be an art to accessibility, one that literary critics haven't yet examined fully.

Critics have also found rich fields for exploration in the activism that sometimes results from these powerful social connections around shared texts. The move toward multiculturalism in college curricula in the late twentieth century, for example, sprang from the belief that students could better negotiate cultural barriers if they could vicariously experience gender and racial difference through reading. Bridging these differences has also been an overt agenda of Oprah's Book Club, from its second meeting where the shared text for the predominantly white audience was Toni Morrison's *Song of Solomon* to a more recent meeting around Sidney Poitier's memoir, *The Measure of a Man.* As many of the chapters in this volume attest, Oprah's intervention into American letters is profoundly evangelical; not only does she insist her that her audience confront personal and social issues (race and gender in particular), but she was also never coy about wanting the Book Club to accomplish nothing less than a transformation of Americans' leisure habits, from mass media back to print culture. Oprah's right to claim this authority to transform lives, literature, and culture has been a recurring question for cultural critics, but her intention is, again, consistent with the history of the novel.

The chapters in this collection investigate these interlocking issues of affect, affinity, accessibility, and activism with originality and vigor. Juxtaposing book history, reading practices, literary analysis, feminist criticism, communication, and political, religious, and cultural studies, the authors map an exciting range and possibilities for future research on Oprah's Book Club.

Juliette Wells and Virginia Wells's "Oprah in the Public Library" looks at Oprah's effect on library patrons and their book selections. A literary critic and a librarian, the authors use the Fairfax County Public Library in northern Virginia as a case study of the Oprah effect, how the Book Club's choices affected libraries and gave librarians new inroads for expanding readership. They offer conclusions on how librarians (and others) can use these best-loved Oprah novels as lessons for buying, displaying, and recommending books, thus increasing their accessibility.

In "Talking Readers," a chapter from *Reading Oprah*, Cecilia Konchar Farr emphasizes that, in reading for connection, Oprah's Book Club reignited the novel's "talking life" by involving readers in conversations about books. Starting with Oprah's encounter with Jonathan Franzen, Farr offers an alternate view of literary value that cherishes emotional as well as intellectual engagement. Oprah's reading practices are valuable, she argues, *because* they build on readers' current consumption practices.

In "Reading Religiously: The Ritual Practices of Oprah's Book Club," Kathryn Lofton analyzes how Oprah's Book Club uses rituals of affinity to construct a community of readers. The "aha" moment is the key to transformation through the Book Club, she argues; reading communally and religiously helps to solve readers' personal dilemmas. These reading practices create an imperative for activism; after reading with the Book Club or watching Oprah, Lofton concludes, "it seems imperative to *do* something."

Yung-Hsing Wu is also interested in the communal potential of Oprah's Book Club. In "The Romance of Reading Like Oprah," she examines the ethics of reading practices on the Book Club and Oprah's emphasis on "what books can do for us." By examining online discussions of selected books, she concludes that Oprah's Book Club creates a communal experience for reading without standardizing that experience.

R. Mark Hall, too, finds value in the varied and often emotional responses of readers, on television and on the related message boards, to three Oprah novels, *Where the Heart Is, The Reader,* and *The Bluest Eye.* In his chapter, "Oprah's Book Selections: Teleliterature for *The Oprah Winfrey Show,*" Hall analyzes how Oprah's Book Club provides a forum for reading that is grounded not just in optimism, but in ethics.

Michael Perry's "Resisting Paradise: Toni Morrison, Oprah Winfrey, and the Middlebrow Audience" provides a detailed study of the Book Club meeting around Toni Morrison's *Paradise,* a complex and difficult book that challenged Oprah readers. Perry contrasts the reading conventions of book clubs with the reading conventions of the classroom, and analyzes how *Paradise* abandoned the egalitarian nature of book clubs for a more hierarchical lesson led by experts. This betrayal of trust, in Perry's formulation, highlights the contradiction between Winfrey's emphasis on affinity and readerly pleasure and penchant for education.

Returning to the idea of affect and connection, Kimberly Chabot Davis argues in "Oprah's Book Club and the Politics of Cross-Racial Empathy" that emotions are essential, not antithetical, to political action. Rooting her analysis in the Book Club's televised encounters of white women with black fiction, Davis argues that critics would do well to reconsider their disdain for the sentimental and recognize that "such cross-racial empathetic identifications in the private sphere could play a crucial role in galvanizing support for anti-racist public policy in America." Affect, then, for Davis, leads to activism.

Timothy Aubry's "Beware the Furrow of the Middlebrow: Searching for Toni Morrison's *Paradise* on *The Oprah Winfrey Show*" demonstrates that reading in community holds a similar utopic promise to that of Morrison's fictional community. At once difficult and accessible, *Paradise* requires "a kind of hard labor that will not thwart but rather attract readers, and that the labor will continue even when the book ends." Rather than violating the conventions of book clubs, as Perry argues, *Paradise* represents the height of the communal book club experience, providing a bridge between serious literature and middlebrow culture.

Ana Patricia Rodríguez continues this interest in race and Oprah's Book Club in "Did Isabel Allende Write this Book for Me?" Analyzing both Allende's *Daughter of Fortune* and the discussion of the novel on Oprah's Book Club, Rodriguez challenges the mass-media construction of multiculturalism and its easy move toward individualism and the preeminent value of self-made fortunes. Oprah's Book Club, in this case, erased difference by mainstreaming an American success story, but also, even if inadvertently, provided openings for unintended valences of difference.

Kelley Penfield Lewis, in her careful observation of two Book Club programs, *House of Sand and Fog* and *Drowning Ruth*, notes a similar flattening of differences in Oprah's Book Club. She observes the constraints of Oprah's reading practices and contrasts them with those of professional literary critics. Her conclusion considers not only what we might learn from the success of the Book Club but also what the dominance of Oprah's reading practices could mean for our larger literate culture.

Kate Douglas's "Your Book Changed My Life: Everyday Literary Criticism and Oprah's Book Club" argues that the Book Club, by putting the everyday reader front and center, has joined forces with other contemporary cultural practices (customer comments on amazon.com, for example) to challenge the hegemony of professional literary critics to decide what books are best. In contrast to Lewis, Douglas celebrates the "everyday literary criticism" of Oprah's Book Club as empowering to nonprofessional readers.

Returning with careful attention to Oprah's encounter with Jonathan Franzen, Kevin Quirk's "Correcting Oprah: Jonathan Franzen and the Uses of Literature in the Therapeutic Age" posits that the eruption of this conflict exposed a broader cultural resistance to the Book Club's "therapeutic multiculturalism." Franzen's anxiety about American culture as therapeutic and multicultural preceded *The Corrections*, but his "solution," to value literature as the only effective therapy, linked him with Oprah in surprising and uncomfortable ways. Franzen's careful reconstructions of *The Corrections* suggest that he has more in common with Oprah's Book Club than he let on in his public comments, and complicates the opposition of "therapeutic" and "literary" on which his Oprah rejection depended.

Simon Stow considers the democratic implications of reading in "The Way We Read Now: Oprah Winfrey, Intellectuals, and Democracy." By contrasting Oprah's reading practices with those modeled by democracy champions like Martha Nussbaum, Richard Rorty, and Gayatri Spivak, Stow suggests that Oprah's Book Club, with its emphasis on discussion rather than debate, and conversation rather than correct interpretation, is a better reading practice to inspire insight and empathy in the practice of liberal democracy. Its accessibility and inspiration to activism make it a crucial literary intervention in American culture.

Kathleen Rooney's "Everything Old Is New Again: Oprah's Book Club Returns with the Classics," an excerpt from *Reading with Oprah*, examines Oprah's move from contemporary fiction to classics and what that move revealed about the divide between highbrow and lowbrow literature. Oprah's refusal to define a "classic," Rooney suggests, is a democratic impulse that views culture not as fixed but as fluid and interactive.

Finally, Jaime Harker's Afterword "Oprah, James Frey, and the Problem of the Literary" considers a more recent crisis of Oprah's Book Club: James Frey's falsified memoir. Frey's deception, Harker argues, was an addiction to the literary modes of masculinity, modes that contradict the basic assumptions of Oprah's Book Club. Oprah's selection of the text reflects her own struggles with establishing her authority in the Book Club, and suggests that her activist impulse has been thwarted by repeated attacks. An articulation of her own gendered literary and activist agenda, Harker suggests, could help avoid pretentiously masculine fantasies like *A Million Little Pieces*.

In these chapters, common themes about Oprah's Book Club emerge— its emphasis on emotion; its insistence on personalizing the novel; its interest in novels as fodder for issues; its general avoidance of the formal qualities of a text; its focus on Oprah as a prism for experience; its opposition to the literary establishment; its primary focus as didactic and therapeutic. But the chapters also share a healthy disagreement about the aims and effects of Oprah's Book Club.

Timothy Aubry finds the difficulty of *Paradise* an inspiring example of what Oprah's Book Club can do for readers, while Michael Perry sees it a betrayal of the trust and egalitarianism that had marked the book club thus far. Kelley Lewis finds the disconnect between online chat rooms and the television show of Oprah's Book Club a disturbing example of how the Book Club's reading practices forestall other interpretations, while R. Mark Hall reads this same difference as a positive example of how readers can gain a variety of benefits from the Book Club beyond the standard message. Kimberly Davis finds Oprah's encouragement of cross-racial empathy a compelling model for political activism, while Ana Patricia Rodríguez is concerned about a sanitized multiculturalism replacing the complex and persistent reality of institutional racism. Simon Stow contrasts the monolithic readings of professional literary critics unfavorably with the open-ended conversation of Book Club participants, while Kevin Quirk's chapter undermines the distinction between "literary" and "therapeutic" on which Stow's comparison depends. Cecilia Konchar Farr and Simon Stow find Oprah's Book Club an inspiring model for cultural democracy; Kathryn Lofton reads it as a consciously religious construction of community; Kathleen Rooney sees a mindful embrace of fluid cultural boundaries; Kate Douglas celebrates an affinity for the ordinary readers; Juliette and Virginia Wells note a dramatic increase in reading. And while Farr, Lofton, Wu, Douglas, and Hall all find the reading practices of Oprah's Book Club empowering for individual readers, Lewis, Perry, and Rodriguez are concerned about how these reading practices may leave readers at the mercy of an ideology of empowerment that actually obscures real oppressions.

These differences are a strength of the collection, we believe, because they demonstrate the diversity of Oprah's Book Club—its book selections, its television portrayals, its readers, and its aims. The chapters' conclusions depend very much upon which episode(s), and which book(s), they focus on. Indeed, simple summaries about the purpose, nature, and consequences of Oprah's Book Club become increasingly untenable the more one reads both critical essays and the books and episodes that inspire them. Oprah's Book Club is a complex cultural phenomenon that cannot be simply described or dismissed, and it invites futures investigation and study.

We would like this collection to challenge literary critics to confront Oprah's Book Club as part of an ongoing and important American literary tradition that has been coded as sentimental. Literary critics have thwarted the development of the culture of the book in America because we have tended to marginalize the books people love. Anxiety about America's ability to foster great art has been a dominant critical mode since Van Wyck Brooks wrote "America's Coming of Age" in 1915. But if we are so afraid of our cultural heritage being defined by the shallow consumerist values of McDonald's or Wal-Mart that we don't claim movements like Oprah's Book Club, we lose the chance to investigate and appreciate the unique American literary culture we have. This mass cultural, consumerist, social engagement with literature is an essential part of the American literary tradition, and *The Oprah Affect* seeks to articulate and even embrace that vibrant, accessible tradition.

Notes

1. For more on Harriet Beecher Stowe, see Joan Hedrick's *Harriet Beecher Stowe: A Life*.

2. For an introduction to eighteenth-century women readers and writers, see Cathy Davidson's *Revolution and the Word*.

3. For more on the *Woman's Home Companion*, see chapter one, "Progressive Middlebrow," in Jaime Harker's *America the Middlebrow: Women's Novels, Progressivism, and Middlebrow Authorship Between the Wars*.

4. For one example of fan letters, see Jennifer Parchesky's "The Business of Living and the Labor of Love: Dorothy Canfield Fisher, Feminism, and Middle-Class Redemption."

5. See Lisa Hogeland's *Feminism and Its Fictions: The Consciousness-Raising Novel and the Women's Libertaion Movement.*

6. And, though women readers and writers were central to this tradition, it freely crossed gender lines, as with the novels of William Dean Howells and John Steinbeck, and, most recently, in the striking success of Dan Brown's novel *The DaVinci Code,* a politically engaged and mildly sensationalized reworking of Christian history that has readers flocking to churches in France and the U.K. to visit the sites where its fictionalized events take place.

7. Some selected studies include Mary Kelley's *Private Woman, Public Stage;* Amy Kaplan's *The Social Construction of American Realism;* Bonnie Kime Scott's *The Gender of Modernism;* Sandra Gilbert and Susan Gubar's three-volume *No Man's Land;* and Molly Hite's *The Other Side of the Story.*

8. This is not to say that women writers are not represented in traditional formulations of literary canon. Women were responsible for the first and most popular American novels and have been at the center of every major American literary movement. Beginning in the nineteenth century with romanticism, writers such as Catherine Maria Sedgwick and Harriet Beecher Stowe defined their age; the contemporary conception of realism is constructed with reference to Kate Chopin and Edith Wharton as well as earlier women regionalists like Rebecca Harding Davis and Mary E. Wilkins Freeman. Women were influential modernists, through the experimental writings of Gertrude Stein and Djuna Barnes, as well as the more realist novels of Willa Cather and Zora Neale Hurston. And they have added nuance and depth to postmodernism, through the novels of Kathy Acker, Louise Erdrich, and Toni Morrison, among many others.

9. Jonathan Franzen's ambivalence about being selected by Oprah's Book Club epitomizes this anxiety—he worried that being seen as too accessible, and too much of a women's novelist, would undermine his claim to be a "literary" writer. The gap between "accessible" and "literary" was, for him, unbridgeable, though in a 1996 essay for *Harper's* magazine he had publicly imagined constructing such a bridge via a successful and socially engaged novel.

Works Cited

Davidson, Cathy N. "Introduction." *Charlotte Temple.* Susanna Rowson. Oxford: Oxford UP, 1986.

———. *Revolution and the Word: The Rise of the Novel in America.* Oxford: Oxford UP, 1986.

Farr, Cecilia Konchar. *Reading Oprah*. Albany: SUNY, 2004.

Gilbert, Sandra, and Susan Gubar. *No Man's Land: The Place of the Woman Writer in the Twentieth Century,* Vol. 1. New Haven: Yale UP, 1988.

Harker, Jaime. *America the Middlebrow: Women's Novels, Progressivism, and Middlebrow Authorship Between the Wars*. Boston: U of Massachusetts P, 2007.

Hedrick, Joan. *Harriet Beecher Stowe: A Life*. Oxford: Oxford UP, 2004.

Hite, Molly. *The Other Side of the Story: Structures and Strategies of Contemporary Feminist Narrative*. Ithaca, NY: Cornell UP, 1992.

Hogeland, Lisa. *Feminism and Its Fictions: The Consciousness-Raising Novel and the Women's Liberation Movement*. Philadelphia: U of Penn, 1998.

Kaplan. Amy. *The Social Construction of American Realism*. Chicago: U of Chicago P, 1988.

Kelley, Mary. *Private Woman, Public Stage: Literary Domesticity in Nineteenth Century America*. Chapel Hill: U of North Carolina P, 1984.

Long, Elizabeth. *Book Clubs: Women and the Uses of Reading in Everyday Life*. Chicago: U of Chicago P, 2003.

Parchesky, Jennifer. "The Business of Living and the Labor of Love: Dorothy Canfield Fisher, Feminism, and Middle-Class Redemption." *Colby Quarterly* 36 (No. 1) 2000: 29–47.

Radway, Janice. *Reading the Romance: Women, Patriarchy, and Popular Literature*. Chapel Hill: U of North Carolina P, 1984.

Scott, Bonnie Kime. *The Gender of Modernism: A Critical Anthology*. Bloomington: Indiana UP, 1990.

Tompkins, Jane. *Sensational Designs: The Cultural Work of American Fiction 1790–1860*. Oxford: Oxford UP, 1985.

1

OPRAH IN THE PUBLIC LIBRARY

JULIETTE WELLS AND VIRGINIA WELLS

On July 2, 1997, ten months after Oprah Winfrey founded her first on-air book club, the American Library Association (ALA) made her an honorary member at the organization's annual awards gala. The ALA, which describes itself as "the oldest and largest library association in the world, with more than 64,000 members" (*American Library Association* screen 1), cited Winfrey for, "through her Book Club, [having] done more to revitalize and promote the importance of reading among American citizens than any other public figure in recent times" ("They Won!" 70). Particularly important to the ALA, naturally, was Winfrey's involvement with libraries: "Through libraries," the citation continues, "she has helped make books available free of charge to many who might not have been able to purchase their own copies. She has refocused attention on the important role of the library in the community" ("They Won!" 70).

At the time of this citation, the ALA, like the rest of America, did not know how long Oprah's Book Club would continue or whether its influence would further grow. Now, several years after Winfrey disbanded her original book club and well into her new club focused on "great books," it is possible to evaluate her effects on public libraries and their readers.[1] To what extent has she significantly promoted the role of libraries in the community, as the ALA commended her in 1997? Has her influence on American readers in general—to which the ALA, booksellers' organizations, and scholars all attest—substantially affected public libraries' mission of encouraging reader-ship among their diverse clientele?

Answers to these questions are to be found neither in the public press nor in academic scholarship, which have focused more on the club's influence on book sales, publishers' strategies, and the literary taste of predominantly female American readers. Libraries are almost completely missing from Cecilia Konchar Farr's and Kathleen Rooney's recent studies of Oprah's Book Club, though both Farr and Rooney provide a valuable theoretical structure for understanding how librarians, and library readers, responded to it.[2] We must turn, instead, to library trade journals (principally *American Libraries*, an ALA monthly publication, and *Booklist*, which runs librarians' reviews of new books), to library system statistics, and to librarians themselves, whose efforts to promote and manage Winfrey's selections have been largely invisible to those outside the profession, and that have, in many cases, left few archival traces.

On a national level, the ALA approached Oprah's Book Club as a matchless opportunity for advancing the visibility of libraries. In addition to conferring an honorary membership on Winfrey, the ALA worked together with Winfrey's staff, publishers, and library book-order services to distribute donated copies of Oprah books and to develop new ordering systems for member libraries. While media coverage of such tactics as "blind" ordering did direct public attention to public libraries, especially during the early years of the original book club, the ALA has been primarily responsible for capitalizing on a very high-profile occasion to promote libraries.

On the levels of the public library system and individual branches, librarians' involvement with and responses to Oprah's Book Club also tell a story of fruitful opportunities identified and seized, albeit often belatedly and with some ambivalence. Many a librarian seems to have become aware only gradually of the power of Winfrey's recommendations and, in some cases, to have resisted or disagreed with them on the basis of the books' themes or literary merit. Nevertheless, librarians endeavored to maintain interest in past selections, to encourage enthusiastic followers of Oprah's Book Club to seek out other works on similar themes, and to increase the number of book clubs based at libraries. Both anecdotal evidence and available circulation statistics suggest that these efforts have had substantial success.

Given the great number of public libraries in the United States and the often profound differences among them, it would be impossible, of course, to offer a complete picture of the influence of Oprah's Book Club. While we will draw on interviews with and Web sites prepared by librarians across the country, we will focus in particular on one of America's largest and most diverse library systems, the Fairfax County Public Library (FCPL) in northern Virginia, outside of Washington, D.C.[3] Our investigation of FCPL's involvement with Oprah's Book Club relies in large part on the experience of Virginia (Ginny) Wells as an information services librarian and popular materials specialist at Chantilly Regional Library, where her duties have included designing and maintaining Oprah's Book Club shelf displays as well as preparing and distributing readers' advisory lists and bookmarks.[4] Her personal records, together with comments and statistics contributed by her colleagues at FCPL, offer incomparable insight into how one major public library has responded to and capitalized on the popularity of Winfrey's book clubs.[5]

Putting Books on the Shelves:
Publishers' Donations and "Oprahsourcing"

"Oprah's Book Club is wreaking havoc in the public library," proclaimed an op-ed piece in the Cleveland *Plain Dealer* in December 1996. "First there was a run on *Song of Solomon*," reported a librarian from Geauga County. "We're backed up with hundreds of requests for it. Now all the patrons are hunting for the January selection, Jane Hamilton's *The Book of Ruth*, and unfortunately the system's only copy is lost" (Kisner 11B).

While not all library systems faced the stampede for Winfrey's latest selection with only one book on the shelf (or missing), they did confront the common challenge of stocking their shelves in very short order with sufficient copies to fulfill reader demand. Books donated by publishers helped, albeit in a small way, to address the need. Beginning in January 1997 with *The Book of Ruth,* according to *American Libraries*, "the publisher, Anchor/Doubleday, donated 10,000 free copies of the book, and Oprah's staff called ALA for help in distributing them" ("Oprah's Book Club Gets the Country Reading" 6). The ALA, which had no way of knowing whether the publishers of subsequent selections would follow suit, "proposed several ideas" to Winfrey's staff, who chose to distribute the copies to about 1,100 ALA member libraries, both public and high school, according to their size (6).

Positive publicity encouraged publishers to maintain the practice, but their donations remained constant in number. Since the ALA continued to expand the recipient list, eventually more than tripling it, each library received fewer books: in 2002, "up to five copies, depending on its size" ("Library/Oprah Ties to Continue" 9). When Winfrey restarted her club, the donation program resumed and, this time, the impetus for it came from the talk show host herself, not from publishers. "Winfrey launched her new book club last June with a focus on classic works of literature," reported *American Libraries*, "and asked publishers of each selection to donate their books to high school, public, and, for the first time this year, community college libraries that are ALA organizational members" ("Oprah's Book Club Selections Distributed" 8).

Even in the early years of publishers' donations, when fewer libraries were sharing the free copies, a large public library system still had to buy many books to meet reader demand, as two statistical snapshots from March 1997 make plain. Before Winfrey's selection of Ursula Hegi's *Stones from the River*, the Houston Public Library owned just two copies of the title; twenty were subsequently donated by the publisher, and the library purchased seventy-seven more ("Libraries Conspire to Stock Books for Oprah's Club" 1). FCPL, which also received twenty donated copies of each Oprah title at the time, ordered forty-two more of *Stones from the River* to fill out existing stock (Davis B1).

While gifts from publishers certainly benefited many libraries, then, the great majority of Oprah's Book Club titles available to library readers were purchased rather than donated. Time, not money, proved the greatest challenge in stocking shelves with newly announced titles, since eager readers did not delay before arriving at libraries hoping to secure precious copies. A Chicago-area librarian recounted in 1997 that one reader "watched the show in her boots and coat with the car running outside. . . . She heard the title, ran to her car and drove here—she got our only copy" (Schultz, "It's Simple" 6). Two aspects of the operation of Oprah's Book Club contributed to this rush, as the ALA explained to its members on a Webpage devoted to the club. The first was Winfrey's tendency toward last-minute decision-making. "We know that you would like a list of books to be featured for the remainder of the year," read the February 2002 version of the ALA's Oprah Web page, but "unfortunately, we do NOT have a list. The decision is not made that far in advance" ("New Oprah Book Club Selection Announced" screen 2). The second factor was the participatory nature of the on-air book club. Of readers who submitted responses to and opinions on the current book, Winfrey regularly chose four to chat with her and the author over dinner. "Many viewers ask about the deadlines for submitting comments on Book Club books," advised the ALA Webpage, "and the response from Oprah's staff is 'the sooner the better,' after the title is announced. They don't set deadlines, because they don't want to be swamped with last-minute entries" ("New Oprah Book Club Selection Announced" screen 2).

In order to accommodate these impatient readers, the ALA at first made arrangements to release to its members the name of the new selection's publisher in advance of Winfrey's official announcement. "When Oprah makes a new selection," *American Libraries* alerted its members in March 1997, "a notice will appear on the ALA Web site at http://www.ala.org/events/ promo-events/. The name of the publisher—but not the title—will be announced so that librarians can call the publisher or their distributor to order copies. The title will not be given out before it is announced on Oprah's show" ("Oprah's Book Club Gets the Country Reading" 6). Before long, a more streamlined system of standing orders emerged, thanks to a collaboration between the ALA and one of the country's largest distributors of books to libraries, Ingram Library Services. Nicknamed "Oprahsourcing," this method allowed librarians to choose in advance the number of copies of the next selection that they wished to order. Ingram promised to ship the books "as soon as they are announced and available from the publisher" and donated two percent of such sales to the ALA ("Ingram Offers Oprahsourcing" 6). Early response from librarians was quite positive: "We were very impressed when Oprah announced the title of her current selection on Friday and by Monday we received our 42 copies of the book," reported the assistant coordinator of collection management for FCPL ("Ingram Offers Oprahsourcing" 6).[6]

A March 1997 *Washington Post* article, which was picked up by wire services, offered a full report of how Oprahsourcing worked at FCPL, with evident relish for what one Ingram employee called the system's "very cloak-and-dagger" nature. "Just before the big announcement each month," wrote journalist Patricia Davis, "the sealed boxes are sent to Fairfax County libraries bearing ominous 'Do Not Open Until . . . ' labels. Inside are dozens of copies of the same book, ordered by library officials who didn't know what they were buying" (Davis B1). Chantilly Library, where Ginny Wells works, was the very first Fairfax County library to receive the just-opened boxes, since it shares a building with FCPL's Technical Operations division, which receives and processes library orders. According to the *Post*, approximately forty library systems across the United States then participated in what Davis termed "this elaborate plan," and FCPL employees applauded it: "We know the demand is going to be so great that it's going to be worth it," stated Michele Leber. A Houston library spokeswoman quoted in a version of the same newspaper story was less enthusiastic: "It's not something we're very comfortable with," admitted Sheryl Berger, "but the track record has been good. . . . Each book she has selected has been an excellent work of fiction" ("Libraries Conspire to Stock Books for Oprah's Club" 1).

In placing orders for unknown books, libraries found themselves in much the same position as booksellers, who also had to commit to purchases before Winfrey's announcement in order to meet demand. "It's the first time I ever bought a book without knowing the title, but I know it will sell," said one Chicago-area bookstore buyer in 1997 (Schultz, "It's Simple" 6). Also like bookstores, which typically have the option of returning any unsold copies to the publishers, libraries have a method of ensuring that their collection of a particular title does not exceed its popularity. Unbeknownst to the average library reader, some books on the shelves of major public libraries are not owned but leased. An internal e-mail sent from Julie Pringle, coordinator of FCPL's Collections Management and Acquisitions (CMA), to system administrators, librarians, and technical operations personnel explains the McNaughton book leasing program, which allows FCPL to temporarily stock copies of so-called high demand titles, at a "slightly lower cost" per book than if copies were purchased. (The library system may permanently keep up to thirty percent of its leased books.) Aside from price, Pringle explains, the McNaughton program offers two important advantages. As a subscription service that runs from January to December, it allows the library system to, in Pringle's words, "bridge that awkward period towards the end of a fiscal year when people still want new library books but the fiscal year is ending." Because the McNaughton books are also distinctively bound, they are easy to locate and pull once they have ceased to circulate, thus "freeing up valuable shelf space with relatively little expense in staff time," according to Pringle.

Although FCPL leases a variety of best sellers through McNaughton, not just Oprah's Book Club selections, the library system's only standing orders for circulating material were for Winfrey's choices, according to Peggy Bercher, also of the CMA office. That FCPL, among many other library systems, adopted and relied on "Oprahsourcing" even with some misgivings reveals librarians' recognition that taking part in the Oprah's Book Club phenomenon by serving their readers' demand for Oprah books could distinctly benefit the public profile of libraries.

Getting Oprah's Books into the Hands of Readers: Circulation and Book Displays

When a library system acquired copies of an Oprah Book Club selection, whether through donations or orders, its job was only half done: It still had to place those copies in the hands of interested readers. "Holds" are a library system's main way of managing demand that exceeds supply: Readers essentially line up—originally by phone, and now often via library Web sites—for popular titles. The larger the library system, the higher the number of holds placed on any book in great demand. According to the Sydney (Australia) *Sunday Telegraph*, 4,000 holds were placed through the New York Public Library system on Jacqueline Mitchard's *The Deep End of the Ocean* on the same day as Winfrey announced this initial selection of her Book Club (Jackman 57). On a smaller scale, but no less dramatic, was the run on Hegi's *Stones from the River* experienced in February 1997 by the Little Falls Community Library in Bethesda, Maryland, where readers placed forty holds in the five minutes following Winfrey's announcement (Davis B1). To cope with the intensity of demand, FCPL eventually developed a system of so-called dummy records for Oprah's Book Club selections, which allowed readers to get in line for the next one—first by phone, then online—even before it was announced and available.

In the early days of Winfrey's original club, newspaper stories covering the phenomenon frequently invoked statistics like those quoted earlier in order to encapsulate the sheer popularity of her selections. Years into Oprah's Book Clubs, the scope and duration of readers' demand for Oprah books continue to be illuminated, if in a somewhat scattered fashion, by such statistics, which are especially valuable since public library systems do not typically retain long-term records of circulation information, including numbers of holds. In other words, it is now impossible to discover from current FCPL records how many holds were placed on a given selection at a given time, or even how many times copies of a title circulated within a particular past year, another important index of reader demand. In the absence of a searchable database of such information, we must draw our conclusions about the initial and enduring popularity of Winfrey's selections from data that is often incomplete.

The history at FCPL of Winfrey's first title, Mitchard's *Deep End of the Ocean*, demonstrates both what can and cannot be determined about the lifecycle of a particular selection from available data. In March 1997, six months after Winfrey's selection of this novel, FCPL readers still had 394 holds on the title, according to the *Washington Post's* Davis. Another statistic from the same article, that *Deep End* "has been checked out 1,020 times so far, or nearly four times as often as the typical book," is more problematic to interpret. Davis is evidently referring here to the circulation of the total number of copies of *Deep End* in the library system, that is, the circulation of the *title* rather than of a particular *book.*[7] *Deep End's* progress from 1997 to 2004, while not fully trackable, can be deduced in some degree from statistics obtainable at the time of writing (December 2004), which show the current status of copies of this title in the FCPL system.

Chantilly Regional Library once owned four copies of *Deep End,* of which it now retains two, both of which most recently circulated in September 2004. One of the copies has been checked out a total of eighty-seven times (an unusually high number), the other only thirty (which likely indicates that it was purchased—or donated by a library reader who had bought it new and finished with it—more recently). A third copy was discarded by the library in March 2003, having been checked out eighty-six times. George Mason Regional Library once had nine copies, of which two remain: one has circulated twelve times, the other fifteen, both most recently in October 2004. Fairfax Library (the central library of the system) retains four copies of an original seven. Pohick Regional Library currently owns five of an original eight, of which one is a "browsing" (paperback) copy, two are on the fiction shelves, and two are "overflow" (stored, usually in the back of the library, because of limited shelf space).

The story told by all these numbers is hardly surprising. Demand was at its highest, and copies at their most numerous, shortly after Winfrey's selection. Copies of this title have continued, and continue, to circulate at a much higher rate than one would expect for what, in the absence of Winfrey's recommendation, would have been the first novel by a relatively little-known author. What cannot be precisely determined from available statistics is the rate at which the influence of that recommendation waned.

The comparative effect of Oprah's imprimatur on the novel selected and on an author's subsequent work is evident in the status at Chantilly Library of Elizabeth Berg's *Open House* (published in 2000, selected in August of that year) and her follow-up novel, *Ordinary Life* (2002). The eight hardback copies (of an original ten) of *Open House* have circulated a total of 487 times; audio versions of the book on cassette and CD have each circulated fifty-six times. Chantilly owns, in contrast, only three copies of *Ordinary Life* (2002), which have circulated a total of 130 times. While an Oprah author, then, can expect higher-than-average circulation of her or his subsequent fiction, the numbers will not match those of the original selection.

So far, the popularity of the "great books" featured in Oprah's second Book Club has also surged at Chantilly, although to a less extreme degree than for the original Book Club selections. Like the other FCPL branches,

Chantilly received new trade paperback copies with colorful, redesigned covers to augment the older, well-worn, often less appealing-looking hardback copies of these titles. In the case of John Steinbeck's *East of Eden*, the first selection of the new club, Chantilly owned four older hardbacks, which had circulated a total of 116 times since the library opened in 1995. At the time of writing, one of these copies is undergoing repair and two are being retired due to heavy use. Chantilly's four new copies of *East of Eden* have circulated a total of fifty-nine times since Oprah's selection of the title in June 2003—half as many times as the four older copies circulated in a decade. Circulation figures for FCPL as a whole show that new copies of *East of Eden* at several branches have been checked out as many as twenty times each, an unusually high number in an eighteen-month period for an "older" title.

One way, albeit an unscientific one, of completing the picture of reader demand that circulation statistics begin to paint is to consult librarians' memories of the popularity of titles at their branches. At FCPL, as at public library systems generally, a professionally qualified librarian gains a sense of which titles are circulating not from actually checking books out, a task that is performed by circulation staff (who are, in any case, not supposed to notice or comment on the books that cross their counter), but rather from readers' questions and from the pace at which themed book displays need to be refilled. Many FCPL librarians developed such displays, which most often take the form of a centrally located shelf with eye-catching headings or decorations, to make it easier for readers to locate Winfrey's selections. Ted Kavich, formerly the popular materials specialist at FCPL's Pohick Regional Library, recalls the success of a display titled "Oprah's Authors" that he and his colleagues put together a few years ago: "We included the titles she selected, plus other books by those authors. The display was an instant smash—we had trouble keeping it filled, so as I recall we branched out and included other book club selections, plus books about starting and running a book club." Safari Wasserman, popular materials specialist at George Mason Regional, attests to the comparable popularity of her library's ongoing table display called "Book Club Favorites," which now includes items from other on-air book clubs as well as from Oprah's Book Club: "I frequently need to replace titles in the display," she reports.

An e-mail sent by Ginny Wells to other FCPL popular materials specialists in March 2002 offers a more comprehensive view of how her library's display worked and how it evolved over time with the help of nonprofessional staff and volunteers:

I want to share something with you that CH [Chantilly Library] has been doing. Perhaps this will give another branch an idea . . . .

Our Oprah display, begun in July 2000 on a whim, proved extremely successful and had outgrown its small bookcase. I, usually with the help of a volunteer, would cull the books from return carts and shelves and keep the display current. Our wonderful clerk-typist designed some graphics (a picture of Oprah, a banner [saying] "Oprah's Book Club"). From the beginning we included a handout of the Oprah titles, alphabetized by title (on the Oprah.com site the alphabetizing is NOT done in a library manner), followed by the author and call number. Each month that Oprah chooses a new title, the list is automatically updated (thanks to the clerk-typist) and printed out in a different color.

Since this display worked so well, I wanted to expand it, so first thing was to find and order a larger, more appropriate bookcase . . . .

Since it is hard to replenish the display from a titles list, I made an alphabetical list by author . . . . That way, I or a volunteer can more easily find the books on the shelves.

As this e-mail makes clear, photocopied lists of the selections, variously organized and formatted, benefit both readers and library staff: A list beginning with titles aids readers who might remember only the title, or only part of it, while a list by author helps staff quickly locate replacement volumes. (Ginny notes, at the time of writing, that demand continues for her lists of the selections of Winfrey's original Book Club, two and a half years after it ended.) Another e-mail, sent by Ginny to the staff of Chantilly Library in February 2002, underscores the popularity of this display, and of the books themselves: "As you all know, we've been featuring the books that Oprah Winfrey selects for her Book Club on a display. . . . Countless 'Oprah' books have been checked out, many times to patrons who read little else. CH staff has been very helpful and supportive of this endeavor!"

Even as Ginny's e-mails proudly celebrate the success of the Chantilly display, they indicate the effort that library staff had to make to accommodate this phenomenon, in which they did not necessarily participate as fans of Winfrey themselves. The first such hint is evident in the birthdate of the Chantilly display: July 2000, or almost four full years after the initiation of Oprah's first Book Club. Ginny's comment about Oprah's website "NOT" alphabetizing in a library manner, while obviously an in-joke among professional peers, also reveals the distinct difference between how librarians and nonlibrarians, such as Winfrey and her staff, view and handle books. Ginny's remark that many who seek Oprah books "read little else" and her encouragement of Chantilly colleagues for being "very helpful and supportive of this endeavor" both indicate the mixed reactions that library staff might well have had about the influx of Oprah enthusiasts. On the one hand, a public library exists to promote the circulation of its collections and the reading that makes circulation happen, regardless of how well educated, literary, or even literate the holder of the library card. On the other hand, librarians were not at all in charge of this reading phenomenon: Inspired by a television personality, people showed up in droves at libraries looking for books that librarians themselves might not necessarily have enthusiastically recommended.

Comparable ambivalence about the Oprah's Book Club phenomenon is discernible in a number of other anecdotes and comments by librarians, both within and outside FCPL. In March 1997, Nadia Taran, then branch manager of FCPL's Tysons-Pimmit Library, described the rush for the latest selection as being "like a stampede, or if you had a sale where the first 100 people get through the door" (Davis B1). While one might expect librarians to be thrilled, in the abstract, by such an enthusiasm for books, they are certainly unaccustomed to being at the head of a "stampede," or of coping with demand that so often exceeded supply. Taran's comparison to a sale highlights how the Oprah phenomenon emphasized librarians' role as providers of coveted objects to customers, rather than as professional advisors or consultants. The advice had already been given by Winfrey, and with a result that helpful librarians can only dream of: Winfrey's viewers were "just eager for whatever it is she said," according to Gail Avery, a librarian at the Chevy Chase Regional Branch in the District (Davis B1).

In part, the gap—and, arguably, the tension—between Winfrey's viewers and librarians can be attributed to substantial differences in education and leisure habits. While public librarians, like Winfrey's viewers, are predominantly (if not overwhelmingly) female, Winfrey draws an audience of all educational levels, as both Farr and Rooney have shown;[8] professional librarians, who hold master's degrees in library science, are among the nationwide minority of holders of graduate degrees. And, while Winfrey has said that she reads at night rather than watching television,[9] it is probably safe to assume that most librarians, by virtue of professional and personal interest, read more and watch television less than the average Winfrey viewer. Class elitism and racism may also have been important factors in distancing librarians, as a group, from Winfrey viewers.

Of course, these factors also profoundly affect how a particular branch library's readers respond to Oprah books. At Great Falls Library (GF), which is located in one of the most affluent areas of Fairfax County, popular materials librarian Lois Glick reports that her "clientele almost appears to avoid the Oprah selections! . . . I think she's been a powerful force in reaching a much wider range of readers than we'll ever be able to, but I must say I've had a lot of reaction to all the dysfunctional themes and angst—at least of her earlier picks. I also should add, I don't think GF's population is typical—possibly higher numbers of motivated, widely-read, educated people than some areas of the county, so my reaction may not be in keeping with the general results. The Oprah effect has been quite minimal here." The reactions that Glick recounts are fully typical of what Rooney and Farr have identified among readers and book-buyers who perceive themselves as being "above" Oprah books (Rooney chap. 1; Farr chap. 3).

Public librarians may, collectively, have been somewhat slow to acknowledge the power of Oprah's Book Club and ambivalent about catering to demand for her selections. Once the phenomenon was established and the process of putting books on the shelves was streamlined, however, librarians across the country recognized that the popularity of Winfrey's selections had created an unprecedented market for their own services.

Fostering the Popularity of Reading:
"Oprahlikes" and Library-Based Book Clubs

Public librarians have long offered "readers' advisory" services, which aid readers seeking inspiration for their next book choice. Readers' advisory can take a variety of forms, from the personal to the technological: Hearing the kind of books a reader has enjoyed in the past, a librarian at the reference or information desk might offer suggestions for a similar read, pass out a photocopied list of popular titles either assembled by local librarians or drawn from a library journal, or (since the rise of databases) demonstrate the use of NoveList, a subscription database that provides title suggestions in response to the name of a favorite author or book. Fundamental to the role of the readers' advisor, in each of these cases, is that she or he begin with and build on the reader's existing taste, rather than pushing a particular kind of book or imposing a particular ideological or literary agenda. In this respect, readers' advisors in the library are distinctly opposed to those members of the literary establishment who, as Farr has persuasively argued, advocate an approach to reading that reflects and reproduces their own perceptions of value and worth (84–88).

Thus, it's not quite accurate to call Winfrey "the nation's number one readers' advisor," as a 2002 *Booklist* article proclaimed her (Wilkinson 1678). Certainly, Winfrey advised, and continues to advise, her audience what to read next, and she is indubitably the most prominent public figure so to do. As Farr has shown, however, Winfrey selected novels that primarily reflected her own interests, not necessarily her audience's, and she aimed to enlist those who had never or rarely read a book as well as those who were committed readers (10–14). Winfrey's recommendations thus have less in common with readers' advisory services at the public library than with the "staff picks" shelf at many an independent bookstore, which promotes books favored by the presumably avid readers employed there.[10]

Public librarians quickly recognized that the phenomenal popularity of Winfrey's suggestions offered them an unprecedented opportunity for revitalizing and capitalizing on their own readers' advisory services. Cathleen Towey, director of adult services at the Port Washington, New York, Public Library, made a case for this in a December 1997 article in *American Libraries*. Arguing that adult services librarians, for a variety of reasons, do not recommend fiction as vigorously as do children's librarians, and noting that the success of Oprah's Book Club proves that "fiction readers crave recommendations," Towey suggests that librarians can also bring lesser-known works of fiction to readers' attention: "Once they [library readers] get beyond the bestsellers, which librarians don't need to promote because publishers take care of that, patrons want help in deciding what to read next. . . . Public librarians can actively provide readers' advisory services by connecting people to authors who are not heavily promoted by publishing houses" (31). In addition to demonstrating how the inspiration for reading initiated by Winfrey can be cultivated in the public library, Towey's remarks call attention to the unique status of librarians and library readers in the financial world of publishing. Though, of course, library systems must buy books, the act of borrowing from a public library is, fundamentally, a noncommercial transaction, one that influences neither a publisher's bottom line nor any best-seller list.

From September 1997 to June 2002, *Booklist* published six compilations of "read-alike" titles keyed to Winfrey's selections, which librarians subsequently adapted for their own reference purposes, for distribution in photocopied handouts, and for posting on library Web sites, many of which still make such lists available.[11] Safari Wasserman of FCPL's George Mason

Regional reports that her library's "Adult Readers' Advisory Notebook" maintains an index tab labeled Oprah, with several relevant lists from *Booklist* and other sources. At Chantilly Library, Ginny Wells included read-alike titles on her Oprah bookshelf display and produced, with the help of a clerktypist, several differently colored bookmarks, each listing approximately six Oprah titles and their read-alikes.

The extent to which being identified as an "Oprahlike" boosted a title's circulation is difficult to determine with certainty, in many cases because such titles were best sellers in their own right or published by best-selling authors. Nevertheless, a glimpse into the circulation histories of one Oprah's selection's read-alikes at Chantilly Library does indicate that librarians' promotion of them via displays and lists has had a distinctly positive effect on their popularity. The "Oprahlike" titles in question are *Breathing Lessons* by Anne Tyler (1988) and *East of the Mountains* by David Guterson (1999), which were identified by *Booklist* as read-alikes for Kaye Gibbons's *A Virtuous Woman* (1990; selected in October 1997). Chantilly currently owns two copies of *Breathing Lessons*, which have circulated a total of 207 times, most recently (in both cases) within the last two months.[12] The circulation of *East of the Mountains* has also been brisk: Chantilly retains three of four original copies, which have circulated a total of 101 times, with two copies having done so within the last two months.

Just as librarians took advantage of the popularity of Winfrey's high-profile recommendations to reinvigorate their own long-standing service of readers' advisory, so, too, did they welcome the reading public's renewed interest in book clubs, which public libraries have long hosted as part of their mission to inspire and bring together readers. In the months following Winfrey's decision to disband her original book club, Deb Robertson, director of the ALA's Public Programs Office, urged librarians to reclaim their historic role as organizers and encouragers of book clubs. Robertson cites a 1998 study showing that more than sixty percent of public libraries reported hosting discussions about books, and she describes book programs ranging from the ALA-sponsored "Let's Talk About It," developed in the 1970s, to the currently popular One Book, One City initiatives. She concludes by reminding librarians that they "are in the ideal—and enviable—position to recommend and initiate discussion of worthy books, and [that] libraries offer the central space for community dialogue, learning, and simple enjoyment of good reading" (52–53).

A February 1997 article in the Chicago *Sun-Times* offers a window onto Winfrey's galvanizing effect on public library reading clubs. Jim Pletz, director of adult services for the Chicago Public Library, reported that that library system's book groups program, begun in May 1996 with twelve groups, was set to expand to thirty-seven by 1998 (Schultz, "Oprah Renews Our Love of Reading" 6). A Cambridge, Massachusetts, librarian quoted in a 2003 *Boston Globe* article likewise reports that, in the Boston metropolitan area, library-sponsored book clubs "are thriving in our branches, even in workplaces" (Mehegan D1). By 2003, of course, more cultural factors than Oprah's Book Club alone were coming together to reignite the popularity of readers' gatherings, as Elizabeth Long's recent study of American women's book clubs has shown.

While the influence of Oprah's Book Club alone is difficult to discern, FCPL's current roster of book discussion groups certainly reflects the nationwide enthusiasm for book clubs. The system's more than two dozen regular book discussion groups for adults include several focused on contemporary or classic novels as well as a mystery readers' group, a "Poetry Group," and a "Black Authors Book Discussion Group." (The Great Falls Library, whose popular materials librarian reported that her clientele "almost appears to avoid" Oprah books, supports two discussion groups.) Meetings happen during the day as well as in the evening, and several libraries, among them small community branches as well as large regional libraries like Chantilly, host two or three groups a month. Chantilly Library's two discussion groups for adults predate Oprah's Book Club, having started very soon after the building opened in 1995; one of them, the "Chantilly Book Discussion Group," has in the past included Oprah titles on its reading schedule. Chantilly Library has also long supported an independent local book group by putting its monthly selections on reserve.

Conclusions

In essence, public libraries' involvement with Oprah's Book Club is a story of professionals' adaptive and opportunity-seizing responses to a phenomenon initiated by a nonprofessional. Faced with unprecedented quantity and timing of reader demand, librarians and library systems coped by reorganizing the ordering of books and improving existing methods of prioritizing readers—for instance, by introducing "dummy holds." To build on readers' interest in Winfrey's selections, librarians developed eye-catching book displays, tailored read-alike lists, and formed more library-based book clubs. With the exception of "Oprahsourcing," none of these initiatives was wholly

new, and all were successful in managing and supporting the interest in reading spurred by Winfrey. Furthermore, these efforts took place at every level
of library bureaucracy, from the ALA and its publications down to the individual popular materials specialist maintaining an Oprah display and photo-
copying lists of titles.

In retrospect, the ALA's citation of Winfrey in 1997, which recognizes
her achievement in placing reading at the forefront of the public mind, can
be read as well as a subtle call to arms to librarians to continue the work that
Winfrey started. If it was she who "revitalize[d] and promote[d] the importance of reading" ("They Won!" 70), it was librarians who possessed the skills
and means to encourage readers to move beyond Oprah selections and find a
community of readers in their own neighborhoods. If it was Winfrey who
"refocused attention on the important role of the library in the community"
("They Won!" 70), it was librarians who, under the unaccustomed glare of
the national spotlight, could ensure that their libraries continued, often cre-
atively, to fulfill that role, during Winfrey's reign and beyond.

Notes

1. Public libraries have, over the years, used a variety of terms—such as
"patron" and "customer"—to denote those members of the community who have
library cards and use libraries. Except when quoting correspondence or articles that
employ one term or the other, we will use the neutral term "library reader," which
distinguishes those who borrow books from libraries from those who buy them at
bookstores. Not all of those who check books out from libraries actually read them,
of course, just as not all who buy copies do, but in both cases reading is at least
intended if not actually fulfilled.

2. Libraries are absent from both Farr's general description of Oprah's Book
Club and her analysis of it. "Here's how it worked," she explains in her introduction.
"Every month or so for almost six years, Oprah chose a contemporary novel and
announced her choice on television. Then, over a million people rushed to their
computers and bookstores to buy it" (2). Her question about why "serious readers,
professors, and teachers [weren't] the first to jump on the Oprah bandwagon" (80)
is, as we will see, equally applicable to librarians. For her part, Rooney makes very
occasional reference to libraries (for instance, in a secondhand quotation on 122),
but they are missing from her overall theoretical framework, most notably her treatment of "the cultural apparatus" (127–29).

3. The Fairfax County Public Library (FCPL) buys or replaces nearly
250,000 items per year. Its twenty-one branches (which include eight regional

libraries, twelve community branches, and an "Access Services" branch for people with disabilities) annually make eleven million loans to the system's more than 700,000 registered users, who reflect the county's mix of recent immigrants, government workers, military service people, and workers in the technology industry ("Fact Sheet").

4. Chantilly Library, which opened in 1995, is the newest of FCPL's regional libraries, located in a fast-growing corner of Fairfax County near Dulles Airport. Ginny Wells describes her position there as follows: I am the popular materials specialist at one of the large regional branches of the FCPL system. "Popular materials" chiefly encompasses adult fiction, mysteries and science fiction, with an emphasis on current titles. My job is to acquaint our readers with these materials by promoting, displaying and discussing them, with the end goal of seeing them circulate (i.e., be checked out).

5. Many thanks to the librarians and employees of FCPL who generously assisted us in investigating the Oprah's Book Club phenomenon. In addition to those quoted and mentioned here, we would like to express our gratitude to Reed Coats, Lois Kirkpatrick, Kathy Tewell, Christine Jones, and Bonnie Worcester for their encouragement and assistance.

6. The *American Libraries* article identifies this employee as "Mike Leber"; as the *Washington Post* story quoted in our following paragraph makes clear, she is actually Michele Leber.

7. Similar confusion between a title and an individual copy is evident in an April 2002 *Milwaukee Journal Sentinel* article, which reported that Ann-Marie MacDonald's *Fall on Your Knees* was checked out twice in the year before Winfrey selected it and sixty-eight times in the three months following (Sharma-Jensen 6E).

8. Farr analyzes the broad range of Winfrey's audience in her introduction (2); Rooney, recalling her attendance at a show taping, likewise testifies to the audience's mix of well-educated and less-well-educated fans (ix–xiv).

9. Quoted, from a 1997 *Mirabella* article, by Rooney, who notes that this article was included in a press kit she received from Winfrey's staff (30).

10. As a 2003 *Boston Globe* article makes plain, independent booksellers also offer readers' advisory services much more similar than Winfrey's to those of public librarians: " 'Customers say, 'I'm looking for something good to read,' " says Dana Brigham, co-owner of Brookline Booksmith. " 'Normally, I like books by so-and-so. What else do you have that is like that?' " (Mehegan D1). Such personal recommendations, according to the article, benefit book-buyers trying to make their way through the vast numbers of newly published books as well as independent booksellers seeking an edge over major chains and superstores.

11. A 2001 posting on the Web site of the Wolfner (Missouri) Library for the Blind & Physically Handicapped, for instance, encourages readers to consult the list

of read-alikes to find "suggestions for further reading that are by the same author, share a similar plot, or evoke the same emotion" (Jochimsen).

12. Ginny Wells notes that the circulation of *Breathing Lessons* (written by a Baltimore author) may well have received an additional boost from being displayed on a "Local Authors" shelf that she also maintains.

Works Cited

American Library Association. 15 Nov. 2004. <http://www.ala.org/>.

Bercher, Peggy. Personal interview. 23 Nov. 2004.

Davis, Patricia. "Oprah's Mystery Stories: Libraries Order Popular Titles Sight Unseen." *Washington Post* 19 Mar. 1997, final ed.: B1+.

"Fact Sheet." *Fairfax County Public Library.* 8 Dec. 2004. <http://www.co.fairfax.va.us/library/factsht.htm>.

Farr, Cecilia Konchar. *Reading Oprah: How Oprah's Book Club Changed the Way America Reads.* Albany: SUNY P, 2004.

Glick, Lois. "Re: Oprah in the Public Library." E-mail to Ginny Wells. 4 Nov. 2004.

"Ingram Offers Oprahsourcing." *American Libraries* 28.5 (May 1997): 6.

Jackman, Christine. "US Literati Honour their Contentious Hero Oprah." *Sunday Telegraph* [Sydney], 14 Nov. 1999: World, 57.

Jochimsen, Vicki. "Beyond Oprah's Book Club." Oct. 2001. 18 Nov. 2004. <http://www.sos.mo.gov/wolfner/bibliographies/beyondoprah.asp>.

Kavich, Ted. "Re: Oprah in the Public Library." E-mail to Ginny Wells. 9 Nov. 2004.

Kisner, Kathleen. "Oprah Winfrey's Subversive Book Club." *Plain Dealer* [Cleveland] 14 Dec. 1996: 11B+.

"Libraries Conspire to Stock Books for Oprah's Club." *Houston Chronicle* 26 Mar. 1997, Houston sec.: 1+.

"Library/Oprah Ties to Continue." *American Libraries* 33.5 (May 2002): 9.

Long, Elizabeth. *Book Clubs: Women and the Uses of Reading in Everyday Life.* Chicago: U of Chicago P, 2003.

Mehegan, David. "Oprah, Book Clubs Help Readers Find Their 'Eden'." *Boston Globe* 3 July 2003: D1+.

"New Oprah Book Club Selection Announced." *American Library Association.* 27 Feb. 2002. <http://www.ala.org/events/promoevents/oprah_undone.html>.

"Oprah's Book Club Gets the Country Reading." *American Libraries* 28.3 (Mar. 1997): 6.

"Oprah's Book Club Selections Distributed." *American Libraries* 35.3 (Mar. 2004): 8.

Pringle, Julie. "CMA BookBytes for January/February." E-mail to FCPL staff. 11 Feb. 2004.

Robertson, Deb. "Oprah and Out: Libraries Keep Book Clubs Flourishing." *American Libraries* 33.8 (Sept. 2002): 52–53.

Rooney, Kathleen. *Reading with Oprah: The Book Club that Changed America.* Fayetteville: U Arkansas P, 2005.

Schultz, Susy. "It's Simple: If She Reads It, They Will Buy." *Chicago Sun-Times* 24 Feb. 1997 News sec.: 6+.

———. "Oprah Renews Our Love of Reading; Book Club Show Sets New Trend." *Chicago Sun-Times* 24 Feb. 1997 News sec.: 6+.

Sharma-Jensen, Geeta. "Oprah's Club Helped Open Minds." *Milwaukee Journal Sentinel,* 14 April 2002: 6E.

Taran, Nadia P. "Re: An Article on Oprah's Book Club." E-mail to Ginny Wells. 22 Nov. 2004.

"They Won! And Did It ALA's Way." *American Libraries* 28.8 (Sept. 1997): 70–77.

Towey, Cathleen A. "We Need to Recommit to Readers' Advisory Services." *American Libraries* 28.11 (Dec. 1997): 31.

Wasserman, Safari. "Oprah Books." E-mail to Ginny Wells. 12 Nov. 2004.

Wells, Ginny. E-mail to FCPL colleagues. 20 Mar. 2002.

———. "Oprah Selections and Oprah Read-Alikes—A Display." E-mail to Chantilly Library staff. 9 Feb. 2002.

Wilkinson, Joanne. "After Oprah: 6." *The Booklist* 98.19/20 (1 June/15 June 2002): 1678–79.

2

TALKING READERS

CECILIA KONCHAR FARR

It could have been the beginning of a beautiful friendship. While Oprah was launching her Book Club in 1996 hoping to get America reading again, novelist Jonathan Franzen was writing an essay for *Harper's* magazine, dreaming of serious socially compelling novels and of a mass audience of readers who wanted to read them. They spent the next five years pursuing a similar ideal down different paths—Winfrey taking serious fiction to that mass audience and Franzen writing a weighty book that America would read—a National Book Award winner and, as it turned out, an Oprah book.

Or almost an Oprah book. Their paths converged when Franzen's novel *The Corrections* became Oprah's September 2001 Book Club pick. Soon after, the two separated less than amicably when Franzen publicly expressed uneasiness about appearing on her show and characterized some of her other Book Club choices as "schmaltzy" and "one dimensional" (Kirkpatrick, "Winfrey" C4). Winfrey rescinded her invitation for Franzen to talk about his novel with her Book Club, saying, "It is never my intention to make anyone uncomfortable" (oprah.com Oct. 2001). This was gossip worthy of *People* magazine and *Entertainment Weekly*, as well as *Newsweek*, the *New York Times*, and even *The Chronicle of Higher Education*.[1] In the midst of my research on Oprah's Book Club, I observed the encounter with eager attention.

"Talking Readers" is reprinted with permission from *Reading Oprah: How Oprah's Book Club Changed the Way America Reads* (SUNY 2004).

33

Think about it. The pedigree on Franzen's book was as good as it gets in American fiction. Critics started calling it The Great American Novel even before it reached the bookstores.[2] The academic acclaim surrounding its publication made waves so large they rocked boats in colleges like mine more than a thousand miles from either coast.

Responding to the critical fanfare, how many copies did Farrar, Straus print for the novel's initial release in early September? According to the *New York Times*, 90,000, a generous estimate for a literary novel and almost twice the total sales of Franzen's first two novels combined. And how many more did they have to run when Oprah selected it for her Book Club later that month? More than 600,000, *seven times* as many as the initial release (Corcoran 6). With five years of experience behind her, Oprah could guarantee that even an unsuccessful Book Club choice would sell that many copies, because, as we have seen, Oprah pulled in a huge group of readers, readers who critics and reviewers still haven't figured out how to access without her.

That's why my favorite part of this story is when Franzen suggested in a National Public Radio interview that he might lose readers, especially male readers, because of the Oprah "O" on the cover of his novel (npr.org Oct. 2001). Monica Corcoran followed up with a story in the *New York Times* about how readers on both coasts were requesting copies of *The Corrections* sans O. "It make me feel mainstream to be reading an Oprah book," one woman commented. "I don't want people to think I have no idea about literature or that I sit home and watch TV all day." But surely these few "bookworms" who considered the seal "a scarlet O," as Corcoran wrote, could not put a dent in the number of new readers the Oprah seal would bring in Clearly, Franzen could only have feared the loss of a certain type of reader. Thanks to Oprah, there was a moment in the fall of 2001 when vast numbers of soccer moms and waitresses in the Midwest were reading the very same thing New York intellectuals were reading. Corcoran's story speaks to which group might find that pairing unpalatable.

But this democratic reading moment was a revealing one for the Book Club, one that highlighted the polarity of responses to it. Love it or hate it, there was little space in between. Franzen, who seemed to enjoy being the darling of elite literary culture, an artist "solidly in the high-art literary tradition," as he told a reporter, couldn't negotiate the divide, despite his belated attempts in that direction (Kirkpatrick, "Winfrey"). After his Oprah's Book Club appearance was cancelled, Franzen quickly backpedaled on the high culture talk. "Mistake, mistake, mistake to use the word 'high.' Both Oprah and I want the same thing and believe the same thing, that the distinction between high and low is meaningless," he said in late October (Kirkpatrick, "Oprah Gaffe" E1).

What was lost in the media hubbub was that Franzen was not the first intellectual to respond to Oprah's cultural clout with measured enthusiasm, to grumble about the erosion of high culture in an MTV world. The real news was that he crossed a line in questioning Oprah's economic clout, calling the Book Club seal a corporate logo. As novelist Rick Moody pointed out, "If you are being published by one of the big houses, you can't object that you are not commercial in some way: what book doesn't have the publisher's logo on the spine?" (Kirkpatrick, "Oprah Gaffe" E1).

And again, who was (and still is) making money from that "corporate O"? Not Oprah. It was, from the beginning, the publishers who requested permission to integrate the seal into the cover art of their books and to keep it on when the novels were reprinted well after they had had their day on Oprah—in fact, well after the contemporary novels version of the Book Club ended. Oprah always does better in the ratings with celebrity and expert shows than she does with the Book Club; she willingly loses ratings points to continue its meetings, if only, now, just a few times a year.[3] Many writers, critics, reviewers, and publishing executives had been careful not to question Oprah's book-selling power because they were the ones who reaped its generous benefits. Even Harold Bloom, notorious defender of elitism (and bestselling author), rushed to claim that he, unlike Franzen, would be "honored" to be invited on Oprah (hint, hint). "It does seem a little invidious of him to want to have it both ways," Bloom said, "to want the benefits of it and not jeopardize his high aesthetic standing" (Kirkpatrick, "Oprah Gaffe").

In truth, the coming together of elite and popular literature that Oprah's choice of *The Corrections* represented had many thinkers furrowing their brows even before the celebrated falling-out. And, ironically, the economic ground that Bloom stood on to negotiate the abyss between high and low culture was the path Oprah walked to success with the Book Club. Americans, even the most elite, are notorious for not arguing with success. That's where Franzen miscalculated.

McLiterature

Yet Franzen's too-public reservations about the Book Club were only a restatement of comments I have heard students and professors making for years. For those "in the high-art literary tradition," the Oprahfication of books was never just about the middlebrow status of the novels or the confessional talk show slant to some of the literary discussions. Rather, it was about the commodification of books, how Oprah transforms books into consumer products, indistinguishable from microwaves or DVD players. The big issue, for many, was the sound of money in Oprah's voice, to paraphrase Jay Gatsby, the clinking of coins every time she announced a new novel.

Just as Gatsby's observation put Daisy in a harsh light, Oprah's endorsement of *The Corrections*, some thought, tarnished Franzen's golden image. Could the book possibly be good, they wondered confidentially, if so many people like it, if it sells like McDonald's hamburgers? I have observed that many arguments condemning Oprah's aesthetic choices are, like this one, arguments on economic principle—and generally uninformed ones. Readers who trash Oprah Books usually can't name more than one title. Literary prizewinners? Respected by other writers? You would never know from the widespread assessment of the Book Club as kitsch. Franzen must have feared being painted with that same brush.

Yet, taken outside of the context of Oprah's marketing success, many of the Oprah novels are, again, aesthetically excellent by academic standards, claiming unquestionable high art literary clout. That doesn't matter when the novels enter the gaudy world of mass production, when they sit on the best-seller list next to Chicken Soup for Dummies. Cultural theorists give context to this divide with their distinction between economic capital, how much money you have, and cultural capital, how "classy" you are. Rich people, most of us have noticed, aren't always classy people. When they aren't, when they build garish mansions and fill them with velvet paintings, they have economic capital and little cultural capital. On the other hand, when I look at my college professor paycheck and realize that it is smaller than my older brother's truck driver paycheck, I comfort myself, as I was subtly but carefully taught to do in graduate school, that my job has cultural capital—not more money but more social distinction.

The way these two types of capital separate themselves in the United States is unique. We are, stereotypically, the world's obnoxious rich cousin, throwing back Cokes and hanging out at the mall in $100 sneakers; we have money but no class. The French are our (irritatingly perfect) prototype of people with cultural capital but little economic capital living in tiny apartments eating gourmet food and talking about art. American attitudes are also complicated by the democratic angel on our shoulder, whispering that if something is worth having, everyone should have a shot at it. If Starbucks coffee really is the best, why hoard it for an elite few in Seattle? Things really get murky when we take books that have cultural capital and try to get them out to more people, thus turning them into consumer products to be bought and sold.

As D. T. Max wrote in the *New York Times Magazine*, critics don't want to see a list like Oprah's that can't distinguish between "Edwidge Danticat, a delicate literary writer whose books sold modestly, and Maeve Binchy, a commercial writer whose perky *Tara Road* was already . . . [a] bestseller [before it became an Oprah Book]." Publishers, he says, "treat one as art and the other as commerce; *one gets prestige, the other money*. But within the world of Oprah, they are equals" (40) [emphasis mine].

Media accounts of the Franzen flap reflect this high cultural unease about the context that Oprah's Book Club creates. Yet, even when the commentators sympathized with Franzen's reluctance to appear on Oprah (why jeopardize high cultural capital?), no one stepped up to condone his kamikaze economic behavior. Instead, they asked how he could bite the hand that would feed him. How could he turn up his nose at the surest shot at financial success a contemporary writer has? And furthermore (maybe a bit halfheartedly), how dare he pretend that his work is too good to share with the masses?

I experienced a similar conflict when, in the midst of researching this book, I began to put the Book Club in the context of other Oprah shows. I tuned into a pre-Christmas program and found myself spun into an hour-long consumer frenzy. It was the much-anticipated, twice-yearly "O List" show, where Oprah gives away literally hundreds of dollars worth of free stuff to every guest in her audience. Pants, candles, shoes, electronics—you name it. If Oprah likes it, she's giving it away on this show. Stuff overflowed from the audience-members' laps into piles of conspicuous consumption all over the studio. I watched open-mouthed, both appalled and envious. Was this incredibly tacky or unbelievably generous? Did I want to run screaming from the room or do my best to get on the next show? Both/and. It was as a moment of genuine American ambivalence.

Serious readers had been trying to resolve these conflicting values since Oprah's Book Club became a phenomenon. As a culture, we were placing increasing emphasis on literacy. Yet, when Oprah publicly demonstrated the joys of reading and encouraged millions of people to make time for good novels, why weren't serious readers, professors, and teachers the first to jump on the Oprah bandwagon? Instead of "You go, girl," we were saying, "I read that before Oprah chose it" and removing the Oprah seal from our books.

Those of us who love reading like to think that books aren't just stuff, and choosing good ones is fundamentally different from finding the perfect pair of black pants. It's a deeper, more intellectual, even spiritual enterprise. On the other hand, we live in a world where "a good writer is a rich writer and a rich writer is a good writer," as *Harper's* Editor Lewis Lapham put it (Kirkpatrick, "Oprah Gaffe"). We can't get past that paradox. On Oprah, in a certain light, the Book Club doesn't look a lot different from the "O List." After watching that show, I observed the big book giveaway at the end of Book Club shows with a little more cynicism.

The split loyalty Americans have when it comes to what we value is rough on critics, who are expected to represent the interests of cultural rather than economic capital. But if they do their jobs well, if, for example, they convince readers that *The Corrections* is a must-read, then the formerly elite product with cultural capital becomes a must-have consumer item, and the critics' reputations expand. Then we have to wonder if the critics' recommendations were self-promoting, aimed at increasing their own popularity and, thus, based on economic rather than artistic standards.

For Americans, artistic standards come trailing shrouds of an aristocratic Western cultural tradition, where real art is supposed to be underappreciated, reserved for a discriminating few. Real artists sacrifice for their art, living in industrial lofts and struggling to put food on their tables (if they take time to think about food at all). In this tradition, our culture holds up the image of a pained and passionate Poe or Salinger, even while most Americans would personally prefer to be Madonna or Andy Warhol. We like our artists lonely and starving in garrets. If they step out into the street in expensive suits, we begin to doubt their commitment.

Claiming Cultural Capital

Because Oprah's Book Club takes place on daytime television and is aimed at women, it is easily assessed as low on cultural capital—it just ain't classy. Because we can't deny its high economic capital, its profitability, we figure it as gaudy or cheap. But, as D. T. Max said, the Book Club blurs the boundaries between cultural and economic capital, art and business. While Oprah is modeling rich reading publicly, she also models public reading richly.

And the "richly" part is essential. For most of the Book Club's regular meetings over its first six years, the smaller dinner groups were held in the studio lushly outfitted as a study specifically for those programs. The stage was complete with thick carpeting, huge armchairs, heavy wooden bookcases, and a globe. Out of respect for their surroundings, no one, not even the writers, wore denim (though leather pants were apparently acceptable), and the guests always looked as if they had just bellied up to the Estée Lauder makeover counter. Oprah presided, often in a cashmere sweater and flashing diamond earrings, offering toasts in crystal wineglasses.

Earlier Book Clubs were linked more closely to the dinner, and guests exclaimed over "seared yellow-tailed tuna roasted with pistachios and black peppercorns" or a perfect crème brulée as they commented on the novels. The show gave up the food talk early on when it pared down its focus to the book at hand. On later Book Club programs, the camera would simply pan the dinner table briefly before settling in on the guests who had retired to the study area.[4] But this link with fine food is significant in situating the work the Book Club does. It blurs traditional class distinctions, placing Oprah's middlebrow novels (and their readers) in the realm of high culture, thus making high culture accessible. You, too, can live like this, the Book Club declares. Not vicariously through the afternoon soaps. Not sometime in the future after you achieve financial security. But here and now. By reading. Reading Morrison's books "is like savoring a gourmet dining experience. This is not like a fast-food read," Oprah said (16 Jan. 1998). So ignore the Boston Market and McDonald's commercials at the station break and pick up this book.

For me, the book is always the fascinating factor. Again, the middlebrow novel has complicated status categories since those sentimental novels and Book-of-the-Month Club books helped to construct us as middle-class Americans. When, in the early twentieth century, professors started to teach American literature and to bring novels more commonly into their courses of study, they had to configure them as high status, as worthy of attention at elite institutions where professors are paid to reproduce cultural capital. So they brought the tools of textual analysis from classical texts in Latin or Greek and from poetry, essays, and scripture.

For American novels, the price of admission into this reflective realm of legitimate literature was that they, too, would need to be sifted and selected, the best elevated and the worst condemned. The standards were ready and waiting, and throughout the early part of the twentieth century these standards were increasingly hostile to the social aspects of novels. So novels became lowbrow or highbrow, bad or good by way of traditional standards of aesthetic merit that, again, were aristocratic in origin and assumed the mediation of a discriminating few. Thus, the early days of the twentieth century were a good time for Herman Melville, for philosophical musings and dense poetic language that sold poorly, and a bad time for Harriet Beecher Stowe, for social engagement and uncomplicated narrative that sold phenomenally well. Poor Harriet was so economically successful that she never made it to college until the feminist critics brought her with them in the 1970s.

But the novel proved much more unruly and harder to control than the (by then) carefully tamed classical texts. Applying aesthetic standards to constantly proliferating consumer products was challenging, especially with that abominable middlebrow novel muddying the waters between the good and the bad. Best-seller lists, established at the turn of the twentieth century, manifest this challenge, as Michael Korda observes in *Making the List, A Cultural History of the American Bestseller 1900–1999.* "From day one," he writes, the list "has always represented a reliable mixture of the good and the bad, of quality and trash, of literature for the ages and self-improvement schemes that now seem merely weird to the extent they're remembered at all" (x).

And because most people insisted on reading without the proper training, they consistently elevated the bad over the good. Korda explains:

> From the very beginning, serious reviewers were dismayed with the bestseller list, and the marked tendency it demonstrated of Americans failing to heed the advice and warnings of book reviewers (then as now). Even today, a reader of the *New York Times Book Review* can hardly fail to note the obvious difference between the books that are prominently and/or seriously reviewed, and those that appear on the list, and there was certainly an initial reluctance, undiminished by time, to "rank" books by their sales, instead of by their merit. (xxi)

The task for the cultural aristocracy, then, was to find a way to guide the novel-reading masses to come around to the elite's definition of "good." The Book-of-the-Month Club is a helpful illustration of how American culture met this challenge.

Learning to Read

In its early days, the Book-of-the-Month Club had an image problem similar to Oprah's because the more popular it became—the more its economic capital accumulated—the more its cultural capital diminished. In the 1930s, high culture critics began to assail it, as Janice Radway explains in *A Feeling for Books*, by arguing that the elite ought to be *naturally* elite, not institutionalized by clubs and lists. The argument was that "one did not need literary authorities [i.e., the Book-of-the-Month-Club Board of Editors] to identify the best because the best books would reveal themselves to individuals who exercised their individual faculties appropriately" ("Scandal" 711). The critics of the Book-of-the-Month Club began to draw a line "between the individual, independent reader capable of actively seeking out real literature and an undifferentiated mass of passive consumers" or "the infantalized, passive dupes of the book clubs who were content with the hand-me-down opinions of eminent book jurors," Radway writes (*Feeling* 210). (This will sound familiar to Oprah's Book Club readers.) The "intelligent minority," they argued, didn't need book clubs. They would choose the best by long-standing, reliable aesthetic standards. The cream would rise to the top, and these autonomous readers would naturally recognize and enjoy it.

Those independent individuals were, of course, hardly self-regulating. Ideally, they would have been carefully taught the reliable aesthetic standards by the proper authorities, and they would apply them just as they had been taught, just as the authorities dictated. As Radway concludes, "It seems evident that what really disturbed the critics of the books clubs was not so much the mob, but the prospect that the mob might now be led by the wrong cultural authorities" (227). The connection to the proper cultural authorities is simple to trace in the choices of the intelligent minority. If you wanted to be among that elite group, you would never admit that you found Joyce's *Ulysses* unintelligible, for example, or that you enjoyed Pearl Buck more than William Faulkner. Yet this emphasis on a false individuality remained throughout the twentieth century.

Harold Bloom is a case in point. He argues in *How to Read and Why* that ideal readers are solitary, not social. He compares his solitary readers to Herman Melville's Ahab, who is "American through and through . . . but always strangely free, probably because no American truly feels free unless he or she is inwardly alone" (238). With this lonely American in mind, Bloom addresses his book to "unfinished" readers, readers who are not yet "wholly [them]selves" and need someone to guide them through literature "in order to strengthen the self" (20, 22).

But the lessons he offers are not suggestive lessons in principle but directive lessons in practice—here are the texts that solitary readers will devote their lives to reading (what to read and who), and here is what they will find, if they read astutely. For example, he lectures readers who hesitate to embrace Jane Austen's directive Mr. Knightley for the hero that he is in the novel *Emma*:

> There is no misandry in Jane Austen or George Eliot or Emily Dickinson. Elizabeth Bennet and Emma Woodhouse are not concerned either with upholding or undermining patriarchy. Being vastly intelligent persons . . . they do not think ideologically. To read their stories well, you need to acquire a touch of Austen's own wisdom, because she was as wise as Dr. Samuel Johnson. Like Johnson, though far more implicitly, Austen urges us to clear our mind of "cant." "Cant" in the Johnsonian sense, means platitudes, pious expressions, group-think. Austen has no use for it, and neither should we. Those who now read Austen "politically" are not reading her at all. (159)

What *Emma* is about, Bloom insists, is not any kind of social or political message—that women need meaningful work and suffer for the lack of it, for example. *Emma* is about the training of the main character's "undisciplined imagination." She must be rescued "through the agency of Mr. Knightley" to see that her imaginings are "mere delusions." When, with Knightley's guidance, she learns "to integrate wit and will" she becomes, for Bloom, "a splendid heroine" (160). With Mr. Knightley by her side, and Mr. Bloom by ours, the right choices become much more obvious; he helps us to distinguish feminist cant from his Truth.

Like Bloom, Charles Van Doren and Mortimer Adler, who first published *How to Read a Book: A Classic Guide to Intelligent Reading* in 1940, aimed to make the lessons of college literature classes accessible to the general public. Their now-classic text has been through several editions and is still readily available in most bookstores.[5] And it shares many of the assumptions of Bloom's book with a similar aim. They argue, revealingly, for example, that "to pass from understanding less to understanding more by your own intellectual effort in reading is something like pulling yourself up by your bootstraps" (8). But here are the esteemed professors ready to give you a hand with those darned bootstraps. To their credit, they don't offer the correct readings that Bloom does. In their brief chapters on "How to Read Imaginative Literature" and "Suggestions for Reading Stories, Plays, and Poems" they offer lessons in principle: "Don't try to resist the effect that a work of imaginative literature [meaning artistic works of fiction, mainly] has on you. Don't look for terms, propositions, and arguments in imaginative literature." But they end their book with a list of 137 great writers and their works that would be "worth your while" to read. The List, they admit, may sound familiar. Much of it comes from "two sets we ourselves have edited," *Great Books of the Western World* and *Gateway to the Great Books* (350).

The List

This seemingly irresistible urge to list is another way of delivering standards of literary merit to the uninitiated. Making sure readers read the right things is a way to guide taste and one that has a history as a cottage industry in our capitalist economy. If upwardly mobile Americans were going to buy novels, why not offer them a lifetime's supply of the ones you recommend (and will make money selling and teaching), at the same time delivering up a little class to the masses? As French sociologist Pierre Bourdieu explains so convincingly in *Distinction*, his influential study of taste, our aesthetic choices are directly connected to our social background, yet we continue to divorce the social and the aesthetic, to insist that taste is "a gift of nature," of sensitive spirit or high intellect. Think of the stock dramatic scene in which a working-class star experiences opera for the first time and can't hold back the tears. But careful observation makes evident that taste is, instead, a predictable product of upbringing and education. "Surveys establish that all cultural practices (museum visits, concert-going, reading, etc.), and preferences in literature, painting or music, are closely linked to educational level . . . and social origin," Bourdieu writes (1). That working-class star, in other words, is more likely to leave the opera at intermission and head across the street to the Garth Brooks concert.

What we choose to read, in other words, is a learned (and thus predictable) behavior. How we were taught to read influences our choices. So when Adler and Van Doren tell us that "imaginative literature primarily pleases rather than teaches," they are indicating how imaginative literature ought to be read (204). It is affective, they say; readers should pay attention to the multiple meanings of words, classify by genre, seek unity and, finally:

> we must remember the obvious fact that we do not agree or disagree with fiction. We either like it or we do not. Our critical judgment in the case of expository books concerns their *truth*, whereas in criticizing belles-lettres, as the word itself suggests, we consider chiefly their *beauty*. The beauty of any work of art is related to the pleasure it gives us when we know it well. (213)

To pay attention to the things Bloom, Van Doren, and Adler suggest, to irony and solitude, to multiple layers of meaning, to the reader and author as coconspirators, to the complexity of characters and the insights they offer for self-understanding, steers us away from social messages. Bloom is emphatic about this. "Western high culture" is in decline because "novels are over-praised for social purposes" (196). He reminds us repeatedly that novels are best when they transcend cultural and political issues, when they enlighten a solitary individual. And thus he obscures the novel's extroverted history, its tendency to engage the imagination in social situations, to urge readers to connect experientially, not just aesthetically through disembodied words or formal qualities.

In summary, if you want to elevate your taste, Adler and Van Doren explain, you should read the way we tell you to. Then you will be "competent to judge." When you find yourself *wanting* to read more of the books we tell you to read, then you'll know you're there. And then "you will probably find a large company of men and women of similar taste to share your critical judgments. You may even discover, what we think is true, that good taste in litera-ture is acquired by anyone who *learns to read*" (214) [emphasis mine].

This final lesson, while sounding democratic, functions in the opposite way. With strange roundabout logic, it invites readers to affirm their posses-sion of cultural capital by exercising it. As Douglas B. Holt, a leading market-ing theorist, explains, "whereas economic capital is expressed through consuming goods and activities of material scarcity and imputed luxury, cul-tural capital is expressed through consuming via aesthetic and interactional styles that fit with cultural elite sensibilities and that are socially scarce" (218). It's not what you buy, then, so much as how you live, what social choices you make. Those with high cultural capital will listen to NPR rather than the eighties rock station; they will live near bookstores and ethnic restaurants, not on one-acre plots at the end of cul-de-sacs. And, as they read their way down The List, they might find a few others who have read what they have read. They affirm each other's "independent" choices by striking up a conversation about the good book they have both read. And, in the end, Bloom's solitary readers are good readers only when they affirm their elite tastes socially, among the culturally approved choices. Thus, Holt continues, "status bound-aries are reproduced simply through expressing one's tastes" (219).

In this way, the distinction between cultural and economic capital is maintained by relentlessly divorcing them from one another. Those with high cultural capital, reinforcing the social scarcity of their elite sensibilities, "tend to disavow mass culture even when mass-produced goods are of high quality, and they camouflage their use of mass-produced goods when using them is unavoidable," Holt explains (239). So when Farrar, Straus put the Oprah seal into the cover art of Franzen's *The Corrections,* it became a different book. It became a mass-produced, popular choice rather than a marker of distinction and taste. And elite readers began to insist on unmarked covers.

Reading for Class

But unmarked covers were a fine distinction, meaningful only to those few Americans who had, in Adler and Van Doren's sense, learned to read. What I encountered in my fall 2001 section of the Oprah's Books course were students marvelously unaffected by Franzen's reputation, as were, I suspect, most Oprah readers. In October, when they read the novel for class, most of them had heard of it only because it was an Oprah book (or because it was assigned), and they felt free to condemn it as "too long and boring." For emphasis (with a touch of high cultural clout), one woman added that she "would rather be at sea with Ishmael and Captain Ahab than read *The Corrections* again."

As part of the final, my twenty-four students, first-years to seniors, traditional college age to retirement age and from various majors (though predominantly nursing and teaching), were required to describe their own standards of literary merit in the context of choosing one of the seven novels we had read as the best and one as the worst. More than half named Franzen's book the worst, twice as many as any other book. Among this half were some of the more experienced readers who appreciated Morrison's *The Bluest Eye* and Danticat's *Breathe, Eyes, Memory.* (Other assigned novels included *What Looks Like Crazy on an Ordinary Day, Deep End of the Ocean, She's Come Undone,* and *Open House).* Their comments on why Franzen's novel didn't work for them were revealing. While several noted that they had learned to appreciate it intellectually through the class discussion, they took it to task on empathic grounds. "I couldn't connect with any of the characters," was the most frequent comment. "I could not get emotionally involved in it," one woman observed. "I wasn't drawn in," said another.

On the other hand, the more popular of the Oprah books I teach are the ones that mix some literary sophistication with an invitation to connection—*White Oleander* or *She's Come Undone,* for example. In fact, many of my students condemn some Oprah novels, as Franzen did, for being too simple, overly emotional, or predictable. They want to be challenged intellectually and philosophically, much in the way my English majors learn to be challenged by texts, but also personally, epathically, and emotionally. They want the rich, multilevel readings that Oprah offered on her best Book Club shows.

My mostly middle-class students, educated for a profession in a curriculum heavy on the liberal arts, are, in my observation, fairly similar to Oprah readers and to what cultural critics call "the general reader." My experience as a teacher convinces me that most of them, even in today's busy dot-com world, want to love to read. They are looking for books that bowl them over, that draw them in, that are unforgettable. Books they can get lost in. And, like good twenty-first century citizens, they want to get to them right now, without having to go through stacks of mediocre stories on the way to that one great read. I suspect that is why students, friends, and acquaintances are always asking me for lists of good books. Traditionally, that's how we have done this—find trusted critics and have them give us titles. Here are the top twenty books every college student should know. These one-hundred are the best novels of the twentieth century. These beautiful leather-bound volumes feature the world's fifty greatest thinkers. These ten books, above all others, have stood the test of time. Variations on Adler and Van Doren's list abound wherever we look.

But as books are ever more readily available, as literacy rates rise and more of us invest in a college education, these old lists and their outworn standards are not enough. Indeed, I sometimes wonder how they survived for so long in a democratic nation. Sure, they simplify our choices, but what do they leave out? In a vast and diverse global information age like ours, the top one-hundred anything is no longer obvious. Top one-hundred for whom? And who says so? Everything around us has changed in the last thirty years in the United States, but The List and the elite standards that maintain it have stayed surprisingly the same. With the rise of social change movements like civil rights and feminism, readers like my students began demanding more connection to their lives, more relevance in their literature. And leading intellectuals, like Adler, Van Doren, and Bloom, kept saying, "See The List." The unspoken What and Who of Bloom's *How to Read and Why* are astonishing. No need to highlight those, his attitude states. They go without saying—Shakespeare, Henry James, Marcel Proust. "See The List."

Since the 1960s, the children of the baby boom have been flooding U.S. universities and colleges. After the influx of veterans on the World War II GI

Bill came generous financial aid programs and growing state university and community college systems, as well as the establishment of merit-based (rather than class or connection-based) admission at our most elite schools. Since mid-century, the face of higher education began to change. As a second-generation Eastern European immigrant and a woman, I was one of those new faces. While the prototypical college-goers were in private schools preparing to get into the Ivy League or the Seven Sisters, checking off The List, reading Dante's *Inferno* and *The Scarlet Letter*, we were watching *Star Trek* reruns and reading Erich Segal. And with television blanketing the nation, mass culture was making a dent in everyone's psyche. It has become the prominent backdrop of our lives—not Homer but Homer Simpson—television and now the Internet.

To be successful, colleges had to take these new students and our different gifts seriously, to meet us where we were, not try to transform us into the privileged preppies we imitated, but would never become. As a graduate literature student, I joined many grad students before me in challenging the centrality of Britain in our literary history, of white men, of New England. We asked to read books by writers from the working class, black writers, immigrants, southerners, women—writers who reflected the America we knew. Colleges responded by creating different kinds of English courses. Many schools even began to take television and mass media seriously. And the traditionalists bewailed the decline of Western Culture. And then came Oprah.

Oprah understood what students have been saying for years, but what many professors and arbiters of taste in our culture have failed to grasp—that today's world demands a different approach to books and to reading. If nothing else is apparent from a close reading of Oprah's Book Club, it is certainly clear that America doesn't read like it used to—though Bloom's *How to Read and Why* typifies the attempts of many professors to correct that. Despite these efforts, Americans aren't going to books seeking classical allusions and Shakespearean quotes as affirmations of our expensive education or cultural literacy, our superior understanding or elite sensibilities. Generally, though William Bennett assumes otherwise, we aren't looking for moral lessons or biblical references. We aren't even hoping for innovation and experimentation. The Modern Library tells us that *Ulysses* is the greatest book of the twentieth century, but even though there are more college graduates among us, Americans are reading *The Pilot's Wife*—because Oprah suggested it. "What," gasps the critic of elite sensibilities, "is going on here?"

Among other things, contemporary criticism is going on. Reflecting the tenor of the times, many critics argue, as I have here, that reading is a social as well as solitary activity. We see reading not so much as the traditionalists do, as building a solid foundation for the preservation of culture and unexamined common values. For us it is as much about challenging and reconstructing (sometimes deconstructing) culture and values in the midst of momentous change. While reading still engages the solitary self in reflection and self-examination, for many readers, inspired by the absorbing worlds of novels, it is also about entering varied social situations, encountering diversity and making connections, even, put simply, starting conversations.

Oprah's Book Club demonstrates that this perspective is a more accurate reflection of where most reading Americans have gone. The Book Club invites readers to talk to each other over books, to share stories, to identify and empathize, to explore new life patterns, and even to change. By emphasizing the novel's talking life, Oprah affirms a democratic shift in what readers value in books. Now I'm not saying that the most popular things are the best. You couldn't pay me enough to watch an *American Pie* movie in any of its iterations, and I'll pass every time on a Danielle Steel or Nicholas Sparks novel. Just as I wouldn't argue that McDonald's hamburgers are the best food because more people buy them, I don't want to make the point that capitalism should guide matters of taste. However, I think we have moved beyond the opposing ridiculous point: that popularity (or femininity) inevitably breeds mediocrity. Again, more Americans are going to college, taking literature classes, joining book clubs, visiting bookstores, and thinking and talking about fiction. They may not know Literature-with-a-capital-L, but they know what they like. And what they like may not be all that bad.

I'm just Jeffersonian enough to believe that the literary tastes that my students and Oprah's readers model are often valuable and informed, and that I can learn something in conversation with them. I am also aware that my role as a professor is to offer them what I have, the skills for more intellectual, reflective reading that I worked as hard to hone as my ex-brother-in-law worked to become a master stonemason. That's what I bring to the conversations. So I approach my students with the skills that allow me to read and understand texts that have been defined as high cultural, but with desires similar to theirs—a desire for authorial generosity and proportion, a driving desire to know, to connect, to communicate, and to share. These are the things that motivate many contemporary readers.

My study of Oprah's Book Club has similarly clarified both my larger understanding of what contemporary U.S. culture embraces as a good book and what my personal preferences look like. Like many Oprah readers, my dream of a contemporary novel demands emotional as well as intellectual commitment. I want to dive into it wholeheartedly. The best novel would meet my expectations; it would engross me on many levels with complex characters, a layered plot, and lovely language. Without talking down or overexplaining, it would trust me as a reader to get it. And it would challenge me on social issues, on my understanding of people and of life, opening new views or values or reinforcing the ones that are central to me. Like many of my students, I don't care if a novel is negative or depressing. I just want it to engage me, to invite me, as Toni Morrison says, into its unique landscape.

Anticipatory Marketing

Though Oprah's staff repeatedly denies the existence of an overt standard of aesthetic merit ("She just picks what she likes"), the Book Club placed these shifting standards in the public eye and institutionalized them. Working from the populist assumptions of a talk show host, Oprah mastered a mantra that Franzen, among others, never learned: Trust readers. This mantra probably springs from a commercial base—these readers are the people who made her rich after all—but it has translated into a broad affirmation of democratic values in a realm where such values are rarely seen, the realm of the aesthetic. While Franzen wondered publicly if serious literature could have a popular audience, Oprah assumed it did. Then she offered her readers good fiction, sometimes a *Tara Road* or a *Pilot's Wife* with a clear, chronological plot and a feisty character to identify with, and sometimes a more difficult novel, a Joyce Carol Oates, Jane Hamilton, or Edwidge Danticat, because she hoped they would like what she likes.

I know many readers found the more serious fiction tough going, but that didn't stop them from buying it in record numbers. By all accounts, they seemed to be *reading* the Book Club novels as well, albeit sometimes only with Oprah's coaching. And, again, what delights me most is that they were also talking about books. Indeed, Oprah's genius may simply be that she captured the book club trend on its way up.

Marketing scholar Malcolm Gladwell calls this "anticipatory marketing"—getting to the future first. In the paradigm he describes in "The Coolhunt," innovators come along first, followed by those who aren't innovators themselves but can spot innovation. When it came to book clubs, Oprah caught cool early. She was, as Gladwell says, an "early adopter," one of "the opinion leaders in the community, the respected, thoughtful people who watched and analyzed what those wild innovators were doing and then did it themselves" (365). So when readers began, in the early 1980s, to band together in book clubs, to negotiate their standards of literary merit publicly and to use novels to make personal connections, Oprah was quick to follow.

Bringing books into American women's living rooms was a good way to get women to embrace them. But a more significant innovation, in my estimation, was in placing those books in a different context from other public book talk. On Oprah's Book Club, the author's voice was never the only voice and often not even the strongest one. Rather than interview an author as the authority sharing banter with the urbane intellectual interviewer, Oprah surrounded authors with everyday readers and staged a conversation—eventually an extended conversation, not just a quick segment at the end of a program devoted to other topics. On Oprah's Book Club, millions of Americans could listen to what cultural critics call "the general reader," just as they had been listening to "real people" since Phil Donohue altered the talk show format in the 1970s.

It is true that like Bloom, Adler, and Van Doren, Oprah has a list, but it is certainly a much different sort of list, perhaps centrally because she begins from different questions, what might be called consumer-driven (I prefer democratic) questions. These questions start from the bottom, with her readers, rather than with a top-down assertion of aesthetic authority. I learned early as a teacher that "Did you like it?" yields responses distinct from "Was it good?" and leads to different literary values. Oprah is looking for books her readers will like, responding to their desire for stories, for strong characters, for connection.

Since I began this study, it has impressed me as a teacher that she used her influence to meet her women readers where they were. She didn't embark on a campaign to have them read what was good for them—a Jane Austen novel or a bit of Virginia Woolf (as I might). Even her move into classics led first to Steinbeck, a solidly middlebrow and thoroughly reader-friendly writer. She took the books many of her readers usually read and went "one click up," as a character in *Midwives* says. And, more important, she modeled how to read these more challenging books in the context of a community of engaged readers. In this way, she rode the wave of the book club movement, but also reinforced it by bringing its methods into the living rooms and minds of her millions of viewers.

Franzen, too, had hoped to bring more serious fiction to "the American mainstream," as he wrote in his April 1996 cover article for *Harper's* magazine. Franzen, then at work on *The Corrections*, wrote in this essay of both his fear that "there was something wrong with the whole model of the novel as a form of 'cultural engagement'" and of his dream that he was wrong. In this time just before Oprah's Book Club began, he lamented how little novels mattered to most Americans and how seldom good ones were read with the seriousness they deserved. "The institution of writing and reading serious novels is like a grand old Middle American city gutted and drained by super-highways," he wrote:

> Ringing the depressed inner city of serious work are prosperous clonal suburbs of mass entertainments: techno and legal thrillers, novels of sex and vampires, of murder and mysticism. The last fifty years have seen a lot of white male flight to the suburbs and to the coastal power centers of television, journalism, and film. What remains, mostly, are ethnic and cultural enclaves. Much of contemporary fiction's vitality now resides in the black, Hispanic, Asian, Native American, gay, and women's communities, which have moved into the structures left behind by the departing straight white male. (5)

Little wonder that despite his yearning for novels to matter, Franzen couldn't see when they did because a lively, inventive cultural center looked like a gutted inner city to his shortsighted gaze. When it came down to it, he was shocked, shocked that his (realistic, social) novel would be placed next to some (realistic, social) Oprah books that were not as serious. Like most high cultural critics, he was blind to changes in reading habits led by the middle or lower classes, by people of color or women, blind to the value of anything that looked like mass market culture. If only he could have let the ladies of the Book Club have at it, he might have been surprised to see, even from his high cultural perch, how comfortably serious novels have always fit in with a little bonding and a friendly hug or two. Sometimes the pages don't even get bent.

Oprah's Book Club was a phenomenal success because it recognized and embraced how most Americans read and value literature. Oprah's unique position in popular culture and, yes, capitalism allowed her to answer the call to give books a public forum, to place them in social contexts, and to take advantage of their power to connect us. The Book Club latched onto a book club movement already gathering strength, especially among U.S. women, and took full advantage of its ties to a long-standing American tradition of novel-reading for literacy, class mobility, and social engagement, a tradition that continues to appeal to deeply held democratic values.

Notes

1. I followed the story in the *New York Times* (see citations below), but articles also appeared in *The Chronicle of Higher Education* (30 Nov. 2001), *People*— twice (12 Nov. 2001 and 31 Dec. 2001), *The New York Observer* (1 Nov. 2001), *Newsweek* (5 Nov. 2001), *The Library Journal* (15 Nov. 2001), *The New Yorker* (16 Dec. 2001), regularly in *Publishers Weekly* through October and November 2001, and in various other places.

2. Some examples of early reviews of *The Corrections* include: *Publishers Weekly* (vol. 248 no. 29 [16 July 2001] p. 164): "This is, simply, a masterpiece"; *Booklist* (vol. 97 no. 21 [July 2001] p. 1947): "Heir in scope and spirit to the great nineteenth-century novelists"; *Library Journal* (vol. 126 no. 13 [Aug. 2001], p. 160): "In this novel of breathtaking virtuosity"; *Book* (Sept. 2001): *The Corrections* "is not only the author's funniest and most focused work, it also hits harder and deeper"; *Fortune* (vol. 144 no. 4 [3 Sept. 2001] p. 256): "Harrowing and hysterical, *The Corrections* is the novel of the year"; *The Economist* (8 Sept. 2001), which panned it, but with this language: "A Great American novel has been expected from Jonathan Franzen since the mid-westerner first appeared on the New York literary scene . . . and this novel proves to be truly great in length alone"; even *O Magazine*, which called it a "dazzling new novel" before Oprah chose it.

3. The spokesperson for Harpo, Inc., who agreed to be interviewed and quoted but not named, in a June 2001 interview explained that the publishers were the ones who requested permission to put the Oprah O on their book covers, and "we granted permission." She added, "We don't require anyone to print that information [the Oprah O] on the book." Later, they asked for permission to reprint books with the logo embedded in the cover art. "The publishers were anxious to get that information on the book," she said.

She also told me that "the Book Club shows on average have slightly lower ratings than the other shows." Ratings winners, she explained were "celebrity shows" or "shows with Dr. Phil." When the Book Club drew a respectable audience, Oprah "was frankly so delighted and pleased when people *were* watching" because "she didn't expect it." From the beginning, she said (and Oprah has confirmed in other interviews) that Oprah wasn't sure the Book Club would work, "but she was committed to trying it anyway."

4. Most early Book Clubs included (somewhat disruptive) comments about the food, the chef, and the restaurant or other venue where the meeting was held. The *Deep End of the Ocean* Book Club ("Newborn Quintuplets Come Home," 18 Oct. 1996) was held at Oprah's house over wild mushroom ravioli and "crème brulée with fresh raspberries and caramel shortbread cookies." The *Stones from the River* meeting ("Selena's Family," 8 April 1997), held in a public library in Riverside, Illinois, featured the seared yellow-tailed tuna.

5. I selected *How to Read a Book: A Classic Guide to Intelligent Reading* by Mortimer Adler and Charles Van Doren, along with Bloom's, because they are the guides for general readers I found most often in bookstores. Though this guide clearly does not reflect contemporary approaches to literature, it continues to be influential and sells well. I also appreciate Mortimer Adler's often-stated commitment to the general reader, a commitment that led him to such a project as *How to Read a Book*. Though his methods eventually undermine his aims, I honor what I understand to be the original spirit of the work.

Works Cited

Adler, Mortimer J., and Charles Van Doren. *How to Read a Book: A Classic Guide to Intelligent Reading.* New York: Simon and Schuster, 1940. Updated edition, 1972.

Bloom, Harold. *How to Read and Why.* New York: Scribner, 2000.

Bourdieu, Pierre. *Distinction: A Social Critique of the Judgement of Taste.* Richard Nice, trans. Cambridge: Harvard UP, 1984.

Corcoran, Monica. "On the Dust Jacket: To O or Not to O." *New York Times* (21 Oct. 2001) 6+.

Franzen, Jonathan. "Meet Me in St. Louis." *The New Yorker* (18 Dec. 2001) newyorker.com posted 17 Dec. 2001.

———. "Perchance to Dream: In the Age of Images, A Reason to Write Novels." *Harper's* 292:1751 (Apr. 1996).

Gladwell, Malcolm. "The Coolhunt." In *The Consumer Society Reader.* Juliet B. Schor and Douglas B. Holt, eds. New York: New Press, 2000. 360–74.

Holt, Douglas B. "Does Cultural Capital Structure American Consumption?" In *The Consumer Society Reader.* Juliet B. Schor and Douglas B. Holt, eds. New York: New Press, 2000. 212–52.

Kirkpatrick, David. "'Oprah' Gaffe by Franzen Draws Ire and Sales." *New York Times* (29 Oct. 2001) E1+.

———. "Winfrey Rescinds Offer to Author for Guest Appearance." *New York Times* (24 Oct. 2001) C4.

Korda, Michael. *Making the List: A Cultural History of the American Bestseller 1900–1999.* New York: Barnes and Noble, 2001.

Radway, Janice A. *A Feeling for Books: The Book-of-the-Month Club, Literary Taste, and Middle-Class Desire.* Chapel Hill: U of North Carolina P, 1997.

———. "The Scandal of the Middlebrow: The Book-of-the-Month Club, Class Fracture, and Cultural Authority." *South Atlantic Quarterly* 89:4 (Fall 1990) 703–36.

3

READING RELIGIOUSLY

The Ritual Practices of Oprah's Book Club

KATHRYN LOFTON

"Behave your way to success" is one of the oft-repeated maxims recited by Oprah Winfrey and her cohort of guest psychologists, columnists, and spiritual gurus. Any study of the products of the Oprah Winfrey empire (represented by her daily television show, her Web site, and her monthly magazine) quickly reveals that prescriptive behavior dominates the substance of Winfrey's message. "Live Your Best Life" columnist and meditation teacher Sharon Salzberg wrote in the January 2002 issue of *O* magazine, "To be able to make an intense effort—to heal, to speak, to create, to alleviate our suffering or the suffering of others—while guided by a vision of life with all its mutability, evanescence, dislocations, and unruliness, is the particular gift of faith" (28). Another month, in the same column, the author made a similar argument that "faith is actually something you *do*" (Medwick 131). Viewers and readers are told to "Make the Connection" and "Get with the Program" in an effort to "Change Your Life." In the narrative landscape of her television program and monthly magazine, "connections" are made, "programs" are designed, and lives are "changed" through the dutiful completion of Winfrey's multimedia prescriptions.

The purpose of Winfrey's programming is reprogramming. After watching an episode, leafing through the magazine, or scanning the Web site, it seems imperative to *do* something. The stories of triumph make you wonder why you haven't; the endless advocacies (eat breakfast, spot prevaricators, write more letters, choose a better dentist, employ more fauna as a decorating strategy) and counsel (discover your relationship sin, reconcile with your estranged relative, find your dream, be more organized, love realistically, work passionately) make you vow to do something—even if it's something small—somehow better. Oprah's voice pervades throughout these instructions, simultaneously ordering and modeling her suggestions. It seems as if her every success demands that you wake yourself to her levels of alertness and action. After all, she is the paradigmatic result of her prescriptions: It is her body, her business, her couture closet, her favorite novel, and her latest breakfast marmalade that stand as the ideal exhibit of her advice fulfilled.

Oprah Winfrey's relationship to reading is perhaps her most publicized prescription. Within her many commentaries on the power of reading, Winfrey embeds countless practices. The Winfrey read is a situational read; according to her repeated recommendations, if done in the right place, in the right clothes, with the right pillows, the revolutionary power of reading is maximized. This emphasis on luxurious rather than ascetic practice is consistent throughout Oprah's discursive realm, as she frequently offers images of herself in comfortable contexts for her readers to enjoy vicariously and ideally to emulate. In a column about her "faith in miracles," she writes that a miracle is "having pomegranate, kiwi, and mango on a pretty tray for breakfast" (Winfrey 2002a: 230). This miraculous moment is supplied by an edible pleasure framed in aesthetic knowing; the practice of savored beauty makes the minor instance a miraculous occurrence. For the consumer, then, Oprah encourages daily practices that create comfortable, sometimes decadent, circumstances. Consider the following description from Oprah's monthly "What I Know for Sure" column in *O* magazine: "In the evenings right before sleep I don't read or watch anything—including late-night news—that would add anxiety . . . I also keep a gratitude journal and, at the end of a workday, I 'come down' by reading a great novel or just sitting with myself to come back to my center—it's what I call going mindless" (Winfrey 2002b: 296). Notice that, here, books are seen as a relaxant. "Great novels" can make one "mindless" as they take a busy woman back to her "center." In other places, great books are also said to "inspire" change and "comfort" women trapped in unhappy personal plots. The point: Reading is a practice, encouraged to be regular, strategic, and situational. By apportioning "down time" and offering alternate worldviews, reading successfully enacts the principles of Oprah's broader spiritual ambition: to encourage "connections" and "success" through regulatory behavior.

Although much can be said about Winfrey's reading practices in her magazine, and in the episodes devoted exclusively to psychological healing, this chapter focuses only on the ritual elements of Oprah's Book Club episodes. Within this distinct cohort of examples, Winfrey's prescriptive tactics congeal into sermonic clarity. Before detailing the ritual themes of the televised Book Club, it is useful to establish a definition of "ritual," and to place the Book Club episodes within the broader ritual paradigm of *The Oprah Winfrey Show*. Scholars of religion emphasize that any definition of ritual must necessarily incorporate a relationship to superhuman beings. For most religionists, ritual is a system of actions and beliefs that has a beginning, middle, and an end, and is directly related to deified figures. Some social theorists, however, have persistently set aside the explicit citation of a divine figuring, focusing instead on the material manifestations of ritual action. For anthropologists, talk of divinity is frequently implicit within behavior, and not explicitly obvious in its ritual performance. This is how anthropologists can define Thanksgiving dinner and Super Bowl Sunday as "ritual events," whereas religionists resist the degradation of the category "ritual" with such vaguely secular instances.

The Oprah Winfrey Show presents a perfect case study in the problem of any methodologically exclusive definitions of ritual. While it would be crude to describe *The Oprah Winfrey Show* as a religious event with superhuman evocations, it is not inaccurate to interpret Winfrey's own commentary as religiously situated. On her show, Winfrey testifies openly about her struggles against authoritarian faith and her own commitment to an omnipotent higher power. She frequently mentions God and the "power of God" on her program, at her inspirational workshops, and in her *O* magazine column. She often mentions her prayers, like her recitation of "I surrender all, I surrender all, I surrender all, all to my blessed savior" when she was waiting to hear whether she was cast in *The Color Purple*. She repeatedly tells employees and audience members that God sets dreams for you, and it is your job merely to listen and surrender to that inner voice.

This is rather flimsy talk, however, hardly the stuff of coherent denominational presence. Such milquetoast spiritual supplication is grounded in Winfrey's particular racial and biographical experience. Her citation of "the black church" is frequent and pronounced in its moral accompaniments. When explaining the virtues of community, she points to all-day Sunday services and church 'mamas' as ideal leaders. When she wants to comfort a despondent guest, she will quote key phrases from gospel songs that "her grandmamma used to sing." Furthermore, her anecdotal offerings are drizzled with references to the church, particularly as it contributed to her professional genesis. "I used to speak in the church all the time, and the sisters in the front row would say to my grandmother, 'Hattie Mae, this child sure can talk'," Winfrey tells her guest audience. During another episode, she describes her informal ordination: "In first grade six white kids were going to beat me up. So I told them about Jesus of Nazareth and what happened to people who tried to stone him. The kids called me the Preacher and left me alone after that." From first grade forward, Winfrey's pastoral purpose was clarion. The superhuman, channeled through her tales and tasks, is the star of the show.

Winfrey's superhuman talk show talk encourages a ritual analysis when pursuing Winfrey's empire. After all, her episodes are not without their plotted redundancies. Viewers who tune in to *The Oprah Winfrey Show* expect the familiar cycle of individual confession, revision, and renewal. This cycle is recycled regardless of topical theme. Every episode of *The Oprah Winfrey Show* incorporates repetition (repetition of advice, of personal revolution, of individual self-sacrifice, of suffering) and parceling (of luxury goods, of extravagant physical makeovers, of spiritual guides, of Oprah-prescribed books). Conducted within the peach and taupe walls of her Chicago studio, the ritual—the regulated parceling of goods and repeated revelation—functions as a corrective to the despairs and inequalities of the world outside her kingdom. Life transformations are described through spotlighted guest montages and monologues, testimonies that mirror the paradigms established within the conversion narratives of evangelical Protestantism. Scholars agree that these narratives have had an analogous structure, moving from contrition ("I'm sorry for my wayward ways") to humiliation ("Everyone can see how awful I am") to volition ("I must and can be better") to exaltation ("Glory to the God that placed me on this holy path") (Stout 39). On the show, spiritual counselors are called on to provide interpretations and translations of these guest testimonials. The guests thus serve as confessors to priest-like spiritual counselors, who in turn defer to the on-site divine mediator—Oprah—for affirmation and the affirming personal anecdote and O-embossed wrapping.

This ritual pattern repeats in episode after episode, year after year. Take any given topic—miraculous weight loss, for example—and the majority of that day's subject will be consigned to first-person testimonial montages, pre-produced and collated into the program. Winfrey introduces the segments and offers sidebar commentaries on the testifying ("She looks like a hot mama now!"). On average, there are four testimonials in any given show, each chosen for their diverse sameness—for their physical and cultural dissimilarity ("we all look different") unified through experiential similarity ("but we all have the same feelings"). Likewise, the narrative trajectory of their experience is programmed into analogy. Case in point: A massive man or woman struggles with obesity due to childhood trauma; this man or woman has a "wake-up call" or an "aha" moment that effectively motivates "change." The man or woman then loses an enormous amount of weight "the right way" (i.e., balanced diet and exercise) and emerges spiritually enlightened and psychologically secure. Also, the individual looks much better (assisted in this last step by a Winfrey-funded total makeover). The man or woman spends time thanking God and Oprah for their never-ending support, but ultimately confessing that, yes, it was they themselves they have to thank for "taking responsibility" for their lives. You could fit any sort of person into this narrative—a rich black woman, a poor Asian woman, an unemployed white woman—and still the moral-driven ritual plot would remain the same.

Book Club episodes are not so neatly narrated. Within any given Book Club meeting, more dissent and discord are illustrated than in the average televised Winfrey therapy. Nevertheless, every episode of Oprah's Book Club does contain repeated organizational and emotive elements. Book Club sessions open with Winfey citing the astonishing number of letters received from viewers about the chosen book. Alongside this epistolary excitement, Winfrey usually proclaims the universal appeal of that text, the message that spawned such testimonial abundance. From the cadre of letter-writers, Winfrey then elaborately selects an appropriate cohort of participants. For instance, in the discussion of *Cane River*, a multigenerational story of slavery in Louisiana, Winfrey picked four perfectly diverse women: Danielle, an African American kindergarten teacher, wife of a white man, and granddaughter of a "proud Creole woman"; Jeanne, a white single mother who read the book in the wake of her mother's cancer diagnosis; Stephanie, an African American still struggling with the darkness of her skin; and Tracey, a white high school teacher who recently discovered that her family had owned slaves. Again, although her cast possesses an apparent variety, their shared emotive response to the text binds them in experiential similarity. Thus, Jeanne and Stephanie, though racially and economically different, will find their universal humanity through their common collusion over *Cane River*. Such elision of difference is a classic attribute of ritual. "Rituals create a setting in which persons can appear, by appearing in their culture, by devising a reality in which they may stand as a part," wrote anthropologist Barbara G. Myerhoff. "In their rituals, we see persons dramatizing self and culture at once, each made by the other" (156). As Jeanne and Stephanie share their biographical empathy with *Cane River*, they will find that the details of their stories are secondary to their driving passion for the book and, indeed, their lives. *Cane River* and the other books of Oprah's Book Club provide a temporary reality, a liminal space for conversation and connection among disparate characters.

Following the announcement of the televised Book Club, Winfrey often supplies a pretaped author montage, including seminal moments in their development, both as an author and as a human being. Accessibility is key. As the author is invited to join the Club, Winfrey seeks to introduce the author as a possible comrade, not an elite figure. Rather than pose the writer as an exiled, idiosyncratic modernist hero, the author is transformed into a gentle-hearted chum, someone with the same familial challenges, sartorial struggles, and self-doubts as Oprah's viewers. A visual thread in these montages is the solitary walk, with the author traversing their backyard, urban neighborhood, or scenic vista while gazing into the distance. "This could be you," suggests the teleplay, as viewers recall the reflective stroll as one of Winfrey's most popular prescriptions.

After this introductory montage and commentary, Winfrey transitions from the studio gathering to the pretaped Book Club meeting. There, women and men gather with Winfrey and the author in a willfully casual atmosphere, such as a living room filled with pillows and sofas, or a dining room table strewn with passable dishes. Candles, food, and luxuriant clothing simulate the sense that this is an elect moment, a performance of exclusive colloquialism. Although the meetings frequently took place in one of Winfrey's opulent homes, the setting is established to suggest that this could be any living room or den or dining room. Focus is on conversation, and the cutlery. Both the discourse and the decorations indicate that the participants are in earnest, both provide "the dramatization of a significant event" requisite for ritual action (Goethals 6). One could certainly host a book club among austere Shaker furnishings or in an unfinished suburban basement, yet the Winfrey Book Club models a decorous importance. This ritual care of the book club context suggests the prescriptive impulse. Roy A. Rappaport has defined ritual as repeated action distinguished in its formality and sincerity. Through the constructed comfort of the conversational situation, Winfrey creates a ceremonial space, a sacred arena for discussion and earnest disclosure.

With the stage seriously set, a conversation can begin. Within that conversation, typical television rules apply: commercial breaks cordon topic distinctions, any major conflict is edited to the second half so as to tempt viewers, and Winfrey's editorial inserts frame any internal messiness to the conversation. While these predictable narrative turns are enough to satisfy a ritual description, the content of the conversation provides even more evidence for the ritual impulse of these dialogues. In his study of the Super Bowl, Gregor T. Goethals observed, "For those who genuinely participate, the rituals offer occasions for identity and renewal." Throughout the Book Club conversations, Winfrey's driving want is to create connection: between the participants and the authors, among the participants, and between herself and her viewing audience. For Winfrey, connection is made through recognition. If participants identify affinities with the characters, and can articulate how their identity mirrors or contradicts their interpretations of the novel, then connection is inaugurated. Through identification with the sacral center (here, the novel), participants may achieve individual reformation. Or, to borrow again from Goethals, they will fulfill the function of ritual, which is "to provide an immediate, direct sense of involvement with the sacred, confirming the world view, indeed the very being, of the participants" (6). Viewers and Book Club guests achieve such ritual success through several rhetorical tropes, including the establishment of relational affiliation, the proclamation of thematic universality, the description of a codified moral, character assessment, communal catharsis. Although each of these tropes will be here assessed individually, in enactment they are overlapping. By outlining them individually, we see how several dialectical threads forge to rope readers into conversion, into a compelling claim of revolutionary selfhood.

For Every Woman

As demonstrated by the sort of Book Club guests Winfrey selects, the best club members are those with clear analogical links to the plot of the novel. Book Club episodes frequently open with Winfrey proclaiming, "For every woman who's ever been [fill in blank], this show is for you." The blank could refer to women who have been divorced or discovered family secrets, or experienced shocking tragedy, debilitating illness, or personal betrayal. Regardless the textual specific, the point of the proclamation is the declaration of relational affinity. "The majority of our e-mails," announced Winfrey at the opening of the *Icy Sparks* discussion, "were from thousands of you who identified with the story of a girl just trying to fit in, like Kerry Strano, our fourth and final guest who grew up biracial in a predominantly white English community." Even though *Icy Sparks* focuses on a girl with Tourette's syndrome,

Winfrey translates that uncommon disorder into common experience. Everyone has access to the experience of "trying to fit in," even if it is not accompanied by debilitating muscular spasms. Introducing the guests for the book club addressing *Fall on Your Knees*, Winfrey describes each in terms of their sense of kinship with the text:

> For Lynne Sherman, this book was a window to exploring her family's secrets, including, she says, the sexual abuse that Lynne hadn't ever discussed with her other siblings. Chaka Reed related to the sacrifices that the siblings made for each other in the novel. And she and her sister adopted their young brother when her mother abandoned them. And Audrey Sytes was struck by the memories that we leave for our children, she says, and how harmful some of those may be. Sue Johnston is another survivor of sexual abuse who says this book helped her see abusers in a different light. And Brenda Zufria is an educator in the prevention of sexual abuse of children.

Again, the guideline for Winfrey's guest selection is a self-described affinity between the women and the text. Through this prefatory profile, Winfrey not only details the participants, she also piques her audience's interest, teasing the upcoming discussion with voyeuristic disclosure. The viewers know that these aren't mere tidbits—these are previews of the confessionals to come. Sue Johnston is not only a survivor; she is a survivor who will speak, bringing to painful light her abuse in the pillowed bower of Oprah's Book Club.

As the conversation proceeds, Winfrey prods the relational touchstones of her participants. "I want to ask this question. What in the book most related to you?" Winfrey repeatedly asks, "When did you think, 'This is my story'?" Regardless of the geographic or historical context of the novel, Book Club guests arrive armed to respond in detail to this ritual question. Right away, the viewers are drawn into the lives of the guests as they offer details to fill the debate and legitimate their reading of the text. Quickly, the subject of the discussion turns from the novel to the guests, to their novelistic retellings of their life stories. "For many of us, it was just a story, but for these women, it was all too real," Winfrey announces at the beginning of a segment. "Most of us only read that story. They lived it" (*We Were the Mulvaneys*, *Drowning Ruth*). Winfrey underlines this transition to the "real" with montages and testimonials from women who may or may not have read the novel, but certainly have access to its plot. "Next, how perfectly normal women just lost their minds during divorce," she warns, "Next, why, if you're harboring a family secret of your own and you're watching this, you need to get it out in the open" (*Drowning Ruth*). These segments involving "real-life women" are inserted to heighten the drama of the episode, to transfer from two-dimensional fiction into three-dimensional contemporary dilemmas. Fictional women provide portholes to deeper interpretations of this televised, but purportedly more real, reality. Winfrey's premise is that real women will feel more comfortable speaking if they have a preexistent vocabulary from which to borrow; the sanctioned ritual text offers an alternate language for self-description, providing one degree of linguistic removal from their own painful reality. Through a conversational affinity with the text, a Book Club participant can achieve therapeutic levels of disclosure. And, as in a Protestant public confessional, the witness will benefit as much as the testifier from the ritual release of the biographic.

Beyond the Work

While useful for establishing relational affinity, the particulars of the selected novel's plot and prose are unnecessary for Book Club viewing. The invited Book Club guests read favorite quotations, and frequently moments from the text are debated, but the driving editorial thrust of the episode is beyond the book. "Truly great books bring out thoughts that go far beyond just the work itself," Winfrey explained in her analysis of *A Fine Balance*. Oprah's Book Club episodes are, by Winfrey's contrivance, not about the book; they are about what people do with books. The conversation is intended to be accessible to a wide viewing audience, for those who may or may not have read the assigned novel. In order to incorporate this diffuse audience, Winfrey emphasizes the inclusive impetus of a given text, gearing discussion toward abstracted versions of character dilemmas. "Now this book gives you a sense from the inside and out of what it is like to have Tourette's or any other affliction that makes you feel different," Winfrey remarked in the *Icy Sparks* discussion. The *Icy Sparks* episode provided a thumbnail discussion of Tourette's and its limited treatments, and spotlighted viewers who had family members with this diagnosis. But a large portion of the conversation focused on communal cruelty to difference, and on the importance of compassionate parenting that breeds children amenable and empathetic toward others. "I just love a book that enthralls you and also teaches, and that is exactly what many took away from this experience," explained Winfrey during the discussion of *Cane River*. "One universal theme that particularly inspired our readers is how the women in the book, with such limited choices, aspired to do so much for the coming generations." The themes highlighted in Book Club books focus on honesty, quality childrearing, and the courage that creates individual redemption.

It has been noted before that the majority of Winfrey's Book Club picks share a unanimous narrative trajectory: A woman, usually of eccentric yet compelling character, experiences an enormous trauma (or has a driving dilemma, such as obesity or a cruel mother). The remainder of the plot follows the character as she manages the psychological, material, or social aftereffects of this trauma. Usually, the stories conclude on a neutral note: The central character (again, usually a woman) is wiser for her experiences, though on the whole not entirely happy with the way her life has resolved. Obviously, Winfrey believes this paradigmatic plotline will not only resonate with her viewers, but also express a universal truth seminal for her spiritual work. This truth can be articulated by Winfrey during the course of an episode, but is often summarized by the author or a precocious participant. Rohinton Mistry, author of *A Fine Balance*, encapsulates an Oprah interpretation in this clean summation of his six-hundred-page novel: "*A Fine Balance* is a story about four characters who, against tremendous odds, endure life, survive, not only endure but manage to find happiness in it and come together as a family." Here, Mistry defines a sprawling, Dickensian rendering of 1970s Bombay as a fable of talk show redemption. Suffering and adversity abound, as they do in real life, and yet are bound up by patience, optimism, and goodwill. Although his novel possesses deep complexity and contradictory conclusions, Mistry and the *Oprah* viewing audience emerge from the episode with a satisfying summary of man's universal plight. Summarizing *We Were the Mulvaneys*, Winfrey remarked, "It is more than a novel. It is about life." The life translated on Book Club episodes is inevitably a careful redaction of accessibility, a tightened slogan often not entirely representative of the chosen novels.

One way Winfrey emphasizes the generic themes within Book Club novels is by acknowledging fictional settings. Social issues are highlighted, yet are conclusively subsumed within the overarching therapeutic impetus of the episode. "I'm telling you the book isn't about slavery," Winfrey explained during the discussion of *Cane River*. "It's about what these women did after they were freed and, you know, one of the things that amazes me is that people are able to, after such degradation, after suffering like that, to be able to love again, to be able to step out of that and say, 'I will now build a family of my own'. That is—to me, is just the most extraordinary thing." The praise embedded within Winfrey's commentary would be evident to any *Oprah* viewer. Regardless their race or genealogy or access to *Cane River*, any *Oprah* viewer with an experience of "degradation" can take something uplifting from this assertion. In other *Oprah* episodes, "learning to love again" and personal regeneration have been central pedagogical themes. Now, in *Cane River*, they are modeled and reasserted. The viewer may have never been to Louisiana, but if they know "degradation," they, too, can access the message of that episode. A white woman who has never left Winnetka, Illinois, can therefore find as much purpose and meaning in *Cane River* as a black woman from Biloxi. The social realities profiled in the selected novels are accessorizing backdrop to the moral dramas of the text.

This moral intention is always named by Winfrey. Oprah's Book Club discussions are discussions, with shared conversational space for all the participants. Nevertheless, Winfrey is the organizing principle. It is her careful liturgy that orders and guides enlightenment. Whether in the editing room or in her bracketing summations, Winfrey steers the moral of the story. Every Book Club episode revolves around an ethical theme, an explicit message that is the "truth" taken from some disarming plot. Winfrey does not moralize without endorsement; the author often provides a validating synopsis of the message. "And you have to get to the bottom before you can turn around and start up again," explained Elizabeth Berg when responding to a panelist's question about the "real truth" of her novel, *Open House*. Oprah cocreates these sermonic centerpieces, as she did in the Book Club meeting for *Drowning Ruth*: "The secret holds so much power for you and when you let it out into the light, you see that was all your big fear." The moral can also emerge in dialogue with a Book Club guest. In her analysis of *Icy Sparks*, Paula, a selected Book Club participant, remarked, "And I think that—that the saving grace in the book—and I find it to be so in my extended family also—is that unconditional love is what will conquer Tourette's." Winfrey didn't miss a beat: "Everything. It can—conquers almost everything." Whether through dialogue or pointed pronouncement, the homiletic thesis is inevitably one that endorses Winfrey's overarching therapeutic intent. In the discussion of *Drowning Ruth*, Patrick, another Book Club guest, articulated Winfrey's ambition:

> Well, one thing that this book helped me to do is see secrets from
> different people's lives. And that's why it really just drew home with
> me is because in my particular situation I had always realized it from
> just my viewpoint and how it affected me, which is very selfish. But
> this book opened my eyes to how it affected other people. . . . If

books are gonna be this good, then I—then I want to read them because—because they—great literature is very powerful and it has the power to affect us all in different ways. And—and it's wonderful.

Winfrey immediately validated Patrick's insight: "That's what I think, Patrick. Literature is powerful. It has the ability to change people's—the way they—the way we think." Regardless of the moral specificity—or ambiguity—of a given novel, Winfrey frames the discussion around the reader's consolidated clarity. In the world of Winfrey, reading is a critical practice of "making the connection," of "behaving" to success.

Taking Issue

Oprah Winfrey's readerly therapies aren't merely proffered in affirming maxims. Indeed, Winfrey communicates as much in her condemnations as in her enthusiasms. Every episode of Oprah's Book Club includes an indignant Winfrey. "The only thing I didn't believe is that she went to Tiffany's and then gave that bracelet away," Winfrey remarked about Amanda, the consumerist divorcee from Elizabeth Berg's *Open House*, "I do not believe she gave that bracelet away to a homeless woman." Despite the protestations of other Club participants (or the author herself), Winfrey persisted in her opinion. Interestingly, Winfrey's disbelief is never couched in textual discontinuity. Never does Winfrey suggest that the text fails to support whatever she rejects; rather, it is the idea of the action or character that frustrates her. For example, the character of Amanda in *Drowning Ruth* receives harsh criticism because of her secrecy. "She's the one I had some issues with," Winfrey announced, "I'm not so sure we love Amanda." Amanda's inability to tell the truth placed her in the lowest echelons of Winfrey's estimation: "I think she had no integrity." Because she could not "live in integrity," Winfrey disdained her. Christina Schwarz, the author, is taken aback, and defends her character from such assignation, noting Amanda's upbringing and context as rationale for her impotence. Winfrey refuses to compromise her position:

SCHWARZ: You really didn't like her.
WINFREY: No, I did not like her.

The irony of Winfrey's dismissal is that her overarching intent of the Club is to counteract such reductive assessments of others. "That's what I love about a book," Winfrey proclaimed during the discussion of *Drowning Ruth*, "it just opens up all those doors." Winfrey consistently argues that books can act as lessons in compassion, yet her own moral compass remains apparently unaltered by her readings. Although she suggests that she has seen new worlds and accumulated new ideas through reading, Winfrey never admits to a personal recalibration through reading. In this public ritual, reading is always confirmation of what she already knew. Winfrey summarizes this conflict with a host's glee. "I love this," she says, "It's like these people are real" (*Drowning Ruth*).

Kathy, from *The House of Sand and Fog*, also garnered little empathy from Winfrey: "You know, I have some issues with her." Even though the character of the colonel from Dubus's novel caused her Club participants more trouble, Winfrey forgave him his transgressions. "I was sympathetic to his culture and him trying to come here to build a better life," she said. But Kathy received tougher treatment. "Why didn't she open her damn mail? That's what I want to know," Winfrey exclaimed, "She is one of those people who sits around and doesn't open their mail because they're trying to hide from their bills. Why didn't she open her mail?" Here, the viewer witnesses the symphonic assimilation of Oprah's varied therapies. Not only is Winfrey responding to the novel in a conversational dialect, she is also signaling her audience that the more banal topics of other episodes can be brought to bear on the elegant abstractions of fiction. Any viewer of *The Oprah Winfrey Show* is familiar with Winfrey's parade of financial counselors and their repeated admonitions to the indebted and those "hiding from bills." Winfrey's degradation of a fictional character reiterates a broader therapeutic plan. For her, any sympathy is diminished by personal irresponsibility and delusion. The bounds of kindness only extend as far as you adhere to her prescriptions. What Kathy really needed was a daily dose of Oprah.

The Lightbulb Moment

All of this conversation and correction, assessment, and moral summation climaxes in the "lightbulb" or "aha" moments. It is Oprah Winfrey's purpose to provoke such moments, which she defines in the following explanation:

> Well, over the years, I know you've heard me talk a lot about light-bulb moments and thousands of you have written to us after experiencing little epiphanies of your own. That's what a lightbulb

moment is. In the magazine, I call it "aha" moments, that moment
when you go, "Aha" while watching the show. I have them all the
time. Lightbulb, aha moments, happen when you hear something
that suddenly clicks for you. What's exciting about a lightbulb
moment is—or one of those aha moments—is that you feel in that
moment you know you discovered something new and important
that can change your life. What's really outstanding about those
moments is usually when you hear something like that, it's—it's—
it's reminding you of what you already know. That's what the aha is,
'cause it feels like, 'I knew this, I just didn't know the words to put
it', you know? That's what it is. That's what's fabulous about it.
("Gary Zukav")

Lightbulb moments, those "little epiphanies" that "change your life," are the
transaction of Winfrey ritual. Whether called "born again" experiences or
"nirvana" or "aha" moments, these instances are conjured through the televised narratives of Book Club participants. The entire trajectory of *Oprah*
show episodes builds to the conjure of such instances. "Today's show is going
to break your heart and heal it again," Winfrey announced at the beginning
of her *We Were the Mulvaneys* discussion, "Break your heart and heal it
again." Meetings of the televised Oprah Book Club follow this plot, moving
from depressive opening confessionals to communal contemplations of character to collective comprehension of the selected sermonic focus. Lightbulb
moments bring closure to the latter portion of the ritual event. Patty Jan,
management consultant and mother of two, had this lightbulb moment
while reading *A Fine Balance*:

I picked up this book to read, and I—I was going through a really
hard time. I'd lost my job and—and things were out of control, so a
really good friend recommended the book for me to read. I was in
awe of how beautifully it was written. But I didn't get it. And one
day I—I just sort of realized through my actions and—and the book
came back to me that what had happened to me was a change that
was thrust into my life, and I had to embrace it in order to move on,
and that is the fundamental message in this book.

Moments like Jan experienced are narrated after some cajoling by Winfrey,
who inevitably concludes most Book Club discussion with the question,

"What did it take for you to get over [fill in blank]?" Again, the blank may refer to a divorce or a death, a familial sorrow or a career disappointment. With this pressing inquiry, Book Club participants happily contribute their "lightbulb" breakthroughs. The message is here redescribed and underlined, with Winfrey framing these disparate tales of triumph with her own peda-gogical ambition. "Well, you know what we have to teach our daughters? Is to give up the fantasy," she decides at the end of one Club meeting. Translat-ing the therapeutic purpose of the text into action is a critical conclusive trope of the Oprah's Book Club. "I celebrate and honor you for the women that you've become, for taking your pain and taking what was a very difficult time and turning it into triumph for your children and for your lives," Win-frey pronounced at the close of her discussion of *Open House*. "Here's to you all and here's to Elizabeth Berg. Here's to books."

The realist reveal of Oprah's Book Club episodes mirrors the sort of con-clusions of her chosen novels. "I'm always accused of not having happy end-ings," Winfrey remarked, "I look for whatever is realistic, whatever is meaningful, whatever is going to take me to the next level with these charac-ters. I don't look for necessarily a happy ending" (*Fall on Your Knees*). The conclusions of Book Club participants are personally uplifted, yet openly pragmatic. Participants agree on the universality of suffering, of secrecy, of generational disappointment. They persist despite these downtrodden senti-ments because of the opportunities for connection and the possibility of the lightbulb. Or, in the words of *Fall on Your Knees* author Ann-Marie Mac-Donald, participants endure in the pursuit of "fairly happy" endings:

> Some people ask me, or they—they ask each other, is it a happy ending? And there is a kind of desire to be reassured that it's going to be okay, and I think that what unfolds over the course of the book is that the truth is told. The story comes out. The secrets come out. Something is released. And something else can rest in peace. You know, when the past is resting in peace and we can go forward with the story, and that's fairly happy.

And so the story moves forward, in a never-ending cycle of truth and mishap.

Anthropologists have suggested that ritual itself necessitates a cycle. Every ritual acknowledges the passage from one stage to another, a transition from one level of awareness to another. Such a description of ritual mirrors the Oprah Book Club, with the individuals achieving temporary relief through the exhalation of personal trial and the connection with correspondent troubles. Through ceremonial observances, "a constant flow of indulgences is spread through society, with others who are present constantly reminding the individual that he must keep himself together as a well demeaned person and affirm the sacred quality of these others," explained Erving Goffman (91). Or, to follow Winfrey's own summation during the 2002 conclusion of her Book Club: "A great book makes us look closer in the mirror. A great book tells the truth of our own experiences. And sometimes a great book offers nothing short of salvation" (*Sula*).

The pursuit of such salvation is at the heart of the ritual enterprise. Although rituals can be tedious and indifferent, routine and vacant, they can also provide the framework for spiritual progress. The question for cultural critics is whether Oprah's progress is a sort of progress to endorse or decry. Because it is clear that there is only one way to read books with Oprah: the way Winfrey does. Reading books "the Oprah way," is to read with the problems of the reader being negotiated alongside the problems of the characters. This is not peculiar to Oprah, or to most readers: We all read texts in part to find comfort, commonality, and resolution through the fictions of others. Yet reading "the Oprah way" is to read only with the intent to solve the *reader's* dilemmas; in the empire of Oprah, the reader is always her. The solipsism of this reader is emphasized over the aesthetic of the text, or the potential social critiques offered within the texts. In Oprah's Book Club, social change and literary beauty are appendages to the primary duty of any text: to make the reader feel better. Yet, like all ritual enactments, reading with Winfrey is rarely a one-time revelation. Inevitably, the predictable exhilaration of episodic television and canny ritual tactics inspires returning participants to consume and exhort this satisfying return. One ritual is never enough; every ritual feeds into another. It is this infinite deduction that makes the Book Club not only good ritual, but also good television.

Works Cited

"Gary Zukav's Light Bulb Moments." *The Oprah Winfrey Show*. ABC. 13 Oct. 2000.

Goethals, Gregor T. *The TV Ritual: Worship at the Video Altar*. Boston: Beacon, 1981.

Goffman, Erving. *Interaction Ritual: Essays on Face-to-Face Behavior*. New York: Doubleday, 1967.

Medwick, Cathleen. "Finding the Connection." *O, The Oprah Magazine*. Sept. 2002: 131.

Myerhoff, Barbara G. "A Death in Due Time: Construction of Self and Culture in Ritual Drama." *Rite, Drama, Festival, Spectacle: Rehearsals Toward a Theory of Cultural Performance*. Ed. John MacAloon. Philadelphia: Institute for the Study of Human Issues, 1984. 149–78.

"Oprah's Book Club: *Cane River*." *The Oprah Winfrey Show*. ABC. 24 Sept. 2001.

"Oprah's Book Club: *Drowning Ruth*." *The Oprah Winfrey Show*. ABC. 16 Nov. 2000.

"Oprah's Book Club: *Fall on Your Knees*." *The Oprah Winfrey Show*. ABC. 5 Apr. 2002.

"Oprah's Book Club: *A Fine Balance*." *The Oprah Winfrey Show*. ABC. 24 Jan. 2002.

"Oprah's Book Club: *The House of Sand and Fog*." *The Oprah Winfrey Show*. ABC. 24 Jan. 2001.

"Oprah's Book Club: *Icy Sparks*." *The Oprah Winfrey Show*. ABC. 16 May 2001.

"Oprah's Book Club: *Open House*." *The Oprah Winfrey Show*. ABC, 27 Sept. 2000.

"Oprah's Book Club: *Sula*." *The Oprah Winfrey Show*. ABC. 2 May 2002.

"Oprah's Book Club: *We Were the Mulvaneys*." *The Oprah Winfrey Show*. ABC. 8 Mar. 2001.

Rappaport, Roy A. *Ecology, Meaning, and Religion*. Berkeley: North Atlantic, 1979.

Salzberg, Sharon. "Choosing Faith Over Fear." *O, The Oprah Magazine*. Jan. 2002: 28.

Stout, Harry S. *The New England Soul: Preaching and Religious Culture in Colonial New England*. New York: Oxford U P, 1986.

Winfrey, Oprah. "What I Know for Sure." *O, The Oprah Magazine*. June 2002a: 230.

Winfrey, Oprah. "What I Know for Sure." *O, The Oprah Magazine*. Oct. 2002b: 296.

4

THE ROMANCE OF
READING LIKE OPRAH

YUNG-HSING WU

One. An entire nation follows the weekly escapades of a neurotic but loveable heroine in a London-based newspaper. The heroine later appears as the protagonist in a best-selling novel and top-grossing film.

Two. An effort to launch the first reading campaign in New York City grinds to a halt when objections are lodged against the novel selected as the campaign's focus. The selection committee eventually retracts the novel in question. The author goes on to critical acclaim and an endowed professorship at Princeton University.

Three. An author becomes the object of public wrath when he turns down an invitation to participate in a book club hosted by a popular talk show personality. The novel continues its ascent up several best-seller lists.

Three scenes of reading—or, more accurately, three scenes in which the public dimension of reading surfaces with unquestionable force. My references to the success of Helen Fielding's column, the controversy over Chang Rae Lee's *Native Speaker,* and the scandal that erupted when author Jonathan Franzen declined Oprah Winfrey's invitation to feature *The Corrections* on her Book Club all make plain that reading, so often idealized as private pleasure, belongs no less to popular culture. Reading in each instance achieves the status of a public event. Thus, Fielding's column became an object of weekly talk around watercoolers (and ultimately the novel *Bridget Jones*), while the Korean-American community's charge that Lee's debut novel trafficked in stereotypical representation fueled discussion across the New York media. Perhaps most infamously, Franzen's assertion that, in some ways, *The Corrections* did not belong on Oprah's Book Club provoked both the ire of Winfrey followers and heated debate about the relationship between authorship and reading. Occurring in the past ten years, these three scenes point to a particular moment in the history of literature when the *communal* potential of reading shapes not only what will be read, but how, why, and to what purpose.

Of course, it has long been commonplace—if not wishful thinking—to claim that literature, through reading, produces the possibility of community. That claim is part and parcel of a larger claim *for* literature. Indeed, this claim is one the academy makes alongside contemporary public discourse, which, in projects like Reading Is Fundamental (RIF) or, more recently, Laura Bush's White House Salute to American Authors, distinguish reading as an act of broad ethical significance. For RIF, the oldest and largest literacy organization in the United States, reading necessitates community, as the program links what happens among families with what happens nationwide: The goal to "ensure that every child believes in the value of books and the importance of reading" demands, as the organization's Web site observes, that volunteers "always" be involved.[1] A similar view prevails in the First Lady's "tribute" series, which gathers "scholars, students, and educators . . . around discussions of the country's important writers" (www.whitehouse. gov/firstlady/initiatives/wh-salute/html). Both programs draw on a rhetoric of citizenship, calling on the populace to participate as either volunteers with RIF or witnesses to the First Lady's public work. In this configuration, reading occupies a national center, acting as a point of convergence around which the vitality of the American literary tradition can be confirmed. Reading emerges as having, indeed, some intrinsic purchase on the national good.

In its consideration of Oprah's Book Club, this chapter is similarly focused on mass readership: I am trying to reckon with what happens when millions read with Oprah. Recent critical attention to the club has framed this question as a debate about value—the value, personal or aesthetic, underlying Winfrey's choices, or indeed the value of the club itself. Of this last, the club's proponents have sought to counter the disdainful view that readers have, lemming-like, followed Winfrey off the precipice of reading. Thus, Kathleen Rooney makes plain her intent to defend Winfrey's choices on aesthetic grounds: "I will explore the books themselves," she writes in the preface to *Reading with Oprah: The Book Club That Changed America* (2005), "and demonstrate that the majority of OBC texts were of higher quality than many critics would have us believe" (xii). Moreover, establishing the merit of OBC novels allows the larger claim that the club not only imbues reading with a sense of social justice, but ascribes to it communal potential. The club is "an important and influential cultural institution" (xii), one capable of all kinds of cultural work—including, for instance, critiques of racism and misogyny. Or, as Cecilia Konchar Farr concludes in *Reading Oprah: How Oprah's Book Club Changed the Way America Reads* (2004), the club has given literature something of a makeover. Oprah-led reading remakes literary status, transforming the long-held notion of literature's cultural inaccessibility and positing in its stead a literature ready to "leap into cultural democracy" (101).

In what follows, I suggest that that debate, while significant, does not address the complex identifications that drive the phenomenal success of the club. Focusing on the host of identifications that swirl among Winfrey's readers, I want to argue that Oprah's Book Club redraws the topography of communal readership. Readership occurs in this club through readers' identifications with texts and across readers, but also between readers and Oprah Winfrey, whose status as "first reader" figures identification in unexpected ways. To disentangle these relationships is to call attention to the ways in which desire, particularly readers' desires, make the club tick. It is commonplace to observe that Winfrey's audience is overwhelmingly female, and that *Oprah!*, by dint of its constituency, produces its own feminization. To the extent that such feminization also defines the book club, how do we understand what readers want when they become Oprah's Book Club members— for themselves, from literature, from one another? What does it mean to think the gendering of the club generically, that is, as a *romance* in which reading *through its association* with Oprah itself becomes an object of desire?[2]

Oprah's House of Reading

On 17 September 1996, Oprah Winfrey announced the birth of a book club for readers everywhere. Drawing on an institution as familiar as the Book-of-the-Month Club, Winfrey's club would also depart from that model, thereby marking for public reading a radical shift. The format of the club would resemble book clubs of the past—with regular meetings of its members, with the selection and discussion of shared texts—but, through the medium of the show and its host's celebrity, Oprah's Book Club (OBC) would turn the very idea of an intimate forum on its head even as it laid claim to that sense of intimacy.[3] Winfrey brought to the club's millions unparalleled access to the living author, performing for her members one-on-one conversations in which they could "get personal" with writers. The book club's television presence created a new kind of reader, a viewer–reader whose awareness of literature is imbued with her experience of having turned on the television in order to watch Oprah read. And with the OBC lottery—in which a select group of viewers are chosen to join Winfrey and the guest author in discussing the novel in question—the show prompted the desire of a public that with each OBC episode grew increasingly hungry for reading, or at least for the spectacle of reading.

If the club was an immediate sensation, propelling the featured novels to overnight best-sellerdom and advancing or even resurrecting the career of many a writer, so did it create what *Publishers Weekly* has dubbed the "Oprah Effect."[4] Publishers have been quick to recognize, celebrate, anticipate, and treasure this effect, recognizing that Winfrey is "the most powerful book marketer in the United States" because she "sends more people to bookstores than the morning news programs, the other daytime shows, the evening magazines, radio shows, print reviews and feature articles rolled into one" (Feldman 31).[5] Indeed, that other media have benefited from this effect suggests that Winfrey's *literary* authority both encompasses the function Foucault ascribes to authorship and marks a newly mediated embodiment of it. This is to observe the rise of similarly "mediated" book clubs—*The Today Show* and *USA Today* followed suit with their own versions—and to say that *Winfrey* confers the author function on to those writers whose novels she selects for the club. For Winfrey's viewers, however, this literary authority means less than the fact that the club offers a bridge to their beloved icon. In the first instantiation, the club's novelty and, as Farr has argued, the variety and scope of Winfrey's selections, moved book club members closer to Oprah by emphasizing how those novels moved her when she read. Readers flocked to Oprah all the more as they watched and read along with her. This dynamic was no less apparent when, after a brief hiatus, Winfrey resurrected the club in 2002. In the club's second incarnation, Winfrey's decision to read "the classics" revivified the authorial signature of writers as various as Dostoyevsky and Steinbeck, not only propelling the sales of *Anna Karenina* and *East of Eden* to historic heights, but leading countless new readers to embrace authors whose works, as many admitted, they had skipped reading in high school. Marrying the traditional with the current, the club forged anew readers' love affair with Oprah by transforming those "great reads that have stood the test of time" into reading events that featured Oprah front and center.

Examining this love affair reveals that the "Oprah Effect" generates readers' desires by making promises to both current and future members. These promises, while made possible by the mediated presence of television and the Internet, also make Oprah more immediate to her fans. Consider here the link from Oprah's Web site to "Oprah's Books" (www.oprah.com/books/books_landing.jhtml). A casual snapshot of the media mogul heads the link; in it, Winfrey sits ensconced in a comfy chair, with open book in hand, looking out toward viewers as if caught in the act of reading, as if, indeed, inviting fellow readers to join her in that act. The scroll down combines the personal touch with a gesture to the educational: the section "What We're Reading Now" not only names the current selection, but provides links to the book club's other features: the reader's guide, complete with background information on authors, "reading quizzes, plot points, and character journeys," and promises of e-mails from Winfrey describing her reading experience.[6] A second link then directs readers to another photo of Winfrey, this time standing center stage on the Oprah show dais, with her most recent selection in hand and the Oprah Book Club logo as backdrop. Finally, a personal review from Winfrey herself concludes the reader's introduction to the club. In the case of a recent selection, Pearl Buck's *The Good Earth*, Winfrey begins her remark by referring to the novel's reputation as "a sweeping saga that's been called 'a universal tale of the destiny of man.'" Her own endorsement, while just as affirmative, takes a slightly different tone: *The Good Earth*, she tells readers, is "juicy as all get out!"

If Winfrey's review of *The Good Earth* typifies the club's emphasis on reading as a communal act, so does it privilege reading as a desire for a "juicy" narrative. The talk show host opens her remarks with a nod to the professional, critical, or highbrow reading of the novel, but her one-liner refuses to give that reading the final word. Her review, like many of the book club's other features, thus hails prospective readers by addressing them as cohorts. The Web link to the book club manages this dynamic by placing Oprah at home *and* on the studio stage, suggesting that the two sites are interchangeable—and that members of the book club are as "at home" with Oprah as they are as viewers of the show. Meanwhile the e-mails from Winfrey—messages only book club members may receive—literally bring Oprah to readers' homes. Finally, it's worth noting that several book club episodes have occurred at Winfrey's Chicago home; there guests are not only *treated to* the experience of hobnobbing with authors but *treated as* friends whom Oprah has invited for a casual but elegant dinner.[7] Taken together, these episodes and the Web link perform double labor for the club. While both seduce readers with the prospect of hearing directly from Oprah, in their framing of that seduction, both cast Oprah as any other reader who simply wants to weigh in on the conversation. The result is a circle of readers who know each other well. Yet this is, of course, no ordinary circle, since Oprah occupies both its center and a point on its diameter.

Living Reading, Reading Lives

"We have become," remarks one online reader about her own book club, "a reading group *family*" (OBCMB, 2 May 2001). While this language of family ties invokes the closeness book club members report about their Oprah reading experiences, it only hints, I believe, at the complex of relations running through the club. I ask, then, what is it that Oprah's Book Club offers its members? What desires do readers bring to the club and, in particular, how do these desires shape expectations about reading and literature? Indeed, what happens to literature when it is knowingly taken up as a shared reading object?

The narratives of reading that pepper the online club provide one kind of answer. In these narratives, members' responses to individual selections perform the negotiations that occur during the experience of reading with Oprah. Writing about *A Map of the World*, Jane Hamilton's novel in which a woman must come to terms with her complicity in the death of a friend's child, one member notes that "the main character was a difficult person to like and very real . . . we have all had moments of self absorption, like when she was so involved in looking at her past, that the present fell apart. It brought up the question for me of how we deal with the knowledge that we all have the power to hurt" (OBCMB, 12 Dec. 1999). From the outset, this reader sounds a familiar note when she privileges characterization as the novel's exemplary feature—it not only prompts her personal and collective identifications but also renders tenuous the line between life and literature. Thus, Hamilton's protagonist is a "difficult *person*" and not simply, or only, a character (my emphasis). Yet this identification does not last long, reversed, in fact, almost as soon as it is made by the reader's reassertion of fictionality: Alice, the comment goes on to remark, is "very real," which is also to admit that she is a representation. In this ongoing referentiality, Alice's status continually shifts, providing the communal "we"—one only partially defined by the universal "we" posited, say, by Eco's ideal readership—a touchstone for judgment and self-reflection alike.

To put it slightly differently, this referentiality results, as two remarks from participants on the show's discussion of the novel reveals, in a rotating

identification in which readers, characters, and *texts* commingle (Oprah.
com, Past shows, 18 Jan. 2000):

Poor Alice, poor us, for not stopping to enjoy what we have (Lori).

I kept saying to the book, Teresa go, be with her. It will help (Anny).

If Lori articulates her identification with Alice through an apposition, one in
which Hamilton's character stands in for readers ("us"), Anny describes her
identification through a direct address to the novel, urging a character to act.
Both the apposition and the direct address invoke intimacy, the sort that
emerges from an acknowledged similarity ("poor Alice, poor us") or the force
of an urgent plea ("I kept saying to the book"). Meanwhile, Lori and Anny
describe their readings of *A Map of the World*—in which both assert their
empathy for Hamilton's protagonist—by underscoring the intersubjectivity
constituting their reading experiences. For these readers, the sense that Alice
and the novel in which she figures are closer at hand than either would have
been without the club's presence compels their identification. A mediated
intimacy, here visibly performed as Lori and Anny sit on the dais next to
Winfrey and Hamilton, fosters reading.

At the same time, narratives about the book club also become an intimate medium in which members write their own lives. The message-board
discussions are replete with these readerly autobiographies; describing one's
reading life before joining the Book Club is a unifying trope, even something
like an obligatory script. Here are three representative examples:

I didn't like to read. I can't remember reading a book since high
school. That is until *The Reader*. I loved that book and have not
stopped reading from Oprah's choices. (OBCMB, 27 Apr. 2001)

I've always wanted to be a reader and I was never able to enjoy it
until I started reading Oprah books. I have finally found books I
enjoy and now I read everyday. (OBCMB, 26 Apr. 2001)

When I was a child I was not a good reader at all. I found it
extremely difficult, boring, and I was embarrassed to be in the "special" reading group. As a mother of two I was determined to have
great readers. I would take them to the public library and read to
them as toddlers. Yet when I went to the library with them I only

went to the books I felt comfortable with . . . my daughters noticed this . . . I knew Oprah had a book club and picked up a list and began reading. This time as an adult I love to read. I hang out at the library and I am totally confident in my "library" skills. The Oprah Book Club has given me a sense of self worth. I am no longer the little girl who hated to read. (OBCMB, 13 Oct. 2001)

As they describe the metamorphoses enabled by the Club, these Book Club members write reading as a new vocation, a longheld desire, even a source of shame. In so doing, they articulate a range of narratives that converges, ultimately, on the epiphanic moment when one can say, "I am a reader." Looking back on that moment, these readers go on to cite reading for its capacity to abstract self-consciousness, to create an identification by which they can claim new terms for selfhood, that is, for making self-generation possible. This gesture of course coincides with the show's discourse of self-improvement, the logic that underlies the segments with Dr. Phil as well as those devoted to "raising your spirit." Reading contributes to the self-awareness Oprah touts on her show; the Book Club makes the case that self-improvement occurs specifically through a literary communion with Oprah and her fellow reader-disciples. Writes one online reader:

I did not read a book since I was in school . . . just couldn't sit still long enough. Oprah's book club inspired me and I made a commitment to read every selection. I have read every selection. Now I love to read and find the time. Never did I dream that commitment would land me on a book club show! What an experience!!!! Since, then, I have come out of my shell. I have no fear of speaking in public or voicing my opinion. (OBCMB, 6 Sept. 2001)

Transformation begins with reading and ends with the assertion of a *fearless* "I" whose emergence means a self in possession of a voice. Perhaps more to the point, the "commitment" to reading with Oprah, with a guest appearance on the show as its reward, gives that voice something to say.

Choosy Readers Choose . . . ?

"I used to feel intimidated when I walked into a bookstore because I wasn't sure what new author to try—I no longer feel that way. For this I am grateful!" (OBCMB, 7 May 2001). The Book Club makes an agency of reading possible: This is the refrain Oprah's Book Club members repeat in their message-board comments. As readerly agents, club members claim that they no longer experience "intimidation" before books; instead, they declare and wield a newfound mastery, one in which literature exists at their disposal, or for their pleasure. Through this agency, readers exert choice in the face of uncertainty: "I saw a show where Oprah was in a bookstore, browsing through books by all kinds of authors," reports one viewer, "I was intrigued, so the next time I was in Barnes and Noble, I started to pick up books from authors I didn't know and read them. I know this sounds sort of infantile, but to me, it made all the difference" (OBCMB, 29 Jan. 2002). An encounter with the unknown, with "books from authors I didn't know": These initially are defined as inimical to agency, perhaps even paralyzing. Having Oprah as a precedent means having a model for overcoming the uncertainty of choice.[8]

Yet even as the club embraces readers' status as agents, as subjects who imagine and define themselves through reading, its discourse also resists the wholesale attribution of agency to Oprah's Book Club readers. Thus, if the language of the message boards brims with readerly confidence, it also speaks, interestingly, an insistence on the continued existence of uncertainty, the center of which is Oprah herself. This insistence, in other words, even as it celebrates Oprah as inspiration for her viewer–readers also figures Oprah *as a kind of agency* without which the formation of readerly subjects could not proceed. In this guise Oprah stands as the consciousness that chooses for the club: this despite the club's dedication to choice as the ground zero of individualism. Oprah emerges as a guiding force, a distinctly visible hand that, in making selections, creates, tautologically, their status as a select group and thereby appears to meet members' unarticulated expectations of what makes books good in the first place. The Book Club perpetuates an ideology of reading in which the act has already been so elevated that it can produce, sustain, and assuage members' anxieties about their abilities to find novels worthy of reading.

Oprah's Book Club maintains a paradox in which reading, figured as an act of self-definition, turns nonetheless on the defining stamp of one reader, Oprah herself. To tell this tale of subject formation is to insist on yoking the promise of improved selfhood with reading. Self-help manuals beckon readers with the assurance of a remade self; Oprah's Book Club asserts that the reading of literature will have already accomplished that makeover. In the meantime, the club also suggests a role for reading that is not simply instrumental, but self-perpetuating:

When Oprah started her Book Club I was delighted to find an
Oprah book discussion group. All my life I have relished reading. I
had a rather lonely childhood and books were a godsend. A year
after the discussion group started, the leader moved away. She asked
me to take over as the leader. I didn't have to think twice before
saying YES! It is a pleasure to be the discussion leader and I love
every minute of it. (OBCMB, 2 May 2001)

This narrative of transformation hails the birth of a new self at its end, but,
importantly, not a new reader. Rather, reading marks this member's one
solace prior to the Club, and the Book Club becomes a social venue where
her earlier, solitary identification with reading has a ready place. Far from
being the mark of her isolation, reading with Oprah context signals both her
belonging and, as the narrative concludes, her embrace of authority. Yet my
point is that if this typical formulation obtains—that reading with Oprah
makes one a better, more confident person—it is preceded by the separate
sense that reading comes *with its own interpellation.* This member recalls that
"books were a godsend," thus describing her formation as a reader in terms
of Althusserian divine intervention. In so doing, she not only suggests that
reading matters as such, but also that reading makes its own subjects. And
indeed more: that of all the identities available, it is the reader who embodies
best the exemplary self.

The Fellowship of Oprah

Such exemplary selfhood does not occur in solitude, however, but in the
company of others. It's not surprising, then, that the message boards should
sound a note of fellowship when the topic of the Club's effect comes up. One
member pens a fairly typical comment when she says that "it is always fun *to
read books knowing that others are sharing* in the same experience" (OBCMB,
18 June 2003); meanwhile another concurs, observing that "I have always
been a solitary reader and to be able to share with so many people and *hear
their thoughts* is priceless to me" (OBCMB, 18 June 2003). Having fellow
readers distinguishes the reading experience for these two book club members. More to the point, an *awareness* of their cohort readers transforms reading into an act at once pleasurable ("fun") and valuable ("priceless"). Out of
such comments reading becomes desirable because it is explicitly and primarily communal—so much so that one circle of friends decides that "after

reading we each [should] sign the front cover" (OBCMB, 8 Nov. 2001). Variations on a theme of mutual reading take center stage: from acts of repeated inscription, each signature not only confirming the fact of reading, but embodying it through readers' written names, to an intersubjectivity that confirms a lifelong passion, the message-board discussions and the Book Club episodes, and not simply or necessarily the novels, compel future members to join and current members to continue. "It is so much fun to see the review after having read the books," one member explains, "*it's as if I am a part of it.* I have truly fallen in love with reading" (OBCMB, 1 May 2001). Securing a place: This is the appeal of the club, its promise to make reading so accessible that members will find their acts of reading repeated—confirmed—on the Club's various outlets.

At the same time, that readers fall in love with reading has everything to do with the possibility of having a place on Winfrey's show, a place next to Oprah, the originary or primal reader whom Book Club members "know" first and best. That this primacy is communicated by simultaneously figuring Winfrey as just another reader demonstrates the richness of identifications taking place between and across the readers of the Book Club. Thus, in announcing the selection of *The Bluest Eye*, Winfrey waxes personal, saying that

> I took this book on vacation with me just a . . . [sic] about a month
> ago . . . I had all of my girlfriends—who happen to be white because
> Gayle couldn't make it—sitting around the pool. I had all these
> white girls crying over *The Bluest Eye*, asking me if this is what life
> was really like as a colored child. ("Ashley Judd" 25)

John Young writes that Winfrey "becomes the point of entry for white readers" because of this assertion of blackness. For Young, the fact of Oprah's racial difference, the fact that she marks it by noting that her girlfriends "happen to be white," opens the door for her predominantly white female viewers. Yet it's also the case that Winfrey frames racial difference in the context of commonality: "I had all of my girlfriends . . . sitting around the pool." This is not to argue that the atmosphere of sisterhood transcends the specificity of race, but to point out that Winfrey emphasizes that specificity through an image of community and, perhaps more significantly, through the desiring identifications made in the name of that community. In other words, when Oprah describes having "all of my girlfriends . . . sitting around the pool" she invites her viewer–readers to imagine their place around that pool. That invitation turns imperative, however, when Winfrey vows to her television audience that

> if you don't like this book, then I don't have nothing else to say to you. You will like this book. OK? I love this book. . . . You cannot read *The Bluest Eye* without having it touch your soul. . . . If it doesn't, then I don't know who you are. ("Ashley Judd" 25–26)

While Winfrey continues to hold out the promise of intimacy with her readers, she does so by demanding that her readers find themselves as moved by *The Bluest Eye* as she is. Indeed she frames that demand as an inevitability, creating the sense that her reading is ultimately the natural one. What's more, Winfrey spells out the consequences of failing that reading. Those who do not "like" *The Bluest Eye*, those whose souls are not touched by the novel, those who do not read like Oprah risk disownment by her: not to be hailed and, worse, not to be recognized.

As for the readers themselves, they respond to such demands with nothing *but* desire, for it is Oprah whose desirability as a fellow reader exceeds all else. For one online member, knowing that "Oprah would be discussing the book I was reading on a later show" is "more exciting" than the books themselves, which for her do not even bear mentioning (OBCMB, 15 Apr. 2002). Whether individual readers come to the Club thanks to a prior identification with Oprah, or come away from the club thus identified, reading provides the sought-for connection, making it possible to imagine and even claim common ground with Oprah, to render her, as Eva Illouz puts it, a "biographical icon," one whose life is as open for reading as the novels she features on her show (30). For some fans, making this connection means remaining in the realm of wish fulfillment: to envision meeting and thanking Oprah for establishing the Club or to fantasize about being "at dinner with Oprah discussing this book" (OBCMB, 20 Sept. 2002). Others go further still, deploying identification to posit a bond between themselves and Oprah:

> The more "Oprah Books" I read, I began to realize that she and I had the same tastes—or maybe it's a woman thing. When the club choice was *Where the Heart Is*, I whooped with delight because I'd already read and loved it. (OBCMB, 24 Oct. 2001)

> One of my biggest pleasures has been when I've already selected and read a book BEFORE Oprah selects it! (OBCMB, 18 June 2003)

Here wish fulfillment gives way to declarations of likeness, and fantasies of being near Oprah become fantastic statements of closeness, of intimacy. Thanks to "Oprah Books," the first reader can close the distance between celebrity and fan, thereby making Oprah accessible through their shared taste and gender. Perhaps more to the point, both readers emphasize their relation with Oprah by asserting that they have beaten her to the punch. Thus, while one "whoops with delight" when Winfrey chooses *Where the Heart Is*, a novel she has "already read and loved," another, in a similar combination of enthusiasm and pride, writes that one of her "biggest pleasures" since joining the club "has been when I've already selected and read a book BEFORE Oprah selects it!" (OBCMB, 18 June 2003). Here desiring to read like Oprah the ur-reader means anticipating or even preempting her. Not so much a statement of hero-worship, this is an appropriative declaration, a kind of hyperidentification, an assertion that through reading one can be, or indeed, better Oprah.

It would be easy to say that readers in choosing Oprah, while they insist on their newfound identification as reading selves, actually abandon themselves as readerly subjects, that is, as subjects whose agency lies in reading. Yet when this romance with reading occurs, when typical readerly identifications with a text (with its characters or author) are reinforced, if not displaced, by identifications that emerge across readers via Oprah, the act of reading itself has radically changed. This shift emerges most forcibly in the Club's articulation of a distinctly literary ethics. As one discussion-board comment puts it, the Club provides readers the experience of "what books can do for us" (OBCMB, 5 May 2002). In this formulation, the situation, or positioning, of readers takes on particular resonance. For a forum so devoted to an advocacy of selfhood, what does it mean to figure readers as selves that receive, to put it somewhat redundantly, themselves? A view emerges in which reading functions as the performative, because willing (as opposed to willed?) reception of ethics. "What books can do for us" hints strongly that books, when read, "do" good and, just as important, that such good does not require readers to be agents of but occasions for said goodness. Oprah's Book Club may insist on the ethical good of reading, but, in so doing, it promotes a view of ethics that, strangely enough, does not need readerly subjects.

Notes

1. Founded in 1966 by Margaret McNamara, RIF's programs share "three essential elements" in the drive to increase children's literacy: "reading motivation,

family and community involvement, and the excitement of choosing free books to keep." The federal government has been involved since 1975 (with the passage of the "Inexpensive Book Distribution Program," whose goal is to provide federal matching funds for local RIF groups); national service organizations have also acted as partners with the program, including Kiwanis, Rotary International, Altrusa, and the Junior League. RIF also has numerous corporate sponsors: MetLife, Verizon, Nestlé USA, the NBA, Toys "R" Us, and Coca-Cola.

2. For an assessment of the ways in which *The Oprah Winfrey Show* has both participated in and turned the gendering of talk shows on its head, see Shattuc.

3. See Janice Radway's *A Feeling for Books* and Elizabeth Long's *Book Clubs: Women and the Uses of Reading in Everyday Life* for thorough histories and analyses of the book club phenomenon.

4. Of this effect, see Bridget Kinsella and D. T. Max. Meanwhile, an interesting example of a noncontemporary author is John Steinbeck, whose *East of Eden* became the forty-seventh selection to hit the best-seller lists. For a thorough and insightful assessment of how Oprah's Book Club has maintained and extended the authorship of Toni Morrison, see Young. Young's analysis is especially useful for its unpacking of the involution of race, reading, and authorship that obtains in Morrison's case.

5. Through the work of the Club, Winfrey has also garnered elevated acclaim as a cultural philanthropist, an icon of good works and good taste. *Newsweek* named her the most important person in the world of books and media in 1997, and the National Book Foundation awarded her its fiftieth Anniversary Gold Medal in 1999. Meanwhile, in 2003, the Association of American Publishers presented her with its highest award, the "AAP Honors."

6. This pedagogic turn has become especially pronounced in the wake of the Book Club's reincarnation in 2002. Since then, in the Club's "return to the classics"—the likes of which has included Steinbeck's *East of Eden*, Paton's *Cry, the Beloved Country*, Garcia Marquez's *One Hundred Years of Solitude*, McCullers's *The Heart Is a Lonely Hunter*, Tolstoy's *Anna Karenina*, Buck's *The Good Earth*, and, most recently, an entire summer devoted to Faulkner—Winfrey has launched an apparatus of reading resources modeled on the classroom. Thus, the Book Club Web site presents a host of materials that ranges from author biographies, plot summaries, character and genre analyses, and historical background. Perhaps most telling of the Club's pedagogic self-image are the "literary guides" Winfrey has recruited for each novel. Often scholars with expertise in the chosen author or text, these guides are "on-call" to answer questions readers post to the site.

7. To take a quick example, consider the case of Toni Morrison, who has had four novels chosen by Oprah for the Book Club (*Sula*, *The Bluest Eye*, *Paradise*, and *Song of Solomon*). In her first appearance, Morrison joined a select group of the Book Club at Winfrey's Chicago apartment for a dinner party discussing *Song of Solomon*.

8. One member notes succinctly of this dynamic: "I like to read but have a hard time choosing what to read." Choice here is figured, interestingly, as a condition of difficulty, an obstacle: hardly an index of agency.

Works Cited

"Ashley Judd/Oprah's Book Club." Oprah Winfrey Show. 27 Apr. 2000. Transcript by Burrell's Information Services.

Feldman, Gayle. "Making Book on Oprah." *New York Times Book Review.* 2 Feb. 1997: 31.

Illouz, Eva. *Oprah Winfrey and the Glamour of Misery.* New York: Columbia UP, 2003.

Kinsella, Bridget. "The Oprah Effect: How TV's Premier Talk Show Hosts Puts Books Over the Top." *Publishers Weekly.* 20 Jan. 1997: 276–79.

Long, Elizabeth. *Book Clubs: Women and the Uses of Reading in Everyday Life.* Chicago: U of Chicago P, 2003.

Max, D. T. "The Oprah Effect." *New York Times Magazine.* 26 Dec. 1999: 36–41.

Oprah.com. www.oprah.com/tows/pastshows/tows_2000/tows_past_20000118_b. jhtml. Noted in text as Past shows.

———. http://boards.oprah.com/Web?13@@.efb862b!DYNID=A104WKHFZRS RLLARA23RQQ. Noted in text by OBCMB and date.

Radway, Janice. *A Feeling for Books: The Book-of-the-Month-Club, Literary Taste, and Middle-Class Desire.* Durham: U of North Carolina P, 1997.

Shattuc, Jane M. "The Oprahfication of America: Talk Shows and the Public Sphere." In *Television, History, and American Culture: Feminist Critical Essays.* Mary Beth Haralovich and Lauren Rabinovitz, eds. Durham: Duke UP, 1999. 168–80.

Young, John. "Toni Morrison, Oprah Winfrey, and Postmodern Popular Audiences." *African American Review.* 35.2 (Summer 2001): 181–205.

5

OPRAH'S BOOK SELECTIONS

Teleliterature for *The Oprah Winfrey Show*

MARK HALL

> I find television very educating. Every time somebody turns on the set, I
> go into the other room and read a book.
>
> —Groucho Marx

R ay Bradbury's 1953 novel, *Fahrenheit 451*, named for the temperature at
which books burn, imagines a futuristic world in which reading is considered dangerous because of the complex and contradictory ideas contained
in books. Literature is incinerated, replaced by wall-sized television sets.
Reading is criminalized, and instead of putting out fires, firefighters are
charged with ferreting out readers and burning books. *Fahrenheit 451* cap-
tures the anxiety among bibliophiles that television leads to a society in
which people no longer spend time in quiet, solitary contemplation, think
independently, or have meaningful conversations with one another. The
heroes of Bradbury's novel are a group of renegade intellectuals, "the Book
People," a network of book lovers who memorize great works of literature
and philosophy. They hope to restore the world of ideas to humankind in the
aftermath of the war on books. Today, this opposition between book culture
and television persists. One example of the continued strength of this opposition is Michael Moore's 2004 documentary, *Fahrenheit 911*, inspired by
Bradbury's premise of a world without books, devoid of critical thinking. In
his revisioning of a society dimmed by too much television, Moore turns a
critical eye on President George W. Bush's war on Iraq. Awarded the Palme
D'Or, one of the highest honors in filmmaking, at the Cannes Film Festival,
Fahrenheit 911 links Bush and his associates to wealthy Saudis, including

Osama bin Laden. Like Bradbury, Moore posits a world in which people no longer read or engage in thoughtful conversation about current events. Instead, we sit passively in our La-Z-Boy recliners, soaking up the narrow, status quo version fed to us via network television.

The accepted wisdom that television harms the culture of reading has made Oprah's Book Club an easy target. Literature presented in the context of daytime talk is guilty by association, so the thinking goes, with lowbrow mass culture, less than serious, easy to dismiss, no matter what its literary merits. What's more, Winfrey's influence on the publishing industry may result, not in the sort of book burning Bradbury imagined, but in another kind of censorship, as she promotes only a small number of books, which sell by the truckload, while many more less profitable books receive little or no attention at all. As Chris Lehmann puts it in *Revolt of the Masscult*, "Even as culture disperses itself more widely and cheaply across the globe, even as technological innovations place the materials of learning more readily at hand to greater and greater numbers of people, there is a waning sense that culture is saying anything meaningful to us—or, for that matter, that we are demanding anything meaningful of it" (77). In Bradbury's dystopia, litera- ture is banned because knotty ideas incite dangerous free thinking. Lehmann's contemporary literary landscape is similarly scorched, but for a different reason. Far from being banned, television and other technologies make books more widely available, yet their association with mass cultural entertainments such as Oprah's Book Club taints books as vapid.

This commonplace view of television as oppositional to books, however, obscures alternative ways of thinking about the relationship between the two media. The distinguishing feature of Oprah's Book Club, after all, is that Winfrey has challenged this old saw to unite television with the culture of reading. Prior to Oprah's Book Club, the two had rarely mixed before, beyond the occasional promotional spot on a daytime talk show, but, in her one-woman literacy crusade, Winfrey has exploited her television celebrity to become a literary cultural force as well. Her star backing alone, however, is insufficient to explain her accomplishment. Winfrey's success is due also, in part, to her ability to fit books into the proven format of *The Oprah Winfrey Show*. Winfrey may promote books on her show, but, as the genre of talk tel- evision demands, she herself, as host, maintains center stage, speaking directly to her audience in her familiar, down-home manner. In order to advance this host-centered emphasis, Winfrey resists the stuffy role of literary critic; rather, in the talk show setting, in which selling something is second only to promoting the image of the host, Winfrey has become a cheerleader for reading, just as she is a cheerleader for yearly breast exams, a new pair of Uggs, and the latest Josh Groban CD. Whatever else Winfrey's book selections may be about, in the context of *The Oprah Winfrey Show*, books embody and promote the themes of self-help and community improvement, which motivate Winfrey's show generally. In this venue, television and book culture combine for what Winfrey calls "the breakdown that leads to the breakthrough." To that end, Winfrey presents reading as a user-friendly entertainment that is, at the same time, both relevant and useful for improving—or at least inspiring the hope of improving—one's life. On *The Oprah Winfrey Show*, literature for television, or "teleliterature," is intended to prompt change, both individual and social, for the better.

But what distinguishes a successful Book Club selection? Writing for *Slate* magazine, Lehmann, deputy editor at the *Washington Post*'s "Book World," sums up Winfrey's selections and use of literature this way:

> The club's principle mission has been to champion recovery, loudly and often. From the first year's Oprah picks, *The Deep End of the Ocean* and the *Book of Ruth*, through 1997's triumvirate of Bill Cosby titles, to your Wally Lambs and Billie Lettses and Anna Quindlens, Oprah's selections have purveyed much the same message that O herself (in both television and periodical guises) continues to hammer away at: Bad things happen, women suffer, and one day, further along, once you undertake that perilous journey from bitterness to forgiveness, you will be vouchsafed the reason for your tenure on earth.

Winfrey's readers recognize this characterization and others like it, which are frequent both in the mass media and even among fans who write to Oprah's Book Club message boards at Oprah.com. But if Lehmann and others are right that Winfrey chooses books whose themes are dull, or at least predictable and didactic, then what gives Oprah's Book Club its currency? What lends the Club its staying power? By limiting attention to an exclusively literary assessment of the books alone, apart from the television setting in which Winfrey presents them, Lehmann reinforces the old opposition and ignores Winfrey's fundamental accomplishment: the union of television and books. This chapter examines three particular Book Club selections *within the context* of *The Oprah Winfrey Show*, addressing the following: What results when literature is brought together with the ideology of daytime talk television, and with what consequences? What do the ways of reading privileged on *The*

Oprah Winfrey Show tell us about Winfrey's literary aesthetic and reading philosophy? My argument is simple: Oprah's Book Club is more than just books. To judge Winfrey's selections as either "good" or "bad" tells only part of the story. If, indeed, even Oprah's Book Club fans find Winfrey's choices "downers" or "depressors"—common complaints on the Book Club message boards—then why do readers keep coming back? What is it beyond the books that catches and sustains the interests of participants? Certainly, Oprah's Book Club does, at times, promote images of the status quo and traffic in familiar platitudes. Rather than condemn Oprah's books out of hand as shallow and banal, however, if Winfrey's choices reaffirm popular wisdom, then we ought to ask what function those bread-and-butter truths serve for readers. How do these themes and the Book Club selections combine to support the ideological work of *The Oprah Winfrey Show*?

Because I'm interested in thematic patterns among Oprah's Book Club selections, my intent is not address all or even most of the Book Club episodes. To do so would be not only counterproductive, but also beyond the scope of this chapter. Instead, my analysis is limited to three novels, Billie Letts's *Where the Heart Is*, announced in December 1998, Bernhard Schlink's *The Reader*, announced in February 1999, and Toni Morrison's *The Bluest Eye*, announced in April 2000. I began the process of narrowing my scope to these novels by choosing from among the books whose message boards are archived on the Oprah's Book Club Web site, since the conversations there among Winfrey's readers have influenced my thinking about both the books and their televised discussions. Second, I chose these three novels because they reflect significant themes and patterns among Winfrey's choices. These novels generated particularly rich discussions on the message boards and on the televised Book Club episodes. They made a splash with readers, and Winfrey herself has remarked on them as especially important. By looking at repeated themes among Oprah's books, reviews in the mass media, the critical reception of these selections, and Winfrey's treatment of them on the show, I hope to uncover some relationships among the books Winfrey chooses for Oprah's Book Club.

First published in 1995, Letts's novel had received some notoriety even before Winfrey called to congratulate the author on being selected for Oprah's Book Club. Winner of the Walker Percy Award and the 1996 Oklahoma Book Award, *Where the Heart Is* was selected by the New York Public Library as one of the 1996 Best Books for the Teen Age (Bingham 1). The novel met with tepid reviews, however. Dwight Garner of the *New York Times Review of Books* says, for example, "Letts unspools this lightweight story with a fair amount of charm, and for a while, 'Where the Heart Is' reads like a Fannie Flagg novel freshened up by Molly Ivins" (7). This reviewer faults Letts for the slow pace of the novel's second half and for clumsy, unconvincing dialogue, which he compares to that of Robert James Waller's *The Bridges of Madison County*. *Kirkus Reviews* characterizes Letts's novel this way:

> A debut novel whose rose-colored glasses yield a happy-go-lucky portrait of the down-home lives of uneducated poor folks in Sequoyah, Oklahoma. Letts's determinedly optimistic novel portrays a world where all races coexist harmoniously, and where the splintery realities of American rural life—poverty, teen pregnancy, single motherhood, homelessness, child sexual abuse—are palpably presented beneath a thick coat of Brothers Grimm varnish. ("Review" 27)

The novel tells the story of seventeen-year-old Novalee Nation, seven months pregnant and heading to California from her home in rural Tennessee with her no-good boyfriend, Willy Jack Pickens. Willy Jack quickly grows bored with her, however, and dumps Novalee out at Wal-Mart. Broke and homeless, Novalee hides inside the discount store for the next two months. She spends her days reading at the public library, her nights inside the store, cocooned in a sleeping bag, eating canned goods and candy bars, trying on maternity clothes. The young girl is befriended by a host of eccentric but loving and generous characters, including the alcoholic town librarian's brother and caretaker, Forny Hull, who helps Novalee give birth to her daughter, Americus, on the floor of Wal-Mart; blue-haired Sister Thelma Husband, who takes Novalee and "the Wal-Mart baby" into her trailer home; and Moses Whitecotton, a photographer, who teaches Novalee his art. The legendary Wal-Mart founder, Sam Walton, also makes a cameo appearance when he gives Novalee $500 and a job. Novalee's life is transformed by the kindness of strangers she meets in the aisles of the ubiquitous superstore. This fairy tale of rural American life is determinately lowbrow. As Garner says, "Her novel seems to have its heart in the right place; its head is a different matter" (7). The same sentiment is expressed by another reviewer: *Where the Heart Is* "is entertaining, good for a tear or two, but lacking in substance" (27). Kathleen Hughes of *Booklist* grants that "although the book's emotional manipulation may be distasteful to some, others may find its soap-opera plot and Forrest Gump-ish optimism appealing" (41).

Although the opinions of literary experts do not find a place on *The Oprah Winfrey Show*, their absence underscores the manner in which Winfrey's presentation of literature reinforces what Cathy Davidson calls in "Toward a History of Books and Reading" "the elite-versus-popular polarity" by defending and promoting the literacy interests of daytime talk show viewers (2). We're all familiar with the cliché that warns not to judge a book by its cover, but the jackets of Oprah's Book Club selections shed light on just how Winfrey negotiates this "elite-versus-popular polarity." In her essay, Davidson suggests that perhaps we *can* judge a book by its cover. Its meaning, she argues, is not found only in the words on its pages; rather, a book's meaning is colored by the design and packaging of the material product itself. If Davidson is right, then we ought to ask how the meanings of Oprah's Book Club books are influenced by Winfrey's stamp of approval. On the cover of each of Winfrey's picks is her imprimatur, the Oprah's Book Club logo, certifying Winfrey's choices as authorized by her, labeling not only the books themselves, but also their readers. Likewise, the logo implies ways of reading and uses of books consistent with those practiced on *The Oprah Winfrey Show*. As Davidson points out, "differences in presentation and, implicitly, audience, also influence the understanding of what is read or what divisions in society are marked by these different readings" (2). One such division marked by the Oprah's Book Club label is the distinction between classroom reading as a specialized and elite enterprise and ordinary acts of reading by general readers. In her on-air presentation of Letts's *Where the Heart Is*, for instance, Winfrey eschews the reading practices of the literary elite and aligns herself, instead, with general readers by championing the popular wisdom and down-home values of the novel.

Winfrey's treatment of *Where the Heart Is* plays up the homespun optimism and emotional manipulations that critics deride, not as weaknesses, but as the chief strengths of Letts's novel. In the Book Club episode titled "Oprah's Book Club Goes to Wal-Mart," Winfrey appears to have two aims. The first concerns the book itself, while the second has more to do with Winfrey's role as host of the show and "literacy sponsor" (Brandt). As for the book, Winfrey sums up *Where the Heart Is* this way: "It's about a seventeen-year-old girl literally barefoot and pregnant who gets dumped on a Wal-Mart store somewhere in Oklahoma, but she gets back on her feet through the kindness of strangers" (19 Jan. 1999). Winfrey's emphasis is important here. While she is often chided by Book Club participants for choosing stories her readers find grim or even depressing, Winfrey underscores that this is *not* one of those picks. "Like people say I do gut-wrenching books," Winfrey says.

"There were some things in there . . . that are pretty disturbing, but overall, wasn't it a fulfilling, uplifting read?" she asks. In this way, Winfrey presents reading as pleasurable, entertaining, and inspiring. Oprah's Book Club is a light entertainment. If Letts's story is one of hardship, it is also, more important for Winfrey, a story of hope and triumph—and, not coincidentally, triumph as a result of reading.

As for Winfrey's role as host turned literacy sponsor, throughout this episode, she establishes her role, in part, by reiterating what she sees as the novel's principle themes. The opening segment sets up the first theme. Here Winfrey shows clips from past episodes of *The Oprah Winfrey Show*, including, as Winfrey puts it, "famous women who say that they were saved by the kindness of strangers." Suzanne Somers, Naomi Judd, Cathy Lee Crosby, and Patty Duke recount their individual hard luck stories. Viewers are offered a glimpse into the dark, often secretly troubled lives of the rich and famous. These vignettes bring to mind Winfrey's own self-disclosures in the construction of her personal bootstraps legend. In this way, these hard luck tales, which parallel Winfrey's, are less about other celebrities than they are about Winfrey. These narratives remind viewers of the intimacy they share with the host of *The Oprah Winfrey Show*, inviting viewers to see these celebrities as like Winfrey in two ways (Haag). First, given our fascination with the rich and famous, their lives are interesting, like Winfrey's, because they are celebrities. At the same time, these stars, whose lives are, like Winfrey's, marked by strength and perseverance, are, paradoxically, just like us. The uneasy life histories of the rich and famous may not be so far removed from our own. Just as Winfrey cultivates a "parasocial" bond between herself and her audience by sharing the personal details of her life, so her talk show extends that bond to include other celebrities as well (Horton and Wohl). By getting to know their secrets of hardship, viewers are positioned to relate to Winfrey's celebrity guests on a personal level, and, further, to be inspired to persevere in the face of their own troubles. She says, "Well, the irony in many cases is that those women not only triumphed at the end, as our character Novalee did, but emerged even stronger than they were before. That's the gift." With this easy embrace, Winfrey establishes a bond with her Book Club audience, extends that bond by introducing viewers to celebrity guests, then deftly yokes their personal narratives to the novel itself, yet another point of connection for all those who have shared the experience of reading as members of Oprah's Book Club.

In addition to triumph over adversity, a second theme of Letts's *Where the Heart Is* suggests that the world is, according to Winfrey, "filled with angels." The hope, of course, is that Winfrey's viewers are themselves among the kind and generous strangers who people "Oprah's Angel Network." If not, perhaps Winfrey's presentation of *Where the Heart Is* will inspire viewers to join. In a neat sound-bite, typical of Winfrey, she sums up another of the novel's lessons: "One of the themes of the book . . . is that . . . many times your family isn't what you're born into but what you're able to create and that you find family among people of the world who take you, literally, into their homes, but more importantly, into their hearts." Three basic assumptions underlying *The Oprah Winfrey Show* and its host's uses of literature are woven together in this statement. First, books are used on *The Oprah Winfrey Show* not so much to teach viewers something new, but to remind them of beliefs and values they already share. In this case, family and community are sacred. Second, the novel echoes a frequent refrain on *The Oprah Winfrey Show*: Doing good leads to doing well. Generosity can bring one into the fold of Oprah's Angel Network. And, third, in this setting, feeling and affect are privileged above other ways of knowing. What is in the heart is what's most important, not what's in the head. What readers "feel," not only about the novel, but also about life, is what counts. Participants are encouraged to explore their feelings about the book, to relate to the characters and their life experiences on a deeply personal level. For instance, after comparing her life to that of the novel's main character, one unidentified woman on the show says, "Yeah. You know? And so I went right—like I said, it went straight to my heart." Winfrey responds with her trademark, "I love the connection that books bring. I just love that." General readers like this one don't want to critically analyze a novel in conventionally academic ways; rather, they want a book to pique their feelings. They want a book to evoke a personal, emotional response. They want to connect the triumphs and hopes of fictional characters to their own lives. On this Book Club episode, like others, Winfrey taps into these literacy goals by valuing and promoting affective reading practices. The lessons of *Where the Heart Is* may seem like unexamined platitudes to critics, but Winfrey's success suggests that we ought to consider the comfort popular wisdom offers. Just as parables such as "The Prodigal Son" and "The Good Samaritan" do not challenge readers with new or difficult ideas, so *The Oprah Winfrey Show* demonstrates that popular fiction likewise provides pleasure in familiarity and straightforward didacticism.

Uniting textual literacy and television literacy, Winfrey reminds viewers that they share an ideology, including common values and feelings. As Winfrey puts it in another iteration of the theme of *Where the Heart Is*, "Even if you didn't read the book though, the story is universal. So many people love this book, how faith and the kindness of strangers can get you through the toughest times." It's not so much the story that's universal, but the emotions it evokes, which regular viewers of *The Oprah Winfrey Show* know, even if they haven't read the text. A close look at the logic here helps to explain the role of literature on *The Oprah Winfrey Show*. In this setting, books are secondary to shared emotions, or, rather, they are a means to that end. Sharing one's personal life and feelings, as Winfrey demonstrates, is central to talk television. Alternative or conflicting interpretations of Letts's novel have no place on *The Oprah Winfrey Show*. The rhetoric of sharing combines with the repetition of commonplace values that no reasonable person would dispute—family, community, generosity, and optimism—to produce the appearance that Winfrey's audience is united not only in what they read, but also in what they believe, and in what they desire for themselves and their communities. Like the politician, who evokes the future of our children to garner support for increased funding for education, so Winfrey unites her audience under themes we can all embrace.

In keeping with the purpose of *The Oprah Winfrey Show* generally, Winfrey also cultivates her parasocial community of likeminded viewers by carefully constructing the setting of this and every episode of Oprah's Book Club. No fancy dinner at Oprah's house to celebrate the triumph of the teenaged mother and her Wal-Mart baby. Instead, this book discussion at a Wal-Mart lunch counter demonstrates how Winfrey uses *Where the Heart Is* to promote the novel's theme of down-home community-building, which is, at the same time, a theme of *The Oprah Winfrey Show*, and especially her Angel Network. In this way, the book and the television show work together to promote one another. First, Winfrey labels Letts "our down-to-earth author," then she connects Letts's novel to the setting for the show: "Each month we hold our book club at a place that will bring out the spirit of the book," Winfrey reminds viewers. "In the past we've dined at Maya Angelou's home. We've had dinner at my house. We've had . . . dinner at a library. We had dinner at a plantation, even had dinner at the Ritz. But this time around the theme of our book brought us to Wal-Mart." Not only does Novalee Nation set up housekeeping in Wal-Mart and then give birth to her daughter there, but also Wal-Mart is, as Letts says of the retail giant in her tiny hometown in rural Oklahoma, "a social center." In the words of *New York Times* reviewer, Anita Gates "Wal-Mart [is] America's new Main Street, just about the only place in a community where all sorts of people cross paths" (3). Winfrey taps into what Gates calls Wal-Mart's "folksy family-first image" (2). Just as Wal-Mart brings together diverse cost-conscious shoppers, so Oprah's

Book Club serves to build a reading community of viewers from all over the world. One participant on the show puts the theme this way:

> But when I'm really homesick, I go to Wal-Mart, because they're all exactly the same. And we've only had—you know, they only made it to Yakima, Washington, about three years ago. . . . I'm from Mississippi originally. So I just go down to the Wal-Mart and go inside, and if I just close my eyes for about 10 seconds, then I'm right back.

While some may find the homogenizing influence of mass marketing, including both Wal-Mart and Oprah's Book Club, disturbing, for this Book Club participant, familiarity alleviates homesickness and provides comfort. By privileging sentiments like this, Winfrey supports not only Letts's message about the importance of kindness and generosity toward strangers, but, at the same time, endorses the multimillion-dollar discount store, which, through its own advertising campaigns, has fashioned itself into a cultural icon, which is meant to represent small-town, working-class American values. As Letts puts it, "The town where I live, Durant, is a small town. We just live a slower life here, I think. We pay more attention to our neighbors and—and to what's going on in the community." The unpretentious setting of this Book Club lunch reinforces Winfrey's lesson concerning, as she puts it, "the spirit and warmth and generosity" that are at the center of Letts's novel. Or, as Letts says in her own folksy way when Winfrey asks what she wanted readers "to feel" when they read her novel, "We have a God's plenty of dark days to go through. I wanted them to think that there are some good people out there, and if we'll just open up and give them a chance, they'll help us in some way."

Through Letts, not only does Wal-Mart represent shared American hometown values, but it also represents the image Winfrey constructs for herself and her Book Club. Via the humble lunch counter at the local Wal-Mart, Winfrey cultivates her "just folks" persona, emphasizing that she, like her Book Club, is not highfalutin. Unlike previous episodes, this Book Club meal is neither glamorous nor intimate. Wal-Mart takes us far afield of Winfrey's own grandiose dining room high atop the Windy City, which we saw during the discussion of Toni Morrison's *Song of Solomon*. Instead of a mark of intimate good taste, this Book Club dinner at the "social center" of Wal-Mart unites the idea of the megadepartment store as the people's store with the idea of Oprah's Book Club as the people's book club, a place where ordinary folk gather to share their reactions to books. Donning the bright blue

apron of a Wal-Mart employee, Winfrey thumbs her nose at literary preten-
sion as she is made honorary store manager during the taping of the show.
Literacy takes a back seat to giddy consumerism. This segment evokes the
yearly "Oprah's Favorite Things" show, for which a seat in Oprah's studio
audience is especially coveted. On these episodes, the "O List," a regular feature in Winfrey's monthly magazine, is revealed, and Winfrey heaps gifts
such as Miss Rona's Lavender Applesauce, an iPod, and anti-aging body
cream on all the guests in her audience. Similarly, in this Oprah's Book Club
segment, *The Oprah Winfrey Show* becomes not a book discussion, but an
extended commercial for Sam Walton's discount empire. As the rules of talk
television dictate, Winfrey remains squarely at the center of attention, seeming to recognize that her performance is steeped in power and authority, not
only as a literacy sponsor, but, more broadly, also as a cultural icon. In accordance with the purpose of daytime talk, not only to entertain, but also to sell
products, as store manager, Winfrey unites her iconic image with that of the
nation's leading discount chain: "That blue apron," Winfrey says, "can give
you a sense of power." Despite her millions, the "just-folks" Oprah likes a
bargain as well as the next Wal-Mart shopper. As a famous celebrity, however,
she can become, paradoxically, Sam Walton's queen-for-a-day, dispensing
deals to her loyal subjects.

Not only is Winfrey "just folks" at Wal-Mart, but the Book Club dinner,
too, is a humble blue plate special. In the nonstandard English, which characterizes such moments on her show, Winfrey explains:

> So you know how people always say I talk too much about the food?
> You won't hear me saying nothing about the food today. They're not
> known for, you know, fine cuisine, so you—this is one time we—we
> really talked about the book because that's what we needed to talk
> about.

Later Winfrey adds, "No frills and self serve. Our menu consisted of chicken
sandwiches, BLTs, corn dogs, cheese sticks and French fries, a Wal-Mart special. Nothing fancy for you, but it's a real Wal-Mart meal." By keeping it
"real" via this humble lunch, Winfrey defines herself, like Novalee Nation
and the other working-class characters of Letts's novel, as ordinary, not fancy,
but down-to-earth and genuine. Oprah and Novalee are themselves the
embodiment of the ideal Book Club participant. Toward the end of the
episode, Winfrey links this characterization explicitly to Oprah's Book Club:
"I read this big article in the *New York Times* about the tyranny in book clubs

where people go and fight over the books and stuff. That doesn't happen here. We're not snobs at all." The article to which Winfrey refers, Eileen Daspin's "The Tyranny of the Book Group," actually appeared in the *Wall Street Journal.* No longer cozy communities of like-minded readers, some groups, according to the author, have degenerated into battlegrounds, with infighting and mean-spirited competition. Daspin explains:

> Out there among America's readers, it isn't always Oprah's book club. While the industry that has sprung up around books is boom-ing—with books on forming book groups, "facilitators" paid to lead them and published guides to decipher bestsellers—book groups themselves are undergoing a decided change in character. No longer just friendly social gatherings with a vague continuing-education agenda, many of today's book groups have become literary pressure cookers, marked by aggressive intellectual one-upmanship and unabashed social skirmishing. In living rooms and bookshops across the country, clubs are frazzling under the stress, giving rise to a whole new profession: the book-group therapist. What started as rediscovery of the literary life has, for some, disintegrated into the tyranny of the book group. (1–2)

Highly paid book-group "facilitators" choose a group's books, formulate dis-cussion questions, and work to keep peace among feuding members. While discordant book groups may need a therapist, for Oprah's Book Club, ther-apy is not a corrective for healing strained relations among members, but the Club's very reason for being (Peck). There is no room on Winfrey's talk show for book-group dissent that may cause what Daspin labels "highbrow headaches and personal grudges" (2). Only snobs would fight about books, Winfrey insists, and Oprah's Book Club is not for snobs, but for common folk, the Wal-Mart set, who, like Winfrey, value community, homogeneity, and consensus.

This points to another aspect of Winfrey's appeal: General readers are drawn to Oprah's Book Club because it taps into their literacy goal of bringing discussions about serious literature down from the ivory tower and into the living rooms of regular people. Just as Winfrey gives voice to the jabs about her penchant for focusing too much attention on the sumptuous food and not enough on the books, Winfrey occasionally highlights book critiques of view-ers. If some don't like her choice, they are allowed—though not often—to say so on *The Oprah Winfrey Show.* But because talk television is host-centered,

Winfrey's own views tend to win out. By contrast, she never mentions the negative views of professional book critics. That the critics thought *Where the Heart Is* lightweight and schmaltzy did not register on *The Oprah Winfrey Show*. Instead, Winfrey plays up its light, affective qualities as strengths. In this way, Oprah's Book Club reminds us that literary interpretations are socially constructed, and the social group led by Winfrey values Letts's folksy wisdom and kooky characters. Because Winfrey and her fans are the book critics whose opinions matter, she seems, in this way, to democratize reading. Toward the end of this episode, another woman in the Wal-Mart audience puts her finger on this theme of equality, which she links to literacy-learning: "I just wanted to say that as a librarian, too, I liked the fact that Novalee, when she needed information, went to the library and got—it's the great equalizer. Everyone can use the library and get information. And in our book club, we have no rules, not anything. We just come, and we love to talk about books." This remark weaves the theme of the novel neatly into the fabric of *The Oprah Winfrey Show*. *Where the Heart Is* is a literacy narrative of liberation and upward mobility, which Winfrey uses to promote a story of literacy consistent with her own life story of transformation and uplift through books.

Reading is a prominent theme in every account of Winfrey's life. Though they were not readers themselves, Winfrey's father and stepmother encouraged Winfrey's love of books. According to *Life* magazine, "Oprah says they regularly took her to the library . . . and they expected her to write reports on the books she borrowed. 'Getting my library card was like citizenship, it was like American citizenship,' she says" (Johnson 48). As with Winfrey, the public library makes possible Novalee Nation's conversion from a helpless teenage dropout into an intelligent, self-sufficient young woman. In *Where the Heart Is*, the library is a mysterious, sacred place, full of promise, pointing the way to Novalee's advancement. Letts describes Novalee's first visit there this way:

> Even before the door closed soundlessly behind her, Novalee knew she had entered a special place. She hardly breathed as her eyes played around the room, a room with dark wood carved into intricate designs, tall windows of thick, frosted glass and red velvet drapes held back with silver cord, chandeliers whose crystal drops caught fragments of light transfused into rich blues and deep greens, paintings in gold frames of nude women with heavy bellies and thick thighs. And books. Racks of books, stacks of books, walls of books. More books than Novalee had ever seen. (58)

In this setting, books—and the knowledge they contain—are more valuable than gold. With its delicate carvings and soaring windows draped in rich fabric, the library of *Where the Heart Is* brings to mind the *Life* magazine photo of Winfrey, seated among the stacks in the elegant Brunswick Room of the St. Ignatius Prep School library. By the novel's end, Novalee has not only read scores of books, but has also enrolled in the university. Winfrey could not have picked a better book to promote her view of the good literacy can do. Novalee tells Forney Hull, "You taught me to learn, Forney. You showed me a new world" (326). Forny is Novalee's Oprah Winfrey. Novalee could be the poster girl for Oprah's Book Club, passing her love of learning on to her daughter, Americus, who, in second grade has already begun to study Latin and reads at the eighth grade level. Americus represents the American dream of education for all. As Novalee's friend Lexie says, "Look what you've done for yourself. You have wonderful child and a home. A family of friends who love you. You have a good job. You're a great photographer—an artist. You've read a whole library of books. You even go to college. You've got it all, honey. You've got it all" (332).

Another literacy narrative among Oprah's Book Club selections is Bernhard Schlink's *The Reader,* which was described on the Book Club Web site this way: "A parable of German guilt and atonement and a love story of stunning power, *The Reader* is also a work of literature that is unforgettable in its psychological complexity, its moral nuances, and its stylistic restraint." *The Reader* was the twenty-second among Oprah's Book Club selections. Schlink's novel tells the story of Michael Berg, a fifteen-year-old German boy who, suffering from hepatitis, meets an older woman one day when he falls ill on his way home from school. The woman, Hanna Schmitz, a streetcar conductor in her mid-thirties, nurses the stricken boy. Later, once he has recovered, Michael returns to thank the beautiful, mysterious older woman for her kindness. So begins a love affair between the two, which is marked not only by their frequent lovemaking but also by Michael's ritual reading aloud to Hanna, who cannot read. Suddenly, however, Hanna disappears. Michael does not see her again until years later when he is studying law at the university. In a courtroom, Michael is shocked to recognize Hanna among a group of accused Nazi war criminals. She is charged with atrocities committed while serving as a guard in a slave-labor camp. For Hanna, however, illiteracy is a shame even greater than war crimes. Rather than reveal that she is unable to read and write, Hanna admits to authoring a damaging report, the principle piece of evidence against her. Michael is also silent on the matter of Hanna's illiteracy, and she is sent to prison. To assuage the guilt he feels at failing to reveal the secret that might have saved Hanna, Michael takes up reading to her again, sending tape recordings to her in prison. Later, Hanna learns to read so that she may study the history of the Nazi regime in an effort to understand own her dark past. As penance for her crimes, Hanna hangs herself on the day set for her release, leaving her small savings to the daughter of one of her victims. Michael, who has been anticipating her happy release, is left at the novel's end, closed off, emotionally isolated, and deadened as a result of his failure to confront both his own responsibility and Hanna's guilt. Using Michael and Hanna's troubled love relationship as a metaphor, Schlink explores the moral dilemma faced by Germany's second generation in coming to terms with wartime atrocities committed by friends, family, and loved ones of the first generation.

In a *New York Times* book review published the day before *The Reader* aired on Oprah's Book Club, Danita Smith reflects on the novel's unexpected success—even before Winfrey brought it to worldwide attention: "'The Reader' is a small, quiet, intellectual book," Smith says, "that asks big moral questions. It has a distinctly Mitteleuropean feel, an air of allegory and moral meditation. Hardly a prescription for a best seller" (1). While critics tended to lump together all of Winfrey's early picks as lightweight "chick novels," the sharp contrast between *Where the Heart Is* and *The Reader* points to some variety among Oprah's Book Club selections, which resists simple, derogatory categories. Like Smith, Daisy Maryles of *Publishers Weekly* reports that Nicholas Latimer, associate publicity director at Knopf publishers, referred to *The Reader* as "'The Little Book That Could'" ("Oprah Goes International" 20). As an unexpected best seller, Schlink's novel itself is apparently imbued with the can-do optimism of Oprah's "change-your-life-TV." Maryles reminds us, however, that Winfrey is not solely responsible for *The Reader*'s success. Prior to its selection for Oprah's Book Club, Schlink's novel, first published in 1997, had well over 100,000 copies in print after eight return trips to the press. Maryles quotes Vintage publicity director, Katy Barrett: "'This has been a tremendous word-of-mouth book—its sales have increased steadily every month.'" Barrett points out, "'It's also hugely popular with book clubs'" ("Oprah Goes International" 20). Although it had an impressive track record prior to being named an Oprah's Book Club selection, thanks to Winfrey's endorsement, Smith points out, at Amazon.com *The Reader* was, at the time, outselling even Monica Lewinsky's biography (2). Here Smith acknowledges Winfrey's power as a literacy sponsor, but she implies that Schlink's "Mitteleuropean" novel is too highbrow, too intellectually sophisticated for Winfrey's audience. *The Reader*, we are told, emerges

from the author's academic and juridical expertise. Schlink, a university professor of constitutional law and philosophy, and a justice of the Constitutional Law Court in Germany, is author of such essays as "Questions of Law,
Guilt and Future After the Third Reich." This and other moral treatises
underscore his interest in the problem of collective guilt, the theme, according to Smith, of *The Reader*. Michael Berg must bear the weight of collective
guilt for Germany's national sins, personified by the woman he loves.

As we might expect of daytime talk television, Winfrey focuses less on
Schlink's philosophical debate concerning collective guilt, and more on his
novel as a sensational story about a sexual relationship between a young boy
and an older woman, which many of Winfrey's American viewers found
taboo. While agreement generally prevails during Winfrey's on-air discussions, there is, in this case, a bit of room for dissensus. On this episode, discussion concerns what guests see as the scandalous nature of Schlink's
fictional May–December relationship. In the parlance of talk television's discourse of recovery and self-help, one reader goes so far as to label Hanna an
"abuser" (March 31, 1999). Unencumbered by the neo-Puritan mores that
lead Winfrey's American readers to view the affair as indecent, the novel's
German author appears taken aback by this characterization. After all, his
intent, he says, is to show how one comes to terms with war crimes committed by a loved one. Hanna may be older than Michael, even emotionally
overwhelming to him, but he is clearly in love with her, an eager partner in
their relationship. Schlink suggests that Winfrey's audience suffers from
sexual priggishness. "I've never had a discussion like that," he tells Winfrey,
"with readers in Germany or France." But Winfrey indulges her readers' way
of thinking because it both reflects a common view among Book Club participants, and, more important, like other hot topics on *The Oprah Winfrey
Show*, a taboo sexual relationship is sensational. Casting Hanna as a sexual
predator makes for good television. More than once during the show, participants ratchet up the debate by comparing Schlink's novel to the real-life
headline-making case of Mary Kay LeTourneau, the married junior high
school teacher who had an affair and two children with a twelve-year-old student. Similarly, the relationship between Michael and Hanna, Winfrey's
Book Club guests insist, is unnatural, unhealthy. Winfrey adds fuel to the
fire when she further advances the aims of daytime talk television by personalizing the discussion and attempting to reveal the author's past. When John,
another Book Club guest, asks a frequent question on Oprah's Book Club,
"My question is how autobiographical is this?" Winfrey leaps at the opportunity to delve into the author's intimate life. Famous for asking questions fans

want answered, Winfrey agrees, "Yeah, that's all of our questions, really."
Again, as we saw in the on-air discussion of *Where the Heart Is,* Winfrey's
presentation of *The Reader* says more about the values and assumptions
underlying daytime talk television than about Schlink's novel. On Oprah's
cozy set, viewers expect the secret lives of guests to be revealed. Schlink, however, refuses to give himself over to tell-all American talk television. Suddenly, distancing himself from the demands of American popular culture, it
is the Continental author who sounds like a prig: "I'm from the old world,"
Schlink demurs, "and I have an old-fashioned sense of privacy, so please forgive that I don't want to specify what's autobiographical and what isn't."
Winfrey, offering a quick lesson on the genre of American talk television, is
forgiving. In a knowing aside to her audience, she says, "Oh, yeah, they're
not used to telling everything over there. . . . He ought to see *The Jerry
Springer Show,* for goodness sakes. I thought we were—I thought we were
being modest." Even while distancing herself from the "trash-pack," Winfrey
underscores what sells on daytime talk.

With Winfrey's self-referential comparison to Springer, we see clearly
what is usually veiled, but always already the case: *The Oprah Winfrey Show* is
first and foremost about itself and its own promotion. For the 1998–1999
season during which Schlink's novel aired, Tim Kiska reported that *The
Oprah Winfrey Show* ranked, surprisingly, second among syndicated talk
shows behind *The Jerry Springer Show* (F1). Winfrey's dip in the ratings suggested that although she was near the top of her game, some fans wanted
more dirt. A 1999 *Detroit News* article titled "Talk-show Viewers Tuning
Out: Audiences Make a Fundamental Shift in the Way They Watch TV"
helped to explain Winfrey's slump. One viewer is quoted as saying, "'I think
Oprah is becoming dull. . . . She doesn't have the pizzazz that she used to
have. (Her talk show) is like going to the library. She is becoming too sophisticated for her audience'" (Kiska F1). Serious books like *The Reader* are a
gamble, and so, to make Schlink's visit more entertaining, and to avoid
seeming dull as "going to the library," Winfrey highlighted the sensational.
As this instance demonstrates, daytime talk shows promise a certain kind of
entertainment, and so in order to keep her Book Club afloat, Winfrey must
carefully balance the ideology of daytime talk television with the goals of
serious literature.

Even so, this Book Club episode does eventually turn from sensational
current events and the private details of the author's past to serious themes of
the book. As Winfrey puts it, "O.K. We love books because they make you
question yourself. For instance, what would you have done if you lived in

Germany during the war, forced to take sides, forced into life and death dilemmas?" For readers who blame Hanna for failing to unlock the doors of a burning church full of prisoners, her question to the judge overseeing her trial, "What would you have done?" calls upon readers to turn the same difficult question on ourselves. Add to this the moral dilemma of young people such as Michael, who must acknowledge—and share responsibility for—the wartime atrocities of their loved ones. According to Schlink, the collective guilt of both generations cannot be easily squared away:

> I think there are irresolvable problems with which we just live and see that things have been done, crimes have been committed that are unforgivable; but at the same time not to try to understand and to make those who committed them into monsters that are so alien that we don't have to relate to them. That's wrong either. So you have to live with the tension.

We may not forgive Hanna, but we mustn't see ourselves as morally superior, for, faced with the same circumstance, we may have done the same thing she did. Here the televised Oprah's Book Club discussion is fairly sophisticated. Of course, under different circumstances, the discussion might be richer, deeper, more nuanced, but the same might be said of most discussions of literature, not just those on daytime television.

The Web-based message boards devoted to Schlink's *The Reader* also exhibit a high level of critical thinking among Winfrey's television viewers. For example, one writer gets fed up with the hand-wringing over the relationship between Michael and Hanna. While theirs is, indeed, a flesh and blood love affair, its metaphorical potential is more interesting to this respondent, who reminds message-board participants that in order to confront the crimes of his parents' generation, Michael had to fall in love with someone much older. This writer goes on to argue that Hanna's illiteracy may also be viewed as a metaphor for her ignorance, however willful, of her wartime behavior and its consequences. Another Book Club participant responds that this writer's post was one of the most insightful analyses on the board. Later, the first writer returns to the discussion, suggesting that Schlink's intention is to provoke readers to consider what we might do if we were, like Hanna, forced by the threat of death, to follow an immoral command. She goes on to say, however, that *The Reader* is about much more than Hanna and Michael. What kind of government, she wonders, preys on uneducated and powerless citizens like Hanna, demanding that they murder their neighbors in order to save their own lives. This post provokes an extended reflection among several participants about the current state of the government, economy, healthcare, and education in the United States. One respondent ends with a common refrain on the Oprah's Book Club discussion boards: discussions in this setting are more interesting and engaging than both the books and Oprah's presentation of them on her show. These readers, who use Oprah's Book Club as a prompt for thinking and talking about significant issues of the day in the electronic social setting of the Internet, are far from the stereotype of Michael Moore's dull-witted couch potato, sitting on the sidelines as the fires resulting from 9/11 rage on.

Like their counterparts who write to the message boards, participants on the televised discussions seem eager to grapple with the complex ideas in Oprah's Book Club selections. They remark on Schlink's ambivalent tone, which invites readers not to judge Hanna, but to put themselves in her position. Another moral dilemma they discuss is the one Michael faces regarding Hanna's illiteracy. Should he, or should he not, reveal to the judge that Hanna can neither read nor write and therefore could not possibly have written the damaging report she is accused of authoring. Once again, Winfrey uses her Book Club selection as an opportunity to promote her message about the transforming possibilities of literacy. Winfrey uses Hanna's shame as an opportunity to highlight the secret pain of illiteracy and the lengths people will go to hide it. Again, we see the tension between discussing ideas in the book and entertaining daytime talk viewers with the kinds of stories they've come to expect on *The Oprah Winfrey Show*. At this point, Winfrey's focus turns to revealing a secret, a regular occurrence on talk television. In this case, the secret is illiteracy. In this way, literacy works as a theme on *The Oprah Winfrey Show* because it fits with the program's underlying values. Winfrey announces, "[Y]ou're going to see in Remembering your Spirit today . . . people . . . who live with the shame of not being able to read." Later, she continues, "but once they're outed, so to speak, once they claim or are willing to proclaim that I don't know but I'm willing to know, it-it-it-it frees them. It frees them." Here Winfrey constructs another bootstraps tale of literacy for liberation, again, much like her own life story, highlighting the literacy narratives of five unidentified men and one woman. Their stories are meant not only to reveal their secrets, but also to promote hope in others. Winfrey says of a ninety-eight-year-old man who confesses that he can't read, but wants to learn, "You are such an inspiration for everybody who thinks they can't turn their life around or can't change." While Letts's *Where the Heart Is* and Schlink's *The Reader* may seem to have little in common,

Winfrey brings them together to convey her message of "Change-Your-Life-TV." As she says of another outed former illiterate in the closing segment of the show, "She's a living example of what can be accomplished when you really set your mind on something. Where there's a will, there's a way." Winfrey proclaims the Horatio Alger doctrine of independence and hard work, which undergirds her show (Decker). Her words are self-referential, for loyal fans understand that this closing comment could be about Winfrey's own rags-to-riches-and-recognition story. In short, as literacy sponsor, and in accordance with the genre of talk television, Winfrey remains the center of the literacy narrative she promotes on *The Oprah Winfrey Show*.

While the novels of Letts and Schlink reflect both diversity and the commonality among Book Club selections, with four titles on Oprah's Book Club list, perhaps Toni Morrison's work reveals the most about Winfrey's literary aesthetic and what makes a successful Book Club pick. *The Bluest Eye* tells the story of Pecola Breedlove, sexually assaulted by her father, abused by her mother, shunned by everyone, including the African American community in which she lives, because she is poor, black, and ugly. After giving birth to her father's stillborn child, Pecola goes mad, praying for the blue eyes that she thinks will make her beautiful. *The New Yorker*'s L. E. Sissman calls the "overriding motif" of Morrison's novel the "desirability of whiteness, or, as the next-best thing, the imitation of whiteness." (5). Though *The Bluest Eye* is set in the 1941 steel-producing town of Lorain, Ohio, not much improved for African Americans, Sissman contends, in the thirty years between the setting of the novel and its publication. In his *New York Times Book Review*, Haskel Frankel calls Morrison "a writer of considerable power and tenderness, someone who can cast back to the living, bleeding heart of childhood and capture it on paper." For him, the theme of Morrison's novel is "the tragic effect of race prejudice on children" (3). Though Pecola's story is a grim one, Frankel finds it, finally, optimistic: "There are many novelists willing to report the ugliness of the world as ugly," he writes. But Morrison is no ordinary reporter. "The writer who can reveal the beauty and hope beneath the surface," Frankel continues, "is a writer to seek out and to encourage" (4). Not surprisingly, Winfrey, too, finds Morrison's "hope beneath the surface" a good fit for "change-your-life-TV."

Unlike some of Winfrey's contemporary "discoveries," *The Bluest Eye* has a long-established place in the literary canon. It is taught in high school and college literature courses across the country and has inspired a wealth of literary criticism. In some ways, this novel is very different from Letts's *Where the*

Heart Is, which Winfrey catapulted to fame, or Schlink's *The Reader,* which had a well-established place among book clubs even before Winfrey picked it. But, like the others, *The Bluest Eye* is significant among Winfrey's picks because of the splash it made within the context of *The Oprah Winfrey Show.* As Winfrey reports in her introduction to the televised discussion, Morrison's novel had a huge impact on Book Club participants: "Over the course of the last month," says Winfrey, "we've been flooded with letters and e-mails from all races and cultures, sometimes over 200 responses a day" (26 May 2000). What's more, Morrison's novel is noteworthy because of the author's special relationship with Winfrey, not only as a writer, but also as a role model of African American womanhood. The following explanation for Winfrey's selection of Morrison's novels appeared at Oprah.com, under "Oprah's Book Club Facts": "Oprah has not chosen [four] Toni Morrison books because she and Ms. Morrison are friends, but because Oprah feels that "Toni Morrison is the best writer, living or dead, and I love her work." For critics who argue that Winfrey panders to an audience of slow-witted television junkies with book selections that are shallow literature-lite, Morrison's prominence on Oprah's Book Club suggests otherwise. Certainly, Winfrey must consider what her viewers will like or dislike as she makes her choices, but her repeated selection of Morrison illustrates the confidence Winfrey has in the willingness of her fans to accept her choices and to adopt her taste solely based on their confidence in Winfrey's judgment. By choosing her favorite author four times, Winfrey highlights the fact that Oprah's Book Club, like *The Oprah Winfrey Show,* is primarily about Winfrey herself, her tastes, her status, her power to set the reading agenda for millions.

At first glance, *The Bluest Eye* seems to have little in common with the novels by Letts and Schlink, but it is consistent with these and other Book Club selections because it, too, presents a story about literacy. Reading plays a central role in both the form and the content of *The Bluest Eye.* As this example and others show, literacy is a persistent concern on Oprah's Book Club. *The Bluest Eye* begins in a prose style familiar to generations of beginning readers, with an excerpt from a Dick and Jane primer:

> Here is the house. It is green and white. It has a red door. It is very pretty. Here is the family. Mother, Father, Dick and Jane live in the green-and-white house. They are very happy. See Jane. She has a red dress. She wants to play. Who will play with Jane? See the cat. It goes meow-meow. Come and play. Come and play with Jane. (3)

This fragment, reprinted three times in the preface, like a spell cast on the life of Pecola Breedlove, becomes progressively more unintelligible with each repetition. The first version is coherent, but in the second, punctuation is removed and capital letters turned to lowercase. Finally, in the third version, the words run together with no spaces between them. Morrison then takes quotations from the run-together fragment and uses them to introduce seven of the novel's subsections. The Dick and Jane reader, the thread that binds Morrison's narrative, reminds readers that words and images have tremendous—and sometimes terrible—power. Sticks and stones may break your bones, but names—and images—too, can hurt you. The primer brings to mind our first school-based literacy experiences, the idyllic pictures of Dick, Jane, Mother, Father, dog, and cat on a deep lawn before a fine house with a white picket fence, the simple sentences securely drilled into our minds. Morrison's deconstruction and repeated use of the primer invites readers to consider the relationship between social class, race, and literacy in the United States. Its scrambled text reflects the dissonance between the dominant white culture's myth of beauty and happiness and the bleak/black experiences of impoverished African Americans. With the primer, Morrison contrasts the white American ideal of family life with that of the Breedloves and McTeers. She underscores the dire effects that this romanticized image has on both the psyche of young black children and the culture of African Americans generally. The Dick and Jane lesson about family love and beauty is damaging because young readers are taught to believe that others are happy because they are white and well-to-do, and perhaps because they are pretty. Unlike Father and Mother in the Dick and Jane story, Mr. and Mrs. Breedlove make only a sad irony of their family name, breeding, instead of love, violence and death. The more poverty-ridden and chaotic Pecola's life, the more she yearns for the primer's norm, which the dominant culture promises provides beauty, love, and happiness. Morrison undercuts the power of this myth, contrasting the flat, dull, mechanical, repetition of the primer with her own richly nuanced descriptions of reality to underscore the blandness of the cultural norms taught by Dick and Jane. On her show, Winfrey uses Morrison's novel to teach her own lesson about beauty and happiness.

Once again, the message of *The Oprah Winfrey Show*—and the books it promotes—is hope and optimism for both individual and community improvement. Winfrey chose *The Bluest Eye* not only because it is her favorite author's first novel, but, more important, because Winfrey could use it to promote herself, her show, and her message. As she did with *The Reader*, pointing to her authority as literacy sponsor and to the theme of "change-your-life-TV," Winfrey sums up her reasons for selecting *The Bluest Eye* during its on-air discussion:

> And that's what's so powerful about "The Bluest Eye." It's why—
> you know, I feel like I would have done my job, I can retire if I get
> the whole country to read the book, because I think it is a way of
> saying to the world, "This is what we're talking about." When
> people say, "Racist. I'm not racist. That doesn't exist," or "What are
> you talking about? I mean, Oprah, look at your life." To be able to
> see through the eyes of Pecola, that that is the world so many of us
> have seen. And that's why it's so exciting to go into a bookstore. Bor-
> ders, which is right across the street from me and to see Pecola dis-
> played. . . . Redeemed. It will change the world. . . . It will change
> the world if everybody read this book.

Positive change can take place, Winfrey teaches, when fans read both *what* Winfrey reads and *how*. In this Book Club discussion, Winfrey demonstrates the reading practice she values most on her show: relating to books on a personal level. In the opening segment, Winfrey begins building a relationship between herself and the text by expressing solidarity with Pecola Breedlove. "And so for me," Winfrey says, "the beauty of this book is that Pecola— Pecola and all the Pecolas of the world have finally gotten our day." Not "their" day, but "our" day. This rhetorical move connects Winfrey not only to Morrison's fictional character, but also to all the Book Club participants who see themselves in Pecola/Winfrey. Like Winfrey, viewers are invited to see themselves and their own lives—"our" lives—played out across Morrison's pages. Winfrey further demonstrates this reading strategy of connecting to the text to the personal when she compares her own grandmother to Pecola's mother, Pauline. Like Pauline, Winfrey's grandmother worked in the home of a white family and seemed to prefer its golden-haired children to her own black granddaughter. Winfrey tells us:

> And when she would come home, you know—and whip me . . .
> chastise me, talk to me, you know, in—in not the most loving
> terms, but every time she would talk about those white children . . .
> she was Pauline. There would be this—this—this sort of glow inside
> her about these white children. And that was—when I—when I
> read what you'd said, I thought, "That's the message"—that's when I
> first got it, that you are better if you are white.

This Winfrey, sharing her painful childhood, is the Winfrey readers have come to trust to select a book because they know her.

Not only does Winfrey connect to Morrison's novel in a deeply personal way, but also, through the book discussion, Winfrey showcases another central theme of *The Oprah Winfrey Show*: building a sense of community, particularly among her mostly female audience. In this case, Winfrey reaches out to incest survivors, as she has before, by sharing her own story, framed this time in terms of "the secret many incest survivors keep inside." Morrison's novel leads Winfrey, in another self-referential moment, to reflect on both the construction of her personal legend in the media and the confusion she herself felt as a child when, on the one hand, she was being abused, but, on the other, she wanted the attention of her abusers, and what seemed, at the time, like their love. Winfrey says: "I know you say, 'People don't talk about it.' I say, 'Oh, she must have missed that show.' But I talked about it. . . . For me, it started with a nineteen-year-old cousin playing footsie, you know? And so you're thinking, 'He likes me.'" In sharing her personal narrative of childhood sexual abuse and relating it to both Morrison's novel and to the stories of other readers, Winfrey emphasizes an important assumption underlying Oprah's Book Club and her talk show in general: You are not alone. Within Winfrey's community of shared experience and feeling, revealing your secret is the first step toward healing. As we have seen before, Winfrey joins books and *The Oprah Winfrey Show* to help foster a sense of parasocial interaction among viewers. By contrast with Pecola's story, which ends tragically, Winfrey's familiar narrative reminds viewers of the intimacy they share with her and, importantly, of her triumph over adversity. Winfrey's life is proof that hope and optimism prevail. In this way, Winfrey's reading of *The Bluest Eye* becomes, by example, a story of the good that books can do when readers see themselves in fictional characters—and, by extension, Oprah Winfrey. That is Winfrey's lesson.

Winfrey's presentation of books always involves a lesson. In this way, Oprah's Book Club has a deliberately didactic purpose. She uses Morrison's novel to teach several lessons, among them, the one above about surviving incest, another about childrearing, and one about racism and the nature of beauty. While this Book Club discussion does cover many of the important themes of Morrison's novel, daytime talk television must sum the book up, package it into neat sound-bites in order for books to remain viable in this electronic setting. Of childrearing, for example, Winfrey says, reflecting on a comment by Morrison:

We do lots of shows on child raising and how to handle your children. I—that's one of the most profound things I've ever heard. For all you moms who are worrying about dirty ears or, "Is your hair combed?" The most important thing, which we all felt when we heard her say it, is do your eyes light up when your child walks into the room. Wasn't that big? That's profound.

Not only does Winfrey succeed as a talk show host by standing in, if you will, for the ordinary viewer, asking the question we all want to ask, but she also embodies and sums up for us the collective feelings of viewers. It would be a stretch to label Morrison's novel a treatise on childrearing, but no matter. Winfrey's lesson about the importance of parental love works in the context of the show because many viewers, who may not readily relate to the plight of a poor, ugly African American girl, are mothers. In this way, Winfrey's brand of popular wisdom fulfills an important need for viewers. Here we see how Winfrey constructs her book discussions to appeal to a broad—mostly white—audience.

In her lesson about racism and the nature of beauty, Winfrey casts a similarly wide net. In the "Remembering Your Spirit" segment of this book discussion, Winfrey ends the show by introducing an African American artist, Cozbi Cabrera, who designs African American dolls. Relating her life to that of Pecola Breedlove, Cabrera represents Winfrey's ideal reader, who is transformed for the better as a result of reading Morrison's novel. Cabrera says, "I very much identify with Pecola, because when I grew up, you know, kids called me ugly. You know, there's something about dark skin that was not really accepted or—or viewed as—as a beautiful thing.'" As regular viewers of Winfrey's "Remembering Your Spirit" segments know, Winfrey's lesson here is not so much about race and beauty, but about the exercise of individual autonomy. In her narrative, Cabrera recounts a successful but unfulfilling career designing packaging for record companies. In this confining role, however, her "voice wasn't really being expressed." Likewise, in her hobby of antique doll collecting, Cabrera felt "despondent" and "totally invalidated as a black woman." At this point, what might be read as a story of black pride, is, instead, personalized according to the dictates of daytime talk television. "Black is beautiful" might be alienating to some of Winfrey's white viewers, but the exercise of personal freedom and entrepreneurial spirit is intended to appeal to all. Winfrey constructs Cabrera's story as one that mirrors her own and, conveniently, Morrison's as well. It is a story about pride in African

American womanhood, certainly. But it is also a more general story, too, about female intelligence, creativity, beauty, and drive. In short, it is the story of what Winfrey's viewers may themselves become through the miracle of "change-your-life TV." Cabrera's "spirit" is mended, her story makes clear, when she throws off the chains of an unfulfilling corporate job and chooses a self-made career that she loves. Winfrey hammers home her lesson about personal autonomy in the close of this segment, in which Cabrera explains that she used to hate going to work, but now every day is "Christmas morning and there's something lying await for me under the tree. And that's an incredible amount of freedom that allows me to share," she says. Not only that, but Cabrera's dolls are turning quite a profit, Winfrey reports. Cabrera's story replaces that of Dick and Jane with a contemporary, but no less idealized, myth of self-love, personal freedom, and hard work, which lead to monetary success in a capitalistic economy. Winfrey's lesson is less about black pride than it is about a more broadly held image of the "American Dream." Her construction of Cabrera's life takes us far afield of Morrison's novel, as Cabrera's embrace of her cultural heritage becomes an effective marketing tool. Self-esteem and following one's passion, as Winfrey sometimes puts it, are worthwhile achievements, but not ends in themselves. Parlay these into a moneymaking venture, Winfrey teaches, and then you'll have genuine freedom, like her own enormous wealth provides Winfrey herself. Who wouldn't be drawn in by this Cinderella story of transformation and uplift so familiar on *The Oprah Winfrey Show*?

As we have seen from Winfrey's treatment of the three books discussed in this chapter, Oprah's Book Club may, indeed, propagate unexamined platitudes about the American way of life, patriotism, democracy, the free world, and—I would add—literacy. Clearly, there are obvious limitations to discussing books thoughtfully on television. But the same might be said of discussing books anywhere else. And so, the persistent false dichotomy between television watchers and book readers seems unhelpful to me because it shuts off the possibility of exploring television and books, not as "either/or," but as "both/and." Television and books work together on *The Oprah Winfrey Show*. In this setting, Winfrey carefully constructs and packages each book discussion to meet the show's own ends, which are to promote the host, her show, its message. While book discussions are necessarily limited, and even shallow at times, within its context, Oprah's Book Club is able to address books in interesting and sometimes sophisticated ways. Oftentimes, as in the example of *The Bluest Eye*, Winfrey's televised discussions controvert what the literary elite might consider *the* themes of the book into others, such as her lesson on childrearing, that book critics may consider insignificant or even misplaced. Oprah's Book Club succeeds with general readers because, by definition, it cannot rest upon the assumption that television watchers are stupid nonreaders. Rather, Oprah's Book Club brings books into a context that viewers already know and respect, in order to encourage readers not only to read, but also to watch television. By applying the commonplace themes of *The Oprah Winfrey Show* to her Book Club selections, Winfrey shows general readers how books can become usefully integrated into their lives, teaching lessons, which she reinforces on her show. Rather than view textual literacies and electronic mass media literacies as mutually exclusive, Winfrey helps general readers fit books into the lives they actually live, which include and value television. Instead of insisting that television fosters low-level thinking, poor reasoning skills, and illiteracy, Oprah's Book Club invites us to value multiple literacies, including mass media literacies, and to consider how these various literacy practices may be brought together to enhance one another.

The notion of multiple literacies points to an important feature of the televised discussions of Oprah's Book Club. As the examples I have discussed illustrate, Winfrey privileges certain kinds of reading practices over others that may also be satisfying. On *The Oprah Winfrey Show*, reading experiences tend to be flattened out to focus on those that the conventions of daytime talk will accommodate. Winfrey values emotional engagements with books, but this sometimes comes at the expense of readings that engage the intellect, judgment, and ethics. The kind of readings Winfrey leaves out include, for example, alternatives to the interpretation of Wal-Mart in Letts's *Where the Heart Is* as the new "social center," an icon of small-town, family values. By contrast, residents of small towns know all too well that when megadiscount stores such as Wal-Mart arrive, long-time family-run businesses frequently go out of business. Letts's novel thus invites us to think about what is lost amid the commercialism that Winfrey rejoices in on this episode of Oprah's Book Club. What's more, that the sameness, rather than the uniqueness, of Wal-Marts everywhere evokes the familiarity of "home" for some may seem sad to others. Likewise, Letts's rosy portrait of a poor, homeless, uneducated, single mother might engage readers to think about the range of social problems that contribute to Novalee's troubles, including the ways minimum-wage employers such as Wal-Mart are complicit in the perpetuation of these conditions. Similarly, Schlink's novel appeals to the desire of general readers to engage thorny ethical issues. Though the televised discussion of Schlink's *The Reader* does eventually address the substance of the novel in a cursory way, there is so much that is interesting that cannot be discussed under Winfrey's reading paradigm. That is not to say, however, that some ways of reading are necessarily better than others; rather, there are a wide range of responses to serious fiction, in addition to the personal and emotional, that are also stimulating and satisfying. For example, some readers on the message board found Hanna's illiteracy unbelievable, given Germany's history of educating its citizens. Others were uncomfortable with the suggestion that Hanna's illiteracy might serve as an excuse for her war crimes. Novelist Cynthia Ozick chides Schlink for imagining a character so anomalous as Hanna. Ozick argues that illiteracy is no exculpation. "It was not the illiterates of Germany who ordered the burning of books," she reminds us. By presenting a character, who is so unusual, Schlink "displaces history," argues Ozick, painting a corrupt picture of wartime responsibility, and wrongly inviting readers to sympathize with a Nazi murderer (28). Likewise, as the wealth of scholarly criticism attests, Morrison's *The Bluest Eye* is also far more nuanced than *The Oprah Winfrey Show* can reflect. What's more, not only literary scholars appreciate that complexity. The message boards at Oprah.com are filled with thoughtful responses by readers eager to think as well as to feel about books. For example, several lively discussions developed concerning the function of the Dick and Jane primer. An excerpt from one respondent explains its significance with the following demonstration: "People'swordsandideasbegin to runtogether and notmakemuchsense. Soon you have an unreadable, or unlivable, mishmash. Pecola couldn't make sense of this life. Couldn't read the text of her life. In the end her refuge is to rewrite reality in her mind." As this and other responses on the message boards indicate, the televised Book Club discussions provide readers something they want, but Winfrey's readers clearly want—and get—more from Oprah's Book Club than *The Oprah Winfrey Show* reflects. Partly thanks to Winfrey's sponsorship of literacy—and partly in spite of the limitations of daytime talk television—Winfrey's readers demonstrate multiple responses to Oprah's Book Club selections, including reactions that engage not only feelings of hope and optimism, the cornerstones of self-help and recovery television, but also the intellect, judgment, and ethics.

Works Cited

Bingham, Larry. "If Oprah Picks Your Book . . ." *Fort Worth Star-Telegram* 19 Jan. 1999, final ed., sec. Life & Arts: 1.

Brandt, Deborah. "Sponsors of Literacy." *College Composition and Communication.* 49.2 (1998): 165–85.

Daspin, Eileen. "The Tyranny of the Book Group." *Wall Street Journal* 15 Jan. 1999, Eastern ed., sec. W: 1.

Davidson, Cathy N., Ed. *Reading in America: Literature & Social History.* Baltimore: Johns Hopkins UP, 1989.

Decker, Jeffery Louis. *Made in America: Self-Styled Success from Horatio Alger to Oprah Winfrey.* Minneapolis: U of Minnesota P, 1997.

Frankel, Haskel. "The Bluest Eye." Rev. of *The Bluest Eye,* by Toni Morrison. *New York Times Book Review* 1 Nov. 1970. 4–5.

Garner, Dwight. "IN SHORT: FICTION—Where the Heart Is." Rev. of *Where the Heart Is,* by Billie Letts. *New York Times Book Review.* 6 Aug. 1995, late ed. 7.

Gates, Anita. "A Sitcom Savant Branches Out." *New York Times* 23 Apr. 2000, late ed., sec. 2: 11.

Haag, Laura L. "Oprah Winfrey: The Construction of Intimacy in the Talk Show Setting." *Journal of Popular Culture.* 26 (1993): 115–21.

Horton, Donald, and R. Richard Wohl. "Mass Communication and Para-Social Interaction: Observations on Intimacy at a Distance." *Psychiatry* 19 (1956): 215–29.

Hughes, Kathleen. "Review of Billie Letts' *Where the Heart Is.*" *Booklist.* 1 Sept. 1995. 41.

Johnson, Marilyn. "Oprah Winfrey: A Life in Books." *LIFE.* Sept. 1997: 45–60.

Kiska, Tim. "Talk-Show Viewers Tuning Out: Audiences Make a Fundamental Shift in the Way They Watch TV." *Detroit News* 12 Jul. 1999, sec. F: 1.

Lehmann, Chris. *Revolt of the Masscult.* Chicago: Prickly Paradigm, 2003.

———. "Oprah's Book Fatigue: How Fiction's Best Friend Ran Out of Stuff to Read." *Slate* 10 Apr. 2002. 2 Jan. 2007 <http://img.slate.com/id/2064224/>.

Letts, Billie. *Where the Heart Is.* New York: Time Warner, 1995.

Maryles, Daisy. "Oprah Goes International." *Publishers Weekly* 1 Mar. 1999: 20.

Morrison, Toni. *The Bluest Eye.* New York: Plume, 1970.

"Oprah's Book Club Goes to Wal-Mart." *The Oprah Winfrey Show.* Auth. Billie Letts. ABC. WHAS, Louisville. 19 Jan. 1999. Transcript.

"Oprah's Book Club: Bernhard Schlink's The Reader." *The Oprah Winfrey Show.* ABC. WHAS, Louisville. 31 Mar. 1999. Transcript.

"Oprah's Book Club: Toni Morrison's *The Bluest Eye.*" *The Oprah Winfrey Show.* ABC. WHAS, Louisville. 26 May 2000. Transcript.

Ozick, Cynthia. "The Rights of History and the Rights of Imagination." *Commentary* 107.3 Mar. 1999: 22–28.

Peck, Janice. "TV Talk Shows as Therapeutic Discourse: The Ideological Labor of the Televised Talking Cure." *Communication Theory* 5.1 (1995): 58–81.

"Review of Where the Heart Is." Rev. of *Where the Heart Is*, by Billie Letts. *Kirkus Reviews* 1 May 1995. 27.

Schlink, Bernhard. *The Reader*. New York: Vintage, 1995.

Sissman, L. E. "The Bluest Eye." Rev. of *The Bluest Eye*, by Toni Morrison. *The New Yorker* 23 Jan. 1971. 5.

Smith, Dinitia. "German's Novel of the Nazi Era Becomes a U.S. Best Seller." Rev. of *The Reader*, by Bernhard Schlink. *New York Times* 30 Mar. 1999: 1–3.

6

RESISTING PARADISE

Toni Morrison, Oprah Winfrey, and the Middlebrow Audience

MICHAEL PERRY

> I warned you going into it.
> —Oprah Winfrey

Twenty-two readers, including one very powerful host and a celebrated author, come together at Princeton to discuss a novel on national television on 6 March 1998.[1] The novel is Toni Morrison's *Paradise*—Oprah Winfrey's selection for the thirteenth Book Club episode (and the second devoted to Morrison).[2] *Paradise* marks the first instance within Oprah's Book Club when a text selected by Winfrey meets considerable resistance. In response, as reader resistance to *Paradise* becomes a "problem" that Winfrey attempts to rectify, she changes the format of the Book Club episode. Striving to maintain authority over her audience, Winfrey instructs her readers that their resistance to the selected text is a result of their misreading, thereby leaving her authority as book selector and host intact. Attempting to adapt the language of Winfrey's daytime talk show, Morrison offers her audience reading lessons meant to both focus and expand their "middlebrow" reading habits. In the end, they offer a "class" designed to *overcome* resistance to *Paradise*, rather than to *understand* it.

The *Paradise* episode illustrates how a class atmosphere imposed on an existing book club proves far less responsive to individual reader concerns, and, in fact, reinforces the image of the solitary reader that Elizabeth Long discusses in *Book Clubs: Women and the Uses of Reading in Everyday Life*.[3]

Furthermore, Winfrey's decision to recast her book club into a class rein-forces the image of the scholar who possesses the keys to unlock meaning for "regular" readers. While both constructs have a place within the classroom, book clubs exist to give support to the group as a whole and voice to the individual while avoiding hierarchal constructions. Therefore, Winfrey and Morrison's attempt to teach, to explain, and to open up becomes one-sided and frustrates the infrastructure of the Book Club. Their attempt simultane-ously illustrates both the potential as well as the obstacles faced when teach-ing practices and book club practices merge in the classroom as both host and author overestimate (in the sense that Book Club members entered *Par-adise* without the necessary tools) and underestimate (in the sense that they do not grant legitimacy to reader resistance) their audience. As a result, the episode offers an instructive, imperfect, and provoking example of the ten-sions that arise between book club and classroom reading experiences through the lens of middlebrow reading practices. The origin of such tension is situated within the twin desires of members of Oprah's Book Club who seek to not only identify with and discern life lessons from the selected books, but also increase their own cultural capital through their engagement with more "literary" fiction. Winfrey's selection of *Paradise* and decision to switch the format of the Book Club disrupts her ability to satiate their need to relate to and identify with the selected texts while simultaneously teaching them "better" ways to read.

Defining Oprah's Contract

Winfrey's selections prior to the *Paradise* episode illustrate her desire to create an atmosphere that, Cecilia Konchar Farr observes, "modeled how to read and talk about books and directly connected reading with The Good Life for her audience" (10).[4] Segments showcased viewers who related to themes in the novels, but not always to the "novel itself or to its characters" (11). At the same time, Winfrey encouraged her readers to bond and identify with the books, "reading the characters as if they [were] real people" (42). Her approach echoes Long's assertion that "the process of 'living' stories other than one's own—whether in books or through hearing other people discuss their own lives through books—may be crucial" (188). More than promot-ing straightforward consumption or focusing on strict textual interpretation, Oprah's Book Club, as noted by John Young, "emphasize[s] the experience of reading" (183). Emphasis on the experience of reading over interpretation

marks not only the source of tension between classroom and book club reading practices but also the implied "contract" between Winfrey and her readers. As will become clear, Book Club members find *Paradise* and the
resultant classroom format of the episode difficult to fit into this "contract."[5]
Book Club members responded with confusion and resistance: Woman #7
notes how she "just quit reading it," then pleads with Winfrey: "I really
wanted to read the book and love it and learn some life lessons; and when I
got into it, it was so confusing I questioned the value of a book that is that
hard to understand" (3).[6] A closer look at the reader's response details the
various levels of connection Book Club members had come to expect with
Winfrey's selections: she wanted to "read it" (relate to it reflectively); she
wanted to "love it" (relate to it empathically); and, she wanted to "learn some
life lessons" (relate to it imaginatively).[7]

In addition to such expectations, participation within Oprah's Book
Club required that members open themselves up not only to the book but
also to the other members of the group—that they actually challenge the
notion of the solitary reader. Oprah's Book Club answered such a challenge
by positing an atmosphere that encouraged engagement with community
values and recognition of individual concerns. While Long asserts that the
"myth" of the solitary reader often "governs our understanding of reading,"
Oprah's Book Club enables readers to expand their understanding of reading
(*Book Clubs* 2).[8] Although Book Club discussions may focus on *individual*
readers (their concerns, their life, their ability to connect with the text), such
discussions do not isolate the reader. Acknowledgment of reader individuality actually strengthens the reading community as well as the individual's
place within it. Morrison concurs, as she informs Winfrey's audience: "Reading is solitary but that's not its only life. It should have a talking life, a discourse that follows" (9). Morrison, a vocal proponent of active reading and
reader participation, has gone as far as calling for her readers to actively
engage in the construction her texts.[9]

The result of Winfrey's implied "contract" supplies Book Club members
with a sense of agency over the texts as they are able to respond to texts under
their terms while also reaping the cultural benefits such reading entails. As
such, Winfrey anticipates a positive reading experience for her audience due
to the trust her readers have in her book selections—a trust that has allowed
Winfrey, spurred by her love for reading and enabled by her status as
celebrity and talk show host, to create an institution intriguingly similar to
early incarnations of the Book-of-the-Month-Club (BOMC).[10] Unlike
being "made" to read a book in a class setting, Book Club members share

expectations similar to BOMC subscribers as investigated by both Joan Shelly Rubin in *The Making of Middlebrow Culture* and Janice Radway in *A Feeling for Books*. Book Club members rely on Winfrey's selections in much the same way as BOMC members: "All news was good news, since the judges [or Winfrey] included only the books they recommended" (Radway 103). The comfort provided by such recommendations from Winfrey "suggests a desire for even greater relief from the anxiety about the ineffectual self— about making wrong decisions in a chaotic world—that reliance on experts could palliate" (103). It appears that early subscribers of the BOMC looked to the editors in much the same way Book Club members look to Winfrey— not only to give them a good read, but also to take away the stress involved in making that choice.

Book Club members trust Winfrey's book selection will both challenge them and offer them cultural capital, yet still give them pleasure. These expectations arise from not only selections prior to *Paradise* but also trust built over the entire run of Winfrey's show. Winfrey's selections display her refusal to adhere to limiting constructs of high and lowbrow literature. Rather, Winfrey seeks to create an atmosphere in her Book Club that combines the marketability of popular television with the cultural capital of literary fiction. And Morrison, as Young observes, illustrates this "clash" of brows as she actively seeks a "popular audience for serious works of fiction" (187). Indeed, such reliance on "authority" to provide proper reading material speaks to one of the many contradictions within middlebrow reading habits, which Rubin explores through one of the Club's editors: "Sherman sensed within his audience longings for a world inhabited by models of character, even as it strove to cultivate personality for the sake of impressing others" (109). This constant struggle between reading on one's own terms while satisfying (even adhering to) existing literary assumptions of cultural hierarchy is indicative of the position Oprah's Book Club holds as it confronts the "problem" of *Paradise*.

A Breach of Trust

During the opening moments of the *Paradise* episode, Winfrey explains the need for a class rather than a discussion; "I heard from many people this month. Some admitted that they could not make it to paradise, that they couldn't make it to paradise. And even readers who did finish still felt a little confused. So for the first time our book club became a class, we needed help"

(2). Winfrey's opening statement clearly identifies the "problem," and the change of format marks Winfrey's attempt to help her audience. However, offering a class to help implies that the reason for the disruption in the Book Club lies solely with the readers—for to implicate either the book or the author would have challenged not only Morrison's but also Winfrey's authority, and, thus, the status of the Book Club itself. In addition, Winfrey's opening comment and decision to conduct a "class" imply that book club members *were* helpless. Therefore, Oprah's Book Club, which had previously displayed "beautifully dressed women sitting in overstuffed chairs in an elegant room, sipping wine and conversing," resituates itself into a classroom within the halls of one of America's most prestigious centers of academia (Farr 10). Without the perceived comfort of home, wine, and food, the very atmosphere of the Book Club changes. Suddenly, as a *class*, Book Club members are told their reaction to *Paradise* constitutes a "problem"; *individually*, they are denied the opportunity to articulate why.

In essence, a book club exists to give voice to each individual (if so desired) within a familiar and comfortable community via discussion. Switching the format of the club into a class disrupted the infrastructure of trust on which Oprah's Book Club was built—a club that has always emphasized a group atmosphere that supports individuals, rather than a class atmosphere that isolates the individual. If "reading thus requires . . . infrastructure as *social base*, in much the same way as modern transportation requires a physical infrastructure of highways, airports, and fuel supplies," then the trust between Winfrey and her audience constitutes a key part of the infrastructure of the Book Club (*Book Clubs* 10). Therefore, if the Book Club acts as a "highway" paved with trust, then Winfrey sets out to repair that highway. During previous selections, Winfrey had carefully developed "an atmosphere of trust" that encouraged "the sometimes tentative and exploratory openness—toward new ideas, about one's own feelings," which Long argues, "characterizes critical reflection in reading groups" (187). Winfrey's selection of *Paradise*, and her subsequent decision to change the format of her book club, breaks the trust she had built over the twelve previous selections and impels her to spend the majority of the episode in an attempt to regain that trust.

Unable (or unwilling) to respond directly to individual readers' concerns, Winfrey voices the mantra that will define the episode and address the group as a whole—a mantra that enables her to champion Morrison and console her readers—"you have to open yourself up" (4). Such a blanket statement, while fitting the discourse of Winfrey's television show, is more problematic when applied to individual reading practices. Winfrey, keen on retaining her authority, attempts to reestablish trust not by challenging *Paradise* and engaging her readers, but by reassuring them of her next book selection: "Next—It's a good one, a lot easier and a love story" (1). Later in the show, she offers: "I'll be announcing our new book that will bring us all back to earth, really." (9). Winfrey struggles to placate her viewers by promising them a return to the status quo, but her attempt only highlights the "problem" before her and hardly instills the trust needed to "open up." This affects members of the book club as well; rather than strive to communicate why they resisted *Paradise*, many expect and simply ask for answers, for help, in order to be able to move on to something "easier."

The search for answers happens in both classroom reading and book club reading communities. In addition, both communities constitute a group reading experience that "not only offers occasions for explicitly collective textual interpretation, but encourages new forms of association, and nurtures new ideas that are developed in conversation with other people as well as with books" (Long, "Textual" 194). But the lack of a clear authority figure physically in the room (not to mention two of them) undoubtedly sets the two communities apart. Morrison, invoking the "talking life" of a text, addresses a key aspect not only of Winfrey's "talk" show but also reading communities in general. However, the *Paradise* episode becomes increasingly one-sided (as classrooms often do, sometimes necessarily so). The "talking" that is supposed to be part of the group experience and a vital aspect of the Book Club made possible by individual readings is conspicuously absent. Situated within a class atmosphere, with a clear authority figure, the power structure is changed and a clear hierarchy is established. Once situated in a class atmosphere (as envisioned and shaped for television), readers, rather than functioning as members of a *group* that supports reader individuality and agency, find themselves in a class atmosphere in which they are isolated and spoken to.

Having lost the agency previously granted them by the Book Club, its members are faced with the enormous "power" that Winfrey holds, which, intriguingly, surpasses that of previous "heads" of middlebrow reading institutions. The editors of the Book-of-the-Month-Club had institutionally accepted degrees that allowed them a certain literary pedigree. Winfrey, despite her lack of formal degrees, offers her readers a similar experience while holding far more "authority" than the editors of the earlier middlebrow institution due to her celebrity status. If, as Long notes, "collective and institutional processes shape reading practices by authoritatively defining what is worth reading and how to read it," then Winfrey single-handedly shapes reading practices on a scale never before seen ("Textual" 192). The "problem," then, could be the break in trust and subsequent challenge to her authority as host. Why this challenge occurs and how she reacts to it constitute the remainder of this study. It would seem, furthermore, that both her selection of *Paradise,* and her decision to switch format, are the actual "problem."

Misreading the Middlebrow

As members of Oprah's Book Club approached *Paradise* before appearing in this episode, they brought their predominately middlebrow expectations (encouraged and shaped by Oprah's Book Club) to Morrison's novel. Of course, the term "middlebrow" can be misleading. Her middlebrow audience, which Farr describes as ranging from "the barely middle class, [and] the less educated [to] the privileged, the college graduates, [and] the stay at home soccer mom longing for intellectual stimulation," illustrates the fluid quality of the middlebrow (2). Middlebrow is more of a fluctuation between high and low, where middlebrow "members" continually oscillate between and among brows. Members of Oprah's Book Club, thus representative of a range of high, middle, and lowbrow readers, indeed had trouble with Winfrey's selection. They were not unintelligent, lazy readers; they were not even necessarily "misreading" Morrison's novel—on the contrary, they were simply bringing a different system of evaluation to the text. Similar to the middlebrow readership that Radway explores, they "read fiction as a way of thinking about key issues in their world and in their personal lives" (73). However, the structure of *Paradise,* its nonlinear nature, and the ambiguity, or what Peter Widdowson refers to as "tropes [that] have moved up a gear so that the complexity of the narrative itself" can cause readers "to underestimate the force of what they are reading," make initial identification with the text difficult (114). As a result, Book Club members were discouraged about participating in discussion, and instead, asked for answers because of disrupted expectations.

Winfrey's selection of *Paradise* displays that she misjudged, or, better yet, misread, what her middlebrow audience was ready (or prepared) to accept. Prior to this episode, a pattern of book selection had emerged in which Winfrey would begin by "leaning lowbrow [*Deep End of the Ocean*], and then quickly shift toward highbrow [*Song of Solomon*]" (Farr 39). Note the qualifiers "leaning" and "toward"—the subjective nature of both labels necessarily demands a certain amount of ambiguity. By alternating between (and around) these two categories, Winfrey highlighted a range representative of what Farr observes as the "parameters of the American middlebrow novel" (39). Therefore, just like her audience, the "middlebrow" novel can be seen more in the movement around and the interplay between brows, rather than in an adherence to a specific (and arguably limited) definition. In whatever direction Winfrey's selection leaned, however, the discussions surrounding the texts remained focused on a very middlebrow sentiment (one integral to the implied "contract" between Book Club members and Winfrey): the simultaneous task of bringing pleasure and lending cultural capital. Early in Book Club history, as Oprah's Book Club approached its second selection, Toni Morrison's *Song of Solomon*, Winfrey had warned her viewers that Morrison would "make you feel and think." (12). Winfrey then skillfully drew her audience's focus back to more comfortable grounding: "It's about motherhood and unrequited love and friendship and family secrets. It's about ten Oprah shows rolled into one book" (qtd. in Farr 12). Such navigation between the twin desires of her readers soon proved more difficult to traverse.

Unable to pursue a similar course in *Paradise*, Winfrey went to Princeton. Instead of empowering members, however, the class threatened the agency they normally possessed within the Book Club, thus highlighting the paradoxical nature of book clubs as members read to gain cultural capital, but consciously employ reading strategies that defy consciously elitist readings posed by the academy. Once within the walls of Princeton, bound by a hierarchy with Morrison on the top and Winfrey at her side as emissary, a room full of readers are left feeling as if they had done something wrong. Early in the episode, Woman #7 says to Oprah: "You should have told us that. It would have been easier" (4). Ms. King states, "I went to college, I'm really kind of smart, but there are a couple of times I would read a page three or four times" (11). Her frustration at having her intellect challenged can be further understood in light of Jennifer Parchesky's observation of middlebrow readers, whose "faith in the intrinsic value of reading and education provided a sense of themselves as intelligent people and book lovers despite their lack of professional or social prestige" (237). Rather than fulfill her "faith in the intrinsic value of reading," King's engagement with *Paradise* left her questioning her own intelligence, and, thus, her own social position. Her questioning originates from the middlebrow culture King comes from, which seeks to "better" itself intellectually (which stems, in part, from guilt at *not* being intellectual enough) while simultaneously resisting elitist claims of superiority by reaffirming the ability to identify with and "simply" enjoy the text. Furthermore, Long asserts that readers draw from their own "strong sense of entitlement that derives from their own position of educational and social privilege, so they can eschew with ease the pronouncements of the academy, which is to them just another fraction of the sociocultural elite" ("Textual" 203). The established hierarchy directly challenges such entitlement.

Further complicating the change of format, the initial need for such change arose because of Winfrey underestimating certain "highbrow" tendencies of Morrison's text, more pronounced (relatively speaking) than in previous book selections, including *Song of Solomon*. Winfrey attempts to spin reader frustration as she interprets Morrison's intentions: "Wise author that [Morrison] is, she knows the rewards are twice as great when we readers get to unlock the secrets on our own" (3). Winfrey approaches Orwellian doublespeak in that she communicates the confusion many readers had without shifting the blame for the confusion onto either the author or the text. Reader confusion is presented as misreading—as a failure to open up. Still, many readers resist the proffered task, despite Winfrey's endorsement— again and again, they want to be told the secrets, thus highlighting the potentially dangerous aspect of Winfrey's comment: that there are indeed "secrets" to unlock.

Morrison, however, "wanted the weight of interpretation to be on the reader" (8). Morrison asserts that her shifting, and at times unreliable and contradictory, narrators create a more realistic portrayal of life within her novel. Her explanation of this effect, through the metaphor of entering a town, clearly and carefully illustrates this to her present audience. Her decision not to limit herself to a single point of view adds multiple layers of possible interpretations to her text: "As for point of view, there should be the illusion that it's the character's point of view, when in fact it isn't; it's really the narrator who is there but who doesn't make herself (in my case) known in that role. It like the feeling of a told story, where you hear a voice but you can't identify it, and you think it's your own voice" ("The Site" 121). However, in order to read *Paradise* in such a manner, the reader indeed must work at reconstructing the narrative she offers. Readers were being asked to interpret and reconstruct before they could relate, before they could identify— before they could apply their own middlebrow reading practices. They felt as though their intelligence was being challenged and called into question. And, in a sense, it was.

Not only was their intelligence questioned, but their perception of pleasure as it pertains to their reading experience was also being challenged.

Radway observes that when certain authors fail "to communicate with their readers or revealed self-indulgently in verbal narcissism, they [produce] an unreadable text or at least one that [cannot] be read with the right kind of pleasure" (67). Certainly *Paradise* should not be categorized as "unreadable"; however, within the context of the Book Club episode, the failure to provide "the right kind of pleasure" applies to many readers. In fact, very few readers on the show are quick to proclaim the *pleasure* it brought. Radway continues, noting how editors of the BOMC reacted negatively to books they considered "autistic," which "displayed [a] sort of literary excess, such as language too crabbed, a plot too convoluted and self-conscious, or an approach to character too fractured" (67). While Book Club members do not direct these specific criticisms at Morrison's text, the language of resistance they employ as they find themselves lost and describe their intellect being challenged arise from a certain "literary excess" within the text as compared with previous book selections that seemingly provided the pleasure desired by the Book Club.[11] Combined with the class atmosphere, the more highbrow tendencies of *Paradise* risk reinforcing the perception that Book Club members misread the novel and that their failure to "get it" was something that could simply be fixed.

From Club to Class

As the class progresses, rather than begin discussions, Book Club members seek answers. The medium of television, when combined with the class atmosphere, disallows for fruitful and potentially powerful discussion, thus creating the perception that Book Club members were not "smart" enough to handle *Paradise*. There are even times when readers seem to believe as much; Ms. King, Winfrey's friend, pleads, "Please. 'splain it to me" (11). Neither Winfrey nor Morrison gives Ms. King the time to explain exactly why she had the reaction she had. Ms. King, no doubt aware of the limitations of the class, is not looking to start a discussion; on the contrary, she looks to Morrison to *tell* her what she was doing wrong. The response by both Winfrey and Morrison begins with the call to "open up." And, throughout the episode, Book Club members learn many valuable lessons from one of America's finest writers who consciously seeks to adapt the discourse of Winfrey's show as she teaches her televised class.

In *Paradise,* Morrison depicts an all-black town in Oklahoma called Ruby and a group of women outside of town who live in a convent. Narrated

by the various women who inhabit the fictional world, Morrison's text offers
her readers not only a constantly shifting point of view but also an experi-
mentally nonlinear and ambiguous narrative. Made aware of audience confusion, Winfrey begins the episode with interviews of a historian, a mayor, a
musician, and a citizen, all with firsthand knowledge of the context surrounding the all-black town on which *Paradise* is based.[12] Presented almost
as a series of lectures, members of Oprah's Book Club (both explicitly on the
show and implicitly throughout the television viewing audience) soon find
themselves immersed in a class atmosphere. When viewed as representative
of what Janet Staiger refers to as a "reception event," it is possible to conceive
how the Book Club's "social formations and constructed identities of the self
in relation to historical conditions explain the interpretation strategies and
affective responses of the readers" (283). In this particular event, Winfrey's
readers employ previously learned interpretive strategies (their cumulative
experience from the previous twelve Book Club episodes) to a text that does
not seemingly mesh with the Book Club's "historical conditions." As such,
Winfrey finds herself in a new position within her Book Club due her selection of *Paradise*—a defensive position. The class, constructed to show how
the book is supposed to be read in order to mitigate confusion and solve the
"problem" of resistance, ignores the "problem" of selection in the process.
Therefore, as Winfrey begins the class by offering background and experts,
she necessarily treats the Book Club members as a single entity, as a class,
rather than a collection of individual readers engaged in a book club—
instruction is valued over discussion.

During this instruction, recognition of the reader's individuality, a hall-
mark of Oprah's Book Club, thus becomes clouded. The failure to address
individual readers stems, in part, from the class atmosphere Winfrey adopts
as she decides to turn the Book Club over to an expert: "foundationally,
reading must be taught, and that socialization into reading always takes place
within specific social relationships" (*Book Clubs* 8–9). The problem with this
particular "specific social relationship" is that the class atmosphere addresses
the needs of the group without addressing the individual. This is not to
argue that *Paradise* (or any novel for that matter) cannot be taught on a college campus in an academic classroom. The reason the class atmosphere is
not as successful is that it disrupts the existing social relations of the Book
Club. The class, in this context, invites both rewards and risks: "At its best,
this social relationship can open up new ways of reading (symbols, structure,
attention to intertextuality), while at its worst, it can produce 'the deadly
serious word,' and a sense of thralldome to a deadening educational process"

(*Book Clubs* 10). Morrison, called on to head Winfrey's class, indeed strives to avoid the "deadening" class experience. Book Club members no doubt benefit from her instruction. Note Morrison's opening statement to Winfrey's audience: "Well, this is a rare opportunity. I have upon occasion been asked to teach my own work and have refused for any number of reasons, one of which is I know too much about it and at the same time not enough. And also, I didn't want to impose on students who have asked me these questions about the fundamental and final reading as though I had it, but this is delightful" (10). While Morrison intimates that her presence represents a "special" occasion, she declares that she will not "impose" her interpretation on the members of the class, thus illustrating her desire to qualify her own role as expert and, thus, her authority.

Morrison goes on to employ various successful methods to "teach" the group, all of which adhere to the "language" of Winfrey's show. But Morrison's presence as teacher and the complicated nature of the text continue to disrupt the "specific social relationship" that the Book Club had thrived on. Winfrey attempts to counter this disruption by paraphrasing Morrison's two primary reading "lessons": "First of all, you have to open yourself up . . . Second of all . . . when you go into a town and you are a new person in town and you're getting to know the people in town, do you know everything at once?" (4). In her phrasing of both lessons, Winfrey, rather than employing literary jargon such as nonlinear narrative and unreliable narrators, offers Morrison a discourse to turn the "lesson" into an act of identification. Compare Morrison and Winfrey's descriptions to Widdowson, who remarks: " [*Paradise* is] an initially puzzling but ultimately vindicated disturbed chronology; a refusal to accept crude ("black and white") binaries and stereotypes; destabilizing strategic thematic ambivalence, mysteries and uncertainties which are never cleared up" (113). His description, while accurate, would not fit within the discourse of Winfrey's show. Morrison understands this and adopts an appropriate discourse.

Morrison, in her taped one-on-one conversation with Winfrey, acutely aware of her audience, uses phrasing similar to Winfrey as she explains how to approach the nonlinear, nonconclusive narration of *Paradise*:

> I intended people to know and remember that no matter what you are doing, you get up in the morning, you do this, and then you do something else and—that's a linear chronological time, but th—we don't really live that way. We're standing at the sink doing the dishes or brushing our teeth, but we're thinking about something that hap-

pened a week ago . . . something that might happen tomorrow or next year, something that happened fifty years ago, because even though we're standing in contemporary time, our minds are not; we're layered in time. (9)

Morrison offers Winfrey's audience a chance to understand the reason behind the "difficult" structure of her novel, and she does so in a way that allows them to internalize her example and relate it to their own lives, setting up new possibilities for connection, thereby revising the social relationship of the Book Club. However, despite Morrison's inventive and successful "translation" of literary discourse into the discourse of Winfrey's talk show, she still offers reading instructions rather than invite open discussion.

The End of Discussion

Winfrey's readers entered *Paradise* "unprepared." Their previous interactions with the Book Club and their middlebrow reading habits left them bewildered with the selection of *Paradise*. Morrison, made aware of reader confusion, offers the following: "I mean, that you enter the landscape of a novel. You enter it fully. You suspend disbelief, and you walk in there like an innocent but who trusts, and you trust the narrator, you trust the book. It's risky, it might disappoint you, but that's the way you go into it" (11). Morrison's language, full of descriptors such as "open" and "trust," draws on the language embraced by Winfrey's audience—a language not often used in literature classes. But it also relies heavily on the existence of a trust that was broken from the onset. Whereas members still respect the authority of Morrison and Winfrey, the level of trust needed to defend their own readings was lost.

What Morrison does not acknowledge (and what Winfrey is unwilling to accept) is that the reason readers are asked to "open up" is that they *resisted* the novel in the first place. How can one trust what one does not understand? Of course, this critique may be unfair, as the myriad of reasons readers resisted *Paradise* could hardly have been addressed within a makeshift class to be aired during a one-hour television episode. Morrison, no doubt aware of the limitations of the format, started out the class by stating, "I would like to begin just by asking you to do a couple of things and putting to you one or two questions. And then I hope that will clarify some things so that the rest of the questions will be in the context of what the novel is about" (10).

While her statement seems to "nurture" only the ideas she wants discovered, within the context of a televised episode, such a statement appears rather prudent. Of course, put more harshly, her statement could be read as: Let us preface this class with a few questions that will keep you from asking irrelevant ones. As part of an existing Book Club discussion, as opposed to a classroom discussion, control over content becomes more problematic. Such control explicitly defies the implicit "contract" defined earlier as it dictates the reflective aspect of reading, hinders the reader's ability to empathize, and curtails their imagination. Even so, the readers *are* learning valuable lessons, they *are* learning new ways of reading, of seeing the world; they may even be developing as students of reading. But too often their expectations from previous Book Club selections are left unaddressed and undervalued as they seek to be given answers.

In such cases, when readers attempt to begin a discussion rather than ask for an answer, the topic is not allowed to continue; one intriguing example occurs when the question of victimization arises. Man #2 asks, "One thing that—that fascinates me about this book is that there aren't any villains . . . they're all victims. Everybody is a victim" (12). Morrison responds, "They're all human" (12). Winfrey repeats Morrison's answer, "They're all human." Morrison, however, does not use the label of victim. She calls them human, and the manner in which Winfrey echoes Morrison's response makes it sound as though an answer has been provided. Morrison then states that they all have a mixture of good and bad traits. Man #2, unwilling to abandon the idea of victim, replies: "And these victims beget other victims, in a sense" (12). Winfrey states that she does not believe in victims, to which Morrison responds: "It's the way we are in the world" (12). Abruptly, the application of the term "victim" to the characters is dropped. What is disconcerting is the fact that the reader's observation is never directly addressed—the discussion is not allowed to develop. Instead, succinct and seemingly final "answers" are provided even though the concept of "victimization" is integral to Winfrey's show and a central aspect/concern of Morrison's work. The solution to the "problem," as is often the case throughout the class, is that the reader needs to "open up" and trust the text.

Another area of inquiry fraught with unexplored questions concerns race. As countless critics and scholars note, Morrison deals directly with race without letting the readers know the race of many of the main characters. Referring to the (almost famous) first sentence of the novel where the reader is told they shoot the white girl first, Morrison claims her intent was "to signal race instantly and to reduce it to nothing" (15). Her explanation is complex, articulate, and dense. Man #4 responds with the cliché: "You did play the race card. From that moment on I was trying to figure out who was the white girl" (15). As if to prevent confrontation, Winfrey calls on Teresa, whom she knows disagrees with Man #4's observation: "I didn't think you played the race card, no" (16). Morrison expresses her dislike of the term "race card," then explains with her often quoted/paraphrased response: "that is why the racial information was withheld, because when you know their race, what do you know?" (16). At that moment the Book Club, stripped of the limitations of the classroom, could have entered into a "discussion" that—far from "answering" the question or "solving" the problem—would have allowed individual readers to enter into the conversation. But the class atmosphere prohibits such discussion and Morrison's provoking questions are left rhetorical. Despite her opening statement, where she warned that she would not give her readers the answer—that she does not deal in absolutes—many readers continued to seek both. Morrison's nonanswers are received as answers rather than springboards with which to enter into further discussion. Thus, readers received instructions as a group, but were unable to respond as individuals.

Covering Up the "Problem"

In apparent response to reader frustration, Morrison states during the episode that she hopes reading *Paradise* offers "a pleasant experience" (12). But for many of the readers to experience such pleasure, they are told that they must open themselves up to a new kind of reading, and, thus, a new kind of pleasure—a sentiment that comes perilously close to dictating taste and value. Failure to appreciate the novel is linked with a failure in one's ability to read and comprehend. Such a demand by Winfrey and Morrison risks implying that Book Club members' current needs, their current reading habits, their current ideas of pleasure, are not good enough, are not valid. It is highly likely that the readers at Princeton, like the middlebrow readership Radway explored, "would rather [have been] entertained and instructed about certain knowable problems and truths . . . than [been] asked to duplicate the artist's own labor," which is exactly what the recursive nature of *Paradise* calls for (69). In order to "duplicate" Morrison's labor, readers needed to, in Morrison's words, actively participate with the text.[13] However, actively participating first requires a deliberate choice—a choice many of Winfrey's readers were unprepared or unwilling to make. More important, the advice to actively participate, to open up, is never presented as a choice in the first place.

Faced with a group of readers whose desires were not met and whose intellect was challenged, neither host nor author asks readers to point out specific places in the book that led to their confusion. In fact, book, author, and host are never implicated as a source of the "problem." Rather, Winfrey and Morrison focus on the reading habits of the Book Club members and instruct them to open up to a new type of pleasure. The class is never meant to challenge Morrison's text or Winfrey's authority: it is a class to instruct Book Club members on "how" to read *Paradise* rather than understand why they resisted it in the first place. And the class atmosphere furthers that agenda, as Book Club members, put into a classroom, focus on asking questions and looking for answers, rather than beginning discussions and relating the book to their own lives. Changing the format of the Book Club successfully avoids examining why the readers' resisted *Paradise*, what that meant for Winfrey as a book selector, Morrison as a writer, and *Paradise* as a novel. Instead, both host and author made the conscious decision to teach, to change, to "open up" the group.

It *is* important to note, furthermore, that the *Paradise* episode not be cast in positive or negative terms. Indeed, Winfrey and Morrison succeeded in that the readers were able to learn from one of America's most respected and talented authors in Toni Morrison. They were instructed to expand their ideas of what it means to read. They were asked, in a sense, to challenge some of their middlebrow reading habits. And, just maybe, some of them did, and became more open readers for it. But Winfrey and Morrison failed to validate readers' concerns and challenge the selection of *Paradise* as it fit into the context of previous Book Club selections. Concurrently, the episode highlighted the forceful change a clear authority figure and class atmosphere can have on an existing book club. Readers were treated as a group of isolated readers to be taught rather than a group of individual readers with whom to engage in discussion. As such, the way in which the readers chose to value and evaluate *Paradise* was often seen as a *misreading*, not simply a *reading*. Morrison, eager to instruct her readers, successfully adopted the discourse of Winfrey's talk show and gave valuable reading lessons to Book Club members, but was unable, in the short time provided, to receive feedback from her readers and, potentially, an opportunity for herself to "open up" to her readers. Winfrey, ever the diplomat, carefully navigated around a disruption to her Book Club and diverted the blame away from those in positions of power and toward Book Club members themselves, who were left to shoulder the burden of constituting the "problem."

Seven years after the airing of the *Paradise* episode, including a brief hiatus, the format of Oprah's Book Club has seen significant changes—many of those changes explicitly appear to work to avoid (but not address) the "problem" of resistance experienced during the *Paradise* episode. In the summer of 2005, the Oprah Book Club turned to William Faulkner, a decidedly "highbrow" and canonized author with intriguing connections to Morrison.[14] Rather than throw her readers blindly into Faulkner's work, Winfrey set up a virtual classroom of sorts on her Web site. In addition to membership perks, which include, "exclusive video lectures, . . . weekly newsletters and . . . worldwide book discussions," members of the Book Club are presented with an extensive online "syllabus" complete with historical context, tips on how to read, video lectures from professors, forums, and more.[15] The Book Club's new format favors increasing one's cultural capital at the expense of identifying with and learning life lessons from the text. The format veers from a focus on reflection, empathy, and inspiration and instead encourages the type of reading and interpretation more endemic to academia—the type that book clubs across the nation both actively resist and secretly aspire to. Had the readers at Princeton been given a similar introduction to *Paradise*, they may have come to the class more prepared. But their concerns, their questions, their "misreadings," would never have been silenced and their own tastes and desires rendered inadequate. Thus, and even more insidiously, such instruction may silence Book Club members' concerns by training them to read a text with a different set of values and disregard their own.

Presently, Oprah's Book Club continues to exist as a premiere middlebrow institution, and furthers what Rubin notes as a "promise that middlebrow ventures [will] put more books in the hands of more people" (xix). Furthermore, as Winfrey highlights more and more canonized literature, she seems to increasingly share with Rubin "the now unfashionable view that learning to apprehend the workings of form and language in the books that critics have, over time, judge[d] 'best' affords readers a richer life—a deeper humanity—than they might otherwise experience" (xix). What is still troubling, however, and representative of the unsolvable condition of middlebrow culture, is the dangerous perception that somehow only through engagement with and adherence to "highbrow" cultural values is this sense of "deeper humanity" deemed available. In fact, such "deeper humanity" exists throughout America in book clubs across not only gender, race, and class lines, but across the brows. The meteoric rise of Oprah's Book Club is evidence of this. The resistance readers felt toward *Paradise* is indicative of how far we have to go. Therefore, when confusion and resistance occur, when a reader, like Woman #7 in the Book Club episode, questions "the value of a book that is hard to understand," the real challenge for scholars and readers alike is to work to not only fix but also understand the "problem." Such an "opening up" invites dialogue across "brows" and calls into question the labeling of such resistance as a "problem" in the first place.

Notes

1. The Book Club began as short segments added to the end of regular episodes of *The Oprah Winfrey Show*. Book Club episodes eventually evolved into "issue oriented shows," where, although the book was highlighted, the issue often "took center stage over the book" (Farr 10). Around the time the *Paradise* episode aired, the shows' transcripts began to carry the title "Oprah's Book Club."

2. The public pairing of Winfrey and Morrison has reignited a fear some critics have of middlebrow culture—a fear that middlebrow response will somehow contaminate highbrow literature. Joan Shelly Rubin alludes to Dwight Macdonald's infamous attack on the middlebrow, when he writes: "[The Middlebrow] pretends to respect the standards of High Culture while in fact it waters them down and vulgarizes them" (qtd. in Rubin xiv). Paranoid that middlebrow culture seeks to "popularize" high art, he desires a clear separation between the "brows" so that "the few who care about good writing, painting, music, architecture, philosophy, etc., have their High Culture, and don't fuzz up the distinction with Midcult" (xv). Similar critiques have been directed toward Oprah's Book Club. Some readers will go out of their way to buy editions without the Oprah seal to avoid the "stigma" her Book Club carries. Regardless, Winfrey's influence on American reading habits is unmistakably huge; her ability to tap into the desires and sensibilities of the lowbrow and middlebrow cultures and, arguably, expand those same desires and sensibilities, undoubtedly becomes more pronounced through her "pairing" with Toni Morrison.

3. I am indebted to Long's book, not only as I extensively quote her throughout, but also because she calls for further study of Winfrey's Book Club near the end of her study, thus enabling and encouraging me to proceed with this chapter.

4. For an in-depth analysis/history of Oprah's Book Club, see Farr's *Reading Oprah: How Oprah's Book Club Changed the Way America Reads*. Farr's work is vital to this chapter as it lays the foundation for the Book Club by noting trends leading up to the *Paradise* episode.

5. These readings were more evident within Oprah's Book Club's treatment of *Song of Solomon*, which placed the emphasis of the episodes on feeling and identification. Mark Hall, in "The 'Oprahfication' of Literacy: Reading 'Oprah's Book Club,'" offers the following example: "Though another guest, Melinda Foyes, arrives at Winfrey's home with her copy of Morrison's novel filled with comments and marked with color coded sticky-notes, prepared to discuss the content of the novel at length, it is not she, but, instead, Messer, crying and self-disclosing, who receives the most camera time at this dinner" (658). Even though Winfrey warned that *Song of Solomon* would make readers think *and* feel, the episode favored feeling. Hall follows with an assessment of the situation: "While Winfrey does not actually discourage intellectual responses to books, this example illustrates that in the daytime talk setting deeply personal, affective responses are more highly valued because they are more consistent with the values and assumptions underlying the show, where one's feelings gets top billing" (658). Hall's observation lends insight into Winfrey's own observation that *Song of Solomon* illustrates a culmination of her show's topics. The response most valued equates with the valued response of the television audience.

6. Taken from the official transcript of the episode, I have chosen to use the title each audience member was given as printed in the transcript. A few are assigned a name; most are given a gender and a number.

7. By emphasizing the selected book's connections to key values upheld on *The Oprah Winfrey Show*, Winfrey teaches her audience theses three lessons that Farr observes run throughout the entirety of the Book Club episodes: "By the end of this second Book Club meeting, Winfrey has affirmed the lessons of careful, *reflective* reading, while still embracing with her audience the skills of connection and *empathy*, both with the fictional characters and with other readers, and driving home the larger *inspirational* message of self-improvement" (49 [my emphasis]). While representations of these three lessons vary from episode to episode, all three are present to some extent during dinner discussions leading up to the class at Princeton.

8. A myth enforced, according to Long, by such constructs as the phenomenological reader, the subjective/psychoanalytic reader, the "ideal" reader, and the "resistant" female reader.

9. See Morrison's "Rootedness: The Ancestor as Foundation." *Black Women Writers (1950–1980): A Critical Evaluation.* Ed. Mari Evans. Garden City, NY: Anchor Press/Doubleday, 1984. 339–45.

10. Parallels between the two include a middlebrow readership, as well as the possible care and time put into the selection process. However, whereas the Book-of-the-Month-Club was created solely to sell books, Oprah's Book Club, through the medium of television and the group-talk atmosphere, also offers a space where readers can come together to interact on a nationwide scale.

11. *Paradise* certainly does not stand alone in novels that employ such tactics. Morrison, in fact, uses these techniques rather sparingly when compared with a novel such as *Ulysses*. However, relatively speaking, in line with previous books selections, *Paradise* indeed offers a considerable challenge.

12. Specialists include: Currie Ballard (historian-in-residence, Langston University); former mayor Viola Jones (Langston, Oklahoma); D. C. Miner (musician, Rentiesville, Oklahoma); Henry Andrews (ninety-nine years old; Langston, Oklahoma).

13. Morrison often mentions that she would like her readers to go beyond simply reading her novels. She wants her readers to actively participate with the text at hand. See "Memory, Creation, and Writing." *Thought: A Review of Culture and Idea.* 54.235 (Dec. 1984): 385–90.

14. For the explanation offered at Oprah.com, see: http://www.oprah.com/obc_classic/featbook/asof/books/books_morrison.jhtml.

15. See Oprah's Book Club online at: http://www2.oprah.com/books/books_landing.jhtml.

Works Cited

"Book Club—Toni Morrison." Host. Oprah Winfrey. *The Oprah Winfrey Show.* 1998 Harpo Productions, Inc. 6 March, 1998. Transcript.

Farr, Cecilia Konchar. *Reading Oprah: How Oprah's Book Club Changed the Way America Reads.* New York: SUNY P, 2004.

Hall, Mark. "The 'Oprahfication' of Literacy: Reading 'Oprah's Book Club.'" *College English.* 65.6 (July 2003): 646–67.

Long, Elizabeth. *Book Clubs: Women and the Uses of Reading in Everyday Life.* Chicago: U of Chicago P, 2003.

———. "Textual Interpretation as Collective Action." *The Ethnography of Reading.* Ed. Jonathan Boyarim. Berkeley: U California P, 1993. 180–211.

Morrison, Toni. "Memory, Creation, and Writing." *Thought: A Review of Culture and Idea* 54.235 (Dec. 1984): 385–90.

———. *Paradise.* New York: Plume, 1999.

———. "Rootedness: The Ancestor as Foundation." *Black Women Writers (1950–1980): A Critical Evaluation.* Ed. Mari Evans. Garden City, NY: Anchor Press/Doubleday, 1984. 339–45.

———. "The Site of Memory." *Inventing the Truth: The Art and Craft of Memoir.* Ed. William Zinsser. 2nd Ed. Boston: Houghton Mifflin, 1985. 101–24.

Parchesky, Jennifer. "'You Make Us Articulate': Reading, Education and Community in Dorothy Canfield's Middlebrow America." *Reading Acts: U.S. Readers' Interactions with Literature, 1800–1950*. Eds. Barbara Ryan and Amy Thomas. Knoxville: U of Tennessee P, 2002. 229–58.

Radway, Janice A. *A Feeling for Books: The Book-of-the-Month Club, Literary Taste, and Middle Class Desire*. Chapel Hill: U of North Carolina P, 1997.

Rubin, Joan Shelly. *The Making of Middlebrow Culture*. Chapel Hill: U of North Carolina P, 1992.

Staiger, Janet. "Taboos and Totems: Cultural Meanings of *The Silence of the Lambs*." *Reception Study: From Literary Theory to Cultural Studies*. Ed. James L. Machor and Philip Goldstein. New York: Routledge, 2001. 282–93.

Widdowson, Peter. "The American Dream Refashioned: History, Politics and Gender in Toni Morrison's *Paradise*." *Journal of American Studies*. 53.2 (2001): 331–35.

Young, John. "Toni Morrison, Oprah Winfrey, and Postmodern Popular Audiences." *African American Review*. 35.2 (2001): 181–204.

7

OPRAH'S BOOK CLUB AND THE POLITICS OF CROSS-RACIAL EMPATHY

KIMBERLY CHABOT DAVIS

While U.S. President George W. Bush has co-opted the affective rheto-ric of liberalism in his oxymoronic doctrine of "compassionate conser-vatism," left-oriented cultural critics have become increasingly wary of the political effectiveness of compassion, sympathy, and empathy as tools in the fight for social justice. Eighteenth- and nineteenth-century philosophers and writers of sentimental fiction viewed these related emotions as key to the development of benevolence, morality, and justice, but many contemporary scholars regard these feelings as imperialist tools that affirm rather than erode hierarchies of race and class. Sympathy and compassion are regularly equated with a condescending form of pity, a "selfish and cruel wallowing in the mis-fortunes of others" (Spelman 65). Cultural critics often argue that crying over the plight of disempowered people does little to challenge the status quo since the emotional catharsis afforded by literature and film all too often results in political inertia and complacency. Although her own analysis is more ambivalent, philosopher Elizabeth Spelman voices the predominant concern that "compassion, like other forms of caring, may . . . reinforce the very patterns of economic and political subordination responsible for such suffering" (7).

"Oprah's Book Club and the Politics of Cross-Racial Empathy" is reprinted with permission from *The International Journal of Cultural Studies*. 12 (2004); vol. 7: pp. 399–419.

This disparaging treatment of sympathy and sentimentality is clearly evidenced in the press response to a recent cultural phenomenon—Oprah Winfrey's Book Club (1996–2002) of contemporary fiction. Although Oprah was widely lauded for reviving fiction reading on a mass scale, her book choices were often derided for blatantly tugging at the heartstrings with sentimental stories of victimization. While journalist Susan Wise Bauer churlishly dubbed the list "Oprah's Misery Index," Emily Prager defended Oprah's talk show as a venue for exploring the "real life of the emotions" (Prager 45). At stake in the critical response to Oprah Winfrey's talk show and Book Club are questions about the value of the "humanizing" emotions connecting the self to others, and the relationship between fiction reading and the public-sphere arena of politics. Oprah's Book Club presents a rich case study for investigating the politics of affect because she has consistently chosen politically charged texts written by black women that poignantly detail the consequences of racism, sexism, and poverty.

While white women constitute the majority of Oprah's talk show audience, ten of the forty-six selections from the original contemporary fiction Book Club were written by African Americans—Toni Morrison's *Song of Solomon*, *The Bluest Eye*, *Paradise*, and *Sula*, Pearl Cleage's *What Looks like Crazy on an Ordinary Day*, Edwidge Dandicat's *Breath, Eyes, Memory*, Breena Clarke's *River, Cross My Heart*, Lalita Tademy's *Cane River*, Ernest Gaines's *A Lesson Before Dying*, and Maya Angelou's memoir *Heart of a Woman*. Oprah's film production of *Beloved* also drew millions of viewers and readers to Morrison's harrowing story of a fugitive slave mother. Invoking tropes of sentimental fiction, many of these texts foster identification with the emotional pain and joyful triumphs of black women. The burgeoning popularity of black women writers among white readers raises important questions about the political consequences of cross-racial sympathy.

Although I concede that such moments of sympathy can devolve into a form of colonizing appropriation, I contend that many critics overstate the case against sympathy and related feelings. Such a totalizing view overlooks the potential for African American literature and culture to elicit a radically destabilizing empathy among white audiences, an emotional experience that could encourage antiracist coalitions by fostering a self-reflective alienation from white privilege. Although scholars tend to equate sympathy, compassion, and empathy, I draw attention to their differences and highlight the important role of *empathetic identification* in galvanizing antiracist political sensibilities. Rather than denouncing or celebrating empathy in a decontextualized fashion, I offer a localized case study of empathetic audience responses on *The Oprah Winfrey Show*. To that end, I examined eight Book Club episodes involving discussions among four or five readers, Oprah, and the author of each novel; another program in which eight audience members were invited to discuss the film *Beloved*; and over a thousand postings on the discussion boards on Oprah's Web site, Oprah.com.[1]

Television Talk Shows: Emotions in the Public Sphere

Although these documents offer useful case studies of audience response, it is important to distinguish between the levels of mediation involved. Virtually uncensored, the online discussion boards for each of Oprah's books provide access to postings by hundreds of readers generating their own discussion topics and engaging in sometimes heated debates.[2] The televised Book Club discussions, however, are clearly mediated and circumscribed by the television context and ideology of *The Oprah Winfrey Show*. From the thousands of letters that she receives in response to each month's book selection, Oprah personally chooses four or five guests to participate in the Book Club discussions. Since Oprah asks the prospective guests to "tell us what you learned about yourself" by reading the novel, the response narratives of the winners are personal testimonials, detailing how their identification with the characters led them to confront their own repressed feelings ("Book Club" 17). For Oprah, reading is a means of therapy, and books are agents of conversion. All of the white women chosen for these shows had strong emotional reactions to the fiction by black women, and they often cried during the discussions. Most identified with the characters on the basis of shared experiences as women, while about a third described moments of epiphany, in which they gained new insight about the evils of racism. Oprah's integrationist politics, her emphasis on female solidarity, and her belief that revelations of pain are instruments of spiritual healing all clearly influenced her choice of guests and clips to air from their discussion.[3]

Since the Book Club participants were carefully selected for the television show rather than randomly chosen, one could argue that any analysis of their commentary reveals more about Oprah's ideology than about the average white reader of African American fiction. Yet even within this constructed subset of liberal white readers, I found significant heterogeneity both in the kinds of sympathy they experienced and in their political attitudes about race, ranging from "color-blind" or more blatant forms of racism to radical critiques of white privilege. Although Oprah's chosen readers may not be representative of the larger reading public, their emotional responses are indeed representative of both the political dangers and the radical possibilities of sympathy and empathy. In drawing connections between these humanizing emotions and racial politics, I build on recent work in philosophy, sociology, and cultural studies aimed at recovering the connections between the private sphere of personal change and the public sphere of political and social movements.

Because television talk shows such as *Oprah* are fertile sites for investigating the intersection of the private and public spheres, they have engendered much debate among media scholars. Some critics denounce the talk show's emphasis on reducing social problems to the realm of the individual. Wendy Kaminer argues that talk shows trivialize the feminist idea that the personal is political, and that such televised revelations of personal pain should not be considered political speech because they ignore the need for epistemic change. Others contend that talk shows offer an alternative counterpublic sphere and a radical "transformation in the nature of the political" (Carpignano et al. 116). In the midst of this debate, Janice Peck analyzed a 1992 series on *The Oprah Winfrey Show* concerning race relations and the L.A. riots. Peck takes Oprah to task for ignoring questions of "politics and power" (Peck 107) by privileging individual changes of heart over public-sphere transformations.

Some of Peck's criticisms of the 1992 series are also germane to Oprah's Book Club programs. For instance, during the televised discussion of *The Bluest Eye*, Oprah made the utopian claim that "the world would be different" if everyone read the story of this unloved black girl ("Oprah's Book Club" 9). While Oprah may be too optimistic about the power of reading to counteract racism, Peck and Kaminer underestimate the ways in which the personal realm of affect and the public sphere of political praxis are intertwined. A private change of heart may motivate an individual to vote differently, volunteer or donate money to minority-interest groups, advocate for minority hiring at work, or influence powerful friends to pursue antiracist policies. As media scholar Jane Shattuc suggests, even if the talk shows themselves do not "advocate changing specific social and political institutions" (174), the audience may independently "connect the discussion of . . . interracial conflict to legislation, elections and news stories" (177). Critics of talk shows often employ a masculine notion of what counts as political, evident in their disdain for a politics of feeling and their underestimation of the power of micropolitical, intersubjective change.

My work on the politics of empathy echoes a recent turn in political science and sociology, exemplified in the essay collection *Passionate Politics:*

Emotions and Social Movements. Collectively reevaluating their earlier dismissal of emotions and the private sphere as apolitical, these sociologists argue that "emotion . . . is a vehicle of political learning" (Berezin 93), and that "personal change and public activism [are] potentially constitutive of each other" (Young 105). Although there is growing interdisciplinary consensus that emotions are cognitive and thus connected to the realm of the political, the dominant position in cultural and literary studies is to see the feelings of sympathy and compassion as routinely or even intrinsically linked to conservative political ideologies.

The "Humanizing Emotions": Sympathy, Empathy, and Compassion

Any discussion of these three terms, often viewed as synonyms for an experience of co-suffering, is fraught with the difficulty of definition. While many dictionaries and scholars conflate the terms, those who distinguish between them still offer quite varying definitions. Sympathy is most often used as an umbrella term, meaning the act of sharing the feelings or interests of another, or feeling concern for another's suffering. Many have suggested that sympathy can take a solipsistic turn toward "self-indulgent and self-congratulatory behavior" (Nussbaum 399), wherein feeling virtuous becomes an end in itself. While empathy could be seen as a type of sympathy, empathy usually signifies a stronger element of identification or "perspective-taking"—imaginatively experiencing the feelings, thoughts, and situation of another.[4] Scholars disagree about whether empathy functions as a metaphoric substitution resulting in erasure ("I am you"), or whether it entails a cognitive recognition of distinctions between self and other.[5] I endorse the latter position. In her book on the emotions, philosopher Martha Nussbaum defines compassion as an emotion of a higher moral order, involving a cognitive component of judgment and action. In her view, compassion entails more than a sympathetic or empathetic consciousness of another's situation, but also a judgment that that person is in distress, and a desire to alleviate the suffering (302). One critic's definition of compassion, however, is another's definition of sympathy. The terms are less important than the experiences they describe, and the value and consequences attributed to them.

While Nussbaum argues that a just society depends upon an education in compassion fostered by reading multicultural literature, many leftist cultural critics are less sanguine about the effects of the humanizing emotions (see Nussbaum 426–31). Critics often view sympathetic feeling as either an

impediment to political change or a colonizing force that erases cultural differences. Treating sympathy, empathy, and compassion as cognates, Lauren
Berlant has been the most outspoken critic of the sentimental strategy of
"privatizing the political," which she views as a "legitimating [device] for sus-
taining the hegemonic field" ("Subject" 54). Berlant's Marxist critical
emphasis on the commodification of feeling within capitalism leaves little
hope for sentimentality to accomplish its "unrealized" potential to "move
people . . . into identifying against their own interests" ("Poor" 640). In
"Poor Eliza," she concludes that sentiment's "ethical imperative toward social
transformation is replaced by a civic-minded but passive ideal of empathy.
The political as a place of acts oriented towards publicness becomes replaced
by a world of private thoughts, leanings, and gestures" (641).[6] Berlant sees in
sentimental discourse "a confusion . . . between changed minds and changed
worlds" ("Poor Eliza" 644) and doubts whether "changes in feeling, even on a
mass scale, amount to substantial social change" ("The Subject" 53). Given
her Marxist leanings, Berlant figures sentimental culture as a consumer dis-
traction, a form of compensatory fantasy that inhibits political action. While
her more recent work on compassion is less damning, she reiterates her concern that "private responses are not only insufficient but a part of the practice
of injustice" ("Introduction" 9).[7]

Rather than viewing empathy as a "passive ideal" and an impediment to
political change, I argue that empathy is an active cognitive process of imagination that can play an important role in catalyzing action.[8] Implicit in
Berlant's argument is a familiar hierarchy of emotions, in which the power of
rage reigns supreme. Despairing about the ability of sympathy to foster
structural change in the public sphere, she places hope only in "political rage,
a discourse of demand and radical critique" ("The Subject" 83). I agree that
rage is central to radical action, but anger is difficult to sustain over time,
and political movements would quickly burn out without reserves of hope.
Among the emotions motivating political action, sociologists include not
only outrage, but also moral shock, guilt, shame, and pride, all of which can
be stimulated by sympathetic feeling (Goodwin 10, 12). The fact that people
may feel sympathy without becoming political actors is not a fault inherent
in the emotion, I contend, but rather stems from multiple causes endemic to
postmodern U.S. society, including a pervasive distrust of the political
sphere, waning communitarianism, and a loss of faith in the power of the
individual to effect change. Given the rise of conservatism and political
apathy in the United States, I suggest that more attention needs to be paid to
the role of affect in galvanizing efforts for radical change. As political theorist

Chantal Mouffe reminds, the Left has for too long ignored the power of affect to engender or sustain radical movements.

While some object to the sympathetic emotions on the grounds that they substitute for political action, other cultural critics and race theorists treat sympathy as an inherently colonizing action, and they reduce empathy to an imperialistic drive to incorporate the other into the self. While some of these critics are informed by postcolonial theories exposing the drive for knowledge of the exotic other as a form of power, others are influenced by the Freudian view of identification as a hostile erasure of the other, "in which the object that we long for and prize is assimilated by eating and is in that way annihilated as such" (Freud 105).[9] In critical race theory, studies of cross-racial sympathy take a decidedly pessimistic tone about the possibilities of coalition, which has the unfortunate consequence of reifying the very racial categories that they seek to undermine.[10] For example, Robyn Wiegman despairs that integrationist novels and films are ultimately wedded to white authority, and concludes that "the transformatory hope of identifying with the pain and suffering of others seems ever more bound to an imperialistic cast" (200). In researching her book *Racechanges*, Susan Gubar sadly concludes that cross-racial masquerade and imitation "inevitably leads to the disappearance of the other's otherness" (245). While these writers take a despairing tone, Doris Sommer aggressively condemns cross-racial sympathy and empathy alike. Focusing on the narrative strategies that ethnic writers use to refuse access to white readers, Sommer dismisses the sympathy of white liberals as an "appropriation in the guise of an embrace" ("Resistant Texts" 543) and a facile form of connection that lasts "hardly longer than the reading of a novel" (529). Arguing that "empathy is the egocentric energy that drives one subject to impersonate another" (*The Politics of Caution* 22), she echoes Freud's view of identification as a metaphoric substitution of the self for the other.

These writers shed light on a problematic possibility of sympathy and empathy—that the privileged sympathizer will ignore differences in his or her zeal to connect emotionally with the sufferer. Erasing the subjective experience of people of color, the white empathizer falsely claims someone else's particular pain as his own. While some critics focus on this desire for sameness as an erasure, others are more critical of the hierarchy they believe is implicit in sympathy's operation. As Berlant puts it, "compassion is a term denoting privilege: the sufferer is over there" ("Introduction" 4) and the observer has the power to either help or turn away. I agree that sympathy may involve power relations between subject and object, and may keep hierarchies firmly in place by granting the sympathizer a feeling of benevolent largesse and denying agency to the sufferer. These consequences, however, are not *implicit* to the operation of sympathetic emotions. Empathetic experiences of seeing from the vantage point of another can lead to a recognition of that person's subjecthood and agency, and can cause the white empathizer not only to become critically aware of racial hierarchy, but to desire to work against the structures of inequality wherein her own power resides.

My case study of Oprah's Book Club addresses both the promise and limitations of empathy and sympathy, asserting that the politics of these emotions depend on how they are experienced and to what end they are employed. While the possibility of appropriation is an important concern, critics also have a responsibility to bring to light moments of empathy or compassion with progressive political significance, lest we lose hope in the potential for change in the racial order. It strikes me as particularly ironic that these despairing conclusions are voiced by *white* antiracist scholars whose own critical work attests to the radical potential of some acts of crossracial affiliation. In our zeal to avoid celebratory analyses that underestimate the power of white hegemony, we need to avoid throwing out the proverbial baby (empathy and compassion) with the bathwater. As many social scientists have argued, empathy can inhibit aggression, and the absence of empathy is a telling feature of intergroup violence, such as the Israeli/Palestinian conflict.[11] In the context of an alarming international rise in hate groups and terrorism, left-oriented scholars cannot afford to give up on empathy's promise of fostering cross-cultural understanding and a desire for social justice and equality.

Reception Analysis

My reception study suggests that sympathy's colonizing functions and its ability to inhibit action are not intrinsic to its structure, but merely one possible deployment thereof. By offering evidence here of the more radical possibilities of empathy visible on *The Oprah Winfrey Show*, I do not claim that the critics of sympathy are categorically wrong, but merely that they are diminishing the complexity of the sympathetic emotions. One could argue that a similarly one-sided argument is put forth by Martha Nussbaum, who optimistically implies that compassion is the cure for what ails modern society. Predicated on the assumption that reading good books produces empathetic and moral people, Nussbaum's philosophical reflections ignore the considerable diversity of reader responses to texts. My reception study, however, exposes both negative and positive strains of empathy and sympathy, while drawing attention to previously under-appreciated progressive effects. While I do not claim that these radical deployments are predominant, either on Oprah's programs or in the reading public at large, I found enough recurrence to warrant attention.

My research also invites several questions related to the nature of the evidence. For example, did the Book Club participants fake or embellish their experiences of cross-racial empathy to look good on television? (This factor is obviously less significant for the anonymous online discussion boards.) Even if one removes the problem of the mediation of television, any academic study of the subjective nature of reading has to admit the possibility of self-censoring and self-promotion, given that such research must rely on the reader's own reporting. However, since Oprah's show tends to foster a color-blind universalizing perspective, I find it hard to attribute the existence of more radical moments in the Book Club discussions (both online and on television) to the participants' desire to replicate Oprah's "liberal" viewpoint, or to seek the approval of the more centrist viewing public (see Peck 94). In fact, the self-critical testimony of some of the empathetic whites involved a remarkable degree of risk, and thus are worthy of study because of, rather than despite, their exceptional nature.

While my reception analysis complicates the overwhelmingly negative critical treatment of cross-racial sympathy and empathy, I did find evidence of their more problematic tendencies and effects. A troubling tendency among the white readers on *Oprah* is that they minimize racial difference in their zeal to connect with the characters "as women." Oprah's emphasis on female solidarity, and the need to cater to her largely white viewing audience, leads her to emphasize her selections' universal or gender-specific themes. Setting the tone of the discussion on *The Bluest Eye*, a novel that addresses a young black girl's desire to be white, Oprah opened the program by saying "regardless of what color you are, there are a lot of women who have defined themselves by what other people think of them" ("Oprah's Book Club" 1). On the Web discussion forum, many white readers thus compared Pecola's self-hatred with their own experiences of being ridiculed because they were fat, ugly, or tall; one even said that "women are all Pecola to some degree."[12] Such universalizing comparisons ignore the specificity of race oppression and merely collapse the other into the self-same, reinforcing the hegemony of whiteness.

Underscoring her focus on female bonding, Oprah included in every Book Club program one white woman who described relating to the characters as mothers, daughters, or sisters. For example, the scene of a child's funeral in *Song of Solomon* caused one "rich white woman from Dallas" to break down in tears at the memory she had repressed of her own stillborn son ("Behind" 4). This woman's prolonged sobbing threatened to derail the discussion of the book altogether, recalling Elizabeth Spelman's complaint about forms of sympathy wherein "I acknowledge your suffering only to the extent to which it promises to bring attention to my own" (Spelman 172). While sharing experiences of female pain and loss may have positive feminist implications, these evocations of sisterhood may indicate a problematic race-blindness that also plagued the early feminist movement. A quest for a bridge across social difference is essential to collective political struggle, but these universalizing moments of female solidarity can also be an excuse to ignore what divides us.

Of course, gender identification does not necessarily result in race-blindness, but it can legitimize a reading process that seeks only reflections of the self, rather than deeper understandings of others. The "rich white woman from Dallas" identified strongly with the mothers in *Song of Solomon*, connecting with their love of breastfeeding, but this woman's identifications belie racist, egocentric attitudes. She states, "I found [the novel] kept sucking me down to a level I've never been before, and that was uncomfortable for me. . . . I had way too much in common with this odd group of characters, and [the book] was making me see pieces of me I didn't like" ("Behind" 6). Because she imagines the African American community of the novel as a space beneath her, her experience of sympathy affirms rather than challenges racial hierarchy. For this woman, reading is a means to greater self-knowledge, to "see pieces of me," rather than an imaginary encounter with other viewpoints. In a recent sociological study of white women's book clubs in Houston, Elizabeth Long observed a similarly "self-serving" move among white readers who "only made use of insights . . . that spoke to their own social situation as white women" (Long 186). Offering a classic example of sympathy as self-indulgent catharsis that reaffirms hierarchy, this reader of *Song of Solomon* lacks an important ingredient of empathy—a respect for the "qualitative difference" of the sufferer as a unique individual of equal value to oneself (Nussbaum 328). Echoing the viewpoint of other scholars, Jessica Benjamin understands empathy as ideally involving "mutual recognition" of the subjecthood of the Other, and the "ability to share feelings . . . without demanding control, to experience sameness without obliterating difference" (Benjamin 48).[13]

The question of whether empathy collapses differences was the subject of a heated debate on the online discussion board for *The Bluest Eye*, a debate that encompassed thirty percent of the 345 total postings on the novel.[14] The disagreement was sparked by two provocative posts, the first from a white woman whose own color-blind ideology was challenged by Morrison's book. She wrote: "I am having a hard time with the [previous] white posters who say they can 'relate' to Pecola. After I read this book I realized that I will never ever know prejudice or pain like the characters have known." Furthering the critique, a black woman argued that the color-blind empathizers were ignoring the issue of racism at the core of the text: "the luxury of bypassing race can only be for those who are not affected by racism." Several middle-class whites echoed these concerns about the colonizing effects of empathy and stressed the importance of respecting difference. Acutely sensitive to the power dynamics of claiming to know how the other feels, one wrote: "as deeply as I have tried to over many years of living side by side with black culture, I can never truly know Pecola . . . or all the truth she speaks." These readers felt empathy for African Americans while simultaneously rejecting the "blanket of shared victimization" that can obscure the particular "ways that racist domination impacts on the lives of marginalized groups" (Rosenberg 83).

While these readers were rightly critical of the universalizing logic of color-blindness, the readers on the other side of the debate celebrated the power of empathy to unite people in common humanity. Defending their identification with Pecola were many working-class, underprivileged whites who shared experiences analogous to those of the African American characters. One woman wrote: "I'm not minimizing racism at all. I see it every day. I'm just saying pain is pain. Is poverty, ignorance, abuse, and cruelty unique to one race? I think we all have to start understanding other people's burdens." This white person recognized that individuals might carry different burdens, and thus analogies are sometimes limited. But she nonetheless seeks a bridge across difference by invoking shared humanity—a concept that critics have located at the heart of the operation of sympathy. As Elizabeth Spelman argues, sympathy succeeds when it results not only in acknowledging "deep and pervasive similarities among suffering humanity" but also in "making a case for mutual care" (Spelman 10). Reflecting on the segregated schooling of her childhood, one woman from an abusive "poor white trash" family declared: "I would have had more in common with Pecola than with the little white girls in my school. I think we've all been cheated. Maybe Pecola would have liked to know me too. We're all going to have to take a chance to bridge the color gap. Start by knowing that we all have pain, and we all have something to offer." Unlike the rich white woman from Dallas who uses Morrison's characters as a cathartic excuse to wallow in her own pain, this working-class woman expresses a desire for mutual care and recognizes Pecola as a subject with "something [valuable] to offer" to society, much like herself. These working-class empathetic whites remind us that experiences of shared humanity need not result in blindness to difference.

While some readers drew on analogous experiences to sympathize with black characters, empathetic "perspective-taking" helped some privileged readers to see the realities of racial inequality in a new light. Rather than simply reaffirming the status quo, empathy had transformative effects for white readers willing to interrogate their own complicity with racist discourse and practice. In her letter to Oprah, one of the white women selected for *The Bluest* discussion confessed that when she had first read it, she did not feel implicated in this story of color-consciousness within the black community; she regarded the novel as a "black book . . . about 'their' problems."[15] On second reading, however, she remembered that her mother had forced her to end a childhood friendship with a black girl, and she then wondered, "Did I make that girl wish her eyes were blue?" This white reader's empathy for Pecola involved looking at herself from the outside in, to experience alienation from the self. Rather than desiring to see the other as "one of us," this reader of *The Bluest Eye* was moved to self-interrogation and to question her previously uncompassionate and personally disengaged reading of the text. While a facile form of sympathy may do little to destabilize the viewer's own subjectivity, empathy can also be radically unsettling.

Since it is often more difficult to feel sympathy for someone of widely different circumstances than one's own, it is important to examine the conditions that enable compassion across racial or class boundaries, particularly when the sympathizer has higher social status than the sufferer. Martha Nussbaum sees empathy as a crucial ingredient in compassionate action because taking up another's perspective facilitates what she calls "eudaimonistic judgment"—the feeling that another person's suffering matters to you and in fact affects your own "flourishing" (Nussbaum 319). Elizabeth Spelman echoes this point, arguing that privileged people will not "think it desirable to lose that privilege . . . unless they see it not only as producing harm to other[s] . . . but also deeply disfiguring to themselves" (Spelman

111). In studying white audiences, I am particularly interested in how iden-tifications with the feelings of African American characters can provoke a critical self-interrogation and a recognition that racism poisons everyone—that it is not merely "*their* problem," but rather *ours* collectively. Such recog-nition, I believe, is a necessary precondition for antiracist political action.

The film version of *Beloved* encouraged several white viewers on *Oprah* to experience such moments of reflective self-alienation through a radical rereading of the racist personal history of their families. Renee, a southern white woman, had been raised with the white supremacist belief that "the black race were animals . . . one step above primates" ("*Beloved* dinner" 7). Although as an adult she had decided "intellectually" that "racism was wrong," she had not felt the true horror of her family's legacy "in [her] heart" (7). Upon viewing the scene in the film when white men drink Sethe's breastmilk, Renee said, "I saw the white men's righteousness from Sethe's eyes, and I felt shame, not pride. Your movie taught me that they weren't the animals; we were. And it's not us and them. It's about what we created" (7–8). Here, her sensitivity to Sethe's sexual violation as a woman leads her to a crucial moment of disidentification with her own family and to acknowledge race and racism as social constructions created by the powerful. Renee even takes personal responsibility for the past, rather than absolving herself of guilt: "What I was raised upon, who I am, a *part of me* is shameful and wrong" (8). Without denying that she belongs to the powerful "we" of whiteness, she is nonetheless trying to move beyond the divisive binary of "us and them." Experiencing shame or guilt over the conduct of whites past and present can be powerful motivators for antiracist action (Goodwin et al. 10). As Spelman contends, "seeing oneself as deeply disfigured by privilege and desiring to do something about it, may be impossible without feeling shame" (Spelman 111).[16]

Another southern woman whose family had been slaveholders experi-enced a similarly guilt-ridden recognition of complicity. After being contacted by a descendant of a slave owned by her family, Audrey discovered her family's records of punishment meted out to their slaves. However, the historical data left her with a feeling of disconnection: "It was so distant from me that they were numbers" ("*Beloved* dinner" 12). On the other hand, when Audrey saw the film *Beloved* and witnessed the whipping scars on Sethe's back, she "felt a gut-wrenching guilt" as her "whole ancestry flashed before [her] eyes" (12). Reading the historical record did not move Audrey as much as this moment of empathetic identification with the bodily pain of a scarred runaway slave. For her, "this is no longer something on paper" now that these numbers have been translated into feeling human beings (12). These women's experiences of *Beloved* suggest that film has "the power to reeducate the look" (Silverman 5), by replacing a voyeuristic or detached gaze at Otherness with an emotional identification that involves a "spectatorial self-estrangement" (Silverman 85). While some may depreciate guilt as an emotion that leads one to seek escape rather than committed action, I argue that the guilt this woman feels is an important step in owning responsibility for perpetuating racism and white privilege—the source of others' pain.

Some critics are concerned that when sympathizers claim responsibility for easing the pain of others, they effectively deprive those sufferers of agency. Such a view equates sympathy with condescending pity, where the boundaries between the powerful and the powerless remain unchallenged. But as Nussbaum and Spelman remind, "compassion can coexist with respect for [the] agency" of those in need (Nussbaum 383).[17] Some of the Oprah readers not only felt empathy for those victimized by racism and shameful guilt for the horrors propagated by white racists, but they also felt joy at the empowerment of black female characters. A white woman responding to *River, Cross My Heart* on the discussion boards wrote in praise of black activism against segregation: "I was so proud of [Johnnie Mae] for being 'unruly' . . . [her refusal] to let the white-pool issue stand was great." In response to Lalita Tademy's *Cane River*, a book that explores the legacy of slavery in the lives of five generations of black women, a white woman was inspired by their defiance in the face of oppression, from the slave girl Suzette "peeing on the rose bushes after being slapped" to Emily "sitting up front on that bus" during the civil rights movement ("Cane River" 7). It strikes me as significant that these empathetic white readers moved beyond co-suffering to take pride in the black characters' insurgency against white domination. Emotional connections with African American characters thus encouraged these readers to feel political solidarity with black protests against injustice. Rather than serving as a substitute for action, feeling inspired these readers to desire political change.

The Political Effects of Reading

But the question still remains: Do such experiences of pain or joy in solidarity with African Americans have any substantive political effects or are they merely fleeting connections in the private sphere that do little to effect social change? Oprah sees her mission as enabling transformations among individuals, but until recently she has shied away from any formal political agenda. When a member of the *Beloved* discussion program implied that the film was made in hopes of provoking white Americans to make a national apology for slavery, Oprah clarified her mission: "I am hoping for just an opening of the heart. I am not asking for a national apology" ("*Beloved* dinner" 15). In response to Oprah's faith in the power of feeling, a black male participant in the discussion urged others to turn feeling into action: "You can't stop there. You can feel it and I want you to feel it, but we have to begin to effect change in this country at whatever level [we] can effect change" (12). The "level" that the white woman Renee chooses is that of the private rather than the public sphere: "Even just passing nonracist ideas on to my daughter, start in my own home" (12). While Renee uses qualifying words like "just" and "start" to suggest that such a strategy would only be a preliminary effort, Oprah falsely concludes that private sphere transformations are enough: "If you do that, then we have already won with this movie" (13). Not only is Oprah claiming a premature victory, but her comments reinforce the gendered division between the public and the private sphere, limiting the scope of women's activism (Nudelman 311).

While I believe that white women must not abdicate a responsibility to counteract racism in the public sphere, I do want to question the tendency among critics of sympathy to undervalue the political power of individual "openings of the heart." Even if sympathizers are not moved to give time or money to a cause, "the sentiment of bystanders can be crucial to a movement's success" (Kemper 70), just as the American public's horrified reactions to televised police brutality played a key role in the success of the civil rights movement. Furthermore, we should not underestimate the role of a change of heart in galvanizing people like Renee or her daughter to take antiracist action, in an effort to transform their communities, workplaces, or even national policy.

Lauren Berlant is right to be skeptical that a reading of a single novel could be solely responsible for producing such radical changes in individuals. However, sympathetic reading experiences can play an important role in a larger chain of events, alongside other moments of critical thinking and encounters with alternative viewpoints that might shift an individual's perspective. As the white woman Audrey said during the program on *Beloved*, "I understand something now that I didn't understand before, and [the film] has made me want to understand more" ("*Beloved* dinner" 13). Reading can clearly alter one's sense of reality, as evidenced by a reader of *Cane River* who noted on the Web-board: "I don't know if it is heightened awareness due to my reading the novel . . . but it seems like there is so much more in the news about racism; just today I read two articles." Reading fiction can help a person to develop an understanding of the plight of others and a sense of moral outrage, often seen as important precursors for action. In her ethnographic study of white women's reading groups, sociologist Elizabeth Long argues that "reading, especially when combined with communal reflection and discussion, provides . . . in some cases, motivation for taking individual or collective action beyond the world of books" (Long 24). Several whites in the online and televised discussions were putting their antiracist feelings to work in the public sphere, in their jobs as teachers and social workers serving minority communities. Although it is unlikely that fiction-reading was the sole catalyst for their occupational choices, their testimony suggests that experiences of empathy in cultural space help to sustain and fortify their ongoing political commitments.

While Berlant doubts that emotional shifts in the private sphere ever get converted into a larger politics of change, Lawrence Grossberg argues persuasively that "affective relations are, at least potentially, the condition of possibility for the optimism, invigoration, and passion which are necessary for any struggle to change the world" (Grossberg 86). While the experience of sympathy may produce merely self-satisfied feelings of benevolence that substitute for committed action, I contend that the larger impediment to radical change is not sympathy itself, but conditions that weaken its effectivity—such as widespread public skepticism that protest can actually accomplish social change in a world controlled by postmodern global capitalism. Like Grossberg, I see affective culture as an underappreciated resource in combating the disenchantment that threatens to nullify political resistance in the United States.

My work on the politics of empathetic reading contributes to a recent shift in American studies, calling for an end to the "separate spheres" paradigm that divided public from private, masculine from feminine, the world of political action from the world of feeling. The essays in the recent collection *No More Separate Spheres!* suggest that the line between the public and the private is a blurry one, and that these two "spheres" are in fact largely imbricated (Davidson and Hatcher). With a similar goal, I have highlighted the political importance of empathetic reading in fostering self-transformation and a radical interrogation of white privilege. In this particular deployment of empathy, such moments of radical understanding could be seen as an incipient form of political action, rather than its antithesis. This form of self-transformation operates on a continuum with larger-scale political

actions in both "private" and "public" settings. Instead of equating the political only with the arena of elections, protest movements, and collective
organizing, scholars also need to consider the importance of local, interper-
sonal encounters in effecting social change. Experiencing empathy for
African Americans in cultural space may move someone to object to a racist
joke among colleagues or friends or persuade an older relative that mixed-
race marriages can produce healthy and happy families. One of the white
participants in the televised discussion of *The Bluest Eye* adopted three
abused black girls and is passionately working to help them to develop self-
esteem. Is her antiracist action any less political because it takes place within
the "private sphere" of the family? I argue that such local and personal examples of taking a moral stand do work to undermine racism, and are probably
necessary stepping stones for individuals to move toward more public-
oriented antiracist acts that require greater risk. The power of culture in fostering personal self-transformation should not be undervalued.

Although many of Oprah's Book Club choices have been disparaged for
their rampant emotionalism, I have argued that their solicitation of sympathy is in fact central to their cultural power. As Larry Grossberg contends,
emotive genres are politically powerful because they provoke identification,
belonging, and investment, providing audiences with "mattering maps" that
reveal "the places at which people can anchor themselves into the world, the
locations of the things that matter" (82). At the end of the *Oprah* discussion
of her book *Song of Solomon,* Toni Morrison revealed her own dream to offer
such mattering maps to readers: "It's the dream of a writer. . . . To have something important, truly meaningful, happen to a person who's ready for the
happening and the key to it is the experience of reading a book. . . . It's not a
lesson that said do this . . . and this is the solution, but to actually engage in
the emotions, the actions, and the company . . . of the characters" ("How'd
They" 18). Oprah's Book Club selections do not provide solutions to social
problems concerning race and gender, but they do offer intense emotional
engagement that is an essential ingredient of political engagement. Although
sympathy has often worked to legitimate the status quo, my analysis of
Oprah's Book Club demonstrates that affective reading experiences can also
disrupt ideologies of racial hierarchy.

Conspicuously absent from most analyses of cross-racial sympathy are
reading experiences such as I have spotlighted here, in which white women's
empathetic encounters with African American fictional characters led to an
increased politicization and desire to combat racism in public forums such as
The Oprah Winfrey Show itself. For some white readers of African-American

fiction, these testimonies of suffering offer merely a vicarious sensory experience that does little to alter their own sense of privilege. These texts produce more radical reading effects when empathetic connections are accompanied by critical reflection, when thought and feeling combine to result in a critique of racism and a deeper respect for cultural difference. While Oprah's utopian claims about the power of individual texts to change the world may seem naively optimistic, she is right about one thing—reading literature and watching films do shape the feelings and ideologies of individuals. This belief, after all, has been central to the academic study of literature, and the motivation behind the move toward multicultural literacy in education. In this academic climate of suspicion toward a politics rooted in affect, critics need to consider that such cross-racial empathetic identifications in the private sphere could play a crucial role in galvanizing support for antiracist public policy in America.

Notes

1. Archived discussions for each novel are available at http://boards.oprah. com. *The Bluest Eye* engendered 345 postings, *Cane River* 799, and *Sula* 207, while a few received only a handful of posts (*Song of Solomon* 1; *What Looks Like Crazy* 4).

2. As in most online forums, there is a standard moderator who eliminates advertisements and solicitations, suppresses posts with "obscene, racist, or sexually explicit language," and checks for relevance to the discussion.

3. Oprah almost always chose two white women and two black women for the discussions of black women's fiction, thus enacting her integrationist politics.

4. C. Daniel Batson prefers empathy ("perspective-taking") over sympathy, which he fears "has become tinged with a paternalistic, moralistic cast" (87).

5. Karl Morrison sees empathy as a substituting logic of domination. Consult John Deigh, pp. 175–79, and Nussbaum, p. 327, for a more generous reading of empathy as involving cognition and recognition of differences.

6. See Cvetkovich for a similar argument about affect as an ineffective "individualist solution to systemic problems" (1).

7. In an essay collection edited by Berlant herself, Woodward echoes my reading: "Berlant's critique of the sentimental narrative, or sentimental liberalism [as morally bankrupt], is severe, even unforgiving" (71).

8. Psychologist Gail Reed notes that empathy may be both active (involving perception and understanding), and passive (involving an immersion of the self).

9. See bell hooks, "Eating the Other."

10. Michael Rogin discusses Jewish affiliations with blackness on film and in political life as a "form of appropriative identification" (18) that ultimately reinforces white supremacy. Similarly, Sanchez-Eppler "uncovers the exploitation inherent" in the nineteenth-century alliance between abolitionist white women and black slave women (10).

11. See Deigh, pp. 218–20, and Andreas Huyssen's analysis of "Holocaust," a television miniseries that offered German viewers the opportunity to identify empathetically with a family of Jewish victims. Huyssen argues that this mass-cultural text provoked a national "collective mourning" (135) that was a powerful agent in combating anti-Semitism in the 1970s.

12. For this and all subsequent references to the discussion boards, see http://boards.oprah.com.

13. Benjamin's term "identificatory love" is synonymous with my understanding of empathy. Other scholars who resist the view of empathetic identification as an appropriating collapse of difference are Nussbaum, Silverman, Deigh, and Spelman, p. 85.

14. The online boards are unstructured, with each post following the other in sequential order. Posters also have the option of responding to any earlier post and creating a discussion thread. Echoing the diversity of the general novel-reading public, the discussion posts ranged widely from enthusiastic generalities and praise for Oprah, to reflections about how the texts spoke to readers' life experiences, to detailed exegesis of themes or passages, and to reasoned debates about larger issues raised by the texts and other posts.

15. These letters are no longer posted on-line, but they were once available at http://oprah.oxygen.com/obc/pastbooks/toni_morrison/obc_letters_20000526c.html.

16. Nussbaum disagrees, viewing shame as an impediment to compassion, pp. 345–48.

17. See also Spelman, p. 60.

Works Cited

Batson, C. Daniel. *The Altruism Question: Toward a Social-Psychological Answer.* Hillsdale, NJ: Lawrence Erlbaum, 2002.

Bauer, Susan Wise. "Oprah's Misery Index." *Christianity Today.* 7 Dec. 1998. 70–74.

"Behind the Scenes at Oprah's Dinner Party." *The Oprah Winfrey Show.* 3 Dec. 1996. Transcript by Burrelle's Information Services.

"*Beloved* Dinner with Oprah." *The Oprah Winfrey Show*. 30 Oct. 1998. Transcript by Burrelle's Information Services.

Benjamin, Jessica. *The Bonds of Love: Psychoanalysis, Feminism, and the Problem of Domination*. New York: Pantheon, 1988.

Berezin, Mabel. "Emotions and Political Identity: Mobilizing Affect for the Polity." *Passionate Politics*. Eds. Jeff Goodwin et al. Chicago: U of Chicago P, 2001. 83–98.

Berlant, Lauren. "Poor Eliza." *American Literature*. 70.3 (1998): 635–68.

———. "The Subject of True Feeling: Pain, Privacy, and Politics." *Cultural Pluralism, Identity Politics, and the Law*. Eds. Austin Stuart and Thomas Kearns. Ann Arbor: U of Michigan P, 1999. 49–84.

———. "Introduction: Compassion (and Withholding)." *Compassion: The Culture and Politics of an Emotion*. Ed. Lauren Berlant. New York: Routledge, 2004. 1–13.

"Book Club—Toni Morrison." *The Oprah Winfrey Show*. 6 Mar. 1998. Transcript by Burrelle's Information Services.

"Cane River." *The Oprah Winfrey Show*. 24 Sept. 2001. Transcript by Burrelle's Information Services.

Carpignano, Paolo et al. "Chatter in the Age of Electronic Reproduction: Talk Television and the 'Public Mind.'" *The Phantom Public Sphere*. Ed. Bruce Robbins. Minneapolis: U of Minnesota P, 1993. 93–120.

Cvetkovich, Ann. *Mixed Feelings: Feminism, Mass Culture, and Victorian Sensationalism*. New Brunswick, NJ: Rutgers UP, 1992.

Davidson, Cathy, and Jessamyn Hatcher, eds. *No More Separate Spheres! A Next Wave American Studies Reader*. Durham, NC: Duke UP, 2002.

Deigh, John. *The Sources of Moral Agency: Essays in Moral Psychology and Freudian Theory*. Cambridge: Cambridge UP, 1996.

Freud, Sigmund. *Group Psychology and the Analysis of the Ego. The Standard Edition of the Complete Psychological Works of Sigmund Freud*. Ed. James Strachey. Vol. 18. London: Hogarth, 1955. 67–143.

Goodwin, Jeff et al., eds. "Introduction: Why Emotions Matter." *Passionate Politics: Emotions and Social Movements*. Chicago: U of Chicago P, 2001. 1–24.

Grossberg, Lawrence. *We Gotta Get Out of This Place: Popular Conservatism and Postmodern Culture*. New York: Routledge, 1992.

Gubar, Susan. *Racechanges: White Skin, Black Face in American Culture*. New York: Oxford UP, 1997.

hooks, bell. "Eating the Other." *Black Looks: Race and Representation*. Boston: South End P, 1992. 21–39.

"How'd They Do That?" *The Oprah Winfrey Show*. 18 Nov. 1996. Transcript by Burrelle's Information Services.

Huyssen, Andreas. "The Politics of Identification: 'Holocaust' and West German Drama." *New German Critique.* 19 (1980): 117–36.

Kaminer, Wendy. *I'm Dysfunctional, You're Dysfunctional: The Recovery Movement and Other Self-Help Fashions.* Reading: Addison-Wesley, 1992.

Kemper, Theodore D. "A Structural Approach to Social Movement Emotions." *Passionate Politics: Emotions and Social Movements.* Eds. Jeff Goodwin et al. Chicago: U of Chicago P, 2001. 58–73.

Long, Elizabeth. *Book Clubs: Women and the Uses of Reading in Everyday Life.* Chicago: U of Chicago P, 2003.

Mouffe, Chantal. "Politics and Passion: Stakes of Democracy." Lecture given at the University of Virginia, Charlottesville. 23 Feb. 1996.

Nudelman, Franny. "Beyond the Talking Cure: Listening to Female Testimony on *The Oprah Winfrey Show.*" *Inventing the Psychological: Toward a Cultural History of Emotional Life in America.* Eds. Joel Pfister and Nancy Schnog. New Haven: Yale UP, 1997. 297–315.

Nussbaum, Martha. *Upheavals of Thought: The Intelligence of Emotions.* Cambridge: Cambridge UP, 2001.

"Oprah's Book Club [discussion of *The Bluest Eye*]." *The Oprah Winfrey Show.* 26 May 2000. Transcript by Burrelle's Information Services.

Peck, Janice. "Talk About Racism: Framing a Popular Discourse of Race on *Oprah Winfrey.*" *Cultural Critique.* 27 (1994): 89–126.

Prager, Emily. "Oprah's Opera." *The Village Voice.* 10 Mar. 1987: 45, 48.

Reed, Gail. "The Antithetical Meaning of the Term 'Empathy' in Psychoanalytic Discourse." *Empathy.* Eds. Joseph Lichtenberg et al. 2 vols. Hillsdale: Analytic P, 1984. 7–24.

Rogin, Michael. *Blackface, White Noise: Jewish Immigrants in the Hollywood Melting Pot.* Berkeley: U of California P, 1996.

Rosenberg, Pearl M. "Underground Discourses: Exploring Whiteness in Teacher Education." *Off White: Readings on Race, Power, and Society.* Eds. Michelle Fine et al. New York: Routledge, 1997. 79–89.

Sanchez-Eppler, Karen. *Touching Liberty: Abolition, Feminism, and the Politics of the Body.* Berkeley: U of California P, 1993.

Shattuc, Jane M. "The Oprahification of America: Talk Shows and the Public Sphere." *Television, History, and American Culture: Feminist Critical Essays.* Eds. Mary Beth Haralovich and Lauren Rabinovitz. Durham: Duke UP, 1999. 168–80.

Silverman, Kaja. *The Threshold of the Visible World.* New York: Routledge, 1996.

Sommer, Doris. *Proceed with Caution: When Engaged by Minority Writing in the Americas.* Cambridge: Harvard UP, 1999.

————. "Resistant Texts and Incompetent Readers." *Poetics Today*. 15.4 (1994): 523–51.

Spelman, Elizabeth V. *Fruits of Sorrow: Framing Our Attention to Suffering*. Boston: Beacon, 1997.

Wiegman, Robyn. *American Anatomies: Theorizing Race and Gender*. Durham, NC: Duke UP, 1995.

Woodward, Kathleen. "Calculating Compassion." *Compassion: The Culture and Politics of an Emotion*. Ed. Lauren Berlant. New York: Routledge, 2004. 59–86.

Young, Michael P. "A Revolution of the Soul: Transformative Experiences and Immediate Abolition." *Passionate Politics*. Eds. Jeff Goodwin et al. Chicago: U of Chicago P, 2001. 99–114.

8

BEWARE THE FURROW
OF THE MIDDLEBROW

Searching for *Paradise* on *The Oprah Winfrey Show*

TIMOTHY AUBRY

Just a few sentences away from finishing Toni Morrison's *Paradise,* an arduous journey almost completed, the reader encounters an image of similarly exhausted travelers and a warning that the real work has only just begun: "When the ocean heaves sending rhythms of water ashore, Piedade looks to see what has come. Another ship, perhaps, but different, heading to port, crew and passengers, lost and saved, atremble, for they have been disconsolate for some time. Now they will rest before shouldering the endless work they were created to do down here in paradise" (318). Morrison awaits seekers of peace or rest with surprises, with reversals of conventional protocols. Labor will not be followed by leisure. Those in search of paradise will, after a long voyage in unfamiliar territory, eventually discover their reward: interminable toil. They should not, however, be dismayed by this realization, since, according to Morrison, such work is not a dreary alternative or an unfortunate but necessary prelude to paradise; such work is itself the essence of paradise—the generous domain of which is no longer up in the air, out of reach, but instead "down here," accessible to all. Or, to understand Morrison's suggestion in a slightly different way, the experience of reading *Paradise*

"Beware the Furrow of the Middlebrow: Searching for *Paradise* on The Oprah Winfrey Show." *Modern Fiction Studies* 52:2 (2006), 350–73. © Purdue Research Foundation. Reprinted with permission of The Johns Hopkins University Press.

may be difficult, may demand substantial work from the reader, even after the book is done, but this work is in fact the point, a gift just as desirable as whatever ends the work might have been thought to achieve. With *Paradise*, Morrison seems to hazard two propositions, both of which rely heavily on the inclinations of her massive middlebrow readership. The first is that her book, like the utopia its title promises, can be at once difficult and accessible, requiring a kind of hard labor that will not thwart but rather attract readers. The second is that *Paradise*'s power will not end on the last page, that the labor Morrison initiates will persist, indefinitely, after readers have put the book down.

Oprah Winfrey's March 1998 Book Club discussion of *Paradise* provides a good test of these propositions. The format of the episode is somewhat anomalous. Because the novel was thought to be so difficult compared to other books featured on the show, Winfrey decided not to host one of her usual informal dinner discussions, but instead invited Morrison to lead a seminar for her and twenty of her viewers. Winfrey's suspicions that *Paradise* might frustrate some people turned out to be correct, but most of the participants, while puzzled, seemed determined to make sense of the text. The episode featured, as D. T. Max and John Young have noted, an unusually rigorous and extensive conversation about the language and meaning of the novel akin to what might take place in a college seminar, but it was nevertheless inflected by the therapeutic and personal priorities that usually prevail on Oprah's Book Club. Thus, the show brought into dialogue the assumptions and inclinations of two very different interpretive communities. The audience's ambivalent reactions and the efforts of Morrison and Winfrey to render *Paradise* accessible reveal a great deal about how serious literature is used by contemporary middle-class readers and what kinds of functions it is capable of performing for them.

Morrison, it turns out, harbors rather ambitious aims. Her novel depicts two ultimately failed utopian experiments: one rigidly policed, patriarchal, all-black town fanatically obsessed with preserving its racial purity and, nearby, a permissive and diverse commune-style household of women who have come to inhabit an abandoned convent. As she describes these two doomed efforts, Morrison seeks to promote a relationship between her text and her readers that can function as yet another model of utopian communal politics, a relationship whose difficult terms she refuses to dictate, insofar as they must be, according to her vision, the product of continual intersubjective negotiation. Nevertheless, Morrison does attempt, in *Paradise* and on *The Oprah Winfrey Show*, to articulate certain conditions necessary for both good reading and good politics. In particular, she insists on a challenging form of social and psychological inclusivity, an openness to unfamiliar experiences, modes of discourse, concepts, and identities seemingly at odds with the restrictive gatekeeping measures typically at work in conventional versions of paradise. Such ideals, one might assume, would find a welcome embrace on *Oprah* where the importance of tolerance and diversity is axiomatic. For Morrison, however, true openness toward the other is not something easily achieved. Notwithstanding the ease with which it is frequently endorsed, true openness requires perpetual work of a very specific and difficult nature. The questions I intend to explore are the following: In what ways does Winfrey's Book Club discussion of *Paradise* promote, or fail to promote, the kind of work that serious literature, in Morrison's view, demands? Do Oprah Winfrey and her audience members adhere to, or do they in fact resist and revise, the protocols of interpretive response that Morrison prescribes? What forms of productive complicity and friction does Winfrey's show illuminate in the negotiation between the aspirations of serious literature and the inclinations of middlebrow readers?

Middlebrow Confusion

Given the unusual character of the *Paradise* Book Club episode, an analysis of its virtues or its shortcomings will not necessarily apply to the format Winfrey typically employs in approaching literature, which involves an emphasis on the author's life and on the connection between the text and readers' personal or psychological problems.[1] Nevertheless, the *Paradise* discussion does stage, in a revealing manner, interpretive inclinations that are broadly characteristic of middlebrow reading culture. But what exactly does the category "middlebrow" denote and how closely does it coincide with the more general category "middle class"? Moreover, if Oprah Winfrey's charismatic allure enables her, as many critics have maintained, to attract an audience that transcends class and race boundaries, then is it even fair to characterize her audience as "middle class" or "middlebrow"?[2] While many historians, sociologists, and ethnographers have attempted to define the essential properties of the middle class, some deferring to economic statistics (an income equal to twice the federal poverty level), others to media-produced images (suburban tract houses), and others to a particular set of values (propriety, industry, narcissism), obviously the proliferation of the term's uses and sites of application makes the task of strictly circumscribing its field of reference rather difficult.[3] But, whether or not all of Winfrey's viewers conform to the standards variously forwarded as conditions for membership within this vaguely defined demographic category, the show's emphasis on self-improvement in fact contributes to the production of rituals and norms that currently define and police the middle class—an interesting development in light of Winfrey's own race and class background.

The term "middlebrow," unfortunately, is no easier to define and its pejorative connotations produce further obstacles for anyone trying to perform a critical assessment of it.[4] In her analysis of Winfrey's Book Club, Kathleen Rooney rejects the term for this reason, but she acknowledges the existence of the reading culture to which it refers (17). Indeed, particular tastes, assumptions, interpretive tendencies, and desires are on full display on *Oprah* that tend to be called middlebrow and that critics often associate with contemporary book clubs. It is important, however, to approach the middlebrow as a tactical, if sometimes automatic, mode of reading rather than as a fixed identity. Many people encounter texts at times as middlebrow readers and at other times through the lens of more scholarly postures, and these motions are enabled by latent conceptual continuities between the two approaches, which Morrison and Winfrey strategically deploy. Finally, it is important to remember that middlebrow modes of interpretation are not necessarily naïve or misguided, as many scholars tacitly assume, but often involve, as Janice Radway has contended, quite complex and critical responses to literature.

In his *New York Times Magazine* article examining the Oprah Winfrey Book Club phenomenon, D. T. Max describes Oprah's reading choices as representing a "therapeutic canon," and this label does a fairly good job of capturing both the kinds of expectations and the kinds of books that tend to prevail within middlebrow culture (36). Audience members on *Oprah* consistently report a desire to read books that can change their lives, and this capacity seems to be the most important criterion for determining a work's literary value. As one participant remarks, "There are good books and there are great books. A great book is a book that changes you" ("Book Club" 2002). While his observation does not specify what kind of change a great book should produce, or how it might produce this change, scholars, such as Elizabeth Long and Janice Radway, have concluded that many middlebrow readers approach literature in the same way they approach self-help books: in search of practical guidance on how to manage various social and psychological challenges, and in search of strategies for self-improvement—a phrase that connotes the acquisition of knowledge, material wealth, status, or some combination of the three.[5]

Such ambitions declare themselves unabashedly, if somewhat obliquely, in the frequently articulated desire to "get" literature. During the discussion of *Paradise*, Winfrey's friend Gayle King remarks: "Ms. Morrison, are we supposed to get it on the first read? Because I've read it—I'm not even trying to be funny—because I've read it once, and I called Oprah and I said, 'Please, 'splain it to me.' So I'm thinking—so I'm now on my second read and I'm hoping I'll get it on the second read" (1998). A few minutes later, Winfrey echoes her friend's comment. "Because I—of course, I started with the epigram. I read it about three or four times. I went, 'Oh, I don't get it, let me move on.'" Why exactly does this expression, "I don't get it," unmask and epitomize so legibly the insecure position of its speaker within the cultural hierarchy that she manifestly desires to climb? Surely those who command expertise or cultural capital often fail to "get it," but they know to remain silent, and so this phrase immediately marks the speaker as uncultured, as middlebrow. Depending on the tone, it can easily betray a self-protective, sarcastically dismissive attitude toward whatever it is the speaker fails to get, which is why Gayle King feels compelled to remark, "I'm not even trying to be funny." Moreover, her comical slip into black English, "please 'splain it to me," while self-mocking, can also be read as self-authenticating, a mark of pride in her own cultural identity, an identity that demands respect *especially* insofar as it keeps her at a distance from the realm of high culture, represented, ironically in this case, by Toni Morrison. Winfrey manipulates the same dynamic when, speaking about the setting of the Book Club discussion, Princeton University, she remarks, "Our thirteenth book brought us to prestigious Princeton University in Princeton, New Jersey, where twenty viewers and I became *Paradise* pupils for a day. It's a natural setting, not only because it's a place of higher learning—whoo, girl, do we need that—but it's also where Toni Morrison teaches. Could we find paradise inside Princeton?" (1998).

Though somewhat playful, the remarks made by Winfrey and King betray genuine reverence for the sphere of high culture as represented by Princeton University and an earnest desire to "get it" based on a veneration for that which defies immediate comprehension. They want very much to understand Morrison's *Paradise*, and they want the challenge that the book's difficulty offers. Still, the urge to "get it" is not entirely auspicious; it seems to entail a disturbing desire for mastery, for possession, rooted in class-climbing pretensions, as if the comprehension of literary works were simply another form of acquisition, capable of procuring for the consumer higher status within a class hierarchy. Moreover, "get it" is so brief that it connotes, not a difficult process of reflection, but instead one quickly completed act of appropriation, no more time consuming than the enunciation of the phrase "get it," which, encased on both sides by hard syllables, sounds as closed and perfunctory as the act it would describe. Somewhat more promising is the fact that both Winfrey and King articulate the idea of "getting it" only in its negation; they *don't* get it, and their uncertainty sustains the potential for Morrison, who treats confusion as the point rather than the problem, to intervene. Indeed, incomprehension propels Winfrey and King to reread the text repeatedly, which would suggest that the author's greatest hopes must reside with the reader's *never* getting it.

Morrison's central project in *Paradise* is to construct, with the help of the reader, new utopian models based on the negotiation between author and reader, and this joint venture of collectively envisioning and producing paradise will necessarily be a difficult, endless task. But not an impossible one; recall that Morrison positions paradise "down here," a phrase that directly opposes the one Winfrey uses, punningly, at the beginning of the show to register her failure to understand the text: "over our heads," another typical middlebrow expression. Morrison's "down here" contests the nearly definitional inaccessibility of paradise implied by "over our heads," which would render, to the satisfaction of the lazy and the complacent, any kind of work pointless and probably painful. In her pursuit of accessibility, Morrison offers readers a text designed to make them struggle and feel challenged, but also designed to make that struggle enjoyable. She remarks at one point during the show, "And I wanted the weight of interpretation to be on the reader," underlining the burdensome hermeneutical labor *Paradise* demands, but, in another moment, she comments: "That's because I want it to be a pleasant experience. I didn't want to write an essay. I wanted you to participate in the journey." In fact, a central purpose of Morrison's text is to impress on its readers the eternal, mutually constitutive relationship between struggle and pleasure, or between struggle and paradise, a relationship Winfrey herself suggests in a revelatory voice-over: "Wise author that she is, Morrison knows the rewards are twice as great when we readers get to unlock the secrets on our own."

But should readers hope to "unlock the secrets" of the text—an aim that sounds suspiciously like the urge to "get it"? Morrison, who refuses to reveal many seemingly crucial secrets in the novel, including the race and eventual fate of many of the main characters, would presumably answer no. Her responses to her readers' confusion and desire for answers are, however, equivocal. After Winfrey declares that she doesn't get the epigram, the two have the following exchange:

MS. MORRISON: I don't believe you Oprah.

WINFREY: It's true.

MS. MORRISON: I don't believe that you—that that happened to you. I think you think it didn't mean anything to you. I think you read it with some heightened expectation that it was in German and you didn't speak German, but what I'm saying is that if I read it to you very slowly, one word at a time, you would know instantly what that meant.

WINFREY: Oh, I knew that it meant we were in for a major journey here. I knew that.

MS. MORRISON: Well, what's left to understand? There is nothing left to understand. That you got it is what I'm trying to tell you.

WINFREY: OK.

MS. MORRISON: You got it and you didn't believe you got it.

On the one hand, Morrison worries that Winfrey has preemptively elevated *Paradise* to such a great altitude in her mind that she has rendered it prohibitively difficult before even attempting to understand it. But, on the other hand, Morrison does want Winfrey to conceive of the text as difficult and she seems pleased when Winfrey acknowledges it as such. Although even Morrison uses the phrase "you got it," what Winfrey has in fact correctly grasped, according to Morrison, is that she will not be able to "get" everything in the text, that *Paradise* will make her work by deliberately evading her comprehension. Morrison's aim here is to validate Winfrey's and her audience's confusion, to reassure them that it is precisely the point that they not "get it." But she also wants to change the way in which they formulate or apprehend, paradoxically, their own confusion—to replace "not getting it" with a different condition, less bent on dominating or possessing what it cannot understand.

What, then, is so difficult about *Paradise*? Probably most baffling is Morrison's mode of exposition, especially in the early sections of the text. The novel centers around the town of Ruby, which has a long prehistory, a complex set of tacit laws, and a host of characters, all of whom are related to each other through an intricate mesh of alliances, bloodlines, commitments, sympathies, rivalries, and feuds. But Morrison defers delivering most of this information at first, almost always narrating, in free indirect discourse, from the limited perspective of individual characters, often visitors who know practically nothing about the town's dynamics. Thus, she depicts a series of scenes, rich with opaque subtexts, but fails to provide the background information necessary to decipher what is happening. Winfrey and later Morrison explain the rationale behind this bewildering method of information delivery in almost identical terms. Morrison tells the audience:

> Because I wanted to force the reader to become acquainted with the communities. I wanted—you have to look at each one of these people and figure out who each one was and then see their relationship to each other and how that changed in each of these paradises. And I wanted the weight of interpretation to be on the reader, the way you do when you walk into a town. When you walk into a neighborhood, you don't know anybody. Do you really just want to know the one person who seems to know everything about the neighborhood?

Her remarks are quite helpful, but also paradoxical. *Paradise* draws the reader into an experience of the unfamiliar. To justify and clarify this alienation effect, however, Morrison compares it to an experience with which her readers are all completely familiar: entering a strange neighborhood—always a potentially disconcerting situation, and one that might thus be called a familiar experience of the unfamiliar. When Morrison later addresses the best method for interpreting some of the apparently unrealistic, otherworldly happenings in the text, she insists that it is necessary to "suspend disbelief of everything that might not be possible in the material world." This advice, in fact, challenges the tendency of Winfrey's Book Club discussions to ignore the fictionality of fictional works, and it clashes slightly with Morrison's previous suggestion.[6] The former justifies her text's difficulty on the basis of its resemblance to the everyday world, the latter on the basis of its removal from the everyday world, and this tension measures her own struggle to locate the paradise she is working to construct, whether "down here," "above our heads," or in some as yet unmappable place in between.

The most disturbing aspect of Morrison's textual challenges is the way they replicate the fictional town of Ruby's paranoid, self-protective methods for dealing with intruders. The community essentially stonewalls Misner, the new liberal-minded minister who has been assigned to work in the town. On hearing the cliché expression, "no harm in asking," Patricia, an acquaintance of Misner's, has the following thoughts: "Yes there is. Harm. Pat sipped carefully from a spoon. Ask Richard Misner. Ask him what I just did to him. Or what everyone else does. When he asks questions, they just close him out to anything but the obvious, the superficial" (216). This closing out is precisely what Morrison does to the reader, at least in the early segments of the book. It is an interesting tactic, given her obvious dissatisfaction with Ruby's exclusionary practices, suggested even in Patricia's sudden disgust with the town's treatment of Misner, and given Morrison's own definition of paradise, at the end of the Book Club discussion, as a state of openness.

MS. MORRISON:	It's being open to all these paths and connections and . . . (*unintelligible*) between.
WINFREY:	And that is paradise!
MS. MORRISON:	That is paradise.

Morrison also comments about her novel, "It's kind of renegoti—or rethinking that the whole idea of all paradises in literature and history and so on and in our minds and in all the holy books are special places that are fruitful, bountiful, safe, gorgeous and defined by those who can't get in" (1998). Why, then, does Morrison put her readers into this position of excluded outsider? Is paradise, as she suggests, available to conceptualization only from a place of exclusion? But isn't Morrison's project to reconceptualize paradise, to imagine ways of rendering it more inclusive? Such questions, presumably, are the kind she hopes many of her readers will ask, thus participating actively in the difficult dialogue necessary to revise a palpably inadequate traditional notion of paradise—but one with such undeniable staying power that even Morrison, with all of her disaffection, cannot resist it—into something more inhabitable.

Frustrating Identification

Ruby comes across as a cruel and cold town, and consequently the avenues of sympathy that readers might seek are often closed. Though Morrison also includes a convent of misfit women outside of Ruby, all of the characters in *Paradise* are elusive, peculiarly fortified against identification. The reader accesses them only glancingly. Their motives are never transparent; Morrison forces idiosyncratic deeds, offbeat metaphors, and cryptic quips to function as synecdoches for their histories, passions, and interior obsessions. Thus, all of the characters seem gestural as opposed to round. And, of course, there are so many of them, no single one of whom assumes the leading role. Morrison herself notes on *Oprah*, "there was no leading character," and one of Winfrey's guests comments, "one thing that—fascinates me about this book is that there really aren't any villains," and he might have added that there are no heroes either. For her refusal to create manifestly deep, multidimensional, stable characters, Morrison has won the admiration of many poststructuralist critics who claim that she is subverting the essentialism presupposed by traditional, realist modes of characterization.[7] But what exactly does her text accomplish by disabling or hindering identification, especially when it represents such a valued interpretive response for so many of her readers and for so many of Oprah Winfrey's viewers?[8]

During the discussion of *Paradise*, the audience's reaction to the antagonistic relationship between two characters, Mavis and her daughter Sal, exemplifies one particularly dangerous consequence of identification. Mavis is, as Morrison acknowledges, an incompetent mother and the victim of abuse from her husband, while Sal appears to be slyly vindictive and coldhearted. Describing the reactions of her readers to these characters, Morrison remarks:

> Somebody was asking me a couple of days ago or—or simply making an observation about this terrible child that Mavis had, her daughter who pinches her—and I kept saying, "Why do you call her terrible?" I said, "Think what it must feel like for an eleven-year old girl to have a mother who permits her as a doormat and you watch this woman get knocked around by the father. She seems totally incompetent. You're terrified as a kid that that might be you" (1998).

At this point, several guests express their agreement and it appears that Morrison will simply offer a somewhat trite lesson in the importance of forgiving, of not judging people too quickly, of understanding the circumstances that drive a character to behave in a certain way. But the discussion takes a more ominous turn: as Sal rises in the group's estimation, Mavis sinks. Although one audience member disagrees, she is quickly silenced, and the consensus, driven notably by Morrison and Winfrey, seems to be that Mavis, for her incompetence, is truly the one worthy of blame. Morrison convinces

Oprah's audience of this interpretation by asking them to project themselves into the mind of the little girl, by soliciting their identification with Sal. Her argument may well be valid, but it nevertheless betrays, unwittingly, a severe economy of empathy, a zero-sum game, undergirding the operations of iden- tification, obviously at work in the consumption of almost all narratives. Empathy for one character, in other words, must be paid for with antipathy toward another; identification with one character means alienation from another. The necessary conclusion is that identification, at least in its typical form, abets divisive hierarchies of preference and modes of exclusion anti- thetical to the kind of paradise Morrison seeks to initiate. Thus, when accounting for her decision not to offer readers a "leading character," Morri- son tells Winfrey, "Because I wanted to force the reader to become acquainted with the communities." Her hope is not to disable identification altogether, but to facilitate another form of identification: a structure of empathy difficult to imagine, less individual-centered, less competitive, and more inclusive. Interestingly enough, Morrison's strategy conflicts slightly with *Oprah*'s tendency to incite compassion through the presentation of individual narratives—a format that, as Corinne Squire has noted, personal- izes social and political problems.[9]

Both identification and empathy by definition are based on actual or imagined similarities between the involved parties, and many scholars have worried that an emphasis on identification might prevent readers from actively engaging with depictions of other races or cultures. Max puts it suc- cinctly: "There's something odd about Winfrey's insistence on teaching novels as springboards for self-reflection. Aren't novels about stepping out- side one's experience?" (36–37). Max's complaint, while reasonable, suggests a misunderstanding of identification, which, as many scholars have noted, almost always involves a fantastical transgression of the borders that enclose the self and an attempt to inhabit an alien perspective.[10] To be sure, identi- fication requires commonalities between self and other, but it also requires alterity, and the insights about oneself that identification promotes origi- nate precisely in the fertile clash between sameness and otherness that read- ers experience as they attempt to view themselves and the world through a fictional character's eyes. Many of Winfrey's choices, such as Andre Dubus III's *The House of Sand and Fog*, which depicts an Iranian immigrant's efforts to start his life over in the United States, or Edwidge Dandicat's *Breath, Eyes, Memory*, which narrates a Haitian girl's development into adulthood, suggest that a wide diversity of characters and situations are susceptible to readerly identification. The greater danger, especially from a political perspective, is that identification's wide net might be cast too far, assimilating and conflating radically divergent experiences, thus effacing crucial particularities. The episode of *Oprah* devoted to *The Bluest Eye*, for instance, features white women claiming that they can relate to the desire of the young African American character, Pecola, for blue eyes, since they, too, have thought themselves to be ugly ("Book Club" 2000). To be fair to Winfrey, she does spend a significant amount of time during the episode discussing race, but her show nevertheless dramatizes the way in which identification can personalize and thus efface important political subtexts, transforming the traumatic effects of an intractable race and class hierarchy into a universal and, in certain moments, even banal psychological problem. Such risks, however, are not necessarily a reason to relinquish identification altogether as a means of mediating various social and cultural rifts, and even the responses of Winfrey's audience members to *The Bluest Eye* could constitute a promising initial effort in a more elaborate dialectic: a fantasy of sameness functioning as a bolstering device necessary to launch oneself into the more dangerous and forbidding territory of otherness.

In *Paradise*, Morrison works to thwart race-based identification by deliberately refusing to reveal the race of most of her characters. The now famous first sentence of the novel, "They shoot the white girl first" (3), which describes the climactic attack of Ruby's men on the convent, produces a mystery that Morrison never solves. Who at the convent is white and who is black? Though the opening sentence implies that only one woman there is white, this unnamed presence destabilizes the racial legibility of all of the characters, provoking an endless interpretive game, an incessant compulsion to read the various clues and markers as unambiguous signs of a particular race, a game that only serves to heighten the ambiguities. If readers choose to identify with a character at the convent, they must do so independently of any certain knowledge about that character's race.

What is the purpose and what is the effect of this experiment? Morrison tells Winfrey's audience:

> I didn't write, "They shoot the tall girl first," or "They shoot the fat girl or the thin girl." I mean, I said, "white," which means race is going to play a part in the narrative. It may not play the part we are used to race playing in identifying who is black and who is white and what does all that mean. It played another kind of role which was to signal race instantly and to reduce it to nothing. (1998)

Morrison evinces a desire to diminish the usually pivotal role race plays in shaping readers' interpretation of fictional characters. A little later in the discussion, she makes a remark that she has made several times on *Oprah*:

> Ms. Morrison: The point is when you—you're right, but the point is you do have to know them [the women in the convent] as individuals. That was why the racial information was withheld, because when you know their race, what do you know?
>
> Several Members of the Group: Nothing.
>
> Ms. Morrison: You don't know anything.

It is possible to interpret Morrison's comments as implying a trivialization of race in stark contrast to the obsession with race and racial purity that characterizes the town of Ruby. Morrison's alternative vision of utopia, one might argue, is a world in which people no longer care about, or even notice, each other's race—a world in which the apprehension and hence the reality of racial difference disappears, as it seems to within Morrison's depiction of the convent. Such an ideal conforms to the racial politics most frequently articulated on *Oprah*: a post-civil-rights position, which holds that focusing on race actually hinders our capacity to understand each other as individuals. Discussing Winfrey's strategy for dealing with race, Janice Peck remarks, "An overriding sentiment in the series, found across all episodes, expressed by those opposed to racism and those who deny it's a problem and by persons of different ethnic and racial identifications (though more often by whites), is that people are, first and foremost, *individuals*" (96).[11] This sentiment is in accord with an increasingly popular notion across the United States, in part responsible for the various attacks on affirmative action programs, that we are, or should aim to be, a post-race society.[12]

While such a position, according to Peck, appeals to many of Winfrey's white viewers, who might be put off by more overt discussions about race, Morrison obviously recognizes that the United States is nowhere near to becoming post-race. Thus, she adds the following qualification: "But at the same time, it is very hard to write race and to unwrite it at the same time. So you have to withhold information, and that means that some readers were, you know, deeply preoccupied with finding out which was the single one, who was white." In her study of white writers' figurations of blackness, *Playing in the Dark*, she contends, in even more emphatic terms, "for both black and white American writers, in a wholly racialized society, there is no escaping racially inflected language, and the work writers do to unhobble the imagination from the demands of that language is complicated, interesting, and definitive" (12–13). *Playing in the Dark* offers a compelling account of what blackness and black characters have been made to symbolize within white literary culture: "illicit sexuality, chaos, madness, impropriety, anarchy, strangeness, and helpless, hapless desire" (80–81). If Morrison is correct, the modes of identification between white readers and black (or otherwise marginalized) characters who populate an increasingly fashionable ethnic literature would be based not on a suppression of race as an important category, but on a paradoxical double gesture, which, to borrow Morrison's phrase, writes and unwrites race simultaneously. In other words, blackness continues to carry its usual freight of otherness, unsanctioned passion, and authentic suffering. But white readers, employing a liberal ethos of individualism, can deny the barrier of racial difference in order to identify with black characters, a denial that allows them to lay claim to all the modes of affect and struggle symbolized by blackness—modes that have become sources of self-valorization—and simultaneously to disavow the metaphorical function race performs in this interpretive act.[13]

Obviously, Winfrey's audience is not exclusively white, and the response I have described is only one among many possibilities, but all the modes of identification her show fosters—both across and within racial boundaries— have the potential to abet reductive, self-serving conceptions of race and racial difference. Hence, Morrison disables race-based identification, but her aim is not to efface the importance of race per se; nor is that the effect of her experiment. Indeed, as Morrison anticipates, many of the audience members on *Oprah* acknowledge that while reading *Paradise* they became all the more obsessed with determining the race of the characters. Most of them agree that racial difference can be a life-and-death matter—it is, as one participant points out, the motivation for the murder described by the first sentence— but they are nonetheless unable to determine who is black and who is white. Readers, in other words, do not encounter the characters in the convent as deracialized, but rather as characters whose race is profoundly unknowable yet profoundly important. Readers' doomed detective work has the potential to make them aware of the multiple attributes, tendencies, and connotations they associate, consciously and unconsciously, with particular racial categories, forcing them to acknowledge the extent to which their concepts of race transcend mere skin color—but, at the same time, to recognize just how inadequate their concepts are for apprehending the complex and contradictory ways that race can be experienced and registered in everyday life. All the obvious markers of race prove unreliable, Morrison never offers conclusive evidence, and thus readers must acknowledge that the meaning of whiteness or blackness defies full and final comprehension. Race, then, ceases to be an easily comprehensible entity; it does not disappear, but rather emerges as a serious epistemological problem, far more elusive than most people suspect in their ordinary apprehension of racial cues. In a sense, Morrison's claim, that when you know the race of another person you know nothing, is true—given the superficial and perfunctory form that most people's knowledge of race ordinarily assumes.

Morrison envisions a utopian mode of racial politics somewhere in between the race-obsessed exclusions of Ruby and the ostensibly race-blind, liberal individualism that characterizes a currently predominant fantasy within the United States. Both of these ideologies entail a striving toward the extinction of racial difference, a movement toward homogeneity, based on reductive racial constructions that elide either the real continuities or the real disjunctions that mediate between various races. For Morrison, racial difference and racial inclusivity are in fact necessary features of paradise. An ongoing, open-minded negotiation with and between different kinds of otherness, in all of their difficulty and complexity, is one of the central pleasures and central challenges that paradise has to offer. Within the novel, the convent is the place that comes closest to approximating this ideal. In stark contrast to the rigorously monitored borders of Ruby, its doors are open to anyone who wants to stay there, and, within its walls, people from all kinds of different backgrounds come together to form a community.

Significantly, however, the convent's inclusiveness relies on one major and ultimately fatal exclusion. Although a few men stay there temporarily, the convent lacks a permanent male presence, and this absence seems to enable its nonhierarchical open-ended structure. When the men from Ruby do appear, their objective is to decimate the community. It would not, however, be accurate to say that Morrison is forwarding a position of gender essentialism or claiming that men are naturally anathema to her utopian vision; she is simply critiquing a historically constituted version of masculinity and its equation with authority in the town of Ruby. Several male characters, including Reverend Misner, and, near the end of the book, Deacon, one of the two patriarchs of the town, question Ruby's repressiveness, and seem ready to embrace a more flexible open mode of communal politics of the kind briefly instantiated in the convent.

Accessing Paradise

Perhaps the most substantial, intricate, and fraught encounter with otherness
that Morrison initiates does not occur within the convent or even within the
text; it occurs, in fact, between the reader and the text. *Paradise* invites readers into a completely unfamiliar puzzling world, occasionally furnishing haphazard clues that sustain bewilderment by promising the possibility of
eventual comprehension. Although many participants in the book club discussion express great frustration with the novel, and although there are parallels between Morrrison's textual devices and Ruby's exclusionary tactics, her
agenda is not ultimately to bar people from entering her world. It is important to observe that her defamiliarizing narrative modes are not merely
secretive but also, in a sense, excessively forthcoming. The way she incites
interpretive frustrations and interpretive desires involves a form of exposition
both guarded and generous, which both cautiously withholds and prema-
turely volunteers information. Morrison frequently saturates her readers with
details about the town of Ruby or the convent, but then fails to provide the
explanations necessary to interpret those details.

The experience of reading *Paradise*, which involves always knowing too
much and, at the same time, never knowing enough, reproduces, significantly, the staggering, uneven trajectory of love. Playing on the metaphorical
associations between darkness and racial otherness, Morrison describes the
love affair between Deacon and Consolata, a resident at the convent:

> He drove, it seemed, for the pleasure of the machine: the roar con-
> tained, hooded in steel; the sly way it simultaneously parted the near
> darkness and vaulted into darkness afar—beyond what could be
> anticipated. They drove for what Consolata believed were hours, no
> words passing between them. The danger and its necessity focused
> them, made them calm. She did not know or care where headed or
> what might happen when they arrived. Speeding toward the unfore-
> seeable, sitting next to him who was darker than the darkness they
> split, Consolata let the feathers unfold and come unstuck from the
> walls of a stone-cold womb. (228–29)

Consolata's relationship with Deacon includes all of the vertiginous gaps of
knowledge and startling leaps of intuition that are peculiar to early intimacy.
In their late-night drive, darkness does not thwart their progress, but rather
invites it. As they "[part] the near darkness" they seem almost to leap ahead

of themselves, to leap ahead of the present moment, apprehending traces of a future not yet arrived, knowing things about each other they should not yet know. But their uncanny vision remains partial and their movement forward simply leads them further into darkness. In fact, unremitting darkness sustains their understanding of each other by demanding continuous interpretive activity, thus constituting understanding as an ongoing, endless process, rather than as a static or instantaneous mode of apprehension. Morrison here is trying to teach readers ways of unknowing that are neither defeatist nor covetous in relation to the subjects that elude their mastery.

Viewing the task of interpreting *Paradise*, and, by extension, the task of approaching otherness, to be akin to falling in love has the potential to recast the difficulty of the text. The serious labor that is required, the frustrated desire for complete comprehension, and the sense of perpetual uncertainty can be understood, like love, to be sources of pleasure. But the other less appealing consequence of this equation is that love, while pleasurable, must also be understood as extremely difficult, a point made in *Paradise*, remarkably enough, by the profoundly unsympathetic, dogmatically conservative Reverend Senior Pulliam: "Love is divine only and difficult always. If you think it is easy you are a fool. If you think it is natural you are blind. It is a learned application without reason or motive except that it is God" (141). Although Pulliam functions as anything but a mouthpiece for Morrison's views, his insights in this instance defy immediate dismissal, and it is significant that Morrison presents his sermon before she identifies the speaker, forcing the reader to assess its validity without the prejudice that his persona is likely to inspire.[14] Here she borrows from an unlikely source an element of rigor for her utopian vision, whose emphasis on nonauthoritarian inclusivity and love might otherwise imply unrestrained permissiveness. The convent runs the risk of becoming too lax, allowing its members to do and think whatever they want, until Consolata, the oldest woman there, decides to impose certain demands and rules on the community, insisting that they do the work necessary to establish a truly fulfilling utopian space: "I call myself Consolata Sosa. If you want to be here you do what I say. Eat how I say. Sleep when I say. And I will teach you what you are hungry for" (262).

In her apparent assumption of power, Consolata seems disturbingly dictatorial, but her methods do not usher in a regime of repression similar to Ruby's. On the contrary, the rituals and regulations she installs incite new unrestrained modes of artistic creation from the convent's residents: self-portraits painted on the floor, lyrical confessions, narrated dreams. Even the central motto of Ruby, inscribed on its monumental oven, "Beware the

Furrow of His Brow," initially designed to elicit from the townspeople strict
obedience to a higher authority, becomes a site of subversive reinterpretation.
The younger generation debates its meaning and eventually rewrites it altogether, so that it reads "Be the Furrow of His Brow." For Morrison doctrines
and protocols are an indispensable feature of paradise, not insofar as they
require strict adherence, but insofar as they provoke the constant, creative
labor of renegotiation and revision.

The rhetoric of *Paradise* often assumes a piously didactic tone like the
inscription on the oven, but Morrison's purpose is not to impose an unambiguous moral or message on the reader, not to silence doubt or division,
since it is, in her view, only through an inclusive, pluralistic dialogue that paradise can be reimagined. As Morrison remarks about *Paradise* on *Oprah*, "I
wouldn't want to end up having written a book in which there was a formula
and a perfect conclusion and that was the meaning and the only meaning"
(1998). And, a moment later, she adds, "Novels are for talking about and
quarreling about and engaging in some powerful way." Winfrey's book club,
Morrison seems to hope, can provide readers a forum in which to debate the
meanings of her text—notwithstanding the danger that her authorial presence might quell a multivoiced conversation. *Oprah* is a promising site for this
kind of discussion insofar as it routinely challenges the exclusive authority of
experts, according to Sherryl Wilson, asserting the validity of knowledge
based on ordinary people's immediate experience (117–18). And Morrison's
hopes do not seem all that far-fetched; the show features robust, if somewhat
truncated, debates about theology, race, and aesthetics, which only occasionally reach a consensus. One reader, apparently not intimidated by Morrison's
purported genius, stridently questions her novel's artistic value: "I was lost
because I came into—I really wanted to read the book and love it and learn
some life lessons; and when I got into it, it was so confusing I questioned the
value of a book that is that hard to understand."

The woman's remark merits consideration. She, like many of Winfrey's
audience members, approaches literature with passion and a readiness to
challenge herself intellectually. *Paradise*'s difficulty, however, effectively
blocks her critical engagement. Her response, to blame the text rather than
herself, echoes some of the comments made by Gayle King and Winfrey that
suggest that *Paradise* might be simply "over our heads," impossibly inaccessi-
ble. Their attitude, which vacillates between awe and dismissal, also includes
as a target Princeton University, a "center for higher learning," as Winfrey
somewhat ironically deems it. Their comments imply a critique of the elit-

ism and exclusiveness that characterize the entire world of so-called high culture along with the academic institutions, such as Princeton, that support, celebrate, and embody this world. The widely acknowledged insularity of high culture and academia remains a justifiably vexed issue, but it is especially pertinent in the case of Morrison, who explicitly thematizes inclusivity in her text. On the show, she remarks that all paradises validate themselves, problematically, by excluding certain individuals—a practice her own institution, Princeton University, unapologetically enshrines as the sine qua non of its high status. Indeed, at the opening of the show, Winfrey underscores the connection between paradise and Princeton, posing a question many, including F. Scott Fitzgerald, must have pondered before her: "Could we find paradise inside Princeton?"

Morrison's answer to this question ought to be an unequivocal no, given that she wants to redefine paradise as a state of openness. But her text runs the risk of denying readers access; its difficulty constitutes a daunting admissions process. Morrison's project, however, is precisely to sever the link between textual difficulty and exclusiveness, which has conditioned the reception of twentieth-century literature at least since the advent of modernism, and to realign difficulty with the task of furthering inclusiveness. All of the challenges *Paradise* offers function as lessons in how to approach otherness, how to negotiate one's relationship with people, practices, and concepts that are profoundly unfamiliar. A paradise with open boundaries, a paradise whose definition and whose practical embodiment remained perpetually receptive to novel interventions would depend on precisely the rigorous modes of dialogue and interpretation that Morrison requires from her readers. Yet the potential consequence of Morrison's demands—made in the hopes of promoting a more inclusive society—may be, if Winfrey's audience is correct, ironically to exclude large segments of enthusiastic readers.

Thus, both Morrison and Winfrey work hard to render *Paradise* accessible to the audience. Their comparison between reading the text and entering a strange town is effective, but also potentially self-defeating. Elucidating the reader's encounter with unfamiliarity through analogy to a familiar circumstance is a way of domesticating the text's strangeness, rendering it recognizable. But part of *Paradise's* power, frustratingly enough, lies in its capacity to leave readers in the dark, bewildered and disoriented, without any conventional map or model for how to proceed, without knowing why or how they have gotten lost, thus forcing them to improvise new strategies of interpretive navigation. Explaining the difficulty, relating it to a common experience, while reassuring, runs the risk of disabling this effect. The woman who complains about the text's inaccessibility responds to Winfrey's guidance in a telling fashion:

WOMAN #7: You should have told us that. It would have been easier for me. I w . . .
WINFREY: But I'm telling you now.
WOMAN #7: OK I'll go home and . . .
WINFREY: I'm telling you now, that you have to open yourself. It's like a life experience. It's getting to know people, getting to know people in a town. It's not everything laid out.
WOMAN #7: No, that makes sense.

The woman wishes she could have been spared any readerly discomfort, any experience of difficulty irreconcilable with a clear agenda. Her comment, "I'll go home," also declares a desire to return to familiar surroundings. She will reread the book only on the condition that she can circumscribe its strangeness within a safe domestic frame.

The reader's wish to return home complements an analogy invoked several times on the show between reading the book and going on a journey. Winfrey, for instance, repeats one reader's warning about *Paradise*: "And someone said—had said that, 'It's challenging, it's like taking a trip, but you'd better have your bags packed. You better not have your bags empty.'" While many an English major at Princeton University has learned the importance of "unpacking" as a mode of interpretation, Winfrey's audience seems dedicated to the reverse process. What exactly does it mean to approach a text with your bags packed? On the one hand, this metaphor could imply refusing to discard, or question, any of your carefully sealed conventional assumptions, associations, and prejudices. On the other hand, it evinces a willingness to leave home behind, to travel somewhere new, even if a condition for this journey is that you carry with you certain familiar items, certain devices that will help you navigate and perhaps domesticate the unfamiliar territory. Both the plan to go home in order to reread the text and the urge to pack your bags constitute the reading process as a dialectical interchange between returning to and departing from the familiar safety of what is known—a paradoxical mode of reflection also at work in the middlebrow experience of identification and in any productive reimagination of paradise.

What the strangely matched pair of Morrison and Winfrey—attempting to embody and enact the reconciliation of serious literature and middlebrow culture—are suggesting is that, as you struggle through this difficult work of fiction, you can bring all of your baggage with you. In fact, it will probably come in handy. Your urge to identify with fictional characters, though dangerous in its favoritism, covert narcissism, and concomitant cruelties, will nevertheless enable you to transgress your own boundaries, apprehend unfamiliar modes of subjectivity, and thus begin the dialogue necessary to constitute a more inclusive community. The desire to "get" literature, while assuming that the task of understanding involves a single, manageable act of acquisition, also evinces a healthy sense of confusion and a willingness to be challenged—a willingness crucial for persevering in the ongoing process of understanding that Morrison hopes to initiate. Finally, the automatic gears of your racial consciousness may grind loudly to a halt as you read *Paradise*, but the dissonant noises they will make are necessary to register the potential for a less routine, more unknowing approach to racial otherness.

One obvious threat to Morrison's egalitarian fantasy is the authorial role she assumes on the show, which places her in a position of superiority relative to the audience, so that she becomes the genius dispensing wisdom for the benefit of the ignorant masses. Her function in this seminar is undeniably pedagogical, but it is important to note that she does not get the final word. By contesting the value of Morrison's book, the audience demonstrates an irreverent skepticism indispensable for producing a paradise based not on answers from above, but on a dialogue from within, "down here." The readers' bold articulation of their dissatisfaction, their claims about the book's inaccessibility, actually comprise just the kind of inclusive, democratic dialogue to which Morrison hopes *Paradise* can contribute, thus continuing the difficult, endless work she imagines on the final page. Moreover, this is work that promises to persist beyond the boundaries of the book club discussion. Almost all the participants on the show express and encourage a desire to reread, an act that may represent a return home, but their return, in this case, has the potential to transfigure home into a disturbingly, auspiciously unrecognizable place.

Notes

1. In their analysis of Oprah Winfrey's book club, Rooney and Illouz both identify these tendencies.

2. Several critics have commented on Winfrey's ability to speak to a diverse audience. See, for instance, Young and Max.

3. For some critical texts that have tried to characterize different facets of the American middle class in the past fifty years see Donaldson, Ehrenreich, Galbraith, Jackson, Jurca, Lasch, Mills, Pattillo-McCoy, Riesman, Spectorsky, and Whyte.

4. For some scholarly explorations of middlebrow culture, see Radway, *A Feeling for Books*; Long, *Book Clubs*; Long, "Textual Interpretation as Collective Action"; and Rubin.

5. See Radway, "The Book-of-The-Month-Club" 535; Long, "Textual Interpretation" 117. Rooney and Illouz also observe that Winfrey and her fellow participants tend to treat fictional works as self-help manuals. See Rooney, 142; Illouz, 143–45.

6. Rooney notes Winfrey's treatment of characters as if they were real people and her lack of emphasis on the fictional status of the novels she introduces (140).

7. For a poststructural approach to Morrison's characters, see McDowell. See also Dubey.

8. Farr, Rooney, and Illouz all point to the centrality of identification on Oprah Winfrey's Book Club. According to Long and Radway, middlebrow readers often seek out role models who can offer lessons in how to navigate—or how not to navigate—particular emotional challenges, or who can function merely as "friends," reminding readers that they are not alone in their problems.

9. In "The Oprahfication of America: Talk Shows and the Public Sphere," Jane Shattuc also addresses the way Winfrey personalizes political issues. And recently scholars have turned their attention to the political complexities of compassion. See, for instance, *Compassion: The Culture and Politics of an Emotion*, edited by Lauren Berlant. See especially Berlant, "Introduction"; Garber; and Woodward.

10. See, for instance, Fuss; Long and Radway, 23; and McDowell, 87–88.

11. For another analysis of Winfrey's approach to race, see Dixon.

12. Pattillo-McCoy comments on Americans' contradictory attitudes about race: "Even though America is obsessed with race, some policy makers and even more average citizens act as if race no longer matters. The sweeping assaults on affirmative action programs are prime examples" (1).

13. Penelope Ingram makes a similar observation about white consumption of ethnic literature:

> While some white Americans are certainly involved in—even, arguably, obsessed with—an appropriation of native culture, whether through New Age, environmental, or certain ecofeminist movements, I find such actions not to be indicative of a *lack* of national identity, but rather perhaps a boredom with, or political rejection of, the one they already possess. . . . "White

American" culture is known to them, familiar, hence seemingly lacking, whereas "ethnic" culture is exotic, dangerous, unknown. (162)

For two other insightful explorations of cross-racial modes of identification, see Dyer and Awkward.

14. In his essay, "Sensations of Loss," Michael Wood notes the difficulty of determining which characters' perspectives we ought to endorse and which we ought to condemn in Morrison's *Paradise.*

Works Cited

Awkward, Michael. *Negotiating Difference: Race, Gender, and the Politics of Positionality.* Chicago: U of Chicago P, 1995.

Berlant, Lauren, ed. *Compassion: The Culture and Politics of an Emotion.* New York: Routledge, 2004.

———. "Introduction: Compassion (and Withholding)." Berlant 1–13.

"Book Club—Toni Morrison." *The Oprah Winfrey Show.* Harpo Productions, Inc. 6 Mar. 1998.

"Book Club—Toni Morrison." *The Oprah Winfrey Show.* Harpo Productions, Inc. 2 May 2002.

Dixon, Kathleen. "The Dialogic Genres of Oprah Winfrey's 'Crying Shame.'" *Journal of Popular Culture* 35.2 (2001): 171–91.

Donaldson, Scott. *The Suburban Myth.* New York: Columbia UP, 1969.

Dubey, Madhu. *Black Women Novelists and the Nationalist Aesthetic.* Bloomington: Indiana UP, 1994.

Dyer, Richard. *White.* New York: Routledge, 1997.

Ehrenreich, Barbara. *Fear of Falling: The Inner Life of the Middle Class.* New York: Pantheon, 1989.

Farr, Cecilia Konchar. *Reading Oprah: How Oprah's Book Club Changed the Way America Reads.* New York: State U of New York P, 2004.

Fuss, Diana. *Identification Papers.* New York: Routledge, 1995.

Galbraith, John Kenneth. *The Affluent Society.* Boston: Houghton, 1958.

Garber, Marjorie. "Compassion." Berlant 15–28.

Illouz, Eva. *Oprah Winfrey and the Glamour of Misery: An Essay on Popular Culture.* New York: Columbia UP, 2003.

Ingram, Penelope. "Racializing Babylon: Settler Whiteness and the 'New Racism.'" *New Literary History* 32 (2001): 159–76.

Jackson, Kenneth T. *Crabgrass Frontier: The Suburbanization of the United States.* New York: Oxford UP, 1985.

Jurca, Catherine. *White Diaspora: The Suburb and the Twentieth-Century American Novel.* Princeton: Princeton UP, 2001.

Lasch, Christopher. *The Culture of Narcissism: American Life in the Age of Diminished Expectations.* New York: Norton, 1978.

Long, Elizabeth. *Book Clubs: Women and the Uses of Reading in Everyday Life.* Chicago: U of Chicago P, 2003.

———. "Textual Interpretation as Collective Action." *Discourse* 14 (1992): 104–30.

Long, Elizabeth, and Janice Radway, "The Book as Mass Commodity: The Audience Perspective." *Book Research Quarterly* 3.1 (1987): 9–30.

Max, D. T. "The Oprah Effect." *New York Times Magazine* 26 Dec. 1999: 36–41.

McDowell, Deborah. "'The Self and the Other': Reading Toni Morrison's *Sula* and the Black Female Text." *Critical Essays on Toni Morrison.* Ed. Nellie Y. McKay. Boston: G.K. Hall, 1988. 77–90.

Mills, C. Wright. *White Collar: The American Middle Classes.* New York: Oxford UP, 1951.

Morrison, Toni. *The Bluest Eye.* New York: Knopf, 1993.

———. *Paradise.* New York: Penguin, 1997.

———. *Playing in the Dark: Whiteness and the Literary Imagination.* Cambridge: Harvard UP, 1992.

"Oprah's Book Club." *The Oprah Winfrey Show.* Harpo Productions, Inc. 26 May 2000.

Pattillo-McCoy, Mary. *Black Picket Fences: Privilege and Peril among the Black Middle Class.* Chicago: U of Chicago P, 1999.

Peck, Janice. "Talk about Racism: Framing a Popular Discourse of Race on *Oprah Winfrey.*" *Cultural Critique* 27 (1994): 89–126.

Radway, Janice. "The Book-of-The-Month-Club and the General Reader: On Uses of 'Serious' Fiction." *Critical Inquiry* 14 (1988): 516–38.

———. *A Feeling for Books: The Book-of-the-Month-Club, Literary Taste, and Middle-Class Desire.* Chapel Hill: U of North Carolina P, 1997.

Riesman, David. *Lonely Crowd: A Study of the Changing American Character.* New Haven, CT: Yale UP, 1950.

Rooney, Kathleen. *Reading with Oprah: The Book Club that Changed America.* Fayetteville: U of Arkansas P, 2005.

Rubin, Joan Shelley. *The Making of Middlebrow Culture.* Chapel Hill: U of North Carolina P, 1997.

Shattuc, Jane M. "The Oprahfication of America: Talk Shows and the Public Sphere." *Television, History, and American Culture.* Ed. Lauren Rabinowitz and Mary Beth Haralovich. Durham, NC: Duke UP, 1999. 168–80.

Spectorsky, A. C. *The Exurbanites.* Philadelphia: Lippincott, 1955.

Squire, Corinne. "Empowering Women? The Oprah Winfrey Show." *Feminist Television Criticism: A Reader.* Ed. Charlotte Brunsdon, Julie D'Acci, and Lynn Spigel. Oxford: Clarendon, 1997. 99–110.

Whyte, William. *The Organization Man.* New York: Simon, 1956.

Wilson, Sherryl. Oprah, *Celebrity, and Formations of Self.* New York: Palgrave, 2003.

Wood, Michael. "Sensations of Loss." *The Aesthetics of Toni Morrison: Speaking the Unspeakable.* Ed. Marc C. Conner. Jackson: U of Mississippi P, 2000. 114–23.

Woodward, Kathleen. "Calculating Compassion." Berlant 59–86.

Young, John. "Toni Morrison, Oprah Winfrey, and Postmodern Popular Audiences." *African American Review* 35 (2001): 181–204.

9

"DID ISABEL ALLENDE WRITE THIS BOOK FOR ME?"

Oprah's Book Club Reads *Daughter of Fortune*

ANA PATRICIA RODRÍGUEZ

> To be totally bicultural was my goal. Why settle for less? The twentieth century was the century of refugees and immigrants; never before had the world witnessed such large numbers of displaced people. My family was part of that diaspora. It is not as bad as it sounds. I thought I could live in Marin County without losing my identity, my background, my language or my beliefs. I could simply keep adding to them.
>
> —Isabel Allende, "Love at First Sight for My California Dream"

On 17 February 2000, Oprah Winfrey announced her book club's next reading selection—*Daughter of Fortune* by Chilean American writer Isabel Allende. A long-standing celebrity writer in her own right, Allende was already well known for her best sellers, including *The House of the Spirits* (*La casa de los espíritus*), *Of Love and Shadows* (*De amor y de sombra*), *Eva Luna* (*Eva Luna*), and *The Stories of Eva Luna* (*Cuentos de Eva Luna*). At the "center of Latin American literature," Allende was unmatched in "her critical and popular reception worldwide" (Jörgensen 128, 143). According to Linda Gould Levine, Allende had long been recognized as "the 'Latin Scheherazade'" because of her storytelling prowess, her personal charisma, and her literary transcendence into popular culture (1). It is not surprising that Oprah Winfrey would select one of Allende's novels for her Book Club. What is surprising, however, is that to date Allende's *Daughter of Fortune* has been the only novel by a U.S. Latina writer to be featured on Oprah's Book Club.[1]

Even more intriguing is that no critic of the Book Club has ever asked, to my knowledge, why U.S. Latina/o ethnic writers have been virtually excluded from the club. This omission is especially telling when Latinos are presently the largest minority in the United States (over forty million people in 2006),[2] and when Latinos/as have produced a significant body of literature, identified by some as a veritable Latino/a literary and cultural *boom*.[3] In 2000, Allende's novel was ripe for the picking by Oprah's Book Club.

With Oprah's endorsement, Allende's *Daughter of Fortune* became an instant best seller in the United States. In his Introduction to *Conversations with Isabel Allende: Revised Edition*, John Rodden explains that following Oprah's announcement of the book as the March 2000 selection,

> Oprah's vast TV audience soon began snapping up Allende's new novel, which rose that week to the no. 1 position on the *New York Times* best-seller list (and shot to the top of the Internet's Amazon.com bookseller list within eight hours). More than a million copies sold during February and March 2000; the novel went on to sell 1.5 million copies in the English edition alone. (34)

Oprah's selection of *Daughter of Fortune* as an OBC pick not only (re)introduced the author and the novel to mainstream readers in the United States, but also inspired Allende to write a sequel, *Portrait in Sepia* (*Retrato en Sepia* 2001), for "many readers, including Oprah herself, had told Allende that they wanted closure to *Daughter of Fortune*" (Rodden 35). Oprah and her readers didn't just welcome Allende to the Club, but rather inducted her into a "national reading project" (Farr 31), laden with "American" values, ideologies, and mythologies. In this chapter, I explore various forces positioning Allende in the culture industry of the Book Club, as well as elements of the novel appealing to Oprah's Book Club readers and addressing dominant U.S. multiculturalist ideologies—namely, the notions of racial and ethnic self-making, uplifting, and integration with a *difference*. Further, I examine how this novel spoke to Oprah's Book Club, and why readers identified with the text, leading Halley Suitt, one of the four guest readers, to ask: "Did Isabelle [sic] Allende write this book for me?" (Letters, oprah.com). Situated at the intersection of cultural traditions, nationalities, and histories, among other things, Allende's *Daughter of Fortune* on Oprah's Book Club could only articulate some of the most pressing issues of our time in regard to immigration, transnationalism, multiculturalism, and the production of Latino/a cultures in the United States.

The Art of Literacy: Oprah's Book Club and Allende

According to Cecilia Konchar Farr, in *Reading Oprah: How Oprah's Book Club Changed the Way America Reads,* Oprah's Book Club is reshaping the reception and consumption of novels and transforming the gendered practice of "social reading" or "group reading" in the United States (54–55). Drawing from research on women's book groups and improvement societies in U.S. women's history, Farr suggests that the democratizing benefits of reading together—promoting critical thinking, making connections, and building community and solidarity (54)—are all potentially redeployed on Oprah's Book Club for readers' edification, self-improvement, and social change (60). Additionally, Kathleen Rooney, in *Reading with Oprah: The Book Club That Changed America,* explains:

> The act of reading [in the United States] has long been venerated—and rightly so—as an autonomous exercise of freedom, imagination, enlightenment, and creativity, one that cultivates benefits not only for the atomized individual but also for society as a whole. Winfrey has proven through her admirably democratizing book club that there are in fact large and largely untapped portions of the population who are willing and eager to interact with literary texts, and through them, with each other. (xiii)

Both Rooney and Farr seem to situate *The Oprah Winfrey Show* and the televised OBC within nation-building projects of literacy dating back to the founding of the United States of America.

In the United States, the democratizing Western tradition of educating and reading has been linked to the master-myths of the *American Adam* claiming, colonizing, and resignifying the new Eden, and the pioneers in their movement westward braving the elements to imprint their presence on the land. Annette Kolodny, in *The Lay of the Land: Metaphor as Experience and History in American Life and Letters,* examines the semiotics of land colonization by the American Adam, who, in taking possession of the "virgin/mother soil" during the U.S. colonial period (22), feminized the American landscape as "nature, not culture" (50), non-European, nonwhite, and uncivilized, hence, opened it for conquest. Out of this colonizing mission would arise the founding mythologies of the United States that naturalized the white pilgrim and settlers' progress through Indian and Mexican territory (Slotkin 1973). In succession, the Louisiana Purchase (1803), the

Mobile Act (1804), the Adams-Onís Treaty (1819), the Treaty of Guadalupe Hidalgo (1848), and the Gadsden Purchase (1853) would bring the Louisiana, Mississippi, and Florida territories and the entire Southwest into the sphere of U.S. expansionism. The Land Law of 1851 and the Homestead Act of 1862 would further legitimize and legalize conquest by U.S. settlers across the "Western Frontier," a movement highly contested by the in situ Mexican and Californio landed class, as represented in María Amparo Ruíz de Burton's novel *The Squatter and the Don* (1885), and in Parts II and III of Allende's *Daughter of Fortune*. In these sections of her novel, Allende reminds us, too, that amid the rush for land and gold in California:

> Racial hostility turned into blind hatred. Mexicans refused to accept the loss of their territory in the war, or to be run off their ranches and the mines. The Chinese bore abuse silently; they did not leave. . . . Thousands of Chileans and Peruvians, who had been the first to arrive when the gold fever blossomed, decide to return to their countries because it wasn't worth pursuing their dreams under such conditions. (*Daughter* 328–29)

In this context of hostile takeover, a culture of vigilantism against Native Americans and Mexicans gained force in the racial hinterlands of the West and Southwest. This scenario of racial violence is most vividly contested by the resistance narrative of the heroic figure of Joaquín Murieta, who makes a fleeting appearance in Allende's novel as the character Joaquín Andieta (*Daughter* 328–30).

Set against this historical backdrop of U.S. western expansion, Allende's *Daughter of Fortune* features two protagonists, Eliza Sommers and Tao Chi'en, who provide insights into the racial history of the United States. Through their eyes, readers witness the exploitation of Mexican, Chilean, and Chinese miners vis-à-vis the Anti-vagrancy and Foreign Miner's laws of the 1850s, as well as the ensuing anti-immigrant violence against "nonwhite" peoples (Takaki 178, 194). After traveling by ship from Chile, Tao Chi'en and Eliza enter the port of San Francisco as "foreigners," one an indentured servant and the other an undocumented stowaway. They join thousands of other newcomers, or "argonauts" as Allende calls them:

> Argonauts [who] came from distant shores: Europeans fleeing wars, plagues, and tyrannies; Americans, ambitious and short-tempered; blacks pursuing freedom; Oregonians and Russians dressed in deer-

skin, like Indians; Mexicans, Chileans, and Peruvians; Australian bandits; starving Chinese peasants who were risking their necks by violating the imperial order against leaving their country. All races flowed together in the muddy alleyways of San Francisco. (*Daughter* 223)

Alone and in the company of Tao Chi'en, Eliza travels through the gold fields of northern California in search of her Chilean lover, Joaquín Andieta. She disguises herself first as a Chinese boy, and then as a Chilean piano player and pastry maker, at times called "Chile Boy" or Elías Andieta. Throughout the novel, she lives among Mexicans, Chinese, Indians, and rogue populations of performers, prostitutes, and convicts. She works as healer's assistant, piano player, and cook, and passes for different ethnicities, races, and genders.

As Elías Andieta, Eliza writes and reads letters for the illiterate miners, and gains deep insights into the lives of others before and after their coming to the United States. As a bilingual entrepreneur in a multilingual land,

Eliza offered her services in English and Spanish; she read the letters and answered them. . . . Some men brought letters for her to read, and she doctored them a little, too, so the pitiful fellow would have the consolation of a few words of kindness. (282)

Indeed, Eliza could be said to have formed her own reading and writing club that allowed her to learn about the harshness of life in California, as when she writes a letter for a Wisconsin miner about to be hung for committing a crime. This particular scene gives Allende the opportunity to allude to the lynching of men "of another race," who were executed amid "the howls of the spectators" (282–83). At key moments in the novel, Allende comments on the social injustices faced by "nonwhite" individuals in California. She describes, for example, the "relentless persecution [that] was waged against the Hispanics" and others (239). Casting its lot with the histories of others—Chinese, Mexicans, African Americans, immigrants, and other "nonwhites"—Allende's novel challenges the notion of the democratizing forces of education and literacy that many U.S. Americans assume as their right and destiny. Literacy and reading have the potential to liberate people, but, as Allende's novel shows, they have also been used to conquer, colonize, and, in the case of the U.S. Southwest, to "Americanize" and acculturate people by force.

As Farr claims, "reading in the United States is, in iconic terms, the way west" (33) and it has served as a way to "teach these others to belong here, to fit in" (33). Literacy has been used to educate others to be "Americans" and it has functioned as a disciplining mechanism whereby ethnic minorities have been (re)made into U.S. American citizens (Macdonald 2004). Although literacy in English almost stamped out other cultural practices, namely, oral traditions in Native American, Asian American, African American, and Latino American cultures on U.S. territory, these traditions survive in signifying oral literature such as *testimonios*, songs, *corridos*, folktales, and oral history, which serve as primary sources for many U.S. ethnic writers. In the hands of Frederick Douglass (black abolitionist), Américo Paredes (Chicano writer, professor, and "dean" of Borderland literature), the women and men who wrote in the Spanish-speaking press throughout the Southwest and Northeast at the turn-of-the-twentieth-century (Kanellos, "A Socio-Historic Study of Hispanic Newspapers in the United States"), and contemporary writers, literacy might be said to serve other critical "democratizing" ends. For them, literacy and reading offered ways to become American while, at the same time, seeking larger liberties and preserving other traditions, cultures, and languages. In this tradition of conflicted "democratizing literacy," Farr situates Oprah's Book Club, through which "Oprah is shaping and advocating cultural democracy in her push to get America reading again" (107). While Book Club readers may be reading to "make their lives better" (Farr 105), they do so in an age of diminishing education, healthcare, and social services, general opportunities, and political and cultural representation for vast segments of the U.S. population. In her shows, Oprah Winfrey, however, craftily weaves personal and social narratives, mixing human-interest stories and celebrity interviews with exposés of some of the most critical issues in the United States today. Her studio and home audience, who "cross class and race boundaries, and . . . feature a multiracial, though largely single-gender audience" (Farr 22–23),[4] are, moreover, exposed to issues of racism, sexism, and homophobia, among other topics.

Read in the light of the extensive popularity and influence of *The Oprah Winfrey Show*, Winfrey's selection of Allende's *Daughter of Fortune* for the Book Club is significant. In their respective book-length studies of Oprah's Book Club, both Farr and Rooney make note of Allende's selection. Rooney identifies Allende as a "highly regarded writer" prior to her appearance on the Book Club (51–52), and Farr points out the novel's literary distinction among the other picks (14, 18), as well as its embedded theme of the American Dream (Farr 65). Farr points out, "The Book Club choices reflect [a multiracial and gender] demographic. Of [Oprah's] first forty-five Book Club books, thirty-five were by women—twenty-four by white North American women, nine by African American women, one by Moroccan Malika Oufkir, and one by Chilean Isabelle Allende" (23). (The other nine or so books are by male writers and have female protagonists or narrators [23]). Read in this context, the selection of Allende's *Daughter of Fortune* for Oprah's Book Club takes on added significance, and thus merits further discussion.

The Global Marketing of Isabel Allende: From Plaza y Janés to HarperCollins

In his review of Allende's *Portrait in Sepia* (*Times Literary Supplement*, 12 Jan. 2001; qtd. in Sokol 90), Ilán Stavans describes Isabel Allende as "a global phenomenon," whose work has been translated into at least twenty-five languages and marketed by major publishing houses of the world. Throughout her writing career, Allende has published her work with prestigious publishers in the United States, Latin America, and Spain, including Plaza y Janés, which was purchased in the 1990s by Random House, a subsidiary of the European Union's Bertelsmann Corporation. Presently with Random House, Allende continues to publish English translations of her first books, including *The House of the Spirits, Eva Luna, The Stories of Eva Luna, Of Love and Shadows,*[5] whose Spanish originals continue to be published under the Plaza y Janés imprint. Before gaining endorsement by Oprah's Book Club, Allende's books, especially those in Spanish, were mass-media marketing successes, benefiting from trends in the globalization of the publishing industry as noted by literary critic Jill Robbins.[6]

Because of her mass-market cachet, some critics have harshly and hastily critiqued the literary merit of Allende's work. According to Stavans, who at times has commented positively on Allende's work and has interviewed her on several occasions (Rodden 87–99):

Allende is the queen of melodrama, a form of oversentimentalized art, popular the world over. Bernard Shaw once cautioned never to underestimate what the public will buy. Her novels are derivative, uninspiring to me, but not to millions of people, whose emotions she massages in novel after novel. Allende has built an audience by means of a shrewd literary agent in Barcelona, first rate—and well-paid—translators, and the undefeatable formula: *repeat, repeat, repeat.* (Stavans qtd. in Sokol 90)

While Stavans and other critics may find Allende's work to be derivative and formulaic in terms of plot, characterization, theme, style, and language (Jörgensen 142), still others discover significant metaphoric and narrative parallels within and between her texts (Rivero 91–111). Her novels are said to have engaged intertextually with Gabriel García Márquez, Pablo Neruda, and other Latin American writers (Coddou 100). In the United States, Allende has been compared to Amy Tan, Barbara Kingsolver, Alice Walker, and Louise Erdrich, all of whom Allende claims as her U.S. literary "sisterhood" (Jaggi). Indeed, Allende's marketability resides in her ability to appeal to varied reception audiences in Latin America, Europe, the United States, and elsewhere. What made possible Allende's selection for OBC was precisely her wide appeal to diverse readers.

Even before Oprah's Book Club, the early marketing success of Allende's first novels established her as a renowned Latin American writer. Her first books published in Spanish by Plaza y Janés introduced Allende to international readers, who were interested in the political history of Latin America, the writing of Latin American political exiles, and Latin American feminisms and women's narratives. She was first read as a Latin American writer of popular and political literature, and more recently as a U.S. Latina ethnic writer. Dating back to her first novel, *House of the Spirits*, Allende's works have been translated into English, securing a place for her in world literature. In his discussion of the translation of Latin American literature to English, Stavans makes the assertion that, "as the lingua franca today, the English language is the ticket to universalism. No writer with aspirations of a global reach can afford to ignore it . . . and also, be ignored by it" (Stavans qtd. in Sokol 91). Allende did not ignore her publishing potential in English, and consequently opened new venues for her work in translation.

In particular two of Allende's texts—*El plan infinito* (1991; *The Infinite Plan* 1993) and *Paula* (1994; *Paula* 1995)—mark a forking path in her writing career. These texts in particular establish Allende as a Latina writer of best sellers in the United States. Based on the life of her second husband, William Gordon, Allende's *The Infinite Plan* tells the story of an Anglo American man growing up in the Mexican American borderlands. Written during the year that her daughter lay in a coma, *Paula* is a personal memoir ruminating on the themes of death, mourning, and renewal, which appeal to wide readerships in Latin America, the United States, and Europe. After *The Infinite Plan* and *Paula*, Allende's new books were published almost simultaneously in English and Spanish by HarperCollins, a subsidiary of News Corporation, which also owns the rights to the HarperCollins Rayo imprint with exclusive focus on Latino/a publications.[7] Allende's publications with HarperCollins include *Aphrodite: A Memoir of the Senses* (1998), *Daughter of Fortune* (1999), *Portrait in Sepia: A Novel* (2001), *My Invented Country: A Nostalgic Journey Through Chile* (2003), *El Zorro* (2005), *Ines of My Soul* (2006), and a series of young adult adventure narratives. The latter includes *City of Beasts* (*Ciudad de las bestias* 2002), *Kingdom of the Golden Dragon* (*El reino del Dragón de Oro* 2003), and *Forest of the Pygmies* (*Bosque de los Pigmeos* 2004).

The publication of Allende's novels also coincides with the cultural boom of Latino/a literature in the United States in the 1990s. During the 1980s and 1990s, a great number of texts by U.S. Latino/a writers was published by mainstream presses, including Oscar Hijuelos's *The Mambo Kings Play Songs of Love* (1989; Pulitzer Prize 1990), Sandra Cisneros's *The House on Mango Street* (1984) and *Woman Hollering Creek and Other Stories* (1991), Julia Alvarez's *How the García Girls Lost Their Accent* (1992), Cristina García's *Dreaming in Cuban* (1992), Ana Castillo's *So Far from God* (1993), to name only a few texts. Anthologies like *Iguana Dreams: New Latino Fiction* (1992), *Growing Up Latino: Memoirs and Stories* (1993), and other collections also brought exposure to Latina/o writers in the mainstream, prompting Earl Shorris, in *Latinos: A Biography of the People* (1992), to claim that with these publications, "Latinos now have a body of work, a literary mirror in which to see themselves, and the images in the mirror grow more interesting to the rest of the society as they represent an increasingly large segment of the population" (395). The anthologies and novels associated with the U.S. Latino/a literary boom seemed to confirm what Nicolás Kanellos, long-time editor of Arte Público Press, had predicted. In his introduction to *Short Fiction by Hispanic Writers of the United States* (1993), Kanellos speculated that Latino/a literature would have its day because it was "an esthetic and epistemological experiment that is preparing the United States for the multicultural, hemispheric reality of the next century" (10).

Indeed, U.S. Latino/a literature has been pushed back to include texts produced in what is now the United States ever since the Spanish conquest of North America in the sixteenth century, as well as those currently being published. As Allende explains: "With Chile and California in my mind, I wrote *Daughter of Fortune* and *Portrait in Sepia*, books in which the characters travel back and forth between my countries" (*My Invented Country* 196). Her novels, as we will see, travel across space and time to speak to contemporary audiences. Her novels, moreover, are published at a significant transnational and *transtemporal* juncture of cultural traditions, histories, and reading markets in the Americas, all "flow[ing] together in the muddy alleyways of San Francisco" (*Daughter* 223), an allusion that refers not only to the historical context of the novel, but also to the contemporary moment of OBC. At this junction, Allende can be read as a transnational literary phenomena—a Chilean-born, U.S. immigrant/ethnic writer, or rather a U.S. Latina author speaking to multiple reading publics gathered around Oprah's couch.

Reading *Daughter of Fortune* Through the Lens of Oprah's Book Club

In many ways, *Daughter of Fortune* was Allende's *comeback* novel after the tragic death of her daughter, Paula Frías, in 1992, and after her transformation into a U.S. Latina writer. Grieving and unable to write fiction, she wrote a best-selling (nonfiction) memoir titled *Paula*, as well as another text of "recovery," *Aphrodite: A Memoir of the Senses*, both of which sold well in English and Spanish versions (Rodden 30). According to Allende, *Aphrodite* "helped her rediscover a capacity to live in the present" (Rodden 29) and to return to one of her greatest passions—novel writing. "In October, having entered the 'light,' Allende completed her sixth novel, *Daughter of Fortune*" (Rodden 30), the story of a California heroine that much paralleled Allende's personal and public writer's life. As Rodden writes,

> Indeed, *Daughter of Fortune* represented an advanced stage in Allende's remarkable program of writing as self-therapy. Allende looked forward to the new millennium and renewed her life by looking backward to the nineteenth century and writing a bildungsroman about a Victorian maiden—and also by looking backward on her own life: the autobiographical resonances of the new novel are manifold. In fact, despite the obvious plot differences between the fortunes of the novel's heroine and Allende's own, it is no exaggeration to call *Daughter of Fortune* another memoir, this time in the form of a historical romance that broadly reinvents Allende's own youth. (31)

With its autobiographical overtones, its woman-centered (if not feminist) narrative of self-discovery, love, and empowerment, its quest for identity and freedom, and its attention to social issues such as those of gender, race, ethnicity, and immigration in U.S. society, Allende's *Daughter of Fortune* was well received by Oprah's Book Club. In Allende's novel, Oprah's readers and public found an engaging story line, covering "love, motherhood, friendship, self-discovery, overcoming adversity, negotiating differences," among other things, and written "by, about, and for women" (Farr 23). According to Farr, "[Oprah's books] aim for an audience that looks like Oprah's audience—women of all colors, classes, ages, and shapes, women who read and those who just picked up a novel for the first time in years" (23). Allende's *Daughter* was a love match for Oprah's Book Club readers seeking an American story of a female coming of age in the present and past Wild West. On the Book Club, Allende found ideal readers that elsewhere she has identified as being overwhelmingly young, female, and "benevolent" (Coddou 129), or, better said, empathic readers who identify with the characters and themes of the novel (Farr 47).[8]

Representing Oprah's ideal readership, four preselected female guest readers and discussants shared preliminary opinions and comments about the novel in the "Letter" section at oprah.com. On 28 March 2000, they appeared on *The Oprah Winfrey Show* for a book-fest with Oprah and Allende. Their initial letters to Oprah expressed how *Daughter of Fortune* cast group members under its spell. Carol Maillard, one of the television discussants, was "touched [by the book] in so many ways" and identified "with so many of the characters" (Letters, oprah.com). Cynthia Greenlee, a twenty-five-year-old African American graduate student of journalism and immigration at the University of North Carolina, was captivated by the book's combined "element of fantasy" and "real-life concerns of people" (Letters, oprah.com). Guadalupe "Lupe" Pfaff, a white Panamanian American woman born into the "ancient landed aristocracy" of her homeland, as she puts it, adopted a line from the novel as her "personal philosophy in life," reiterating "'what matters is what you do in this world, not how you come into it'" (Cf. Allende, *Daughter* 5). Finally, Halley Suitt, a Los Angeles-based businesswoman married to a Chinese man and raising biracial children, asked, "Did Isabelle [sic] Allende write this book for me?" Suitt's interrogative suggests that the appeal of the novel lies not only in its personal relevance to the lives of its readers, but also in its contemporary cultural relevance, for, as Suitt says, "it's such a wink to what's going on in California right now" (Letters, oprah.com). Indeed, historical fiction is known to be as much about the past as it is about the present.

Following genre conventions associated with historical novels, *Daughter of Fortune* is about past and present constructions of multiracial and interethnic societies in the United States. Updating the "national romance," as defined by Doris Sommer in *Foundational Fictions: The National Romances of Latin America* (1991), *Daughter of Fortune* uses the metaphor of erotic and romantic coupling to represent larger issues of national history, politics, and social and racial engineering. In national romances, the romantic couple represents different socioeconomic, racial, and/or ethnic groups, political agendas, and competing visions of the nation. Allende's *Daughter of Fortune* can be read as a contemporary revisioning of Latin American nineteenth-century national romances, but set in the current context of the United States or, more specifically, northern California, where Asian Americans and Latino Americans are redefining and reconfiguring national identity.⁹ It is telling that the protagonists and romantic partners in Allende's novel are Tao Chi'en and Eliza Sommers, a Chinese American man and a Latino American woman, read in light of today's ethnic categories.

The romantic family plot of the novel begins as the infant Eliza Sommers is mysteriously found in a basket on the doorstep of a British expatriate family living in Chile. Adopted by the Sommers family, Eliza grows up in a Victorian household run by a spinster, Miss Rose, and her unmarried brother, Jeremy. No one knows Eliza's true parentage, although by the middle of the novel readers discover that she is the illegitimate daughter of Miss Rose's older brother, the seafaring John Sommers and an unidentified Chilean woman (*Daughter* 256–58). By the time of this revelation, however, Eliza has slept with and has been impregnated by a young Chilean revolutionary named Joaquín Andieta, who flees to the California gold fields. In pursuit of Andieta, Eliza has herself stowed away in a ship traveling to San Francisco with the help of a Chinese medicine man and ship cook, Tao Chi'en. Disguised as a boy, Eliza subsequently roams "the golden landscape of California," looking unsuccessfully for Andieta, yet finding that "she was flying free, like a condor," shedding her "armor of good manners and conventions," and repeatedly remaking herself (275–76).

Like the gold miners (all men), Eliza learns that she can be the master of her destiny (277), as California unfolds before her like "a blank page; here I can start life anew and become the person I want" (280). In a disguised bildungsroman of sorts, she becomes a self-willed, hardworking individual who breaks all social conventions when she eventually marries her soul mate, Tao Chi'en. Somehow, all along, she had known that she and Tao Chi'en "one day . . . will be together again" (280). The narrative brings to the fore the questions posed by many women, past and present: Love or freedom? Either, or? Why not both? In the novel, Eliza and Tao Chi'en's coupling challenges sociohistorical conventions prohibiting interracial relationships in the nine-teenth century (Pan 1990; Yung 1986), thus announcing the creation of present-day hybrid interracial and interethnic communities. The voice of the present-future, Tao Chi'en affirms, "to white people I am just a revolting Chinese pagan, and Eliza is a greaser" (363). Together, however, "their simi-larities had erased differences of race" (363); thus, the novel proposes a cou-pling and interracial national identity for the Americas, north and south.

The last chapter of the novel, titled "An Unusual Pair," closes with Tao Chi'en and Eliza living together and working jointly in the underground movement to rescue Chinese prostitutes from the Chinatown brothels of San Francisco (367). In this rescue narrative, allusions are made to the sexual abuse and exploitation of immigrant sex laborers, which continue to this day and are recurrent topics on *The Oprah Winfrey Show*. By the end of the novel, Eliza gives up her useless search for her ex-lover Andieta, learns "the rudiments of Chinese necessary for communicating on an elementary level," and works with Tao Chi'en to provide medical care for the indigent and marginalized of Chinatown (368). Their story is retold in the seclude, *Portrait in Sepia*, by their mixed-race, transnational granddaughter, Aurora del Valle (Lin Mei), who although raised as a child by Eliza and Tao Chi'en in San Francisco, lives most of her life in Chile. Forming a trilogy, the nar-rative that begins in Chile and travels to California with *Daughter of For-tune*, and returns to Chile in *Portrait in Sepia*, closes with the preclude that started it all—*The House of the Spirits*. Read as a trilogy, Allende's *Daughter of Fortune*, *Portrait in Sepia*, and *The House of the Spirits* weave national (hi)stories into a transnational, interracial romance plot that acutely appealed to Oprah's readers.

In their conversations, Oprah's four guest readers were captivated by Allende's romantic plot. In fact, on the day of the airing the "discussion dinner with the author" video clip and general discussion of *Daughter of For-tune* with the audience, the show was literally framed by the topic: "The crazy things people do for love" (*Oprah Winfrey Show* Archives for 28 March 2000; oprah.com). On the air, Oprah introduced Allende's novel as the story "about one young woman's bold adventure." In the dinner video clip with Allende, the discussion focused on the topics of women's love, passion, courage, and self-fulfillment, as well as Allende's alleged inspired romantic writing process. Indeed, Allende claims that as she wrote the book, "some-how [the characters like spirits] just emerged from someplace" (Transcript of Past Shows, oprah.com). Identifying with Eliza's passionate search for iden-tity, independence, and empowerment as a woman, Oprah seemed to insist in her conversation with Allende that a main theme of the novel was the pursuit of happiness not only as a feminine pursuit, but also as "a very American thing." The transcript from the televised exchange between Allende and Oprah went as follows:

> ISABEL: It's a very American thing, this right to search for happiness that is in the Constitution. What are we talking about here? Right to be happy? Life is about both. It's about being happy and not being happy. It's about terrible pain and great joy—and you can't have one without the other.
>
> OPRAH: You're right. It's a very Americanized feeling and philosophy that you're just supposed to be happy. I'm telling you, all the time I do shows where women say, "I just want to be happy. I just want to be happy."[10]

In the context of Allende's novel, Oprah insists that women's pursuit of happiness vis-à-vis romantic love fulfills an American dream, ethos, and destiny, echoing in fashion the U.S. Declaration of Independence. Acknowledging Oprah's singular American reading while also complicating it, Allende adds that, at least for her, "the book is not [just] about the search for love [= happiness]. It's about freedom. It's about choices." In Allende's book, pain, abandonment, crises, and contradictions accompany happiness, love, relationships, and freedom. Full of contradictions, tensions, and choices, *Daughter of Fortune* is thus an "American" novel, for it is about becoming "American" and assimilating the images that U.S. Americans have of themselves as free, happy, loving, courageous, and empowered people, who overcome the predicaments of the modern world. As represented in the novel, Eliza and Tao Chi'en are models of this American destiny set in the context of 1850s San Francisco, where on learning to love one another across differences, they overcome obstacles, gain freedom, and are "better off" than in their homelands (*Daughter* 364).

An opportune pick for Oprah's Book Club, *Daughter of Fortune* not only fulfilled the affective reading criteria and expectations of an ideal Book Club readership, but it also affirmed romantic narrative conventions and ideals, mainly that love conquers all—in the United States. Despite all odds, Tao Chi'en and Eliza Sommers choose to love one another across racial lines, promising an interracial marriage of freedom, happiness, and good fortune in the diverse social context of the United States. Indeed, Halley Suitt, in her letter, explains that the novel is really about the "vital brew of diversity" and "the lovely ying and yang balance of Male, Female, Asian, Hispanic, Indian, Black and White and all other races together to create this new world" (Letters, oprah.com). A declared postfeminist businesswoman married to a Chinese man, raising a Chinese American child, and starting her own business in the network industry, Suitt talks candidly about diversity as a "new start-up business," bringing about "a revolution of tolerance and opportunity" and possibilities of self-reinvention. She celebrates Allende's novel for offering "strong, powerful women AND men choosing the freedom to reinvent themselves over and over again, jumping barriers of race, gender, family, class, poverty, you name it" (Letters, oprah.com).

Along these lines, Carol Maillard (another of the guest readers), in her letter, refers to the "melting pot" theory of multicultural identity, which she timidly calls into question at various points. She explains that the novel represents "what it is/was to be disenfranchised in this country particularly during that time of history." (Her imprecise use of verb tenses is significant.) Although she identifies the "melting pot" as a cliché and suggests that "under that pot is a great deal of fire and heat working the ingredients and the pot is always being stirred," Maillard situates racism as part of U.S. past history and as a misguided series of "concessions, intimidations, lies and deceit" (Letters, oprah.com). In her comments, Maillard identifies moreover with "this land of ours" and "our history" as "Americans." Clearly, she is troubled by a history of racial and ethnic injustices in the United States, but she neutralizes her critique with the historical cliché: "Those that do not embrace and acknowledge history will be doomed to repeat it" (Letters, oprah.com).

Perhaps the most personally revealing of the four guest readers is Guadalupe Pfaff, a privileged, educated Panamanian woman married to a U.S. military man (from the former Canal Zone) now living in the United States. In her letter to Oprah, Pfaff draws parallels between her life and Eliza's, including being raised in "two opposing cultures," leaving her homeland, marrying for love, adapting to U.S. culture, and overcoming cultural obstacles. Pfaff claims that she has taken as her own mantra a line spoken by Tao Chi'en: "What matters is what you do in this world, not how you come into it" (*Daughter* 5). Re-cited by Pfaff, this maxim seems to serve as an apology for socioeconomic privilege, deferring to the ideology of meritocracy, individual uplifting, and self-making. Pfaff recalls her father saying to her that "a man could do and accomplish anything he wanted if he was smart, wanted it enough, and worked hard to achieve his goals. Education was the key . . . for men" (Letters, oprah.com). The words of Pfaff's father seem consequently to shape and condition her personal identification with Eliza, who "rebelled and forged her own path and destiny" (Letters, oprah.com).

Finally, the fourth woman reader of *Daughter of Fortune*, Cynthia Green-lee (an African American graduate student at the University of North Car-olina) reads beyond the romantic narrative: She is not sure that she would give up her career path to follow her boyfriend. In her analysis, Greenlee addresses what she considers to be the most important themes in the novel, among them, historical memory, immigration, acculturation, and interracial and interethnic relations. Greenlee situates these issues in the present moment. She makes note of the current anti-immigrant movement and the resurgence of Ku Klux Klan activity throughout the United States. According to Greenlee, the novel speaks to us about the condition of immigration today: "The 'becoming,' as I call it, is really the most important [thing], for though immigrants are always tied to home and the myth of home, they occupy a new reality when they step foot on foreign soil" (Letters, oprah.com).

In her reading of the novel, Greenlee draws significant connections between the practices of racism experienced by African Americans, Asian Americans, Latinos, and others. She explains,

> I have a newfound appreciation for how Asians and Latin Americans shed blood, sweat and tears—as much as my black ancestors. Some-times, people of different ancestries seem to quibble and—yes—even fight over who has seemed to suffer the most. *Daughter of Fortune*, as a work of fiction, really put those questions to rest for me. (Letters, oprah.com)

In her critical assessment of the book, Greenlee reads beyond the dominant narrative of multiculturalism (getting along) and draws parallels between the experiences of ethnic groups, much like Ronald Takaki (1993), Tomás Alma-guer (1994), Gloria Anzaldúa (1990, 2002), and other scholars of critical interethnic and interracial relations have done in their respective works. Finally, in what to me is a key statement, Greenlee deconstructs the tenets of multiculturalist ideology and historical revisionism in the United States, concluding that:

> This was not a history I learned in school; it was a history I sought, reading books about Japanese women who were also sold into bondage overseas or the black cowboys. Reading *Daughter of Fortune*

made me pause and think—did this happen? Did this happen the way I heard it? Who didn't I hear? Allende does a wonderful job explaining why people migrate, even those cultural reasons that are difficult to discuss, and not belittling them or their places of origins. Honestly, before when I thought of the Chinese in the frontier, the image was not flattering; it comes from the "The Wild, Wild West." You know, the show with the American spy who wore tight, Spanish-style pants and the shuffling, subservient Chinese manservant with a long braid and a limited vocabulary. (Letters, oprah.com)

In the end, Greenlee demonstrates that a text of popular fiction like Allende's *Daughter of Fortune* may be read meta-reflectively, combining empathy, personal identification, and critical inquiry. Seeking other U.S. histories and using other interpretative frameworks, Greenlee interrogates her own naturalized and hegemonic reading practices, as she asks herself: "Did this happen the way I heard it? Who didn't I hear?" Greenlee's critical reading of Allende' novel demonstrates, thus, that it is possible to read with and beyond the Oprah's Book Club reading schema. As we have seen, the four guest readers of *Daughter of Fortune*, each in their own turn, represent different Oprah's Book Club reading practices and positions, from empathic to more critical ways of engaging with texts. They identified with the book on key terms—love, freedom, self-making, and the construction of multicultural, if not multiracial societies, in the United States. In her critical comments, however, reader Greenlee used Allende's book to interrogate romantic and transparent notions of U.S. multicultural society, which *The Oprah Winfrey Show* and the Book Club seem to promote.

Conclusions

In her article titled "This Is Your Book: Marketing America to Itself," Lori Ween argues that "the 'original text' of a novel should not be seen as a pure, untouched document that is corrupted or changed by the publishing industry and marketing schema" (Ween 91). According to Ween, an "original text" like *Daughter of Fortune* under the lens of OBC becomes itself "another layer of meaning that is influenced by the demands and desires of cultural norms" (91). Selected and read by Oprah's Book Club, Allende's *Daughter of Fortune* was successively reshaped for consumption by Oprah's readers through the packaging, marketing, collective reading, and discussions of *Daughter of Fortune* on the Book Club. Although Ween does not study the Book Club explicitly as a *paratext* (following the work of Gerard Genette),[11] her analysis of the function of literary reviews could be applied to the Book Club. Ween suggests that book "reviews are often the first access the larger public has to an educated opinion of what they should be reading and enjoying and how they should be reading it" (97).

Today, because of Oprah Winfrey's mega-media persona, power, and influence, Oprah's Book Club may be the first exposure to fiction and nonfiction for many potential readers. Thus, it would be safe to say that, like book reviews, a *paratext* like Oprah's Book Club reaches a greater public and shapes more extensively "public opinion" of a book—even before it is read. (For many, the emblematic "O" on a book cover verifies and certifies the readability of an Oprah book.) In the case of Oprah's Book Club, the selection, framing, and discussion of books shape public opinion via public broadcasts. When the televised discussions of Allende's *Daughter of Fortune* endorsed love, freedom, and transformation as American destiny or good fortune, the Book Club imposed a standard reading schema on Allende's novel, as well as (re)produced "image[s] of ethnicity and, further, of Americanness for its audiences" (Ween 91). As I have shown in my analysis of the four guest readers' letters and live discussions of Allende's *Daughter of Fortune*, Oprah's Book Club generated dominant ideologies of race, ethnicity, class, gender—in sum, *difference*—as expressed in multiple references to the melting pot, social uplifting, individual remaking, and cultural hybridization.

By analyzing discussants' commentaries against my own close readings of the novel, I have situated the Oprah's Book Club reading of *Daughter of Fortune* within a larger critical "multicultural history" of the United States, or what Ronald Takaki has called the "imbricated histories" of Latinos/as, African Americans, Asian Americans, and others. The characters of the novel—Eliza Sommers, Tao Chi'en, Joaquín Andieta, and others—speak to the cultural anxieties of living in the United States, then and now. Oprah Winfrey's selection of Allende's novel for her Book Club activated and negotiated points of identification based on multicultural self-images of the United States. In Oprah's studio, *Daughter of Fortune* became a bookmark for discussing the quest for self-made fortunes, the place of (new) immigrants in a transnational era, and the right of *everywoman* to cross every mountain, if not every border, in pursuit of happiness, independence, and freedom. In the end, perhaps Isabel Allende *did* write *Daughter of Fortune* for Halley Suitt and the diverse multicultural readers of Oprah's Book Club.

Notes

1. In April 2004, during the second run of Oprah's Book Club, *One Hundred Years of Solitude* by Gabriel García Márquez became the only other Latin American novel to be read by the Book Club.

2. For up-to-date Hispanic population statistics, see tables compiled by the U.S. Census Bureau, at the Web site http://factfinder.census.gov/home/en/pldata.html.

3. Some scholars see this boom as part and parcel of market forces shaping cultural consumption practices in the United States (Campos 2001; Dávila 2001).

4. Still, Farr admits that Oprah's audience is "a largely white audience in an industry dominated by white writers" (22).

5. See the Random House Web site http://www.randomhouse.com.

6. In "Neocolonialism, Neoliberalism, and National Identities: The Spanish Publishing Crisis and the Marketing of Central America," Jill Robbins examines the globalization of the publishing industry in Spain. According to Robbins, a case in point is "the purchase of important publishers like Lumen and Plaza y Janés by Random House," which in turn is owned by the European conglomerate Bertelsmann. Originally published by Plaza y Janés, in this merger, Isabel Allende's books are now published on a global scale by Random House. For writers like Allende, opportunities have opened up in the global book industry, while for a larger number of Latin American regional and local writers, the possibilities of publishing their works have been greatly diminished.

7. The Web site for the HaperCollins Rayo imprint states, "Rayo publishes books that embody the diversity within the Latino community, in both English and Spanish-language editions, connecting culture with thought, and invigorating tradition with spirit." No doubt the success of Isabel Allende, for whom HarperCollins lists no less than fifty-three texts, has contributed to the publishers' interest in the U.S. Latino/a reading market. Other Latino/a authors listed include Rudolfo Anaya, Carolina Garcia Aguilera, Yxta Maya Murray, Jorge Ramos, Esmeralda Santiago, Ilán Stavans, Victor Villasenor, and Alberto Fuguet, among others.

8. Farr suggests that Oprah's ideal reading strategy on Oprah's Book Club, like the viewing of her show, is generally one of affect, empathy, inspiration, experience, and identification, sometimes reaching reflective or critical levels, but not necessarily meta-reflective ones (47–50). The modus operandi of Oprah's Book Club, according to Farr, is that "reading is about the effort to understand" (44), in most cases oneself, one's world, and the social issues that affect one. "One" is key in this discussion. For Oprah's Book Club, reading is transformative at the level of the individual who seeks self-improvement. Oprah's Book Club social reading may lead to larger social transformations; however, as I see it, reading with the Book Club is not

about resistance, revolution, "oppositional consciousness," or the interrogation and transformation of systemic inequities in the United States, as advocated by ethnic writers with social justice agendas, particularly those identified with women of color feminisms (i.e., Audre Lorde, Alice Walker, Gloria Anzaldúa, Chela Sandoval, et al.). That is another story. Hence, the leading questions asked of and by almost all Oprah's Book Club readers have been, "Did you like this book?" "What did like you like about it?," almost inevitably triggering a singular reader response: "'I identified with' the setting, characters, situation, or 'I responded personally' to the main character" (Farr 41). In literary criticism, this would be called the psychological or affective approach, only one of many possible receptions that could serve as a starting point for more critical readings of any text. Academic "classroom" discussions and analyses of literature, on the other hand, "focus almost exclusively on reflective, intellectual approaches" (45). The ideal would be to integrate and channel these modes into what Farr calls a "hybrid approach to reading" (45).

9. In 2000, the U.S. Census Bureau reported the population of San Francisco County at 776,733 persons, of whom approximately 50% are non-Hispanic whites, 31% are Asian, 14% are Latinos, 8% are African Americans, 4% are Native Americans, .5% are Hawaiian or other Pacific Islander, 7% other races, and almost 4% are multiracial. See tables with state population totals at the website for the U.S. Census Bureau, on the Web site http://factfinder.census.gov.

10. See transcripts of past shows, oprah.com.

11. The literary critic Gerard Genette identifies as "paratexts" all those devices and conventions that "enable a text to become a book and to be offered as such to its readers and, more generally, to the public" (1). Further, "peritexts" would include those devices such as book covers, forewords, illustrations, typeface, pocket-size and/or other formats, review inserts, and special series or imprints, which are generally used by publishing houses for the purpose of selling texts (16–36). The Oprah's Book Club with its emblematic "O" printed on selected books would fall into the category of "peritexts."

Works Cited

Allende, Isabel. *Daughter of Fortune.* Trans. Margaret Sayers Peden. New York: Perennial/HarperCollins, 1999.

———. *Portrait in Sepia.* Trans. Margaret Sayers Peden. New York: Perennial/HarperCollins, 2001.

———. *My Invented Country: A Nostalgic Journey Through Chile.* Trans. Margaret Sayers Peden. New York: HarperCollins, 2003.

———. "Love at First Sight for My California Dream." *Guardian Unlimited, The Guardian Weekly,* 10 Nov. 2002. 19 Dec. 2006. http://books.guardian.co.uk.

Almaguer, Tomás. *Racial Fault Lines: The Historical Origins of White Supremacy in California.* Berkeley and Los Angeles: U of California P, 1994.

Anzaldúa, Gloria, ed. *Making Face, Making Soul / Haciendo Caras: Creative and Critical Perspectives by Feminists of Color.* San Francisco: Aunte Lute Books, 1990.

Anzaldúa, Gloria, and analouise keating, eds. *this bridge we call home: radical visions for transformation.* New York: Routledge, 2000.

Campos, Javier. Rev. of *Escritores latinos en los Estados Unidos,* ed. Alberto Fuguet and Pablo Paz-Soldán. *Ventana Abierta* 3.10 (2001): 81–85.

Dávila, Arlene. *Latinos Inc.: The Marketing and Making of a People.* Berkeley and Los Angeles: U of Berkeley P, 2001.

Coddou, Marcelo. *Isabel Allende: Hija de la Fortuna, rediagramación fronteriza del saber histórico.* Valparaíso, Chile: Universidad de Playa Ancha Editorial, 2001.

Farr, Cecilia Konchar. *Reading Oprah: How Oprah's Book Club Changed the Way America Reads.* Albany: State U of New York P, 2004.

Jaggi, Maya. "The Guardian Profile: Isabel Allende, A View From the Bridge." *Guardian Unlimited, The Weekly Guardian* 5 Feb. 2000. 19 Dec. 2006. http://books.guardian.co.uk.

Jörgensen, Beth. E. " 'Un puñado de críticos': Navigating the Critical Readings of Isabel Allende's Work." *Isabel Allende Today: An Anthology of Essays.* Ed. Rosemary G. Feal and Yvette E. Miller. Pittsburgh: Latin American Review P, 2002. 128–46.

Kanellos, Nicolás. "A Socio-Historic Study of Hispanic Newspapers in the United States." *Recovering the U.S. Hispanic Literary Heritage.* Ed. Ramón Gutiérrez and Genaro Padilla. Houston: Arte Público P, 1993. 107–28.

———. Introduction. *Short Fiction by Hispanic Writers of the United States.* Houston: Arte Público P, 1993.

Kolodny, Annette. *The Lay of the Land: Metaphor as Experience and History in American Life and Letters.* Chapel Hill: U of North Carolina P, 1975.

Levine, Linda Gould. "Weaving Life Into Fiction." *Isabel Allende Today: An Anthology of Essays.* Ed. Rosemary G. Feal and Yvette E. Miller. Pittsburgh: Latin American Review P, 2002. 1–28.

Macdonald, Victoria-María, ed. *Latino Education in the United States: A Narrated History from 1513–2000.* New York: Palgrave, 2004.

oprah.com. *Daughter of Fortune.* 19 Dec. 2006.

———. Isabel Allende, "Exclusive Essay." 19 Dec. 2006

———. "Finding Freedom Through Writing." 19 Dec. 2006.

———. *Letters.* 19 Dec. 2006

———. Transcript of Past Shows, OBC–Allende. 19 Dec. 2006

Pan, Lynn. *Sons of the Yellow Emperor: A History of the Chinese Diaspora.* Boston: Little, Brown, 1990.

Rivero, Eliana. "Of Trilogies and Genealogies: *Daughter of Fortune* and *Portrait in Sepia.*" *Isabel Allende Today: An Anthology of Essays.* Ed. Rosemary G. Feal and Yvette E. Miller. Pittsburgh: Latin American Review P, 2002. 91–111.

Robbins, Jill. "Neocolonialism, Neoliberalism, and National Identities: The Spanish Publishing Crisis and the Marketing of Central America." *Istmo 8* (2004), 19 Dec. 2006 http://www.denison.edu.

Rodden, John, ed. *Conversations with Isabel Allende: Revised Edition.* Austin: U of Texas P, 2004.

Rooney, Kathleen. *Reading with Oprah: The Book Club That Changed America.* Fayetteville: U of Arkansas P, 2005.

Ruiz de Burton, María Amparo. *The Squatter and the Don.* 1885. Ed. Rosaura Sánchez and Beatrice Pita. Houston: Arte Público Press, 1992.

Shorris, Earl. *Latinos: A Biography of the People.* New York: W.W. Norton, 1992.

Slotkin, Richard. *Regeneration through Violence: The Mythology of the American Frontier, 1600–1860.* Middletown: Wesleyan UP, 1973.

Sokol, Neal. *Ilán Stavans: Eight Conversations.* Madison: U of Wisconsin P, 2004.

Sommer, Doris. *Foundational Fictions: The National Romances of Latin America.* Berkeley and Los Angeles: U of California P, 1991.

Stavans, Ilán. "Beginnings: Interview with Ilán Stavans." *Conversations with Isabel Allende: Revised Edition.* Ed. John Rodden. Austin: U of Texas P, 2004. 87–99.

Takaki, Ronald. *A Different Mirror: A History of Multicultural America.* Boston: Little, Brown, 1993.

U.S. Census Bureau. 19 Dec. 2006 http://factfinder.census.gov/home/en/pldata.html.

Ween, Lori. "This Is Your Book: Marketing America to Itself." *PMLA* 118.1 (Jan. 2003): 90–102.

Yung, Judy. *Chinese Women of America: A Pictorial History.* Seattle and London: U of Washington P, 1986.

10

THE TROUBLE WITH HAPPY ENDINGS

Conflicting Narratives in Oprah's Book Club

KELLEY PENFIELD LEWIS

*O**prah* is a loaded sign in American popular culture. The word is more than a name; it refers to not only the individual successful business-woman Oprah Winfrey, but also to a carefully designed and highly influential cultural construction that reaches a mass audience daily via an array of entertainment, educational, and merchandising projects. The term alone, *Oprah,* evokes a powerful narrative that embodies a specific set of values. As television viewers and pop culture consumers, we are aware of an identifiable story that accompanies the word "Oprah" and is always implicit in her presence, her endorsement. Recent critical attention that has focused on the "myth" or "legend" that is Oprah can help us to explore the shape and nature of the Oprah narrative and interrogate how it functions as a text and is read by her audience, both as a discrete entity and as a filter through which other texts are viewed. In the case of Oprah's Book Club, especially in its earliest incarnation as a televised book discussion, selected books contend with the Oprah narrative; readers must read through the template proposed by Oprah in order to access the text. Oprah's personal narrative overlays the Book Club Selection, creating a kind of palimpsest that potentially obscures reader response. Several episodes of Oprah's Book Club perform this kind of dual reading of narratives. The uplifting and individualist tone of the Oprah philosophy supports a favorable reading of those texts that follow a general pattern of personal empowerment and uplift. Conversely, on other episodes, guest readers can find their reception complicated by the omnipresence of the Oprah perspective. What is the trajectory of the Oprah narrative and how might it impose interpretive limitations and repress alternative reading practices?

The Construction of a Cultural Icon

One of the most widely recognized cultural icons in the United States today, Oprah's empire includes a daytime television talk show,[1] a monthly lifestyle magazine (called simply *O*), an international charitable organization ("Oprah's Angel Network"), a multinational group of corporations, and, of course, Oprah's Book Club. Every novel that has been selected for Oprah's Book Club has become a best seller; she is "the King Midas of modern letters—what she touches turns to sales" (Anft). Her press bio lists her various public roles as talk show pioneer, actress, producer/creator, magazine founder and editorial director, creator of Oxygen Media (an Internet and cable company), educator, and philanthropist.[2] In 2003, *Forbes* magazine estimated her net personal worth in excess of $1 billion and growing, making her the first black woman billionaire in history ("Economy's Down"). Her recognizability factor is high; she is known internationally on a first-name basis; she is, simply, Oprah. The conflation of Oprah's cultural products with her personal identity is strengthened by the fact that almost all of her projects are, in some way, self-named.[3]

Oprah's rise to fame reflects a correlative climb through cultural hierarchies. The initial incarnation of *The Oprah Winfrey Show* featured guests with scandalous family conflicts or celebrity gossip as a staple of the program. In 1994, Oprah made a conscious move away from the "Jerry Springer"-style narrative toward a more therapeutic and positive approach, a "transformation from the trailer parks' chief bear-baiter to empress of self-improvement" (Sweet 1). Program content elevated from petty domestic dramas to subjects such as self-help, stories of individual triumph, literacy, and charitable works.

Oprah's private and public biographies play a significant role in the construction of her image. She has effectively written an "Oprah narrative" into the American (and possibly international) public consciousness that is not confined to a single autobiographical volume. Her triumph over a difficult childhood, poverty, history of abuse, weight problems, and other struggles against adversity are integral components in the identity she presents to her audiences. It might even be said that Oprah's identity is all about life history; her public image is equated with the story of her private, personal life.[4] The construction of Oprah's celebrity has been the subject of an explosion of recent critical writings.[5] Her biography (recounted by way of interview, anecdote, and televised 'testimony') is the vehicle by which her persona is repeatedly disseminated, and Oprah's biography is a classic story of individual suffering surmounted by hard work, determination, eventual self-empowerment, and extraordinary, unprecedented success.

This narrative has a particular power in the United States, where the American Dream is built on concepts of independent spirit and personal responsibility. As critic Dana Cloud puts it, "The story of individual triumph over humble beginnings is a staple of a culture steeped in Horatio Alger mythology, in the service of an inegalitarian economic order buttressed by an ideology of individual achievement and responsibility" (115). The endless appeal of this kind of self-determining achievement is the subject of Jeffrey Louis Decker's book, *Made in America: Self-Styled Success from Horatio Alger to Oprah Winfrey*. Decker discusses Oprah's development of "prosperity consciousness," a philosophy that "explains her rise from poverty to prosperity as a sign of a higher calling. It emphasizes not only the individual's responsibility for amassing wealth. The alteration of self-image is a prerequisite to ascending the ladder of success" (118). This "self-image" is necessarily related to one's own self-construction in terms of gender, body, class, and, to some extent, race. These elements problematize Oprah's narrative of success as they function within political and social structures, whereby Oprah's simplified biographical narrative resists larger dynamics of power and insists on personal self-empowerment as primary determinant. As Cloud notes, Oprah's biography " 'proves' that the American Dream is possible for all black Americans" in a "bootstraps philosophy" that "obscures the collective nature of oppression and the need for collective social action" (117). Oprah's insistence on the primacy of personal choice and responsibility follows a tradition of television talk shows that tends to privilege the individual's ability to choose freely regardless of the constraints of social or political systems (Carbaugh).

Oprah's narrative is propelled by a series of public self-disclosures that she credits for her progress beyond challenges. The revelation of intimate secrets is consistently treated as an empowering process that allows others to identify with the speaker, while the confessor can reconsider his or her own self-understanding and transcend the pain/shame/fear associated with the secret. This formula is applied to a catalogue of experiences that Oprah has endured, from childhood sexual abuse, to overeating, to drug experimentation, to relationship problems, to family tensions. Oprah frames these struggles as formative experiences, but it is not enough to endure hardship or to fail personally; one must share one's weaknesses and difficulties with others in order to fuel the natural progression from privation to empowerment. This sharing is best performed as public confession.

It is through her own confession that Oprah facilitates others' testimonies.[6] The concept of confession is so entwined with the Oprah narrative that in 1993, *Jet* magazine reported that the term *Oprah* was common parlance among American youth to mean engaging "in persistent, intimate questioning with the intention of obtaining a confession. [The term is] usually used by men of women, as in 'I wasn't going to tell her, but after a few drinks, she *Oprah'd* it out of me'" (Mair 267). Although Jane Shattuc uses the term favorably to describe a certain kind of public discourse in which personal identity takes precedence, a shift toward "the authority of everyday experience, whether in reactionary or progressive form" (109), it is mostly with a negative or dismissive intonation that the term *Oprahfication* or, variably, *Oprahization*, is used by cultural critics.[7] In 1997, *The Wall Street Journal* picked up on the word as a term for the "psychotherapeutic feelingness" that has come to be the norm:

> This upending of tradition—from keeping one's heart under control
> to wearing it always loudly and tearfully on one's sleeve—has come
> to be known as *Oprahfication*, after the famous talk-show host who
> popularized public confession as a form of therapy. ("Queen" A22)

The cultural movement toward emotion-oriented discussion is controversial, with some seeing it as a "wholesale makeover of the nation, and then the world," resulting in a civilization that values surfaces over content, image over substance (Steyn 30). In the *National Review*, Mark Steyn criticizes to the *WSJ*'s limited understanding of Oprahfication to "refer to anything as piffling as a partisan creed or a stylistic voice"; he applies it to a much broader cultural outlook that falsely preaches that everything can be overcome ("the road from Denial to Rehab is spoken of as if they were stops on a vaudeville circuit") and anything can be accomplished. Unfortunately, in the whirlwind of this emancipatory trajectory, certain nuances can be lost, such those of a literature that does not always end on such a happy note.

There has been an absolute flood of cultural criticism about Oprah in recent years, with as many critics supporting her—for empowering women and other marginalized groups to tell their stories—as there are detractors who find fault with her willful blindness toward the larger social and political structures that affect our lives.[8] This project aims to give perspective to these variant positions by tracing how Oprah's narrative of her own life and world-view is reiterated through her cultural productions, specifically, how it is read into, over, and against the selected texts of her Book Club.

Oprah's life philosophy is widely understood as "you are responsible for your life" (Lowe 19). Her methodology of self-empowerment through books is recognized as a process of reading, identification, confession (or testimony), and self-change followed by empowerment or uplift. The impli-cations of this narrative structure extend through the reading of selected texts to the book discussion. Her personal biographical narrative is so well housed in her viewers' psyches that it is, in effect, read simultaneously with the texts she promotes. This "dual reading" works to reinforce the positive reception of those texts that conform to the narrative structure and mes-sages of Oprah's biography. However, this mediating narrative screen can create conflict when the text in question does not agree with the narrative of Oprah, but in fact offers an alternative view, or resists reduction to truisms altogether. In the case of the Club's discussion of Christina Schwartz's *Drowning Ruth*, Oprah's narrative of personal empowerment complements the text's reader reception; however, in a later discussion of Andre Dubus III's *House of Sand and Fog*, the differences between the tone and trajectories of the two narratives (the text and the program) make the discussion con-tentious. In the first case, we could say that the program "works" because of the fit of narratives; in the second case, each narrative exposes the flaws of the other and the narrow reading practices of the program no longer "work" for the book discussion.

The Interpretive Community of Oprah's Book Club

Books showed me there were possibilities in life, that there were actually people like me living in a world I could not only aspire to but attain. Reading gave me hope. For me, it was the open door.
—Oprah qtd. in Ebert 62

The way in which literature is considered by Oprah and her guests can be understood within a tradition of populist, "middlebrow" approaches to read-ing. In "The 'Oprahfication' of Literacy," R. Mark Hall looks at how Oprah's Book Club succeeds in promoting literacy "as a means of individual and

cultural advancement" (646). Hall describes Oprah's authority as constructed in part through her self-presentation as a "trusted friend" to the
viewer by creating an "illusion of intimacy" in her weekly broadcasts in
which she rations out details of her private life (651). Much of Oprah's literacy work is accomplished by promoting the "usefulness" of reading. She
focuses on the experiential aspects of reading and frames it as an activity that
can be both enjoyable and therapeutic. By explicitly linking reading to self-
improvement, she encourages readers to access "the transforming possibilities
of serious fiction" (Hall 655). In this way, books play a role similar to the
guest therapists on the program; they are presented as vehicles of "self-
improvement and cultural uplift" that attract viewers interested in the promise of change:

> Books are central to [Oprah's] theme of self-improvement. . . . the
> 'lifestyle makeover' of both herself and her show—including the
> addition of "Oprah's Book Club"—suggests that self-making within
> an electronic media culture can be realized, not just along the sur-
> face of the body, but through cultivation of the mind and spirit.
> (Hall 655)

Oprah's approach to books echoes the middlebrow book clubs of the
Modernist period. In the first quarter of the twentieth century in America,
book clubs were selling "culture" as a status signifier; books were the vehicle
for accessing prestige and cultural authority (Radway, Rubin). At the beginning of the next millennium, Oprah's Book Club sells self-improvement and
empowerment; books are packaged as the keys to accessing a better, fuller
life.[9] Both the Book-of-the-Month Club and Oprah's Book Club approach
texts as commodities through which the consumer may gain specific, valuable benefits.

As Elizabeth Long makes clear in her detailed study of twentieth-century
book clubs, the predominant approach of national book clubs is personal:
books are meant to be experienced in an emotional and even visceral way.
Although Oprah does not explicitly state that she prefers certain narrative
patterns to others, many commentators argue that Oprah tends to opt for "a
certain *type* of book, telling a certain type of story" ("A Book, An Author"). If
one considers her initial Book Club selections, this storyline might be considered the troubled family narrative or the self-empowerment saga. Critic
Martha Bayles describes Oprah's selections: "[they] reflect a coherent sensi-
bility: she favors novels about people, mostly women but some men, who are

up against hard circumstance but who manage to endure, if not prevail, in the spirit of what Ralph Ellison called heroic optimism" (35).

Each month, from 1996 to 2002, Oprah announced her next book "pick" to give readers a chance to read the novel and write in to tell her how the book had affected them. A typical book club episode from this period began with a pretaped biography of the author, excerpts from the book club dinner discussion, and an interview with the author in front of a studio audience. There has been a slow, although unspoken, literary elevation in the books Oprah chooses, from 1996's "wrenching drama" *The Deep End of the Ocean* (Jacqueline Mitchard) to the 2005 selection of William Faulkner's *The Sound and the Fury*. Interestingly, regardless of the relative literary merit of a selected text, the reading and discursive practices brought to each novel remain fairly consistent. The televised book discussion tends to focus primarily on the experience of reading and how the messages in the book can be applied to readers' personal lives. Attention is paid to subjective emotions and accessible, uplifting messages that can be extracted from the book. Despite the variety of issues touched on in Oprah's Book Club selections, there is a remarkable uniformity in the tone of the discussion: It is colloquial, comforting, and enthusiastic. The tone of Oprah's Book Club is connected to the medium itself: Like most talk shows, the televised book discussion and dinner is personality driven. The show's impact comes from the performance of Oprah's persona with the help of any drama provided by the guest author and guest readers. By identifying pleasure and self-improvement as the preferred "uses" of a text, certain elements of the text are necessarily emphasized. Especially during the early Book Club episodes, little or no attention was paid to style, language, or other formal elements. This approach is not new to recreational book clubs and discussion groups; it is the unprecedented influence of this individual club's reading practices on American cultural tastes that makes it unique.

At the risk of oversimplifying these issues, it is impossible to deny the role of gender, class, and race in the construction of the Oprah narrative and her selection of books for the Book Club. An important factor influencing anxieties around the approach of Oprah's Book Club is related to Oprah's racial identity as an African American.[10] The framing of literature on *The Oprah Winfrey Show* is heavily influenced by traditional African American approaches to storytelling as a vehicle for spiritual uplift and liberation.[11] Folktales and spirituals were used for community advancement and cultural pride throughout the Harlem Renaissance, and this approach is echoed in the language and themes that Oprah draws on when discussing the importance of literature. The complexity of these subjects has also warranted numerous compelling studies on gender and popular culture in relation to Oprah.[12]

For the purposes of this discussion, I am interested less in the literary validity of Oprah's approach to reading than the way that her narrative performs when faced with dissimilar texts on her Book Club. My approach to reading practice is guided by the idea of reception according to Stanley Fish's well-established theory that "interpretive strategies" are responsible for defining the "shape" or meaning of texts for readers. These strategies are directly determined by the "interpretive communities" to which an individual reader belongs. They are both inclusive and exclusive in that they "at once enable and limit the operations" of the reader's consciousness and his or her ability to produce meaning. Fish was careful to note that these communities are built on shared strategies beyond the text in question; that is, they "exist prior to the act of reading and therefore determine the shape of what is read rather than, as is usually assumed, the other way around" (Fish 14). In the case of Oprah's Book Club, readers bring into play a set of interpretive conventions based not on the selected text, but on the Oprah narrative that has developed over years of familiarity with her talk show and other productions. As Fish notes, interpretive strategies work successfully *as long as* the text in question can be considered as belonging to the same set of conventions as the community. In this sense, episodes of Oprah's Book Club function as constraints on the activity of reading and interpretation for the guest readers, as they are asked to apply one set of conventions to a text that may or may not be of that same community. In addition, guest readers are simultaneously reading the (con)text of *The Oprah Winfrey Show* environment (be it the televised dinner party or the show in front of a studio audience) and trying (as "good" guests) to conform to that narrative.

As Fish notes, the "shape of [reading] is determined by the literary institution which at any one time will authorize only a finite number of interpretive strategies" (342). In the case of a text that follows an Oprah-approved trajectory of struggle to self-empowerment, there is no problem assimilating narrative interpretations. Although individual reactions may vary, there is a way of speaking about the text, or "*producing*" the text that has been validated. For example, the Oprah narrative insists that we are each responsible for our own life, we each have the power to make change. But what happens when Oprah's book selection violates one or more of the tenets of the Oprah narrative? What happens when the forces at work in the narrative are larger than individual agency? Or when there is no extractable, single, life-affirming message in the text in question? What happens when there is no opportunity for reader identification, or when that identification produces sour results, or when the narrative ends with nary a speck of evidence of uplift or self-empowerment? What happens when there are no happy endings?

Complementary Narratives: The *Drowning Ruth* Discussion

OPRAH: This is what amazes me about fiction. Somebody else reads it and they say, "You know, that's like my life." ("Oprah's Book Club [*Drowning Ruth* Discussion]")

OPRAH: I mean, look—I mean, for goodness sakes, we're all more open. We've had *The Oprah Show* in our lives now for fifteen years. People know that you have to, you know, get to the truth of who you are and express that to your family. ("Oprah's Book Club [*Drowning Ruth* Discussion]")

Oprah's relationship with books can be understood as having its own discrete narrative. The rhetorical strategies of this narrative vary; however, there are consistent elements that can be distilled down to the simple "Books change lives." That is, books as framed and discussed on *The Oprah Winfrey Show* have the power to change readers' lives. This maxim is repeated throughout the discussions and is reinforced by her guest readers both directly and indirectly:

OPRAH: "Literature is powerful"
GUEST: "It's wonderful."
OPRAH: "It has the ability to change people's—the way they—the way we think.
GUEST: "It does." ("Oprah's Book Club [*Drowning Ruth* Discussion]")

This power is attributed to books' ability to help readers know themselves better, and share that with the world. Book club members are encouraged to read, identify with the text, testify to its impact, heal the original wound, empower themselves, and experience emotional or spiritual uplift. This mandate is fully realized in Oprah's Book Club discussion of Christina Schwartz's first novel, *Drowning Ruth*. By recognizing this episode in a later program about the impact of Oprah's Book Club ("Letters to Oprah's Book Club"), the importance of this particular discussion is confirmed. It is no longer books alone that can change lives; it is the reading of books through the filter of Oprah's Book Club that is truly transformative. In the *Drowning Ruth* episode, Oprah opens with an explicit statement of her goals for the discussion:

> OPRAH: That's what I'm hoping will happen to a lot of people who are holding their own secrets because, really, the secret holds so much power for you—you know, keeping it in the darkness. . . . And when you let it out into the light, you see that that was all your big fear. The people who love you will always love you and will still love you. ("Oprah's Book Club" 16 Nov. 2000)

As in most episodes, the "lesson learned," whether from the chosen book or the show's topic of the day, is not proposed; it is stated as an objective "commonsense" fact. The book is used as "evidence" proving the validity of the thesis set out by Oprah. The accuracy of her conclusions is never questioned; that is, the claim that those who love you will always love you after the disclosure of a serious family secret goes uncontested.

The objective—to extract a unified and life-changing message from the text—is reached in several ways. First, the program is always framed with a "topic," which by its naming becomes the overriding theme of all discussion. Oprah can refer back to this "topic" whenever the conversation digresses. Another method is to ask guests for their "big takeaway," meaning the single message they leave the text with:

> OPRAH: Your big takeaway, Kati, was?
> GUEST: You know, it reinforced something I think I've spent the last five years learning, and that is I can only control me, my integrity, my honor.
> OPRAH: Oh, that's big.

Oprah enthusiastically rewards her viewers for identifying the succinct and positive life-changing elements from the book. The more they can integrate the text into their understanding of their personal lives, the better. In addition, the connection between books and self-disclosure is emphasized. In this episode, the link is explicit:

OPRAH: Next, why, if you're harboring a family secret of your own and you're watching this, you need to get it out in the open. This book . . . might just help you do that. . . . It is just remarkable to me—more remarkable to me how a work of fiction can touch and, really, begin to help heal the lives of readers in ways that a lot of self-help books and therapy and conversations cannot. Our lesson . . . is this; that if you are harbouring any kind of family secret, y'all need to let it out; let it go. . . . Just ahead, you'll meet others like Ruth whose lives were affected by family secrets" ("Oprah's Book Club" 16 Nov. 2000)

During the period of 1996 to 2002, in order to appear on an Oprah's Book Club episode, readers were asked to write letters detailing how the chosen book had affected their lives. Out of these letters, several lucky readers were chosen to participate in a taped book discussion and meal. Later, Oprah would invite the author (and sometimes other readers) onto the show for interview and conversation. Readers were encouraged to write testimonies about the personal impact of the book; on the program, these testimonies were repeated and applauded by Oprah and the studio audience. This unspoken, though uniformly supportive, approach to the text can be seen to preclude discussion of any limitations or problems in the text; Oprah's "rah-rah enthusiasm . . . doesn't allow for critical consideration of the books" ("A Book, An Author"). As Rona Kaufman notes, "In Oprah's Book Club, a successful text was one that sent a reader back into his or her own life, a text that made a reader rethink his or her life and that led to some type of change on the reader's part" (228–29). Interestingly, the narrative of Oprah's biography is also a text that sets out to achieve these same ends.

In the *Drowning Ruth* discussion, Oprah explains: "Many of the readers chosen for our discussion this month had their own family secrets. That's what I love about a book, it just opens up all those doors." Letters show how readers have integrated their understandings of the Oprah narrative into their reading of the chosen text. Keep in mind that prospective guests are well aware of the selection process for appearance on the show. To make it onto the program, they must engage in the rules of the narrative, which, although not homogenous, operate within a limited set of assumptions. In these letters, the overwhelming tendency is to conform to the narrative of reading set forward by Oprah, that is, to personally identify with the experience portrayed in the text and apply a positive message from it to one's own life. It is this identification that is emphasized in the introduction to each guest in the discussion:

> The family secrets in *Drowning Ruth* rang true for Bo, a forty-year-old mother of two. . . . The book *stirred troubling memories* for Ginger. . . . Ellen Marie *related to* Ruth's loyalty . . . Kati *related to* the damage secrets can do to a family. . . . But the book *was comforting* for Patrick, whose family learned of a half brother only last year. (emphasis added)[13]

Compare the uniformity of these responses to other, more difficult or resistant readings, say, "Wenda was appalled at the need to disclose such personal issues, Jamie was bored by the prevalence of popular self-help techniques in the novel, and Stanley found the characters unconvincing, the tone condescending, the diction limited and the themes hackneyed and unoriginal." Clearly, these imagined responses are not acceptable readings for Oprah's Book Club as it has been constructed.

The Book Club formula often involves beginning with the author's explanation of the genesis of the book. This approach is not unique to Oprah's Book Club; it is a standard trope of celebrity interviews in many pop culture venues. The author's testimony of "why" answers to the audience's need to understand the motives of the artist and, hence, to establish authorial intention in their reading. Interestingly, this part of the discussion allows for more resistance than other portions of the show, perhaps because it is performed by the author, who may be more familiar with directing narrative schemas than guest readers. Still, Oprah rarely concedes control of these narratives of genesis, exerting her authority and phrasing over the author's testimony. For example, author Christina Schwarz reports that her idea began with a single character in her mind: "I could hear her tone; like the way she would respond to things." Oprah reacts mockingly to this description saying "I love writers, don't you? 'I heard her tone.' Yes, go ahead." After this jab at writerly rhetoric, it is Schwartz's turn again, and she tries to explain the motivation for writing in her own terms, "I wasn't really sure what she would respond to. Like a lot of writers say—oh, they just let the characters talk and it sort of writes itself. I—I wish that would have happened to me." Schwartz's testimony is ambiguous and vague—the antithesis of the way Oprah wants to frame the story. Oprah, being the professional and efficient host that she is, quickly grasps the reins of the tale and steers it back on course: "So this is a story about a drowning, but it's also . . . about family secrets." In case there is any question, Oprah clarifies what the book is about for the author: "Also about family secrets and how holding on to a secret until it literally, practically destroys you." Ironically, in this search for authorial intention, the concept itself is compromised; *Oprah* tells the *author* what the book is about. Schwartz consents with ("mm-hmm"). I don't mean to imply that this struggle for narrative control is confrontational. The mediation is done in a lighthearted way and the pattern and its purpose are well understood by both host and guest. The conversation must remain focused and clear for the program to work and maintain viewers' attention.

When the discussion finally turns to the book itself, it revolves around themes of self-disclosure, self-help, and empowerment. Schwartz's characters are criticized for their lack of integrity, shame, and moral strength, and she defends her creations against charges from Oprah and the guest readers. At one point, Oprah diagnoses a character as "manic depressive" in order to explain her actions. Schwartz resists this, struggling to retain some of the ambiguity around her character: "I don't know—I don't know how to diagnose it, but, yeah, I think she—I think she did—I think she wasn't well." This exchange reveals the program's tendency to interpret along psychological lines using a language of self-help. This dialogue conforms to the narrative of Oprah's life more generally, the need to classify, testify, and experience self-empowerment.

The *Drowning Ruth* discussion is characteristic of the narrative pattern of Oprah's Book Club episodes. Through Oprah's introductory remarks, the on-screen book discussion, author interviews, and supporting online materials, simplified moral lessons are extracted from the books chosen, and these truisms always conform to the Oprah narrative. For example, in the discussion of Joyce Carol Oates's *We Were the Mulvaneys*, the lesson is boiled down to one reader's assertion that "it's not what happens to you; it's how you react to it" and Oprah's pronouncement that she has "learned to surrender and forgive all characters, all things." Similarly, the lesson of (Wally Lamb's) *She's Come Undone* is determined to be the uplifting, "Accept what people offer . . . take their love"; for Barbara Kingsolver's *The Poisonwood Bible*, it is (according to Oprah) "There's always a price for not owning yourself."

Some authors—and, presumably, their books—corroborate conventional Oprah readings: Billie Letts, author of *Where the Heart Is*, explains, "I wanted people to think this is a better world than maybe sometimes they believe it is. Even on the darkest days . . . I wanted people to think that there are some good people out there. And if we'll just open up and give them a chance, they'll help us in some way." Author Sue Miller gives her book,

While I Was Gone, an equally edifying gloss: "It's . . . a book about forgiveness and the need for forgiveness . . . that human impulse to connect with someone else and to have that other person say, 'I love you. No matter what. I love you.'" Finally, if no one on the show articulates it succinctly, there are always the Web site blurbs to remind readers what the chosen books are really about. There, viewers will find the authorized reading for Elizabeth Berg's *Open House:* "In order to emerge from grief and the past, she has to learn how to make her own happiness. In order to really see people, she has to look within her heart." More insidious than a review that makes plain its subjectivity, the short and snappy (and happy) book description is there to tell readers how to read this text and what messages to take away from it.

Conflicting Narratives: *The House of Sand and Fog* Discussion

When Oprah taped the book discussion for Andre Dubus III's *The House of Sand and Fog* in early 2001, she may have already known that the selected text was not working well within the established Book Club formula. Letters from readers expressed anger that she had chosen the book, undoubtedly contributing to a book discussion "where people could not shut up" ("Oprah's Book Club [*House of Sand and Fog* Discussion]"). At the beginning of the episode we learn that one guest was "very upset" about the selection and had assumed that Oprah must be "out of books" to have chosen this one. In the edited episode, Oprah characterizes the discussion as "lively" and "more of a book battle than a discussion." In retrospect, she concedes that the conflict and debate obscured the program so much that she deems the episode a "false move." According to a later episode, "the message boards lit up with controversy" after the "pandemonium" of the program. Viewers felt that the conflict among the readers made them "mad" and even Oprah found the show's conflict and constant interruptions of viewers "frustrating" enough to make the program "bad for TV" and deserving of her regrets six months later: "My apologies to everybody disappointed in (*The House of Sand and Fog* Discussion)" ("Letters"). Whether or not anything that makes "the message boards [light] up" is really bad for television is debatable; however, the episode did not correspond with the Oprah narrative in the usual way.

The book in question, *The House of Sand and Fog*, is about the struggle between an ex-general of Iranian descent and a troubled young American woman for ownership of a California house. It is a tale that problematizes issues of race, class, and gender and grapples with multicultural power dynamics and differing cultural values. Because it resists closure and generally fails to deliver an uplifting or even easily articulated ending, simple "life lessons" are difficult to express from the text.

The book's deviation from the Oprah narrative is reflected in the televised book discussion. Guest readers were dissatisfied with the book's lack of unambiguously "good guys" or any characters with whom they could easily identify. One male reader explains that he put the book down for three weeks because of the "darkness" of the text and the absence of positive role models in the story. In one exchange, Peggy, a woman of no visible minority, and Shahdi, an Iranian woman, argue over the implications of the main character's decisions. Peggy has wholeheartedly internalized the Oprah narrative and tries desperately to apply it to the text. On the videotaped introduction, we learn that, for Peggy, "the book was about the choices we make in life and paying the consequences for those and how they affect all the other people in our lives as well." In contrast, Shahdi reads the text with an eye to broader racial power structures and sees the book as "not fiction but an autobiography of thousands and thousands of people." Her reading, although informed by personal experience, does not conform to the Oprah narrative because it privileges cultural and class influences over the individual's ability to choose freely. She defends one character's decision to hide his livelihood from his family out of cultural pride:

SHAHDI: What was his bad choice, though? There were no . . .
PEGGY: I mean, I've been—I've been at this level and I've been
            at this level and I've been back at this level, but . . .
SHAHDI: We all have been at those levels. But, see . . .
MR. DUBUS: I love this.[14]
PEGGY: . . . have choices.
SHAHDI: . . . it's about America. It's probably hard for you guys
            to see it. ("Oprah's Book Club" 24 Jan. 2001)

How *can* they see it? Within the narrative of the world of Oprah, there is no excuse for abdicating responsibility because of social or cultural factors. Consider these celebrated Oprah quotations:

Don't complain about what you don't have. Use what you've got. To do less than your best is a sin. Every single one of us has the power for greatness, because greatness is determined by service—to yourself and others. (qtd. in Culhane 10)

> I understand that nothing happens to you without your deserving it
> or creating it in some way for yourself. . . . I believe from the time
> you are born you are empowered with the ability to take responsibil-
> ity for your life. . . . You can allow yourself to be a victim, or you can
> be the kind of person who understands that you have to take charge.
> (qtd. in Adler 244)

To be fair, later in the episode, Oprah concedes that class and race might play
a role in the conflict of the novel, and that "a lot of what people call racism in
this country is really classism . . . and we deny it," a sentiment with which
Dubus agrees enthusiastically, adding that it "goes against the American
Dream to talk about being classist." Unfortunately, this line of inquiry is
quickly dropped as Oprah shifts the discussion abruptly to a tried and true
element of the Oprah narrative: the genesis of the book's idea and its writing
(Oprah: "Tell us how the voices come . . ."). Oprah consistently steers the
conversation away from potentially divisive exchanges, even when she seems
personally moved by the issue. She tends to shy away from a structural or
social analysis for a more individual-centered explanation of behaviour or
decisions (Peck, "Mediated" 541).

In this particular episode, the discussion strays from the Oprah formula
so frequently that several times Oprah is compelled to scold guests for disagreeing ("would you give us a break, George?") or later for failing to change
their mind ("You people are tough . . . You people are tough"). At another
point of tension, Oprah raises the issue of a romantic relationship in the text
as a way of returning the discussion to the safer and more familiar terrain of
intimate relationships. Finally, struggling to make sense of the responsibility
for the tragedy in the book, Oprah decides to blame the book's main conflict
on one character's failure to open her mail, an arguably ludicrous return to the
narrative of personal responsibility that convinces no one on the panel, least
of all the author. Oprah struggles to bring about a moment of self-transformation among the viewers, an effort that is thwarted because the book in question simply will not conform to the reading practice promoted by the Oprah
narrative. Failing to make the book selection work with her reading practice,
Oprah ends the episode with expressions of exasperation and resignation.

While several other Book Club selections do not have unqualified
"happy endings," *The House of Sand and Fog* is arguably one of the darkest
texts chosen in the early incarnation of Oprah's Book Club. It is a difficult
selection for the Oprah format for its refusal to conform to the Oprah narra-

tive of self-empowerment and personal choice. Recent critics have suggested that Oprah's insistence on self-help prevents her from recognizing the more literary qualities of her chosen books. Kathleen Rooney explores this in detail in her book, *Reading with Oprah*, claiming that Oprah

> damaged these complex, sophisticated narratives of her own choosing by treating them as corollaries to her program's doctrine of mindless American optimism . . . that via pluck and forgiveness, everything can be worked out for the best. [Most of her choices] portray human suffering in all its unresolvable complexity; their characters aren't always able to simply get better. (142)

Although Oprah has said, "I don't look for a happy ending. I look for whatever is realistic. Whatever is meaningful, whatever is going to take me to the next level with these characters" ("Oprah's Book Club [*Fall on Your Knees* Discussion]), it is the happy ending that more readily yields memorable apothegms; it delivers feel good moments to its viewers; quite simply, it makes for good television.

The Consequences of Oprah's Book Club

What, if any, are the larger repercussions of the limitations of Oprah's reading practice on reader response? The Club's long-term effect on literary culture is yet to be fully assessed. In both the popular and academic press, Oprah's supporters emphasize the role of the club as a literacy advocate and educator.[15] The most common assumption of her defenders is that the widespread success of Oprah's Book Club, and book clubs more generally, has led to increased reading in America, and that this is unequivocally a good thing for people; it is a good thing for American culture.[16] However, the popular consensus on Oprah's Book Club has yet to be convincingly proven. The declaration that "America is reading again!" tends to be based on anecdotal evidence of a vocal enthusiasm for and increased visibility of reading. Literacy changes are difficult things to measure; even more difficult to ascertain is how much reading qualifies as literary, however we may define that term (literary texts? literary reading practices?). In fact, empirical research fails to support the existence of any increase in reading activity in the years since the incarnation of Oprah's Book Club. According to a 2004 survey by the

National Endowment for the Arts, literary reading in the United States is in a critical state of decline (Bradshaw and Nichols). Less than half of adult Americans engage in reading literature (defined loosely as fiction, drama, or poetry), with the most dramatic rate of decline in the youngest age groups.

One could argue that these reading rates don't take into account how Oprah's literacy promotion is working to slow the tide of new media (Internet, television) as it supplants traditional reading. Perhaps Oprah's Book Club has helped readers approach books they would have avoided in the past. Her approach to reading cannot be dismissed; as a social activity, Oprah's Book Club seems to offer positive experiential effects for many individuals and has certainly raised the profile of reading as a therapeutic activity. Still, in terms of literary culture and reading practices, there are other pressing issues to consider. What if Oprah's work has not really increased reading at all, preaching only to the converted and determining their interpretation for them? Worse, from my perspective, is the possibility that Oprah's Book Club has standardized the reception of books and has changed the way America approaches reading. The unprecedented cultural authority of Oprah, a single tastemaker with self-professed idiosyncratic literary preferences, is perhaps symptomatic of a nation hungry for cultural leadership. Perhaps her success should be a wake-up call to traditional institutions of academia and criticism that their discourses have, through their increasing inaccessibility, become irrelevant to the majority of readers. What can we learn from her experientially based reading practice that consistently privileges personal response and self-transformation? Is there a way to integrate the empowering aspects of Oprah's reading practice without adopting the restrictions that accompany her approach? I believe that this work begins with an effort toward getting over a traditional distaste for middlebrow reading practices in order to observe and analyze Oprah's interpretive conventions more objectively. It might involve reexamining the assumptions and the interpretive conventions that we, as literary scholars, assume to be correct. Jumping off from Stanley Fish's work on reader response, Steven Mailloux remarks how readers always look to context for their "appropriate procedures" for interpreting a text (405). Perhaps the power and explicitness of the Oprah narrative can help to reveal the more insidious yet equally grand narratives that inform professional readers' work. The talk show embrace of the happy ending is only the flip side of the literary disdain for the same. The effectiveness of the Oprah myth over reading practice is fundamentally a triumph of rhetoric, no more seamless than those systems of cultural rhetoric that govern our academic interpretive conventions.

Notes

1. According to her bio on Oprah.com, since 1986, *The Oprah Winfrey Show* has been the highest-rated talk show in television history, boasting an American viewing audience of forty-eight million each week and broadcast internationally in 123 countries.

2. Kathryn Lofton characterizes the magazine as "liner notes to [Oprah's] televised therapies." She describes how these various projects work together to achieve a single vision: "Taken together, her show, magazine, and Web site provide the text of her movement, the instruction manual for viewer consumption and her inner revolution."

3. Including Harpo, Inc., Harpo Productions, Inc., Harpo Studios, Inc., Harpo Films, Inc., Harpo Print, LLC and Harpo Video, Inc.—all an inversion of the word Oprah.

4. For detailed analyses of the formation and operation of Oprah's celebrity, see Abt and Mustazza, Cloud, Farr, Illouz, Rooney and Wilson.

5. See Epstein and Steinberg, Haag.

6. See Jane Shattuc's "The Oprahfication of America?: Identity Politics and Public Sphere Debate," R. Mark Hall's "The 'Oprahfication' of Literacy: Reading 'Oprah's Book Club,'" Chuck Colson's "Oprahfication and Its Discontents: Our Mile-Wide, Inch-Deep Religious Culture," Dale Meador's "The Oprahfication of America" and John R. Hill and Dolf Zillmann's "The Oprahization of America: Sympathetic Crime Talk and Leniency."

7. Some cultural commentators argue that the Oprah approach could lead to a dangerous moral relativism that privileges the personal above all collective or cultural experiences or moral precepts. In more recent popular writing, *Oprahfication* is shorthand for a national cultural condition, one that is characterized by "the exaltation of victimhood, the no-fault moral universe, the abuse of public discourse for private therapy" (Terzian). The word can be uttered with a tone of light mocking, or it can be a damning label meant with dead seriousness.

8. Numerous recent studies explore the empowering and even subversive potential of Oprah's approach, such as Illouz, Masciarotte, Peck, Shattuc, Wilson, and Young. While some critics have found favor with Oprah's approach to race and gender, the program's emphasis on individual empowerment typically overshadows any broad political analysis.

9. Recent research suggests that some of the large book clubs associated with retail chains are moving toward a more academic approach, promoted as an elevated alternative to the common colloquial approach of the televised talk show book discussion. In a study of recent publishers' book club guides, researchers McGinley et al. found that these guides tended to "steer readers toward analytic,

text-based practices" (204) and that they "at once assume a 'readerly' identity . . . one that consequently distinguishes the guide reader from more colloquial or 'everyday' readers" (209).

10. For analysis of the influence of race on Oprah's celebrity, see John Young's "Toni Morrison, Oprah Winfrey, and Postmodern Popular Audiences" and Janice Peck's "Talk about Racism: Framing a Popular Discourse of Race on Oprah Winfrey." For a broader discussion of the traditional uses of literature in African American culture, see Lawrence Levine's *Black Culture and Black Consciousness: Afro-American Folk Thought from Slavery to Freedom*.

11. See Bernard Bell's "Folk Art and the Harlem Renaissance."

12. For focused discussion of the role of gender in the public response to Oprah, see Elizabeth Long's *Book Clubs: Women and the Uses of Reading in Everyday Life*, Andrea Press's *Women Watching Television: Gender, Class, and Generation in the American Television Experience*, and Gloria Masciarotte's "C'Mon Girl: Oprah Winfrey and the Discourse of Feminine Talk." The influence of gender on literary hierarchies also informs Jane Elliott's take on the Oprah incident, "O is for the Other Things She Gave Me." Discussing the link between femininity and "light" fiction, Elliot observes "literary categories [have come] to reflect the same set of oppositions that were once used to distinguish men and women: thinking vs. feeling, public vs. private, hard vs. soft" (Elliott).

13. See Peck's "The Mediated Talking Cure" for an analysis of formulas for ideological containment on talk shows.

14. Note the author's interjection in the midst of the conflict: Dubus "loves" the controversy, the debate between reading practices.

15. Notable book-length studies include Cecilia Konchar Farr's *Reading Oprah: How Oprah's Book Club Changed the Way America Reads*, and Kathleen Rooney's *Reading with Oprah: The Book Club That Changed America*.

16. See Robert McHenry's "tentative conclusion."

Works Cited

"A Book, an Author, and a Talk Show Host: Some Notes on the Oprah-Franzen Debacle." *The Complete Review Quarterly* 3.1 (2002). 20 June 2004.

"A Million Little Lies: The Man Who Conned Oprah." *The Smoking Gun*. 13 Jan. 2006 http://www.thesmokinggun.com.

Abt, Vicki, and Leonard Mustazza. *Coming After Oprah: Cultural Fallout in the Age of the TV Talk Show*. Bowling Green, OH: Bowling Green State U Popular P, 1997.

Adler, Bill, ed. *The Uncommon Wisdom of Oprah Winfrey: A Portrait in Her Own Words*. Secaucus, NJ: Birch Lane Press, 1997.

Anft, Michael. Review of *The Corrections* by Jonathan Franzen. *Baltimore City Paper Review.* 7 Nov. 2001. 20 June 2004. <http://www.citypaper.com/arts/review.asp?id=1626>.

Bayles, Martha. "Imus, Oprah and the Literacy Elite." *The New York Times Book Review.* 29 Aug. 1999: 35.

Bell, Bernard. "Folk Art and the Harlem Renaissance." *Phylon* 36 (1975): 155–63.

Bradshaw, Tom, and Bonnie Nichols. *Reading at Risk: A Survey of Literary Reading in America—Research Division Report #46.* Research Division, June 2004. National Endowment for the Arts. 8 July 2004. 11 July 2004. <http://www.arts.gov/news/news04/ReadingAtRisk.html>.

Carbaugh, Donal. *Talking American: Cultural Discourses on Donahue.* Norwood, NJ: Ablex, 1989.

Cloud, Dana. "Hegemony or Concordance? The Rhetoric of Tokenism in Oprah Winfrey's Rags to Riches Biography." *Critical Studies in Mass Communication* 13.2 (1996): 115–37.

Colson, Chuck. "Oprahfication and Its Discontents: Our Mile-Wide, Inch-Deep Religious Culture." *Christian Examiner* May 2002. 10 Nov. 2002. <www.christiantimes.com/Articles/Chuck%20Colson/Art_May02_Colson.html>.

Culhane, John. "Oprah Winfrey: How Truth Changed Her Life." *Reader's Digest* Feb. 1989: 10.

Decker, Jeffrey Louis. *Made in America: Self-Styled Success from Horatio Alger to Oprah Winfrey.* Minneapolis: U of Minnesota P, 1997.

Dixon, Kathleen. "The Dialogic Genres of Oprah Winfrey's 'Crying Shame.'" *Journal of Popular Culture* 35.2 (2001): 171–91.

Ebert, Alan. "Oprah Winfrey Talks Openly about Oprah." *Good Housekeeping* Sept. 1991: 62.

"Economy's Down, Oprah's Not." *CBS World News* 28 Feb. 2003. 10 July 2004 http://www.cbsnews.com/stories/2003/02/27.

Elliott, Jane. "O Is for the Other Things She Gave Me: Jonathan Franzen's *The Corrections* and Contemporary Women's Fiction." *Bitch Magazine.* Feb. 2002. 20 June 2004 <http://www.bitchmagazine.com/>.

Epstein, Debbie, and Deborah Lynn Steinberg. "All Het Up! Rescuing Heterosexuality on the Oprah Winfrey Show." *Feminist Review* 54 (1996): 88–115.

Farr, Cecilia Konchar. *Reading Oprah: How Oprah's Book Club Changed the Way America Reads.* Albany: SUNY, 2004

Fish, Stanley. Is There a Text in this Class? *The Authority of Interpretive Communities.* Cambridge: Harvard UP, 1980.

Gamson, Joshua. *Claims to Fame: Celebrity in Contemporary America.* Berkeley: U of California P, 1994.

Haag, Laurie. "Oprah Winfrey: The Construction of Intimacy in the Talk Show Setting." *Journal of Popular Culture* 26.4 (Spring 1993): 115–21.

Hall, R. Mark. "The 'Oprahfication' of Literacy: Reading 'Oprah's Book Club.'" *College English* 65.6 (2003): 646–67.

Hill, John R., and Dolf Zillmann. "The Oprahization of America: Sympathetic Crime Talk and Leniency." *Journal of Broadcasting and Electronic Media* 43.1 (1999): 67–82.

Illouz, Eva. *Oprah Winfrey and the Glamour of Misery: An Essay on Popular Culture.* New York: Columbia UP, 2003.

Kaufman, Rona. "'That, My Dear, Is Called Reading': Oprah's Book Club and the Construction of a Readership." *Reading Sites: Social Difference and Reader Response.* Eds. Patrocinio P. Schweickart and Elizabeth Flynn. New York: MLA, 2004. 221–55.

"Letters to Oprah's Book Club." *The Oprah Winfrey Show.* 6 July 2001. Transcript.

Levine, Lawrence W. *Black Culture and Black Consciousness: Afro-American Folk Though from Slavery to Freedom.* Oxford: Oxford UP, 1978.

Long, Elizabeth. *Book Clubs: Women and the Uses of Reading in Everyday Life.* Chicago: U of Chicago P, 2003.

Lowe, Janet. *Oprah Winfrey Speaks: Insight from the World's Most Influential Voice.* New York: John Wiley, 1998.

Mailloux, Steven. "Convention and Context." *New Literary History* 13.2 (1983): 399–407.

Mair, George. *Oprah Winfrey: The Real Story.* Secaucus, NJ: Birch Lane P, 1994.

Masciarotte, Gloria-Jean. "C'mon, Girl: Oprah Winfrey and the Discourse of Feminine Talk." *Genders* 11 (1991): 81–110.

McGinley, William, Katanna Conley, and John Wesley White. "Pedagogy for a Few: Book Club Discussion Guides and the Modern Book Industry as Literature Teacher." *Journal of Adolescent and Adult Literacy* 44.3 (2000) 204–15.

McHenry, Robert. "All Hail Oprah's Book Club." *The Chronicle of Higher Education* 48.35: B17.

Meador, Dale. "The Oprahfication of America." Razormouth.com 24 Feb. 2003. 10 Nov. 2004 <www.razormouth.com/NewsPub/Stories/2003/02/24/10461007921.php>.

Mittell, Jason. "Audiences Talking Genre: Television Talk Shows and Cultural Hierarchies." *Journal of Popular Film and Television* 31.1 (2003): 36–46.

"Oprah's Book Club [*Drowning Ruth* Discussion]." *The Oprah Winfrey Show.* 16 Nov. 2000. Transcript.

———. [*Fall on Your Knees* Discussion]." *The Oprah Winfrey Show.* 5 Apr. 2002. Transcript.

———. [*Fall on Your Knees* Discussion]." *The Oprah Winfrey Show.* 5 Apr. 2002. 5 Jan. 2006.

———. [Final Book Club Episode]." *The Oprah Winfrey Show.* 2 May 2002. Transcript.

———. [*House of Sand and Fog* Discussion]." *The Oprah Winfrey Show.* 24 Jan. 2001. Transcript.

———. [*Open House* Discussion]." *The Oprah Winfrey Show.* 23 Aug. 2000. 20 Jan. 2001.

———. [*She's Come Undone* Discussion]." *The Oprah Winfrey Show.* 22 Jan. 1997. 14 Dec. 2005.

———. [*We Were the Mulvaneys* Discussion]." *The Oprah Winfrey Show.* 8 Mar. 2001. 10 Jan. 2005.

———. [*Where the Heart Is* Discussion]." *The Oprah Winfrey Show.* 19 Jan. 1999. 10 Jan. 2005.

———. [*While I Was Gone* Discussion]." *The Oprah Winfrey Show.* 23 June 2000. 10 Jan. 2005.

———. [*The Poisonwood Bible* Announcement]." *The Oprah Winfrey Show.* 23 June 2000. 10 Jan. 2005.

"Oprah Winfrey's Biography." oprah.com. 2006. 12 Jan. 2006.

Peck, Janice. "The Mediated Talking Cure: Therapeutic Framing of Autobiography in TV Talk Shows." *Gender, Race and Class in Media: A Text-Reader.* 2nd ed. Eds. Gail Dines and Jean M. Humez. Thousand Oaks, CA: Sage, 2003. 534–47.

———. "Talk About Race: Framing a Popular Discourse of Race on Oprah Winfrey." *Cultural Critique* 27 (Spring 1994): 89–126.

Press, Andrea L. *Women Watching Television: Gender, Class, and Generation in the American Television Experience.* Philadelphia: U of Pennsylvania P, 1991.

"Queen Oprah" (Editorial). *The Wall Street Journal.* 17 Sept. 1997: A22.

Radway, Janice. *A Feeling for Books: The Book-of-the-Month Club, Literary Taste, and Middle-Class Desire.* Chapel Hill: U of North Carolina P, 1997.

Rooney, Kathleen. *Reading with Oprah: The Book Club That Changed America.* Fayetteville: U of Arkansas P, 2005.

Rubin, Joan. *The Making of Middlebrow Culture.* Chapel Hill: U of North Carolina, 1991.

Shattuc, Jane M. "The Oprahfication of America?: Identity Politics and Public Sphere Debate." *The Talking Cure: TV Talk Shows and Women.* New York: Routledge, 1997.

Steyn, Mark. "Comic Oprah: American's Talker-in-Chief is the Perfect Embodiment of the Virtual Culture of the Nineties." *National Review* 50.5 (1998): 30–34.

Sweet, Matthew. "Jonathan Franzen: The Truth about Me and Oprah." *The Independent.* 17 Jan. 2002. 20 June 2004.

Terzian, Philip. "The Love Tour." *The Wall Street Journal Opinion Page.* 25 June 2004. 12 Nov. 2004.

Wilson, Sherryl. *Oprah, Celebrity and Formations of Self.* Houndmills, UK: Palgrave MacMillan, 2003.

Young, John. "Toni Morrison, Oprah Winfrey, and Postmodern Popular Audiences." *African American Review* 35.2 (2001): 181–204.

11

YOUR BOOK CHANGED MY LIFE

Everyday Literary Criticism and Oprah's Book Club

KATE DOUGLAS

The rise, fall, and resurrection of Oprah's Book Club has resulted in the emergence and convergence of fervent debates concerning commercialism in contemporary literature, the rise of the "the everyday reader," and the state and future of literary criticism. In its initial incarnation, Oprah's Book Club was a monthly event that focused primarily on recent literary fiction. The Book Club foregrounded everyday readers (mostly women) and celebrated their critical responses to literature. These critical responses were commonly based on autobiographical or humanist critical responses, and Winfrey facilitated these responses by putting them center stage on her international daytime television program.

However, this apparent challenge to the literary establishment was fraught with trials. After being credited with revolutionizing reading in the mid to late 1990s, in April 2002, Winfrey announced the closure of her television Book Club (it was revamped and resumed in 2003, an issue I will take up further on in this discussion). Upon its closure, Winfrey explained that "the truth is, it has just become harder and harder for me to find books on a monthly basis that I am really passionate about . . . I have to read a lot of books to get to something that I really passionately love, so I don't know when the next book will be. It might be next fall or it could be next year" (Rooney "Oprah Learns" 56). Much of the commentary that followed this announcement focused on the possible economic reasons behind the termination of the Book Club, the suggestion that its popularity was waning, or that Winfrey was tiring under the weight of responsibility and criticism leveled at the Book Club.[1] The Book Club's entrenchment within the empiric *Oprah Winfrey Show* placed a particular impetus on the club beyond its reading books: the Book Club had to be engaging television—fresh, innovative media that sustained its viewers and longtime host. Furthermore, the Book Club had to endure within a particular cultural moment—amid a range of involved observers and stakeholders that included booksellers, librarians, book critics, television critics, and media analysts who saw themselves as being directly affected by the choices that Winfrey made. Though bookselling and criticism have long been commercial enterprises, influencing reader choices, and inscribing value on certain books and not others, Oprah's Book Club proved offensive to many critics because it influenced these choices so openly and so widely; its impact was there for all to see.

The debates that surrounded the Book Club provide an absorbing insight into contemporary literature, literary values, and their gatekeepers. Unlike Winfrey's critics, I am not suggesting that, in closing the Book Club's first incarnation, Winfrey failed in her efforts to open reading to the masses or, more specifically, to facilitate "reading communities." Quite the contrary, this chapter observes the cultural significance of Oprah's Book Club to the study of contemporary reading practices. In focusing on the Book Club's first manifestation—as a Book Club for literary fiction—I argue that Winfrey's readers, and the approach to reading celebrated by Oprah's Book Club, represented a confrontation to literary fiction and its "middlebrow" readership. In opening up and even claiming literary fiction for the everyday reader: the popular-culture fan, the housewife, the occasional reader, and the television viewer, Oprah's Book Club celebrates the everyday reader and everyday reading practices.

The Book Club has played an integral role in a more general cultural departure from professional literary criticism. Though Oprah's Book Club has propelled the everyday reader into prominence in an unprecedented way, the Book Club developed in a cultural climate in which autobiographies of previously marginalized persons were the boom literary product, and Web pages and Internet diaries have become key cultural artifacts. Significantly, Oprah's Book Club strengthened alongside other models of nonprofessional literary criticism, for example, amazon's "customer comments," to name one example. Critics have too often disregarded such interactive strategies as commercial manipulation; while the commercial motives of such sites are incontrovertible, to deny readers any critical agency in these reader-response initiatives is shortsighted. Thus, in an age when the everyday reader has become increasingly visible in institutions of reading, what can the rise and fall of Oprah's [literary fiction] Book Club suggest about the cultural position of this particular form of critical response to literary criticism? What happens when "everyday reading" goes corporate, with a dominant central role model like Oprah attached? I attempt to unpack the particular reading performances elicited by the Book Club and their effects as everyday literary criticism. In using an episode of Oprah's Book Club from 2001 as a case study—as well as the publicity material, viewer responses on the Book Club's Web site, brief references to other episodes of Oprah's Book Club, and significantly, intertextual media responses to Oprah's Book Club—I am interested in the reader responses encouraged by Oprah's books, and the discursive effects of such constructions for the readers involved in Winfrey's program (and beyond).

Reading with Oprah

Though reading "famously went mass media in 1996 in America with Oprah's Book Club," and now the practice of reading in groups is currently at the peak of its popularity, as Jenny Hartley suggests, book clubs have been around as long as there has been reading (1–4). There are more than 50,000 book clubs in the UK, and more than 500,000 in the United States; with twelve or fifteen members belonging to each book club, these signal huge commercial possibilities for publishers (Hartley qtd. in Hope R4). Book clubs have become even more widespread through the Internet, where thousands of different book clubs can be found.[2] The reasons for the existence of these clubs varies from a shared love of reading, social and intellectual stimulation, fashion, friendship, support, self-help, or therapy. Yet at the heart of all book clubs would seem to be a belief in the value of everyday literary criticism, an assertion of the value of critical discussion on books by persons who may have no formal skills or knowledge of literature.

Oprah aimed to "get America reading again" (James NA). It is a recurrent point of humor on Oprah's Book Club that Winfrey has encouraged people into reading who have not read a book since leaving high school. As Paul Gray suggests, "if Oprah can make books inviting and exciting to nonreaders, who are the purists to complain?" (84). Yet the purists did complain—that the books chosen were predictably uniform or simply just "bad," or that if the books were "good," the attachment of an "Oprah sticker" became a "mainstreaming" stigma to these works of literary fiction. Others complained that Winfrey's methods of reading were condescending and uncultured.[3] And other literary critics soon observed that, ironically, television icon Oprah Winfrey had become the "patron saint of book publishing" (Chin and Cheakalos 112).[4]

According to "Oprah's Book Club Facts" on the Oprah.com Web site, "Oprah's Book Club is the most non-exclusive club in the world. To be a member, all you have to do is read!" (oprah.com). In other words, the club's ethos is accessibility via the consumer's interactivity with the television program, host, live audience participants, and perhaps also the Webpage message boards, which advise viewers, among other things, how to form their own (sub) book clubs. Its framing within a "club" format implies a community of shared values and goals. The club's immersion within the culture of Winfrey's program in general assures participants that the Book Club will extend on the particular values espoused in the show's more general format: comprehensible popular culture-based responses to social issues, the importance of self-reflexivity in reading social texts, and the value of autobiographical disclosure in interpretation, meaning-making, and ultimately the overcoming of adversity.

In Oprah's Book Club, guests are chosen for "dinner discussions" that air on Book Club episodes.[5] According to the Web site: "guests are chosen based on their reaction to the book. . . . A personal connection to the book helps, but isn't mandatory" (oprah.com). Yet a viewing of any episode of Oprah's Book Club reveals that a personal connection is not only mandatory, it will be the primary critical position from which the book will be read. Winfrey and her guests continually assert that the value of reading lies in its encouraging you to "appreciate your own life." Following, perhaps predictably from its therapeutic-media foundations,[6] Oprah's Book Club is driven by the very public autobiographical-therapeutic performances of its participants, signaling a celebration of a particular mode of everyday literary criticism that can be found within any episode of Oprah's Book Club.

Case Study: *We Were the Mulvaneys* and Critical Readings of Oprah's Book Club

A case study of an episode of Oprah's Book Club illuminates the type of literary criticism employed within the club's format. This episode discusses Joyce Carol Oates's novel *We Were the Mulvaneys*, and the program begins with Winfrey's introduction of the book, including her personal responses. Following Winfrey's introduction is a short true story segment that becomes the focal point of the program. This takes the form of a brief documentary film about the experience of "the Hanson family of Minnesota." The short film recounts the rape and suicide of their teenaged daughter Susie and the aftereffects for the family. Jane Hanson, the mother of Susie, is one of the participants in the Book Club discussion of *We Were the Mulvaneys*.

Winfrey's introductory comments[7] to the program encourage the viewer or would-be reader to personalize the novel chosen for the Book Club. Interestingly though, this suggested personalization takes a very specific form. Winfrey and each of the guest readers chosen for the discussion of *We Were the Mulvaneys* (all of whom are female) discuss the book in terms of the ways in which it affected them emotionally. The principal task for the guest readers is to initially make connections between the events within the fictional novel and their own lives and to continue to articulate these connections during the program. The guest readers discuss the book entirely in popular therapeutic terms, for example, the book's "power to heal" or its ability to "change your attitude."

Unmistakably, the dominant motivation for reading inherent within this reading community is personal development. Winfrey says during the Book Club discussion: "there's no question—reading changes your life." Consider also the topics on the message forum on the Book Club section of Oprah.com. These message boards work as an extension of the program's book discussion. Two of the discussion topics are "Has Oprah's Book Club changed your life?" and "What authors have inspired you?" Though it is arguably an axiom that reading is personally enriching or stimulating, the reading practices of Oprah's Book Club have raised a range of alarm bells for literary criticism: rampant relativism or reductivity, evocations of therapeutic individualism, or even solipsism.[8] Others decried its lack of social contextualization, or the Book Club's nonacknowledgment of intertextuality.[9] Encouraging individual, therapeutic responses does not necessarily incite readers to consider the book in terms of the broader social lives of others. As Janice Peck writes (of *The Oprah Winfrey Show* more generally),

> the therapeutic discourse [of programs such as *Oprah*] strives to confine social conflict within narratives of individual and interpersonal dysfunction . . . therapeutic discourse proposes that we change ourselves, our attitudes and behaviour, without also recognizing that our identities and actions are determined by and respond to social conditions that will not change simply because we decide to interpret and handle them differently on an individual basis. (152)

These concerns provoke a number of questions: Does Oprah's Book Club place everyday readers in a position of presumed disempowerment, while elevating the institutions of literary production and distribution to the role of therapeutic provider? Does the Book Club disempower readers to empower them, or diminish the consideration of reading and writing as political acts? As Wendy Parkins suggests, many critics of therapeutic talk shows have marked them as an unfortunate retreat away from social politics into remedial individualism (146). A shallow assessment of the development of the *We Were the Mulvaneys* Book Club session would seem to confirm these concerns. During the program, Winfrey asks guest reader Jane Hanson if she believed that reading *We Were the Mulvaneys* prior to her daughter's suicide might have prevented it. Jane Hanson responds by suggesting that this is a possibility and that the book was a "slap in the face" for her. The book discussion is again framed in individual narratives, where questions of individual agency and personal responsibility are implicated. Another guest reader, "B. J.," describes being ostracized by her family as a result of being a teenage mother. Yet ultimately B. J. explains that she survived as a result of personal change. Interestingly, despite the group's acknowledgment that *We Were the Mulvaneys* explores momentous social concerns such as female inequality, the readers ultimately agree that the primary message underlying the novel relates to individual's taking responsibility for their own lives and relationships.

Lawrence Grossberg offers a discussion on the role popular culture plays in empowering its consumers. Grossberg argues that although popular culture forums often inspire social awareness, passionate involvement, accessing resources, and goal setting, this empowerment tends to remain in the private domain because "everyday life" is all consuming (305). According to Grossberg's theory, involvement in popular culture is more likely to result in individuals taking personal action in their everyday lives, than in social or political action in broader communities. This theory is problematic due to its assumption that personal action and social action have no immediate relationship. Furthermore, as Parkins argues, the presence of predominantly female consumers (as *Oprah* participants) complicates this theory considerably, because everyday life, for many women, is the primary site of cultural and political life. To deny female popular culture consumers' political agency via their consumption of the Book Club may be to deny them any sociopolitical agency. Parkins writes: it is "precisely because they [talk shows] address the everyday that they are such significant sites of cultural and political mediation for women" (147). Talk-show therapeutic activities can be considered conducive to political aims such as feminism:

The "helped self" need not be seen as antithetical to feminism by some kind of inevitable association with a cult of individualism but may in fact enable a form of imaginative identification with other "helped selves" with similar aspirations, offering a way of re-inserting some of the collective aims of feminism into the often post-feminist world of TV and everyday life. (147)

More specifically, reading in a book club within a talk show format carries particular associations: access to intellectual tools, cultural capital, knowledge, and community. The Book Club's implicit promise is that it will encourage its participants to understand their relationship to the characters in the books they read, and also to each other. In the case of *Oprah*, Parkins argues, "self-transformation is always linked with relations with others and with a broader community" (148). The Book Club, according to its participants, provides a forum not only for self-reflexivity but also for conflict resolution, social awareness, and the discussion of social justice issues such as racial inequality, women's rights, mental illness, and a range of human relationships, responsibilities, and connections. Via this frame, the seemingly therapeutic individualist events in the *We Were the Mulvaneys* discussion can be read in a much different light.

Yet the cultural commentaries surrounding the Book Club suggest that this mode of reading is not valued as an appropriate approach to literary criticism. One of the criticisms of the club is its choice of a certain "type" of texts—predominantly female authored and overwhelmingly stories concerned with people overcoming adversity.[10] Interest in such texts has been disparaged as a popular culture trend: These texts have experienced a wave of popularity beyond Oprah's Book Club. However, such books have traditionally been marginalized as literary texts, particularly absent from "high" literary canons. As D. T. Max argues, "Oprah's Books" redraw the literary canon for everyday criticism, challenging established notions of what kinds of books are socially valuable. Within a cultural climate rapidly absorbing the notion that literature is didactic and constantly implicated in questions of social justice (particularly via contemporary autobiography), Oprah's Book Club champions women writers who write about women, for women's consumption.[11] Within the club, "Oprah books" are never read with the expressed purpose of raising readers' cultural capital, again suggesting the particular celebration of alternative critical methods that are not commonly distinguished as literary criticism. As Eva Illouz argues, such dialogue should be considered as consequential "social" interchange. Illouz argues that "emotion talk" should not be dismissed as solipsism but considered as "talk about social relations" (118), by persons who have previously been denied access to critical methods.

In her introduction to the discussion of *We Were the Mulvaneys,* Winfrey says: "As with all of our Book Club shows it's more about life than about a novel." Significantly, even though it is a book club, members are absolved from reading the novel. One of the most prevalent criticisms of Oprah's Book Club is that it has little to do with the appreciation of literature.[12] The most famous example of such criticism is Jonathan Franzen's skeptical acceptance of Oprah's choosing his book for the Book Club. Franzen expressed concerns in interviews over Winfrey's corporate logo being placed on his book, and also criticized some of Winfrey's previous choices for her club, citing their lack of sophistication and their narrow appeal (to mostly women) (Kirkpatrick A1). As a result, not only was Franzen's book *The Corrections* removed from the club's list, the incident created much debate over elitism in the literary community.

At the heart of these debates is Winfrey's choice of books. Oprah's Book Club presents almost entirely fiction.[13] Traditionally, fiction has enjoyed a higher literary esteem than autobiography.[14] Within the recent and current waves of interest in autobiography,[15] this form would have perhaps been the form chosen for the Book Club forum. However, significantly, Oprah's Book Club made a bold claim on fiction, much of it award-winning, critically acclaimed literary fiction.[16] This occurred, much to the surprise of critics, such as David D. Kirkpatrick, for example, who writes:

> Ms. Winfrey's project—recommending books, *even* challenging literary novels, for viewers to read in advance of discussions on her talk show—initially provoked considerable skepticism in the literary world, where many associated daytime television with lowbrow entertainments like soap operas and game shows (emphasis added). (A1)

In choosing fiction, the Book Club designated this form of writing as accessible, and appropriated it to its own receptive frameworks: namely, the Book Club reads these fictional texts almost entirely via auto/biographical literary readings. Though highly prescriptive, this strategy is not particularly notable considering the proliferation of regulatory promotional material on contemporary literature. Presumably, readers have become very used to and comfortable with being told what to read and why. Elizabeth Long argues that cultural and institutional authorities constantly shape popular reading practices, telling readers what books to read and how to read them:

> Authoritative framing has effects on what kinds of books are published, reviewed, and kept in circulation in libraries, classrooms and the marketplace, while legitimating, as well, certain kinds of literary values and correlative modes of reading. Academics tend to repress consideration of variety in reading practices due to our assumptions that everyone reads (or ought to) as we do professionally, privileging the cognitive, ideational, and analytic mode. Further, recognizing the importance of the collective activity . . . inevitably brings into view both the commercial underside of literature and the scholar's position of authority within the world of reading. (192)

Oprah's Book Club was particularly offensive to some critics, perhaps because it was so openly assertive of its reading intentions, and on a much broader scale than book catalogues or book jacket blurbs.

Another consequence of choosing fiction is that the Book Club avoids the responsibility of having to address the biography of authors in any depth, in favor of centering the autobiographical narratives of guest readers and viewers.[17] At one point in the *We Were the Mulvaneys* discussion when Winfrey offers, "you can't help but read it and think about your own family," it becomes clear that this is the primary speaking position for Book Club articulations. In the *We Were the Mulvaneys* episode, despite her presence on the program, author Joyce Carol Oates is almost entirely marginalized in the discussion of her book. The discussion of her book does not begin until a third of the way through the program. Oates's book is a key to the reader's self-discovery and, like self-help books, is used to promote the cathartic unraveling of adverse life experiences. Moreover, when *We Were the Mulvaneys* is being discussed, whenever the dialogue moves toward textual analysis it quickly veers again into the readers' personal narratives of healing. The invited guests, who represent Winfrey's viewers, consistently take center stage. In turn, guests tell of how the book affected them. As Caryn James suggests "[Winfrey] does not function as a literary critic, but as a cheerleader for reading, reassuring viewers that books are user-friendly and relevant to their lives" (NA). At the end of the show, viewers are encouraged to write in, or discuss on the Web site, the book's effect upon them. Kelly Blewster suggests that Oprah's Book Club "demonstrates how books affect the lives of everyday people" (21); conversely, Max argues that these autobiographical reading frames are merely part of Winfrey and the program's convenient commodification of both the books and the participants' (and viewers') autobiographical disclosures; their involvement ensures their consumption (36). Yet, arguably, the consumer involvement involves a very active consumption— that is, beyond merely buying books and watching a television program. The consumers are reading, engaging with others either in person, or via Web site message boards, as well as experiencing the encouraged self-reflexive articulations relating to the cultural product they consume. Furthermore, these methods ensure the reader's critical agency—each person has access to critical tools via their own autobiographical narrative, making this form of criticism innovative and accessible.

This everyday reading position is celebrated on Oprah's Book Club precisely because of its marginalization in other forms of formal literary criticism. Though, as critics such as Paul John Eakin and Jeremy D. Popkin suggest, autobiographical criticism (and by this I refer to the use of autobiographical self-reflexivity in critical writing) has experienced a relative boom in recent years, it remains on the margins of much of academic practice. Michéle Roberts notes that "the autobiographical" is considered by many critics as lacking "art" and "imagination" (5), and thus in criticism would be the marker of inferior critical capacities.[18] Roberts argues the opposite, that autobiography and imagination are "deeply connected" (14). Similarly, Jane Tompkins argues that the marginalization of autobiographical readings excludes a great deal of female critical knowledge. Tompkins quotes a lecture by Alison Jaggar:

> Western epistemology, she argued, is shaped by the belief that emotion should be excluded from the process of attaining knowledge. Because women in our culture are not simply encouraged but *required* to be the bearers of emotion, which men are culturally conditioned to repress, an epistemology which excludes emotions from the process of attaining knowledge radically undercuts women's epistemic authority. (1105)

Tompkins suggests "the public-private dichotomy, which is to say, the public-private *hierarchy* is a founding condition of female oppression. I say to hell with it. The reason I feel embarrassed at my own attempts to speak personally in a professional context is that I have been conditioned to feel that way" (1104). Tompkins and Jaggar, like Parkins's discussion of *Oprah*, suggest the ways in which the marginalization of certain literary critical practices has primarily affected female critics and consumers. Conversely, they suggest that these critical practices should be celebrated precisely as a measure for balancing such conditionality:

> I think people are scared to talk about themselves, that they haven't got the guts to do it. I think readers want to know about each other. Sometimes when a writer introduces some personal bit of a story into an essay, I can hardly contain my pleasure. I love writers who write about their own experience. I feel I'm being nourished by them, that I'm being allowed to enter into a personal relationship with them. (Tompkins 1104)

Though suspicions and defenses abound concerning the value of autobiographical-criticism, as I have suggested in earlier research, "the personal" is highly profitable in a variety of forms of everyday cultural consumption (Douglas 806–26), and Oprah's Book Club brought the personal into literary criticism, via the everyday, on an unprecedented scale.

Conclusion: The Demise of Oprah's Book Club and the Everyday Reader?

The termination of Oprah's [literary fiction] Book Club provoked further debates among media commentators and other cultural gatekeepers concerning its role as an effective facilitator of reading communities. Kathy Rooney regrets "that the club was never discussed as the rich cultural phenomenon that it really was" ("Oprah Learns" 56). Conversely, Francine Fialkoff and Thomas Leitch regret the reasons Winfrey chose for ending the Book Club (Fialkoff 76; Leitch 587).[19] Fialkoff refers to Winfrey's suggestion that there are not enough books around that she is passionate about as "careless words" from someone who reengaged so many people with reading (76). It is fascinating to consider how, despite the success of the Book Club in terms of generating reading communities and everyday critics, comments such as these attribute overwhelming influence and agency to a single, powerful mediator of reading practice. Though it seems fair to argue that the club facilitated reading, it does not necessarily follow that people will stop reading because Winfrey ceased the Book Club.

Sheridan Prasso writes that a "slew of other media outlets" are seeking to fill the void left by Winfrey (including ABC's *Good Morning America* and *Live with Regis and Kelly*, NBC's *Today Show*, *USA Today*, and *The Washington*

Post) (12). But, as Rooney predicted, those eulogizing or seeking to replace Oprah's Book Club were premature: In 2003, Winfrey revived the book club with a new focus "Traveling with the Classics" ("Oprah Learns" 56). It is impossible not to read such a development in terms of the criticism leveled at the Book Club. For instance Robert McHenry discusses how the cancelation of Oprah's Book Club was met with "a surprising amount of gloating and what one can only infer is some long-suppressed hostility among the intelligentsia. Some of the commentary has been harsh, haughty, not to say bitchy. 'So many bad books, so little time,' was one newspaper reviewer's arch dismissal" (B7). A move away from contemporary literature marks a potential move away from the realist immediacy and autobiographical transference that has been a feature of Oprah-style literary criticism—toward the contained meanings and formal literary criticism often associated with canonical literature.

In this chapter, I have offered an examination of the reading practices inherent within Oprah's Book Club, as well as a consideration of the criticisms and celebrations surrounding this reading forum. The club had a particularly unsustainable conditionality inherent within the reading practices it celebrated. Yet rather than affecting the reader/participants, this conditionality affected the broader stakeholders of Oprah's Book Club. For example, despite its resolve to use only contemporary fictional texts for the club, Oprah's Book Club was heavily dependent on the therapeutic autobiographical performances of the host, the author, and the reader/participants. These performances affected limits whereupon the fictional texts, without being overtly "self-help" books, were nevertheless established as books that readers could form a therapeutic bond with. Indeed, within Oprah's Book Club, such an articulation was typically the most valorized response to a book. The very public nature of the club meant that the culturally laden act of reading was brought under the media gaze, and Winfrey suffered constant skepticism regarding her commercial motives and criticism of her apparent destruction of reading cultures.

Yet rather than damaging literary criticism, via its celebration of subjectivity, the club became part of a move away from the exclusive and perhaps impenetrable trappings of other forms of literary appreciation. The Book Club joined the challenge to "high," "middle," and "lowbrow" reading, which has long been fought by analysts of popular culture, by asserting an alternative model: everyday literary criticism—employing reading methodologies that were applicable to the everyday life of the participants. Those who were offended by this "use" of literature failed to recognize that literature has been used to justify and consolidate human relations, intellectual debates, and social values for as long as it has existed. Though Oprah's Book Club's style of literary criticism was appealing to participants, spurred book sales and reading figures to exceptional levels, and endured for six years, its actions met constantly with either suspicion or ambivalence from a number of media commentators. Considering the career of Winfrey, and the run of the Book Club, it is unlikely that these criticisms caused its demise. Most likely, a combination of factors contributed to its end—including the demands for fresh television, and the pressures and responsibilities leveled at Winfrey. Of most interest is, and will continue to be, how the life and death of the Book Club were received by readers, professional and recreational. This social experiment in reading revealed the different social engagements and investments in contemporary literature and literary criticism to suggest that spaces for reading and criticism are paradoxically as liberated and controlled as they ever have been.

Notes

I would like to thank the editors—Cecilia and Jaime—for their comments and suggestions on this chapter.

1. See Kirkpatrick, Max, McHenry, "Oprah Demurs," and Rooney.

2. Hartley writes that "Internet reading groups are legion, transient, and diverse, forming excited and impermanent communities of talk. . . . Any account of the net's assets runs the risk of obsolescence, but the resources it offers are unique" (*Reading Groups* 2).

3. See Kirkpatrick, Max, and McHenry.

4. Paula Chin and Christina Cheakalos observe, "A Pulitzer Prize is nice. A Nobel even nicer. But to hit the literary jackpot these days, what an author wants is an Oprah" (112). There are many examples of pre-Oprah, post-Oprah dramatic sale comparisons. The first three books chosen by Oprah's Book Club in 1996 became instant best sellers (see Gray). One of these books was Toni Morrison's then nineteen-year-old novel *Song of Solomon*. As Gray suggests, its inclusion in Oprah's Book Club provokes more sales than Morrison's 1993 Nobel Prize. Before Oprah, *Song of Solomon* had sold 374,000 copies. By 1996 and after its inclusion in Oprah's Club, it had sold 900,000 copies (p. 84). A. Manette Ansay's novel *Vinegar Hill* had sold 18,000 copies pre-Oprah. After the book had been selected by Oprah's Book Club, *Vinegar Hill* sold in excess of 800,000 copies (see Maryles "When Oprah Called"). Janet Fitch's *White Oleander* had 100,000 copies in print before Oprah chose her book. After Oprah, there were 850,000 copies in print (see Maryles "The Latest from

L. B"). In 1999, another Oprah selection, Anita Shreve's *The Pilot's Wife* was in its sixth paperback printing (it had first been published in paperback that year), bringing its paperback in-print total to 1.3 million (Maryles "The Latest from L. B").

5. According to Kelly Blewster, "Winfrey decided to invite viewers who had read the book to dinner with her and the author. She and her staff cull the four guests from letters and e-mails hopeful viewers have sent expressing their response to the book. The book discussion dinner is taped, and portions are shown on her show's book club segment" (21).

6. Parkins suggests that the 1998–1999 Oprah television season marked a shift in focus toward 'Change Your Life TV', a move to distinguish her talk show from "the Jerry Springers of the talk-show world" (145).

7. "Today's show is going to break your heart and heal it again . . . don't worry if you haven't yet read [*We Were*] *The Mulvaneys* because as with all of our book club shows it's more about life than about a novel." Winfrey explains that when this book was announced as the book club selection "letter after letter poured in" [from viewers] saying "this is our story."

8. Gavin McNett, writing for online magazine *Salon*, suggests that "most Oprah books 'play on sentiment' and only help readers 'learn what they already know'" (Chin and Cheakalos 112). Max writes: "There's something odd about Winfrey's insistence on treating novels as springboards for self-reflection. Aren't novels about stepping outside one's experience?," and then explains that this particular approach is part of the program's commodification of books and therapy: "This therapeutic approach has made Winfrey the most successful pitch person in the history of publishing" (36). Max also suggests that Winfrey's approach to reading is highly prescriptive and condescending: "At the end of each book club show, Winfrey announces the name of a new book that she has read and loved. She doesn't just name it. She sings it out: "'*PAR-A-DISE.*' CAN YOU ALL SING WITH ME? '*PAR-A-DISE.*'" Or she exclaims, "'*BREATH, EYES, MEMORY,*'" and exhales, blinks her eyes, and then pats her forehead. Then she and her staff go into the audience with a stack of the books under their arms and hand them out. People reach up timidly to take theirs. But Winfrey charms with her smile, reassuring them they have several weeks to do the reading." (36)

9. Janice Peck argues that on chat shows such as *Oprah*:

Audience members privilege individual experience as the "primary source of truth." Through their self-help logic, the shows encourage taking responsibility for one's own feelings and behavior, basing the encouragement on an assumption that participants are powerless to change anything beyond [their] own lives. Through the discourses of Protestantism, liberalism, and the therapeutic, the shows reproduce the dominant ideology of "self-contained individualism"—the foundation of the existing American social order. (qtd. in Shattuc 98)

10. Max writes: "I knew the names of only half the authors before I started. Winfrey's canon does not conform to New York's literary fashions; she draws from a separate sense of what an important book is. For one thing, the narratives she has chosen are overwhelmingly by women—22 out of 28. In eight novels, young women are abused, raped or murdered. A dozen men commit adultery or act abusively toward their families. Women nurture, men threaten. The book club includes no novels of soldiers in war or old men dealing with mortality. Only five novels have male protagonists. The implication is this: we are women, and we are going to read about women" (36). See also Fitzgerald, James, and Kirkpatrick.

11. Max describes "Oprah's Book Club" as a "vast experiment in linked literary imagination and social engineering. Toni Morrison calls it " 'a revolution,' because Winfrey's rapport with the camera cuts across class and race. . . . Women from the inner city to the suburbs rush out each month to buy Oprah's pick" (36).

12. See James, Kirkpatrick, and Max. Also, one viewer, Maggie Smith Barr, asserts that "some book club dinner guests are chosen less for their grasp of the book than because they will elicit an emotional response from the audience, because it will make 'good TV'. . . . The Maya Angelou show was good TV. It was not, however, a book discussion. . . . A good discussion would include some praise, some criticism, some differing viewpoints, some ideas I have never heard of, some thoughts from a person who has a different life experience from mine" (Blewster 21).

13. One frequently asked question on the Oprah.com Web site is "why doesn't the Book Club choose any nonfiction books?" The answer: "Oprah has chosen only one nonfiction book, *Heart of a Woman* by Maya Angelou, but Oprah highlights so many other nonfiction books on the show that she feels Oprah's Book Club should be a forum for fiction" ("Oprah Book Club Facts" Oprah.com). When an autobiography was chosen, it was revealed as a "surprising choice for her 41st Book Club selection—the first nonfiction book since 1997! . . . *Stolen Lives: Twenty Years in a Desert Jail* by Malika Oufkir. Have you read the latest Oprah's Book Club selection? How did it affect you? We want to hear from readers who have been moved by this powerful true story" (oprah.com).

14. For example, see Roberts 5–14.

15. See Egan, Egan and Gabriele Helms, Gilmore, and Smith and Watson.

16. As one critic suggests, "The list [of books chosen for the book club] has included some truly distinctive writers, like Ms. Morrison, Bernhard Schlink and, notoriously, Jonathan Franzen. And it has also included a string of sentimental works by unmemorable writers. In all fairness, Ms. Winfrey's batting average isn't notably worse than that of the Nobel Prize committee." ("Oprah Demurs" A24). Daisy Maryles writes that Oprah chooses well-written, accessible yet often sophisticated contemporary literature for her club ("Behind the Bestsellers" 18).

17. An example of this is the episode of Oprah's Book Club when Malika Oufkir's autobiography *Stolen Lives: Twenty Years in a Desert Jail* is discussed. The

book is read almost entirely through a biographical reading (i.e., no attention to
other literary or textual aspects) and the book's nonfiction status results in the
author of this text being given much more discussion time and attention than Joyce
Carol Oates received in the previous installment of Oprah's Book Club. As with the
discussion of Oates's novel, guest readers of Oufkir's autobiography are encouraged
to read the book in terms of their own lives and to articulate their responses to the
text autobiographically through the discussion. However, due to the centrality of
the autobiographical author, less time is available for guest readers' autobiographies
on this occasion.

18. Though Roberts is discussing autobiographical writing, I believe that the
same values hold true for other autobiographical acts in culture.

19. Similarly, Kirkpatrick writes: "Some admirers of her efforts, however, said
the notion that worthy books were harder to find seemed to contradict her testimonials to the pleasures of reading. 'I don't buy that at all', said John Leonard, a literary
critic for *The Nation* and a television critic for *New York Magazine* and the former
editor of *The New York Times Book Review*. 'You have 55,000 to 60,000 new books
being published each year. If 10 percent of that is worth paying attention to, and I
think it is, then it shouldn't be hard to come up with something once a month'" (A1).

Works Cited

Blewster, Kelly. "Oprah Winfrey: Testifying to the Power of Books." *Biblio* (Jan.
    1998): 21.

Chin, Paula, and Christina Cheakalos. "Touched By An Oprah: How does it feel to
    be embraced by the patron saint of book publishing?" *People Weekly* 52.24 (1999):
    112.

Douglas, Kate. "Blurbing Biographical: Authorship and Autobiography." *Biography:
    An Interdisciplinary Quarterly* 24.4 (2001): 806–26.

Eakin, Paul John. "Foreward." Philippe Lejeune, *On Autobiography*. Ed. Paul John
    Eakin. Trans. Katherine Leary. Minneapolis: U of Minnesota P, 1989.

Egan, Susanna. *Mirror Talk: Genres of Crisis in Contemporary Autobiography*. Chapel
    Hill:U of North Carolina P, 1999.

Egan, Susanna, and Gabriele Helms. "Autobiography and Changing Identities."
    Biography: An Interdisciplinary Quarterly 24.1 (2001): ix–xx.

Fialkoff, Francine. "12 Good Books: Despite Oprah's careless words, there are
    dozens of books worthy of attention." *Library Journal* 127.9 (15 May 2002): 76.

Fitzgerald, Sarah. "Inside Oprah's Book Club." *Writer's Digest* 80.10 (Oct. 2000):
    24–27.

Gilmore, Leigh. *The Limits of Autobiography: Trauma and Testimony.* Ithaca: Cornell UP, 2001.

Gray, Paul. "Winfrey's Winners: Oprah recommends a book on TV and bingo!—her viewers turn it into an instant bestseller." *Time* 148.25 (1996): 84.

Grossberg, Lawrence. *We Gotta Get Out of This Place: Popular Conservatism and Postmodern Culture.* New York: Routledge, 1992. 305.

Hartley, Jenny. *Reading Groups.* Oxford: Oxford UP, 2001. 4.

Hope, Deborah. "Eat, Drink and Be Literary." *The Weekend Australian.* 11–12 August 2001: R4–R5.

Illouz, Eva. "'That shadowy realm of the interior': Oprah Winfrey and Hamlet's Glass." *International Journal of Cultural Studies* 2.1 (1999): 118.

James, Caryn. "Harnessing TV's Power to the Power of the Page." *New York Times* (21 Nov. 1996): NA.

Kirkpatrick, David D. "Oprah Will Curtail 'Book Club' Picks, and Authors Weep." *New York Times* (6 Apr. 2002): A1.

Leitch, Thomas. "After Oprah." *Kirkus Reviews* 70.9 (1 May 2002): 587.

Long, Elizabeth. "Textual Interpretation as Collective Action." *The Ethnography of Reading.* Ed. J. Boyarin. Berkley: U of California P. 1992: 180–211.

Maryles, Daisy. "Behind the Bestsellers." *Publishers Weekly* 244.9 (1997): 18.

———. "The Latest from L. B.: How Oprah Winfrey's book club selection helped sales of Janet Fitch's *White Oleander.*" *Publishers Weekly* 246.20 (1999): 23.

Max, D.T. "The Oprah Effect." *New York Times.* 26 Dec. 1999: 36.

McHenry, Robert. "All Hail Oprah's Book Club." *The Chronicle of Higher Education* 48.35 (10 May 2002): B17.

"Oprah's Book Club." *Oprah Winfrey Show.* Channel 10 Australia. 12 Apr. 2001.

Oprah Winfrey Show Web site. http://www.oprah.com (16 May 2001).

'Oprah Demurs.' Editorial. *The New York Times* (10 Apr. 2002): A24.

Parkins, Wendy. "Oprah Winfrey's Change Your Life TV and the Spiritual Everyday." *Continuum: Journal of Media and Cultural Studies* 15.2 (2001): 145–57.

Peck, Janice. "The Mediated Talking Cure: Therapeutic Framing of Autobiography in TV Talk Shows." *Getting a Life: Everyday Uses of Autobiography.* Ed. Sidonie Smith and Julia Watson. Minneapolis: U of Minnesota P, 1996. 152.

Popkin, Jeremy D. "Coordinated Lives." *Biography: An Interdisciplinary Quarterly* 24.4 (2002): 781: 805.

Prasso, Sheridan. "Apres Oprah." *Business Week* 3788 (24 June 2002): 12.

Roberts, Michéle. *Food, Sex and God: On Inspiration and Writing.* London: Virago, 1998: 5–14.

Rooney, Kathy. "Oprah Learns Her Lesson." *The Nation* 274.19 (20 May 2002): 56.

———. "The Final Chapter: Oprah's Book Club." *The Economist* (US), 13 Apr 2002: NA.

Shattuc, Jane. *The Talking Cure: TV Talk Shows and Women.* New York: Routledge, 1997. 98.

Smith, Sidonie, and Julia Watson, *Reading Autobiography: A Guide for Interpreting Life Narratives.* Minneapolis: U of Minnesota P, 2001.

———. *Getting a Life—Everyday Uses of Autobiography.* Minneapolis: U of Minnesota P, 1996.

Tompkins, Jane. "Me and My Shadow." Ed. Robyn R. Warhol and Dianne Price Herndl. *Feminisms: An Anthology of Literary Theory and Criticism.* New Brunswick, NJ: Rutgers, 1997. 1105.

12

CORRECTING OPRAH

Jonathan Franzen and the Uses
of Literature in the Therapeutic Age

KEVIN QUIRK

In his effusive praise of Jonathan Franzen's 2001 novel *The Corrections*, one early reviewer declared it "a conventional realist saga of multigenerational family dynamics . . . and love's mutating mysteries," but insisted it had "just enough novel-of-paranoia touches so Oprah won't assign it and ruin Franzen's street cred" (Gates 10). Yet soon after this review—and only weeks after the novel's publication—Winfrey did indeed select it and her decision turned into a minor media story but a major literary fracas. For his repeatedly expressed ambivalence about being chosen for Oprah's Book Club, Franzen was labeled "an elitist curmudgeon," insensitive and condescending toward Winfrey and her readers (Dyson 29). As a result of his comments, Franzen became the first author to have his invitation withdrawn. But this distinction raised his "street cred" with some, who applauded him for "encouraging readers to think for themselves . . . instead of waiting like sheep for Ms. Winfrey's pronouncements" (Czarnecki A24).

As these statements suggest, media coverage and the public response generally characterized the controversy as a clash between high art and middlebrow taste. While this is not inaccurate, it overlooks crucial differences between Winfrey and Franzen over therapeutic values and their relation to literature. Jonathan Franzen has consistently positioned himself—and literature in general—in opposition to a mainstream culture whose therapeutic values, he implies, are tainted by their feminine and multicultural associations, while Oprah's Book Club stressed the therapeutic value of multicultural reading.[1] For these reasons, this chapter argues that the apparent high/middle divide hinged primarily on conflicting views of the Book Club's therapeutic reading pedagogy in particular and the therapeutic ethos in general. More specifically, I claim that although the club promoted literary reading in a politically progressive, multicultural manner, the Book Club failed to distinguish between literature and self-help or to define a unique set of *literary* values, a task that has been central to Franzen's career. At the same time, however, I demonstrate that although Jonathan Franzen's discomfort with Winfrey's Book Club was rooted in often outspoken hostility toward therapeutic values, his work—both *The Corrections* and an earlier essay—actually veers between a straightforward antitherapeutic stance and a profoundly ambivalent one. The astonishing success of both Oprah's Book Club and *The Corrections* and the strident partisanship the conflict provoked indicate that they tapped deep currents in contemporary American culture. Overlooking the central concerns and differences of the two adversaries not only simplifies their dispute but also obscures serious questions it raises about literary and therapeutic values and their relationship to one another.

Prelude to a Controversy—Literary Value in "The Harper's Essay"

The incendiary remarks that cost Jonathan Franzen his invitation to Oprah's Book Club should be examined in light of his previous statements about literature, therapy, and multiculturalism. At no time during his dustup with Winfrey did he directly address the club's therapeutic orientation. Nevertheless, his somewhat famous 1996 essay published in *Harper's* magazine—like a number of his later declarations and *The Corrections* itself—explicitly identifies therapeutic culture and the preoccupation with psychic health as among his major concerns. Before the publication of his third novel, the "*Harper's* essay," as Franzen himself refers to it, was the novelist's best-known work and reviewers often used it as touchstone for evaluating *The Corrections*. In this earlier piece, "Perchance to Dream: In an Age of Images, a Reason to Write Novels," critically acclaimed yet commercially unsuccessful, Franzen writes in despair of his own "obsolescence," likens "the institution of writing and reading serious novels" to a "depressed inner city," and questions the novel's ability to "engage the culture" in the context of "the banal ascendancy of television; the electronic fragmentation of public discourse" (36–38). The social novel, the medium of social reportage and instruction that once commanded large audiences and delivered them meaningful news, is dead, he declares, replaced by television news magazines and Hollywood film. Anguish over this and his own insignificance had thrown the author into a depression and stymied progress on his third novel.

More relevant to the brush with Winfrey is the fact that this lament is rooted in Jonathan Franzen's frustration with simplistic understandings of mental health and the function of literature in today's therapeutic society. Eva Moskowitz has demonstrated how contemporary Americans subscribe to a "Therapeutic Gospel" that constitutes a sort of secular faith, a program for individual and social development that stresses that the individual's happiness should be our supreme goal and that all other measurements are contingent upon the measure of this happiness. What is more, this faith presumes, personal problems and discontent stem principally from internal, psychological causes rather than external, social forces and therefore demand psychological remedy (1–7). Because of this, Moskowitz and other scholars have tended to characterize the therapeutic outlook as intellectually, politically, and morally evasive.[2]

In the *Harper's* essay, Franzen expresses similar views. Despite openly acknowledging his own debilitating depression, the author refuses what he regards as the obvious fixes and remains reluctant to categorize his condition as a disease because, he says, "A disease has causes: abnormal brain chemistry, childhood sexual abuse, welfare queens, the patriarchy, social dysfunction. It also has cures: Zoloft, recovered-memory therapy, the Contract with America, multiculturalism, virtual reality." He would rather treat himself with art, one of "the historically preferred methods of coming to terms with [the] Ache" that defines human existence (47). Yet he is careful to distinguish literature from self-help, arguing that "strong works of fiction . . . [are] everything that pop psychology is not." Quoting Shirley Brice Heath, an anthropologist who has studied contemporary reading practices, Franzen contends that, in contrast to reading self-help works, "reading serious literature impinges on the embedded circumstances in people's lives in such a way that they have to deal with them. And, in so dealing, they come to see themselves as deeper and more capable of handling their inability to have a totally predictable life" (49). Franzen characterizes mainstream American culture as distinctly therapeutic and defines literature in opposition to that most salient quality. Therapeutic society is anti-intellectual and promotes an inauthentic emotional certainty that is ultimately damaging to individuals and society, while literature is cerebral, open-ended, and genuinely healthful.

Franzen's criticism of therapeutic culture in the early sections of the *Harper's* piece echoes what Nina Baym has labeled "melodramas of beset manhood," theories of American literature that depict the white male writer as marginalized by an "encroaching, constricting, destroying society" against which he, like his fictional protagonists, does battle (133). In his updated version, Franzen finds himself at odds with a consensus culture that he perceives as not only feminine, as in earlier theories, but also multicultural and therapeutic. He links the recent popularity of novels by women and minorities to academic multiculturalism and distances himself from the "therapeutic optimism now raging in English literature departments [that] insists that novels be sorted into two boxes: Symptoms of Disease (canonical work from the dark Ages before 1950), and Medicine for a Happier and Healthier World (the work of women and of people from non-white or non-hetero cultures)" (47). Although he does not decry, as Nathaniel Hawthorne once did, any "damned mob of scribbling women," he does contend that women and what he terms other "tribal" writers have clearly defined audiences for their work. White men, on the other hand, are ignored by all but a few steadfast readers and are unable to shape the culture in the ways their predecessors had. In a telling footnote, Franzen explains, "Writers like Jane Smiley and Amy Tan today seem conscious and confident of an attentive audience. Whereas all the male novelists I know, including myself, are clueless as to who could possibly be buying our books" (48).[3] He also approvingly quotes novelist David Foster Wallace, who avers:

it's not an accident that so many of the writers 'in the shadows' are straight white males. Tribal writers can feel the loneliness and anger and identify themselves with their subculture and can write to and for their subculture about how the mainstream culture's alienated them. White males are the mainstream culture. So why shouldn't we angry, confused, lonely white males write *at* and *against* the culture? (51)

Interestingly enough, however, the essay concludes with an apparent disavowal of such alienation and strikes a note of compromise in which Franzen modifies his ambition for grand cultural authority. The personal story he tells reads like an *Oprah* narrative—a triumph over emotional deprivation and a journey from the margins into the mainstream. Indeed, the essay moves from the profound pessimism summarized above to hope and reconciliation. In the later sections, the author declares that his next novel will abandon the "crushing imperative to engage explicitly with all the forces impinging on the pleasure of reading and writing" (54). He characterizes this adjustment (or correction) in intellectual, aesthetic, *and* therapeutic terms, explaining that only by ending his social and artistic isolation and jettisoning the ambition to "Address the Culture and Bring News to the Mainstream" did his work begin to progress. Having abandoned the conviction that novels must effect cultural change, Franzen embraces the more modest idea that "novelists are preserving a tradition of precise, expressive language; a habit of looking past surfaces into interiors." Above all, he resolves, as a novelist, to help preserve "a community of readers and writers" who subscribe to literary fiction's "tragic realism," a complex view of the world that "raises more questions than it answers . . . [and] doesn't resolve [conflict] into cant" (52–53).

Here is where the essay's stance on therapy and literature veers revealingly toward contradiction. When he says his depressive condition "didn't need curing," Franzen is apparently referring to the contemporary cures mentioned earlier (54). At the same time, however, he suggests that, though it is "anything but straightforward," the tragic realism in strong fiction has functioned as a cure for him, not by making him "fit into the 'real' word" (as Zoloft or self-help presumably might) but rather by making him understand his place in it as reader and writer (53–54). This allows him to overcome his personal and artistic despair and restores the pleasure of reading and writing. By implication, one of the primary values of literature lies in its *genuinely therapeutic utility*, which differs from the falsely simplistic promises of the other cures Franzen shuns. While the distinctions he makes may be real and worth investigating further, what is notable here is the way this ostensibly antitherapeutic writer ultimately falls back on therapeutic language to valorize literature.

Therapeutic Multiculturalism in Oprah's Book Club

An invitation from Winfrey might seem like a perfect opportunity for a writer determined to reenter the mainstream of American life and serve a community of readers and writers. In light of his views on literature, therapy, and multiculturalism, however, having his novel associated with Oprah's Book Club looks like Jonathan Franzen's worst nightmare. Despite his claims to be unfamiliar with the Book Club, the therapeutic preoccupations of *Oprah* and her club were hardly news at the time of Franzen's selection; indeed, "Oprahfication" had become shorthand for the spread of the

therapeutic outlook in American culture, and it is hard to believe that an
author who once wished to "address the culture and bring news to the
mainstream" would find Winfrey's basic approach to books surprising. Not
long before the Winfrey/Franzen fracas, in a feature article in the *New York
Times Magazine* D. T. Max argued that Book Club selections constituted a
"therapeutic canon" and club segments modeled a self-help approach to
reading (36). Max's article demonstrates that Oprah's Book Club structured
reading fiction as a means to self-fulfillment, but the piece overlooks the
way the Club consistently synthesized its therapeutic approach with the
broad goals of multiculturalism—recognition and respect for racial, cultural, and gender differences. This section of my chapter illustrates the
Club's reading pedagogy by looking at one Book Club episode and one
selection and then comparing them briefly to critical work on middlebrow
reading and the therapeutic ethos. In doing so, I demonstrate how the
Club's therapeutic orientation helps bring multicultural reading practices
into the mainstream, but, in doing so, both diminishes the importance of
cultural difference and evades questions of literary value.

Its second anniversary show, aired in September 1998, encapsulates the
Book Club's therapeutic multiculturalism. Like most segments, it celebrates
the power of books and reiterates a vision of reading as an intense, transformative emotional encounter. By way of introducing that month's selection,
Winfrey declares, "[The] beauty of books is . . . that books connect us . . .
and bring us all closer. That's what many family members of the mentally ill
wrote to us about Wally Lamb's book, *I Know This Much Is True*" ("Oprah's
Book Club" 1–4). The crux of Club segments, however, is the dinner party
where Winfrey, invited guests, and the author discuss the novels. The
dinner/discussion is a tightly edited session that repetitively enacts the therapeutic and multicultural value of reading—sometimes quite movingly,
sometimes to the point of banality. Lamb's novel is the story of twin broth-
ers, one of whom suffers from schizophrenia; the second anniversary show
therefore orients its discussion around how the novel helped readers cope
with the disease and develop a healthier sense of self. For guest Kathleen,
who also has a schizophrenic twin, the book served as a healing experience
that saved her "a trip to the shrink . . . [and] . . . thousands of dollars" (8).
Molly, who has suffered from mental illness herself and spent years in therapy, says that the main theme for her was the book's message: "With
destruction comes renovation." She explains, "I found the most success . . .
when I could face my fear, when I was willing to let go of the way it was,

look at the way it really is, and then be open to what it could be. It only came after I was willing to look at my past, face my fears, rip it apart and build it back up again" (9). The most dramatic illustration of the power of club pedagogy comes for guest Monica, who finds affirmation of her biracial heritage in the book. Tired of narratives in which being multiracial is tragic and sad, she finds empowerment in the novel's affirmation of the multiple heritages the central family unearths.

A number of novels mirror the therapeutic and multicultural reading protocols reiterated throughout Book Club segments. This is especially true of Billie Letts's *Where the Heart Is*, a January 1999 selection. As the story opens, the protagonist, Novalee Nation, seven months pregnant and on her way to California, finds herself abandoned by her boyfriend in the middle of rural Oklahoma. Though young, alone, and broke, through the support of a makeshift family consisting of the racially diverse denizens of Sequoyah, Oklahoma, Novalee matures into a strong, independent single mother and professional photographer. Together with community support, books play a crucial in her transformation. Once, while perusing the works she has read, she realizes the ways they have changed her identity and her outlook:

> And suddenly, Novalee knew—knew what she hadn't known before. She wasn't who she had been. She would never again be who she was before. She was connected to those women she had read about. Untouchables. Black women. Arab women. She was connected to them just as she had been connected to girls in seventh-grade gym class. (157)

Novalee's early life in a small, poor, largely white town warped her self-understanding, limited her potential for personal growth and professional success, and denied her familiarity and friendship with those culturally and racially different. In her new home, cross-cultural reading experiences play a crucial role in her emotional and intellectual triumph over the limitations of her past.

This therapeutic multiculturalism suggests that middlebrow reading practices have moved in a progressive direction since the mid-twentieth century. Janice Radway's work on the Book-of-the-Month Club, for example, demonstrates that what she labels the club's "middlebrow personalism" promoted reading as "narrative therapy"—a technique for consolidating a coherent sense of self and achieving personal connection. However, as she shows, that club targeted a largely white male middle class and narrowed the range of possible identifications by shying away from works about people "too different from the white middle class . . . at the center of middlebrow culture" (283, 306, 285). In contrast, through its selections, reading strategies, and audience address, Oprah's Book Club embraced a much wider range of identities. Monica, the biracial guest from the second anniversary show, serves as an example. By identifying vaguely with one of the characters and a particular passage about him, even she, who appears to have no direct connection in her life to schizophrenia, manages to interpret the novel in ways that affirm important aspects of her identity and thus shore up her self-esteem. The process she exemplifies mixes psychic healing with validation for marginalized identities and reiterates the club axiom that ostensible differences mask underlying commonalities.

The club clearly worked to mainstream multicultural values. Though American culture may be saturated with therapeutic discourse, it most certainly does not embrace multiculturalism and female empowerment to the extent that Oprah's Book Club does. Following philosopher Richard Rorty, we might say therefore that the "sentimental education" encouraged by Oprah's Book Club "gets people of different kinds sufficiently well-acquainted with one another so that they are less tempted to think of those different from themselves as only quasi-human . . . [and] expand[s] the reference of the terms *our kind of people* and *people like us*" (10).

However, while it points to a politically progressive development in middlebrow reading practices, the therapeutic optimism on Oprah's Book Club tended to push cross-cultural identification to the point that, as Franzen would say, it resolved into cant. Historian Jackson Lears might use the term "evasive banality" (*No Place of Grace* 17). Lears's work suggests that, at the end of the nineteenth century, the emergence of the therapeutic outlook in American culture—an outlook first formulated by the white male bourgeoisie—was characterized by banality and "platitudinous vagueness" that trivialized the very large-scale socioeconomic problems therapeutic practices were designed to counteract ("From Salvation" 9). We can see a similar pattern in Oprah's Book Club and this pattern compromises its political and intellectual import. While "difference" in its various forms emerged as a widespread concern at the end of the twentieth century, as the second anniversary show illustrates, the Club emphasized the importance yet trivialized the difficulty of addressing racial and cultural difference. Monica's identification with the text seems almost mechanical and the Club's discussion of differences works at times to render them ultimately insignificant. The Book Club's therapeutic multiculturalism functions as a tactic of recognition and evasion of difference.

Its failure to distinguish between differences and interrogate them in rigorous fashion makes the Book Club susceptible to the same criticism scholars have made of the therapeutic worldview: It is not only vaguely platitudinous, but also morally relativistic. If personal growth and psychic health are ultimate values, then identifying with difference serves merely as a means to those ends. In turn, the moral and political challenges these differences pose become subordinate to personal fulfillment. Indeed, on Oprah's Book Club, racial or cultural differences are constructed principally as tools to help the individual reader become whole rather than dilemmas to confront on emotional, intellectual, and political terms. For similar reasons, Lears and other scholars regard the therapeutic as a conservative, if not reactionary, ideology, and although there is much to this characterization, Winfrey's show clearly indicates that the therapeutic can play a far more ambiguous social and political role. Careful examination of Book Club practices points to the fluid ideological nature of therapeutic values and serves as a necessary corrective to the prevailing scholarly view that they are fundamentally conservative.

However, the Club's political and moral ambiguities parallel its uncertainty about the particular value of literature. Although Winfrey consistently celebrated books as unique, selected literary novels and expressed awe toward writers, the club's therapeutic rhetoric consistently obscured discussions of specific literary values. Like the cross-cultural identifications it promotes, the Club consistently valued reading literature primarily as a means to personal growth or psychic healing. As the second anniversary show illustrates, the Club characterized literature as like therapy, only better. By validating it almost exclusively in this way the Club failed to differentiate literature from other therapeutic practices and texts. Indeed, the Club's reading practices would seem to confirm Jonathan's Franzen's contention that literary and therapeutic values are fundamentally at odds. Although the decision to feature literary fiction at first seemed to be a dramatic departure from talk show values and practices, and commentators were surprised by the Club's ratings and the sales of its selections, Oprah's Book Club clearly managed to energize readers and sell an astonishing number of "serious" novels by avoiding literary concerns and centering its reading practices squarely within the show's standard frame of value.

Crossing Over/Pulling Back—Gender
and the Therapeutic in *The Corrections*

The Club's reading pedagogy stands at odds with Jonathan Franzen's views on literature, therapy, and multiculturalism, suggesting therefore that these differences were at the root of the author's later discomfort. However, concerns for literature and therapy not only divide Winfrey and Franzen but also bring them together. They share a general belief in the value of literature and a desire to enlarge its audience. Oprah's role as therapist at-large is well known, while in his essays, novels, and public statements Franzen returns to the issue of therapy repeatedly. Moreover, in recent years, both have tried to reposition themselves within their own fields, each moving toward a sort of middle ground. The Book Club served as a means, among others, for Winfrey to distinguish her program from trash talk shows such as *Jerry Springer* and *Jenny Jones*; *The Corrections* likewise marks a shift away from the brainy postmodernism of Franzen's early career and toward more accessible, traditionalist storytelling.

What follows outlines some common ground Winfrey and Franzen share, then concludes with a more careful analysis of their differences on literature and therapy. This section first examines the reception of *The Corrections* as a hybrid, crossover, if not specifically middlebrow, text in order to suggest how Franzen and Winfrey were moving toward the cultural middle. Then, after considering Franzen's comments about the Club, I conclude by offering a close reading of the ways *The Corrections* explores the issues raised by Franzen's *Harper's* essay and his later statements—the elite/popular cultural divide, the effects of media culture and the nature of the female audience, and the role of therapy in American culture. This reading suggests that Franzen's views on gender are more sympathetic than his comments alone indicated. Most important, I argue that despite the author's ostensibly antitherapeutic inclinations, the novel concludes with its own profoundly ambivalent depiction of therapeutic adjustment. This not only demonstrates that the controversy was more than a simple highbrow/middlebrow split but also suggests that the tense intersection of literature, gender, and therapy in this controversy might serve as fertile ground for investigating questions of literary value in contemporary culture.

The Corrections was published in the early fall of 2001 amid a level of hype emblematic of the media culture Jonathan Franzen had bemoaned in his essay five years earlier. Farrar, Straus & Giroux distributed 3,500 advance copies to reviewers and booksellers, issued an initial print run of 85,000 and budgeted $100,000 on advertising—numbers far in excess of those typical of most literary fiction (Lacayo 78). The promotional blitz paid off. *Publishers Weekly* noted that Franzen's work had been the buzz at that summer's Book Exposition of America and, by the time of its release, *The Corrections* had already been optioned by major Hollywood producer Scott Rudin (Zalesky 164). Even before Winfrey announced it as a selection, it had risen to #7 on the *New York Times* best seller list (Zeitchik and Nawotka 26). Despite being mired in controversy, in November of that year, *The Corrections* won the National Book Award for Fiction and was later nominated for (but failed to win) both the National Book Critics Circle Award and the Pulitzer Prize. It remained on best seller lists for most of its first year in print and by March 2002, over 960,000 copies had been shipped and sales of the novel totaled over $12 million (Buchanan S11). It became that holy grail of the publishing industry—a critical and commercial blockbuster.

The novel was widely reviewed and lavished with almost unanimous praise. Reviewers used the *Harper's* essay as a touchstone for assessing *The Corrections*, but tended to overlook the author's decision to abandon his grand ambition to write a great social novel. Citing the essay as an implied declaration, *San Francisco Chronicle* reviewer David Kipen proclaimed that the novel "stands as the literary equivalent of Babe Ruth's famous 'called shot.'" Like Ruth, Franzen predicts a home run, "swings for the fences and clears them with yards to spare" (D1). The *New York Times* published an admiring author profile in its magazine and glowing reviews in both its *Book Review* and daily edition. Reviewers invoked the predictable superlatives: "the first great novel of the twenty-first century," "wildly brilliant, funny, and wise," and "simply a masterpiece" (Charles 19; Zalesky 164). Announcing it as a selection, Winfrey called it "the best 568 pages I've read in years" (qtd. in Jacoby A19). Arguably, *The Corrections* was the biggest sensation in the American literary scene since the appearance of Oprah's Book Club almost five years before.

In different ways, both Franzen and Winfrey were hailed as literary saviors and celebrated for crossing cultural boundaries. The Book Club's phenomenal early success had the mainstream press wondering if Winfrey was "saving the novel before our eyes?" (Schwartz C7). She was depicted as a guardian angel for authors—*People* published an article titled "Touched by an Oprah"—and was credited with bridging the gap between literary high-mindedness and ordinary readers (Chin and Cheakalos 112). Reviews and profiles contended that in *The Corrections* Franzen had produced a hybrid work that served to "correct" past literary errors by synthesizing tradition and innovation, ideas and action, emotion and analysis, the personal and the social. Novelist Adam Begley declared, " *The Corrections* is mostly aimed at the heart, in a way that makes it an agreeably accessible novel, poised halfway between postmodern chic and plain, old-fashioned storytelling. . . . What Mr. Franzen does—brilliantly—is to risk sentimentality to get at emotional truth" (10). Gail Caldwell of the *Boston Globe* deemed it "a big, showy powerhouse of a novel, revved up with ideas but satisfyingly beholden to the traditions of character and plot" (E3). Contrasting this novel to his earlier fiction, *Time* reviewer Richard Lacayo described it as "A more personal book. The social disorders of the 21st century are expressed mostly through the personal distempers of the three siblings and their flight to the false consolations of sex, careerism and consumerism." *The Corrections*, it averred, corrected "certain problems in the postmodern novel—its cartoonish character. Its repetitive paranoia and absorption in Big Patterns" (78).

Franzen's change in course mirrors changes Oprah Winfrey made on her show a few years before. Fed up with the sensationalism of daytime talk television, Winfrey used the book club (among other programming changes) to claim cultural legitimacy and thus reposition her show "upward" toward the cultural center.[4] Similarly, Franzen himself has suggested that he has used a strategy of triangulation to bridge gaps and reach a more mainstream audience. He has spoken of his retreat from the "systems novels" of Pynchon, DeLillo, and Gaddis that he had admired and tried to emulate in his earlier work, and has repeatedly expressed a wish to create the kind of fully realized characters that postmodernism foreswore.[5] As he told one interviewer, "For better or worse I'm . . . an emotions guy"—perfect, as one commenter noted, for *Oprah* (Klinkenberg A16).

Yet, though Franzen had finally grabbed the spotlight he had once coveted, Oprah's embrace became a badge of shame. Once selected, in interviews and at readings, the author quickly distanced himself from the Book Club. Like one of his characters, he seemed reluctant to appear "crappy and middlebrow" (*The Corrections* 415). He cringed at Winfrey's choices, explaining: "She's picked some good books, but she's picked enough schmaltzy, one-dimensional ones that *I* cringe, myself, even though I think she's really smart and fighting the good fight" (Weich, par. 53). In an interview on National Public Radio, Franzen further elaborated on his unease: "I feel like I'm solidly in the high-art literary tradition, but I like to read entertaining books and this maybe helps bridge that gap, but it also heightens these feelings of being misunderstood." He called the club's dinner/discussion a "Kaffee Klatch" and described the videotaped author profile he was forced to endure as "bogus" in its stagy sentimentality (qtd. in Kirkpatrick C4). He fretted that having the Oprah logo, a seal of "corporate ownership," on his book would compromise his authorial autonomy and put off readers who "have suspicion of anything with a mainstream stamp of approval. My chief worry now," the author explained, "is that I will lose readers that I'm interested in attracting" (qtd. in Thorn 1E). More particularly, he "had some hope of actually reaching a male audience," which he feared would balk at the Oprah stamp of approval (Gross).

Partisans who spoke out in defense of Franzen echoed these sentiments. The *New York Times* reported, "to some bookworms, [the Oprah logo] is a scarlet O," and one such person explained, "It makes me feel mainstream to be reading an Oprah book. I don't want people to think that I have no idea about literature or that I sit home and watch TV all day" (Corcoran J6). The Oprah label, literally and symbolically, compromised the independence of both writer and reader. Book Club readers were "sheep" who passively followed Winfrey's dictates and, like the author, Franzen's defenders positioned themselves firmly in opposition to a mainstream culture they devalued as passive and feminine.

The author's remarks suggest that he had reverted to the outsider stance purportedly abandoned at the end of his *Harper's* essay. There is little doubt that Franzen put his foot in his mouth and he has expressed his regret, albeit at times unconvincingly, for his awkwardness. His discomfort, however, can be better understood when viewed alongside the novel, which treats similar issues. *The Corrections*, in fact, demonstrates much more complex and sympathetic views of audience response, commodification, and female empowerment. And while I am not suggesting, as D. H. Lawrence insisted, that we should simply "trust the tale not the teller," examining parts of *The Corrections* will illustrate Franzen's views in more comprehensive fashion and offer a more precise analysis of the way questions of gender and therapy intersected in this literary controversy.

The following close readings maintain that in many interesting ways *The Corrections* avoids the crude high/middle, masculine/feminine, active/passive oppositions the author and his defenders invoked during his dustup with Winfrey. Nevertheless, this analysis shows that, despite its eagerness to bridge these divides, *The Corrections* sustains a distinctly masculine perspective. Yet surprisingly, by critiquing therapeutic culture from this masculinist angle, the narrative moves ultimately toward not a disavowal but rather a reformulation of the therapeutic in more masculine terms.

Franzen's depiction of his character Chip Lambert offers an object lesson on elitist contempt for mainstream sentimentality and commercialism, while the story of Chip's mother, Enid, reads like a parable of female empowerment and liberal tolerance. An assistant professor of Textual Studies, Chip teaches a course on Consuming Narratives. As a test for the final meeting of the course, Chip shows the video of an advertising campaign called—of all things—"You Go, Girl." The ad campaign mirrors the therapeutic, multicultural optimism of *Oprah* episodes and Book Club segments, but the satire focuses primarily on Chip's self-inflating, knee-jerk anticommercialism. The campaign consists of six episodes shown once a week during a prime-time hospital drama and has been celebrated in the mainstream press as a revolution in advertising. It tells the story of four diverse female office workers— "one sweet young African American, one middle-aged technophobic blonde, one tough and savvy beauty named Chelsea, and one radiantly benignant gray-haired Boss"—who bond together when Chelsea is diagnosed with breast cancer. Although Chelsea dies, the experience of coming to her aid not only brings the women together but helps them learn the wonders of technology by utilizing W_____ Corporation's Global Desktop Version 5.0 to research treatments and support networks. As the series concludes,

> The Boss is scanning a snapshot of the departed Chelsea, and the now rabidly technophiliac blonde is expertly utilizing the W_____ Corporation's Global Desktop Version 5.0, and around the world, in rapid montage, women of all ages and races are smiling and dabbing away tears at the image of Chelsea on their own Global Desktops. Spectral Chelsea in a digital video clip pleads: "Help us Fight for the Cure." The episode ends with the information, offered in sober typeface, that the W_____ Corporation has given more than $10,000,000 to the American Cancer Society to help it Fight for the Cure. (39–40)

Chip is dismayed with their response when he asks the class whether it is truly revolutionary "to engineer a surefire publicity coup for your ad campaign" by having Nielsen rate episodes, by rebroadcasting it during sweeps week, and by floating a rumor on the Internet that Chelsea is a real person. Students do not notice the campaign's cynical exploitation of women's fear of breast cancer and fail to understand that as "Baudrillard might argue . . . the evil of a campaign like 'You Go, Girl' consists in the detachment of the signifier from the signified." In fact, the entire class feels the ads are "good for the culture and good for the country," and even Chip's star pupil, Melissa, refuses to share his contempt for the campaign. She argues, "It's celebrating women in the workplace. . . . It's raising money for cancer research. It's encouraging us to do our self-examinations and get the help we need. It's helping women feel like we own this technology, like it's not just a guy thing" (43). The incident almost directly mocks the intellectual certitude with which Franzen condemned television, therapy, and multiculturalism in the *Harper's* essay.

The Corrections also evokes the seductive lure of consumer culture. Melissa ridicules the course's assumption that "making money is inherently evil" and that " 'corporate' is a dirty word," and Chip later comes to wonder "if the Great Materialist Order of technology and consumer appetite and medical science really *was* improving the lives of the formerly oppressed; if it was only straight white males like Chip who had a problem with this order" (44–45). Later, when Chip finds himself isolated on a Thanksgiving morning in suburban Connecticut, he takes

comfort in the sturdy mediocrity of American commerce, the unpretending metal and plastic roadside hardware. The thunk of a gas-pump nozzle halting when a tank was filled, the humility and promptness of its service. And a *99¢ Big Gulp* banner swelling with wind and sailing nowhere, its nylon ropes whipping and pinging on a galvanize standard. And American sedans moving down the access road at nearly stationary speeds like thirty. And orange and yellow plastic pennants shivering overhead on guys. (62)

Whereas Franzen the public figure squirms about having the Winfrey's "corporate seal of approval" on his book's dust jacket and seeks to avoid commercial taint, Franzen the novelist explores corporate capitalism and consumer culture in far more sympathetic and nuanced fashion, evoking their ambiguities, their frightening challenges to personal autonomy, and their uncanny ability at times to satisfy personal needs and serve the social good.

The novel's portrait of Enid Lambert, Chip's mother, likewise appears at odds with Franzen's aversion to the book club, therapeutic culture, and multiculturalism. As A. O. Scott remarked in the *New York Times*, Enid "is the kind of person who might watch Oprah, and buy a book with the telltale O

on the cover" (D4). She embodies the very middle-American, kitschy sentimentality at which Chip and his creator recoil. For Enid, the pageantry of
Middle American weddings evokes "the paroxysmal love of place. . . . [A]t a
Saturday wedding in the lilac season, from a pew of the Paradise Valley Pres-
byterian Church, she could look around and see two hundred nice people
and not a single bad one." Her white suburban community outside the mid-
western city of St. Jude seems to her "like a lawn in which the bluegrass grew
so thick that evil was simply choked out: a miracle of niceness" (118). She
"loves Christmas the way other people love sex" (432) and the tiny plastic
Christ child figurine she places in the Advent calendar every year is "an icon
not merely of the Lord but of her own three babies and of all the sweet baby-
smelling babies of the world. She'd filled the twenty-fourth pocket for thirty
years, she knew very well what it contained, and still the anticipation of
opening it could take her breath away" (471).

Notwithstanding the irksome banality of Enid's optimism, Franzen has
repeatedly called her his favorite character and the hero of the book. Interestingly, in contrast to the heroes in the classic American fiction identified by the
theories Baym discusses, she is neither male nor an outsider. She embodies the
mainstream consensus—suffocating her children and driving them away—
and is victim of it—constantly acceding to its patriarchal mores at the expense
of her own happiness. Moreover, her ability to endure and change bears striking similarity to the transformations undergone by the protagonists of
Oprah's Book Club selections, as well as by Club guests. Enid moves from
being stifled by her family's needs and her husband's authority to exercising
the personal agency she has long found elusive, and in achieving that agency
she quietly rises above the stuffy prejudices of middle-class suburbia.

In the novel's epilogue, entitled "The Corrections," her husband Al has
been committed to a long-term care facility. With Al out of the house, Enid
sees "everything more clearly now" (563). At her bridge game, when her
partner begins "to vent her Christian disapproval of a famous 'gay' actress,"
Enid, "no champion of 'alternative' lifestyles," retorts that being gay is not a
choice and "that with so many people hating 'gays' and disapproving of
them, why would anybody choose to be 'gay' if they could help it?" (564)
Enid's self-assertion is redolent of the ethos of Oprah's Book Club and the
novel's final lines exemplify its trademark themes of endurance and personal
growth. After two years in a home, Al finally passes away, and when Enid
"pressed her lips to his forehead and walked out . . . into the warm spring
night, she felt that nothing could kill her hope now, nothing. She was sev-
enty-five and she was going to make some changes in her life" (568). Despite

her often exasperating conformity, Enid lacks the kind of feminine passivity Chip (like Franzen's defenders) perceives in the unenlightened and unironic masses. And unlike the heroes of canonical male fiction—Natty Bumppo, Huck, Ishmael—she does not light out *from* but rather reasserts herself squarely *within* society—a move that parallels her creator's own efforts to succeed within the mainstream of American culture.

Regardless of his reputed postmodern orientation and his concern with large cultural, social, and economic forces, Franzen's novel reads much like the "Illness Stories" Richard Ohmann has identified in canonical and pre-canonical postwar American fiction. Ohmann argues that novels by John Updike, J. D. Salinger, Saul Bellow, and Philip Roth are characterized by this narrative in which deep social contradictions produce an individual crisis that is resolved not through transformation of those social contradictions but instead through personal transformation. By concluding their narratives with the "achievement of personal equilibrium vis-à-vis the same untransformed external world," these authors identify "individual consciousness, not the social or historical field, [as] the locus of significant happening" (80, 89). Like these narratives, *The Corrections* ends with Enid's transformation and implies that individual self-discipline holds the key to personal survival, if not happiness, amid the social contradictions elaborated throughout the novel.

In his criticism, Ohmann rendered visible postwar American fiction's unacknowledged investment in therapeutic transformation. Jonathan Franzen shares similar goals for his fiction. He has stated, "I'm pretty impatient with realist fiction written today that tells these stories of family conflict or bad marriages and that pretends that those conversations can now happen without a discussion of drugs or therapy" (Miller 4). But although his depiction of Chip and Enid suggest sympathy for the kind of female empowerment Oprah so vigorously promotes, in many ways the novel evokes hostility toward the therapeutic ethos and its tendency to view emotional strife as a simple matter of personal adjustment—that is, correction. For Franzen the issue of treatment is a fraught one, one in which he rejects psychotherapy and psychotropic drugs and insists that individuals work through their difficulties independently. One should achieve mental health the old-fashioned way, he implies, by stoically earning it.

Indeed, the novel's depiction of psychological remedies reveals striking parallels to the author's take on corporate ownership and authorial autonomy. Early in the novel, Chip argues, "the structure of the entire culture is flawed. . . . The very definition of mental 'health' is the ability to participate in the consumer economy. When you buy into therapy, you're buying into buying" (31). Chip's brother Gary accuses his father of being clinically depressed, and Al responds evenly, "So are you." (176). The novel makes it clear that both men are right, but it favorably juxtaposes Al's manly stoicism to Gary's laughably clumsy attempts to avoid confronting his depression. Gary is comically tormented by the question of whether or not he is depressed and he resents that his wife Caroline has been in treatment because it has "given her a lifelong advantage over [him] in the race for mental health" (159). Al's struggle with depression is quiet, dignified, and tragic; Gary's frantic, craven, and ridiculous.

What is more, in speaking of his own depression, Franzen suggests his affinity with the long-suffering, drug- and therapy-free Al. His public statements structure the story of his recovery around a key moment of refusal. After a friend has arranged an appointment with a doctor willing to prescribe antidepressants, "unsure about how a substance like Prozac would affect a writer's brain," Franzen chooses not to go (Eakins, para. 45). Instead, he resolves to fight the disease on his own terms and to retain his sense psychological, physiological, and artistic autonomy. Though Franzen calls Al "a government that could no longer govern" (7), we are asked to admire his, *and Franzen's*, noble desire to strive, to fight, and not to yield his self-control. He presents himself—suffering artist in his Harlem loft—and Al—the solitary tinkerer in his basement workshop—as the last of an outmoded breed of men beset by a cultural milieu that needs but can no longer find a place for their kind.

One would be tempted to characterize this as straightforward male fantasy were it not complicated by the story of Enid's refusal to succumb to Aslan, an Ecstasy-like wonder drug that appears to offer the ultimate correction to her unhappiness. Aslan is an illicit street drug in America, but a fully legal European prescription medication—a "personality optimizer" (321). Ironically, it relies for its effectiveness on a process Al developed and patented years before. The Axon Corporation has bought the rights to that patent, but because he refused to negotiate beyond their initial offer, Al received only a pittance while the corporation stands to make millions.

The novel thus frames the lure of the drug as potentially a double betrayal for Enid, not only of her authenticity and autonomy but also of her husband and the integrity that led him to refuse to capitalize excessively on his patent. Though the drug works wonders for her disposition and helps Enid cope with the uncertainty of her Christmas plans, she fails to get more Aslan in time for the holidays and is forced to face the inevitable chaos of the family gathering on her own. Amid intense squabbling and Al's sudden deterioration, when her daughter, Denise, lets her know the drug has arrived, Enid chooses not to keep the pills. She becomes the hero of the novel, then, by acting like Al, like Franzen, like a man. In refusing the drugs, she tells Denise, "I want the real thing or I don't want anything" (530).

Though Franzen's public statements express a desire for distinction from Oprah's audience, making Enid the hero of the novel makes that audience central and her example instructive. Enid's refusal of a neurochemical solution to her unhappiness mirrors the desire for authenticity and independence Franzen craves as an individual and artist. But whereas the pedagogy of Oprah's Book Club contends that drugs and therapy may be the keys to authenticity and independence, Franzen's work depicts them as threats and suggests that personal empowerment and cross-cultural solidarity, like literature, are more authentic, more real, when achieved through disciplined masculine self-control rather than therapeutic evasion.

Conclusion

Just as Jonathan Franzen insists that realist novels of family conflict or bad marriages ought to address the topics of drugs and therapy, the controversy between Franzen and Oprah's Book Club suggests that the discussion of literary value in mainstream American should not take place without discussing the complicated relationship between perceptions of literary values, therapeutic values, and gender. Before this incident, Winfrey's success in selling books and generating excitement about reading had left little room in the mainstream press for serious, engaged assessment of the ways she framed literary value. Franzen's discomfort ignited the first and most sustained criticism of Oprah's Book Club. While his comments may have tapped elitist and antifeminine sentiment in literary culture, there is good reason to suppose that concerns may have been deeper and broader than that and may have been rooted in similar ambivalence about therapeutic values, particularly their perceived challenge to masculinity and the sometimes rote, unintellectual manner in which they have been conflated with literary value.

Even the champions of the book club conveyed ambivalence similar to Jonathan Franzen's. At the time of the controversy, many defenses of Winfrey's Club were remarkably lukewarm and unassertive. *The Cleveland Plain-Dealer* described her picks as "not anything close to an embarrassment," and novelist Jay Parini asked, "Who would not want to be in the company of

Toni Morrison and Joyce Carol Oates?" (Sandstrom E1; qtd. in Mahegan F1). Michael Eric Dyson credited Winfrey with having "almost single-hand-edly boosted the nations' literacy level. . . . [T]he most powerful woman in America," he claimed, "has used television—a medium often disparaged by cultural snobs—to achieve what thousands of programs aimed at increasing our cultural I.Q. have failed to do" (29). Like Dyson, a number of commen-tators shied away from defending the quality of her selections and instead elaborated what *Washington Post* book critic Jonathan Yardley called the "Classic Comics theory: It's better to read something—comics, box tops, skywriting—than nothing at all, and maybe reading bad stuff will lead some people to read good stuff" ("Oprah's Bookend" C2). Though he faulted her picks as melodramatic, Yardley claimed, "But she doesn't pick genuinely bad books. . . . The literary taste of the American mass market is execrable. Oprah Winfrey is doing her part to elevate it" ("The Story of O, Cont." C2). These defenses reveal a strong faith in a fairly traditional cultural hierarchy in which great works of literature fend off the same media-fueled philistinism that concerns Jonathan Franzen. Oprah's Book Club and middlebrow cul-ture in general are deemed most valuable as conduits for connecting readers to the very same high literary tradition with which Franzen allies himself. If Franzen's purported snobbery is objectionable but "high" literature remains desirable, we must ask: What is desirable about it? As previously mentioned, Franzen himself has tried to answer, citing intellect, linguistic precision, irony, and open-endedness. He has also explained: "It's a tonal thing and a stylistic thing as well as an ability to be funny. I need to be persuaded that . . . I'm going to be protected from icky, embarrassing sentimentality or leaden earnestness" (qtd. in Canfield).

   Is this a representative view? What else do contemporary literary actors indicate is at stake? The insensitivity of Franzen's comments and Oprah Win-frey's summary disinvitation turned the event into media melodrama and shut down discussion. But by engaging Oprah's Book Club in more critical yet nonpartisan fashion, we can begin asking some larger questions about lit-erary value that the controversy raises. To what extent, we might ask, are therapeutic and other values mixed or conflated in other reading communi-ties and mainstream discussions of literature? What nontherapeutic (aes-thetic, intellectual, political) criteria shape popular discussions of literature and reading practices? What qualities do gatekeepers and readers perceive distinguish high, middle, and lowbrow fiction and how are gendered and therapeutic terms invoked to make distinctions? Like so many other com-mentators, Jonathan Franzen and Oprah Winfrey both agree that literary reading performs an invaluable role in American culture—their conflict points us toward a more precise understanding of perceptions of that role.

Notes

1. My chapter treats Oprah's Book Club in its first incarnation, from 1996 to 2002. Because of this, I speak of it in the past tense.

2. In addition to Moskowitz, see scholarship on the therapeutic in American culture: Robert Bellah et al., *Habits of the Heart: Individualism and Commitment in American Life*, (Berkeley: U of California P, 1996); T. J. Jackson Lears, *The Culture of Consumption: Critical Essays in American History, 1880–1980* (New York: Pantheon, 1983); Ann Douglas, *The Feminization of American Culture* (New York: Knopf, 1977); Philip Rieff, *The Triumph of the Therapeutic* (New York: Harper & Row, 1966); Christopher Lasch, *Culture of Narcissism: American Life in an Age of Diminishing Expectations*, rev. ed. (New York: Norton, 1991) and *The Minimal Self: Psychic Survival in Troubled Times* (New York: Norton, 1984); Dana. L. Cloud, *Control and Consolation in American Culture and Politics: Rhetorics of Therapy* (Thousand Oaks: Sage, 1998); and Elayne Rapping, *The Culture of Recovery: Making Sense of the Self-Help Movement in Women's Lives* (Boston: Beacon Press, 1996).

3. It is important to note that here and in other essays and interviews, and unlike the theorists of American literature Baym criticizes, Franzen does not exclude novels by women and minorities from the category of literature. He instead attacks the ways works by women and minorities are taught and understood, not their specific content or value. In fact, in this same essay, Franzen cites Paula Fox's *Desperate Characters* as an exemplary work of fiction that has been unjustly ignored.

4. Besides the book club, in the mid-1990s Winfrey launched The Angel Network, an ongoing charitable campaign featured regularly on the show, and created the programming feature "Change Your Life TV." She also became involved in *Oxygen*, a television company for women, and began publishing *O* magazine. All these moves constitute a clear effort to claim greater cultural legitimacy.

5. Franzen has expressed this sentiment in numerous instances, including his notorious *Harper's* essay and, most recently, in Jonathan Franzen, "Mr. Difficult," *The New Yorker* 30 Sept. 2002: 100–11.

Works Cited

Baym, Nina. "Melodramas of Beset Manhood: How Theories of American Fiction Exclude Women Authors." *American Quarterly* 33.2 (1981): 123–39.

Begley, Adam. "'But Dad!' The Joys of Family, Up Close and Scarily Lifelike." Rev. of *The Corrections* by Jonathan Franzen. *New York Observer* 16 July 2001: 10.

Bellah, Robert et al. *Habits of the Heart: Individualism and Commitment in American Life*. Berkeley: U of California P, 1996.

Buchanan, Patricia. "Seroy Gets Author Franzen's Honesty to Come Out in Oprah Flap." *Advertising Age* 25 Mar. 2001: S11.

Caldwell, Gail. Rev. of *The Corrections* by Jonathan Franzen. *Boston Globe* 9 Sept. 2001: E3.

Canfield, Kevin. "The Perfection of 'The Corrections.'" Rev. of *The Corrections* by Jonathan Franzen. *Hartford Courant* 9 Sept. 2001: G2.

Charles, Ron. "That Warm Family Feeling." Rev. of *The Corrections* by Jonathan Franzen. *Christian Science Monitor* 13 Sept. 2001: 19.

Chin, Paula, and Christina Cheakalos. "Touched by an Oprah." *People* 20 Dec. 1999: 112–22.

Cloud, Dana. L. *Control and Consolation in American Culture and Politics: Rhetorics of Therapy*. Thousand Oaks: Sage, 1998.

Corcoran, Monica. "On the Dust Jacket, to O or Not to O." *New York Times* 21 Oct. 2001: J6.

Czarnecki, Paul. Letter to the Editor. *New York Times* 2 Nov. 2001: A24.

Dyson, Michael Eric. "Read Him and Weep." *Chicago Sun-Times* 30 Oct. 2001:29.

Eakin, Emily. "Jonathan Franzen's Big Book." *New York Times Magazine* 2 Sept. 2001: 18+. LexisNexis Academic. DePaul University. 11 Jan. 2007.

Franzen, Jonathan. *The Corrections*. New York: Farrar, Straus & Giroux, 2001.

———. "Mr. Difficult." *The New Yorker* 30 Sept. 2002: 100–11.

———. "Perchance to Dream." *Harper's* April 1996: 35–54.

Gates, David. "American Gothic." Rev. of *The Corrections* by Jonathan Franzen. *New York Times Book Review* 9 Sept. 2001: 10.

Gross, Terry. Interview with Jonathan Franzen. 15 Oct. 2001. http://freshair.npr.org. 3 May 2003.

Jacoby, Jeff. "Too Good for Oprah." *Cleveland Plain-Dealer* 5 Nov. 2001: B7.

Kipen, David. "Big Franzen Novel Aims High." Rev. of *The Corrections* by Jonathan Franzen. *San Francisco Chronicle* 15 Sept. 2001: D1.

Kirkpatrick, David D. "Winfrey Rescinds Offer to Author for Guest Appearance." *New York Times* 24 Oct. 2001: C4.

Klinkenborg, Verlyn. "The Not-Yet-Ready-for-Prime-Time Novelist." Editorial. *New York Times* 30 Oct. 2001: A16.

Lacayo, Richard. "Great Expectations." Rev. of *The Corrections* by Jonathan Franzen. *Time* 10 Sept. 2001: 78.

Lasch, Christopher. *Culture of Narcissism: American Life in an Age of Diminishing Expectations*, rev. ed. New York: Norton, 1991.

———. *The Minimal Self: Psychic Survival in Troubled Times*. New York: Norton, 1984.

Lears, T. J. Jackson. "From Salvation to Self-Realization: Advertising and the Therapeutic Roots of the Consumer Culture, 1880–1930." *The Culture of Consumption: Critical Essays in American History, 1880–1980*. Eds. Richard Wightman Fox and T. J. Jackson Lears. New York: Pantheon, 1983. 1–38.

———. *No Place of Grace: Antimodernism and the Transformation of American Culture, 1880–1920*. Chicago: U of Chicago P, 1981.

Letts, Billie. *Where the Heart Is*. New York: Time Warner, 1995.

Mahegan, David. "Franzen Not Alone in Oprah Dilemma." *Boston Globe* 10 Nov. 2001: F1.

Max, D. T. "The Oprah Effect." *New York Times Magazine* 26 Dec. 1999: 36–41.

Miller, Laura. "Only Correct." Interview with Jonathan Franzen. *Salon.com* 7 Sept. 2001.

Moskowitz, Eva. *In Therapy We Trust: America's Obsession with Self-fulfillment*. Baltimore: Johns Hopkins UP, 2001.

Ohmann, Richard. "The Shaping of a Canon: U.S. Fiction, 1960–75." *The Politics of Letters*. Middletown, CT: Wesleyan UP, 1987. 68–93.

"Oprah's Book Club." Transcript from *The Oprah Winfrey Show*. Burrelle's Information Services, 25 Sept. 1998.

Radway, Janice A. *A Feeling for Books: The Book-of-the-Month Club, Literary Taste, and Middle-Class Desire*. Chapel Hill: U of North Carolina P, 1997.

Rapping, Elayne. *The Culture of Recovery: Making Sense of the Self-Help Movement in Women's Lives*. Boston: Beacon, 1996.

Rieff, Philip. *The Triumph of the Therapeutic*. New York: Harper & Row, 1966.

Rorty, Richard. "Human Rights, Rationality, and Sentimentality." *Yale Review* 81.4 (October 1993): 3–20.

Sandstrom, Karen. "Author's Snub of Oprah Reveals His Own Literary Bias." *Cleveland Plain-Dealer* 25 Oct. 2001: E1.

Schwartz, Amy E. "Will Oprah Save the Book?" *Washington Post* 15 Dec. 1996: C7.

Scott, A. O. "Seizing the Literacy Middle." Editorial. *New York Times* 4 Nov. 2001: D4.

Thorn, Patti. "Too Hip for Oprah?' *Rocking Mountain News* 3 Nov. 2001: 1E.

Weich, Dave. "Jonathan Franzen Uncorrected." Interview with Jonathan Franzen. 4 Oct. 2001. http://www.powells.com/authors/franzen.html. 3 May 2003.

Yardley, Jonathan. "Oprah's Bookend." *Washington Post* 15 April 2002: C2.

———. "The Story of O, Cont'd." *Washington Post* 5 Nov. 2001: C2.

Zalesky, Jeff. Rev. of *The Corrections* by Jonathan Franzen. *Publishers Weekly* 16 July 2001: 164.

Zeitchik, Steven, and Edward Nawotka, "Franzen Hits the Road." *Publishers Weekly* 10 Oct. 2001: 26.

13

THE WAY WE READ NOW

Oprah Winfrey, Intellectuals, and Democracy

SIMON STOW

I might begin with a confession that will possibly resonate with many read-ers of a collection such as this, and, in so doing, pose it as a problem: I am embarrassed to be seen reading a novel that Oprah Winfrey has recom-mended. This extends to any novel on her now long list of recommended texts, but especially those identified with the circular symbol, the inscribed "O," the not-quite-scarlet letter that marks out a text as having the Winfrey seal of approval. When Oprah has recommended books that I have also wished to read, I have gone to great lengths to obtain a non-Oprah copy: ordering Toni Morrison's *Paradise* over the Internet from the U.K.; persuad-ing (for which you should read begging) a sales clerk to sell me the window display copy—the last one without the symbol of shame—of Jonathan Franzen's *The Corrections*; and when, all else had failed, simply obliterating the Oprah logo with a black marker (how I long for the days when it was simply a removable sticker, not an integral part of the book jacket). I would like to justify this foible with some high-minded explanation, but the sad fact is that my motivation is sheer snobbishness. I simply worry that I, an academic and as such an ostensible intellectual, should be seen reading a book recommended by Oprah Winfrey; more accurately, I worry that people will think I am reading a book *because* Oprah recommended it.

I offer this confession not to alleviate my latent, antipopulist guilt—though I do feel better for having done so—but as a starting point for a reflection on Oprah Winfrey's Book Club and its troubled and troubling relationship with intellectuals and the ivory tower. It is a relationship that is made all the more troubling by the recent resurgence in interest among certain academics in the power of literature to offer us insight into other ways of living, thinking, and being in the world: insight that is said, by some at least, to be of benefit to the practice of liberal democracy. By liberal democracy is meant here, of course, a system of government with a commitment to popular rule, individual rights, and the rule of law, one that draws on the work on John Locke (1988), John Stuart Mill (1998), and John Rawls (1971). This interest in the alleged "othering" power of literature has its historical roots in Aristotle (1997), and in the nineteenth-century work of Adam Smith (2002) and Matthew Arnold (1993), but more recently it has come to play a significant role in the work of such philosophically and politically diverse luminaries as Martha Nussbaum, Richard Rorty, and Gayatri Chakravorty Spivak.

Martha Nussbaum's *Poetic Justice: The Literary Imagination and Public Life* is an impassioned plea for the expansion of our moral imaginations as citizens, jurors, judges, and social scientists through the act of reading novels about those from whom we differ in numerous ways. Similarly, Richard Rorty has argued that reading novels generates "solidarity"—akin to the sort of "fellow feeling" identified by both Adam Smith and Martha Nussbaum—making us more attentive to the needs of others. In addition, he suggests that novels can also show us the kinds of cruelty of which we ourselves are capable, alerting us to the contingency of our own deepest convictions, and making us more tolerant of other perspectives. Nussbaum also believes that literature can alert its readers to the contingency of their own positions simply by depicting difference. "There is," she writes, "no more effective way to wake pupils up than to confront them with difference in an area where they had previously thought their own ways neutral, necessary and natural" (*Cultivating* 32). Spivak has made similar claims about these values of contingency and solidarity in her *The Death of a Discipline*, arguing—in part at least—for a move away from the high Theory that has dominated literary studies in recent years, and a return to reading as a source of insight into practical social and political problems.

In light of this apparent convergence of literary theorists, political thinkers, and philosophers on the power of literature and reading to generate all sorts of useful moral and political insights, one might be forgiven for thinking that academics and intellectuals would welcome Oprah's Book Club as an opportunity to see their pet theories put into political, philosophical, and literary practice. None of these thinkers has, however, seen fit to comment—in print at least—on Oprah's undeniable success in getting

America reading, and those intellectuals who have chosen to comment on the Oprah phenomenon have been somewhat less than kind. Jonathan Franzen's public ambivalence about his novel *The Corrections* being selected, and then deselected by Oprah, was relatively mild compared to the late Alfred Kazin's (in)famous description of the Book Club as the "carpet bombing of the American mind" (Braun 8). Even when Winfrey was lauded by the organizers of the National Book Awards, receiving a medal on the fiftieth anniversary of the organization, they were keen to stress—in a "doth protest too much" kind of way that alerted everybody to their real motivation—that Oprah was being recognized for "a literary reason, not a marketing reason" (Minzesheimer 47).

What seems particularly galling to the literati is not just the rather predictable type of books that Winfrey chooses—for a long time they tended to be tales of individuals overcoming racial, sexual, or some other injustice—but also the way they are read. Rebecca Pepper Sinkler, for example, complains that:

> The discussion on Oprah's Book Club is hardly rigorous. The conversation consists mainly of breathless enthusing—as much for the wild mushroom ravioli on a shallot reduction sauce as for the fictional fare. The novels seem to supply emotional rather than aesthetic epiphanies: There are frequent tears. One white guest, outspoken about she hadn't wanted to read about poor black people, underwent a conversion after reading *Song of Solomon*. On camera, she bore witness to the power of fiction to broaden the mind, and she was gathered back to the flock as a repentant sinner. (1)

Pepper concedes that although Winfrey has on occasion "displayed perfectly respectable literary judgment" in her choice of books, often the reader "response is more therapeutic than critical, more pop-psych than post-mod." She speaks for many perhaps when she confesses her fear, albeit in a somewhat tongue-in-cheek way—though only somewhat, that "Oprah was threatening my life's work" (1).

Ironically, however, it may well be that in provoking this kind of highly personal, often emotional, and surprisingly confessional response in her readers, Oprah Winfrey is doing more to engender the democratic values and insights sought by thinkers such as Nussbaum, Rorty, and Spivak than the thinkers themselves. For, at least as far as moral and political values are concerned, there appears to be an important difference in the way that academics and intellectuals write and talk about novels and the way that non-intellectuals or "lay readers" do so. The former tend to speak in the objective or impartial voice, personifying the text and telling us what it or the author (who is similarly constructed) intends, along with the moral and political lessons that we should derive from our reading. Lay readers, such as those in Oprah's Book Club, are, by contrast, notable for the frequency with which they draw attention to the contingency or subjectivity of their position, prefacing their comments with "I" statements such as "I thought," "I think," or "it seems to me." It is a difference that suggests that it is Oprah, not the intellectuals, who offers us the best model of the use of literature to generate values that are necessary to the practice of liberal democratic society. Establishing this claim requires, however, a brief exposition of the most recent attempts to establish the connection between literature and liberal democracy.

Of the three thinkers who have recently sought to revive the connection between literature and liberal democracy, only two—Martha Nussbaum and Richard Rorty—offer a detailed account of the alleged link. Spivak simply gestures toward the claim in her typically elliptical style. Despite their deep philosophical differences, both Nussbaum and Rorty suggest that reading novels about people from whom we differ in a multitude of different ways will expand our moral imaginations, making us more sensitive to the needs of others, and, as such, better citizens of a liberal democratic society. Nussbaum's and Rorty's claims are predicated upon a similar approach to reading the novels they recommend: Each reads the text and tells us the lessons that readers will or should derive from it. Mr. Gradgrind will, according to Nussbaum, alert us to the dangers of excessive abstraction and formal modeling (*Poetic* 13–27); Charles Kinbote and Humbert Humbert, according to Rorty, to the need to be more sensitive to the suffering of others (*Contingency* 141–68). In this, both seem to be advocates of a "supply-side" theory of the novel; neither seems to be terribly concerned about the role of the reader. Nussbaum, for example, argues that the very form of the novel "constructs compassion in readers, positioning them as people who care intensely about the suffering and bad luck of others, and who identify with them in ways that show possibilities for themselves" (*Poetic* 66). Similarly, in his introduction to *Pale Fire*, Rorty presumes "to describe the reader's reactions in the course of a first reading of the book" (v) simply by reading the text without any reference to an actual reader. In this, both seem to be guilty of what Jonathan Rose has called the "Receptive Fallacy": identifying the response of readers by studying the text rather than the readers themselves (4). This focus on the text at the expense of actual readers is further evidenced by the apparent need of Nussbaum and Rorty to champion their own interpretation of a given text at the expense of all other readings.

It is a distinctive feature of the contemporary work of literature and democracy that the thinkers involved identify the lessons one will, or should, derive from reading the books they recommend. All seem to be advocates of specific readings—precisely those that support the lessons they wish us to derive from our reading. While Martha Nussbaum is prepared to accept that different readers might draw different meanings from the text, she is never-theless determined that through a process of "coduction"—a sort of conver-sational equilibrium identified by Wayne Booth—they will come to agree on the proper interpretation of the novel—that is, the one identified by Martha Nussbaum. She rejects, for example, Oscar Wilde's reading of *The Old Curiosity Shop* in which he famously declared that "one would have to have a heart of stone not to read the death of Little Nell without laughing" on the grounds that it is "not a properly responsive reading of Dickens's text" ("Defense" 353). For Rorty, too, despite comments elsewhere that would seem to commit him to some version of a reader-response theory (*Conse-quence* 151), there is a definite sense that his project requires agreement on a particular interpretation of given text. At times, Rorty seems to be something of a boo-hooray literary critic: awarding bouquets to those whose reading of the texts corresponds to his own, and brickbats to those whose does not (*Pale Fire* v–xvii). At others, he is similarly prepared to construct the author and his intentions. In reading *Lolita*, he writes, we are alerted to our own cruelty because we forget about the eponymous heroine of the text, and then remember in shame and guilt. We forget, he writes, "because Nabokov arranged for us to forget" (*Pale Fire* viii). Rather than simply assigning the books that they believe to be morally and politically beneficial and sitting back to watch as democracy flourishes, both Nussbaum and Rorty feel the need then to set out their own readings of the novels that they recommend. It is a somewhat puzzling trope.

Given that Nussbaum and Rorty spend so long setting out their own readings of the texts that they recommend, it is not obvious what is actually to be gained from reading in their thought. For it is not clear that having read, say, Nussbaum on Dickens or Rorty on Nabokov, that there is any benefit to be derived from reading the novels themselves. Reading about reading is, furthermore, unlikely to produce the outcome that they both appear to desire: It is rather like expecting to benefit from watching some-body else exercise. Nor is this the only problem associated with their approach to the texts. The suggestion that reading is simply a matter of coming to an agreement on the meaning of a text seems not only to fly in the face of much contemporary literary theory, but also the everyday experience of reading. Almost all of us have probably had a friend who has urged us to read a particular book that changed his or her life, only to read the book and find it truly turgid. Both thinkers accept that some readers might draw different conclusions from a given text—hence Nussbaum's theory of coduction—but both seem to suggest (Nussbaum explicitly, Rorty implicitly) that a failure to see the text in the way that they prescribe arises from some deficiency on the part of the reader, be it irrationality or a simple lack of perception. This account of reading is not only theoretically and empirically flawed, but also politically problematic.

Both Nussbaum and Rorty turn to literature because they believe it will expand the moral imagination of a liberal democratic citizenry, thereby generating greater tolerance and respect for other viewpoints. It is somewhat ironic that it does not appear to do the same for the thinkers themselves. Both write as if they have some unique insight into the texts that they recommend, insight that they are keen to impose on a citizenry in the latter's own interests. Neither seems very interested in textual interpretations that do not match their own. As such, both seem to be guilty of a distinctly illiberal lack of tolerance for other viewpoints. Liberalism seems to demand listening to those other viewpoints and at least considering the possibility that they might be correct. It is precisely this that the "professional" approach to moral and political reading, that which constructs the novel and/or the author's intent and the moral and political lessons to be drawn from the text, seems to prohibit. Nor are Nussbaum and Rorty alone in this. Valentine Cunningham complains about the third recent advocate of literature and othering: "Spivak can't ever avoid thinking about herself in these thoughts about Others. And her namings of Third World women usually involve the loud naming of herself" (52). The point is, perhaps, that honed by years of experience in the demands of academic discourse and debate, Nussbaum, Rorty, and Spivak seem to be somewhat strident in their readings of the texts that they recommend. As academics, they all speak as if the text alone will do all the work on the citizenry, even as they seek to shape the responses of that citizenry with their own textual readings. Juxtaposing the professional responses to Bernard Schlink's novel *The Reader* with those of the lay readers of Oprah's Book Club illustrates the way in which it is the latter that seems more likely to promote the values of contingency, and solidarity, that the theorists of literature and democracy so desire.

Until Oprah reinvented her Book Club in June 2003, possibly bowing to the intellectual snobbery of Kazin and his ilk by deciding to choose "classics" such as *Anna Karenina* and *East of Eden*, her selections tended not to be of a sort to elicit too much academic discussion. Along with the works of Toni Morrison, Bernard Schlink's *The Reader* was an obvious exception, drawing comment in *The New Republic*, *The London Review of Books*, the *Times Literary Supplement*, and the journal *Philosophy and Literature*. In it, Schlink tells the story of Michael, a fifteen-year-old boy in postwar Berlin who has an affair with Hanna, a thirty-six-year-old woman who is later tried for having been a prison guard in the Nazi death camps. Hanna's exact role in the atrocities and her guilt are somewhat complicated by the secret of her illiteracy: Although she is clearly guilty of some of the crimes for which she is charged, her inability to read means that she is also innocent of others. With questions of guilt and responsibility, and with dramatic ironies arising from the disparate levels of information available to the reader and to the characters in the text, the book seems almost tailor-made for moral and political discussion.

In almost every instance, the critics who wrote about the book adopted the previously identified "professional" approach to the text, constructing both the author and the novel's moral and political intent. Martin Conway's 1999 article "Compassion and Moral Condemnation: An Analysis of *The Reader*" was a particular case in point. Conway uses the events of *The Reader* as evidence to support his rejection of Martha Nussbaum's theory of compassion. In so doing, Conway happily constructs the text and the author. "The novel" he writes, "questions the hard and fast distinction that one is either responsible or one is not" (287). Elsewhere Conway claims that "part of the power of the novel is that it operates in the midst of this conflict, refusing to simplify the tension. It does not dismiss the need for moral judgment about Hanna's acts, yet it also refuses to sacrifice compassion" (287). Indeed, Conway personifies the text at various points: "the novel shows" (290); "as the book points out" (291); "the book thereby suggests" (291); "*The Reader* makes this plea" (297); "the novel questions" (297); and "the story acknowledges" (298). Conway's construction of the text and the author not only obscures the origin of the claims that he is making—with his criticism becoming a kind of ventriloquism in which the text is made to speak for the critic's claims—it contrasts sharply with the way in which the lay readers in Oprah's Book Club responded to the text.

In a letter to Oprah read out on the 31 March 1999 show, Julie, a viewer, wrote "I can't get over the fact that Michael was fifteen and Hanna thirty-six. Hanna was a pedophile. I don't know why it's acceptable for a woman to behave in this manner and yet we as a society would be outraged if it were a fifteen-year-old-girl and a thirty-six-year-old-man. I just don't get it."[1] In the studio, Linda, a fifty-one-year-old mother of teenage boys, declared: "I know I am a good mother with high standards and morals. However, I am going out on a limb by saying that if my sons were to have had an early sexual experience, I would not be terribly upset if they had encountered someone like Hanna." In sharp contrast to the approach of Conway, both the letter-writing viewer and the Book Club participant presented their claims as their own, prefacing it with an "I" statement. Nor were they alone in doing so; every participant in the discussion made a similar move, either prefacing their claims with an "I" statement or otherwise identifying it as their own: "I didn't like the book"; "I thought it was a wonderful book"; "the book reached me"; "the book touched me"; "I think"; "I believe"; "I'm saying"; "I look at it this way"; and "If I was [sic] a Nazi." In response to one of the moral dilemmas depicted in the text, even the host herself declared, "I'm now saying he should have gone to her and not the judge. I'd have marched my butt up to the judge but now I'm going to reconsider."

This distinction between the way in which lay readers and professionals talk about the moral and political implications of the novels they read is hugely significant for the possibility of engendering democracy through literature. Unlike professional readers who appear to struggle for some methodology that will lift them out of their own subjectivity and allow them to talk with some degree of impartiality about the texts, lay readers instinctively seem to understand that, when they are talking about the novels they have read, they are talking about their own moral and political reactions. As Oprah Winfrey notes in her discussion of responses to *The Reader*, "the we that you refer to, yourself [sic] is based upon your own personal history." Professional critics, on the other hand, who are more accustomed perhaps to talking about the literary qualities of a text, its structure, or the way in which it seeks to impact on a reader—questions that can be spoken of with a certain degree of impartiality—seem to seek this same impartial voice in the moral and political discussion. Their motivations for so doing may be mere conceptual error, or a rather more insidious desire to gain some kind of authority in moral and political discussions, seeking the cultural weight that comes from adopting the "objective" voice. Either way, however, it is clear that as far as generating values of benefit to liberal democracy are concerned, the lay approach to texts characterized by Oprah Winfrey's audience is a far superior source, not least because it appears that the professional critics misunderstand the source of any possible moral improvement that arises from literary discussion.

Implicit in all the recent attempts to theorize the relationship between literature and democracy is a conversational element, be it Nussbaum's theory of "coduction," Rorty's conceptualization of liberalism as an ungroundable conversation into which he seeks to draw as many people as possible (1989), or Spivak's attempt to make us more sensitive to the demands of the "Other" (2004). In *The Structural Transformation of the Public Sphere*, Jürgen Habermas argues that, in the seventeenth and eighteenth centuries, conversations about books in literary salons "provided a training ground for critical public reflection still preoccupied with itself—a process of self-clarification of private people focusing on genuine experiences of their novel privateness" (29). Such literary debates were, he claims, instrumental in the development of the public sphere and the rise of democracy. It may well be, therefore, that if we do indeed see any moral and political benefit arising from reading certain novels, then it is the conversation about the book, rather than the book that itself, that is doing the work. This would seem to be corroborated by David Miller's work on deliberative democracy. Miller notes that participants in games modeling resource allocation were more likely to choose altruistically when they were permitted a few moments of conversation with their fellow choosers than when they entered the process with no prior contact (190–91). Literature may provide the common ground for such discussions to begin. Furthermore, in their undeniable capacity to draw us in to situations to which we might not otherwise attend, and to consider possibilities that we might otherwise overlook, novels are particularly well suited to their role as the ostensible subject matter in a political conversation, though no more so, perhaps, than films, or even some poems and songs. Nevertheless, this should not blind us to the real source of the potential moral and political improvement: the conversation with and among our fellow citizens. In their tendency to construct the author and the text and to adopt the impartial voice, the ventriloquism of the professional critic may obscure the origin of these values, and, in so doing, potentially undermine them in two ways: first, by simply diverting attention away from the real source of moral and political improvement, and, second, by promoting a self-defeating form of political dialogue.

"Despite their familiarity with the classics," wrote K. K. Ruthven famously, "professors of literature do not appear to lead better lives than other people, and frequently display unbecoming virulence on the subject of one another's shortcomings" (184). The archness of much contemporary professional literary discussion is, perhaps, a function of the adoption of the objective voice—especially now that so much of literary critical discussion is concerned, in one way or another, with the political—a mode of discourse that encourages academic debate rather than moral or political discussion. The difference between a debate and a discussion is, of course, that one can win a debate but not a discussion. In bringing the professional approach to texts into the moral and political realm, thinkers and critics such as Nussbaum, Rorty, and Spivak are, perhaps, turning what might better be a moral and political discussion (which may in and of itself generate the values of contingency and solidarity that they all claim to seek) into a moral and political debate. It is a mode of discourse that is less likely to produce the values alleged to be of benefit to liberal democratic societies, evidence of which is, perhaps, to be found in the shrillness of the exchange between Richard Posner and Martha Nussbaum over the ethical value of literature (Nussbaum "Defense").[2] In Oprah's Book Club, by contrast, the conversation about moral and political values generated by the novel *The Reader* is clearly very much of a discussion, not least because each of the participants is prepared to acknowledge themselves as the source of their claims. As such, the ensuing discussion is, it seems, far more likely to generate the values of contingency and solidarity that Nussbaum, Rorty, and Spivak all desire than the approach that these theorists adopt in their own work.

In the first instance, there appears to be a greater degree of civility in the moral and political discussions generated by the mode of reading in Oprah's Book Club. In response, for example, to Linda's suggestion that she would not mind too much if her sons had an early sexual encounter with somebody like Hanna—in which she implied that the relationship between a thirty-six-year-old woman and a fifteen-year-old boy was not as problematic as other discussion participants had suggested—Cassandra strongly disagreed. Far from adopting the objective or impartial voice of the professional critic, however, she simply said "I disagree with you." Her measured tone, far different from the shrillness of much of our contemporary moral and political discourse, then allowed her to articulate her reasons for disagreeing. Cassandra says of Hanna: "she was really a classic abuser to me. Because she—he never really knew where he stood. He even toward—to the end, he really never knew. He was always somehow trying to turn himself inside out to please her." Even as she makes her claim, Cassandra personalizes it ("to me") and in so doing mitigates her apparent moral judgment, facilitating a more productive exchange. The personalization of the claim and the presentation of reasons stand in stark contrast to the professional approach in which the text is presented as if it decides self-evidently between competing moral and political claims. It may be, of course, that in the studio context the Leviathan-like figure of Oprah or the presence of the book's author imposed a certain amount of discipline of the discussion, and we cannot entirely discount this possibility, but it seems that there is a qualitative difference between the lay and professional moral and political debates arising from textual discussion, and that Oprah is not the only variable. In her memoir of quite a different reading group *Reading Lolita in Tehran*, Azar Nafisi notes a similar difference between the way in which some academics and lay readers read and talk about the texts they read (69), noting how "the novels we escaped into led us finally to question and prod our own realities, about which we felt so hopelessly speechless" (38–39).

The suggestion here then is that we might rethink the way in which recent attempts to establish a connection between literature and democracy by recognizing that it is not so much the books themselves that generate values of benefit to liberal democratic societies, but rather the discussions *about* the books. We might also recognize that despite the apparent disdain of academics and intellectuals for Oprah's Book Club, it is her approach to reading that seems to generate the most profitable discussion of moral and political issues. Indeed, there seems to be a double benefit here: First, Oprah's approach seems to encourage moral and political discussion, rather than debate; second, it also seems to encourage participants to bring up topics that they might not normally feel comfortable in bringing to the public sphere. Like Winfrey who identifies herself as "a survivor of sexual abuse" in *The Reader*-based discussion, Lynn declares that she is "a Jew, a lawyer, a mother, a daughter, [and] a victim of an abusive relationship." Such self-identification, though mocked by professional critics, may allow Book Club participants to recognize that a different position from their own on the events depicted in a novel may well arise from a different life-experience in a way that promotes the sort of empathy valued by Martha Nussbaum. Indeed, that one from whom one differs so significantly—the Book Club's studio participants are generally drawn from a diversity of socioeconomic, ethnic, and religious backgrounds—shares an interest in a novel may well be the first step on the road to some sort of solidarity, the kind that comes from recognizing a fellow reader, or even a fellow enthusiast for a particular author. One cannot, perhaps, imagine other circumstances under which a group as diverse as the one Oprah assembled for her Book Club on *The Reader*—they included a young mother, a middle-aged African American man, and a Jewish woman—would actually be able to engage in so civilized a discussion about the central moral and political values of empathy, compassion, and responsibility, especially one that concerned the always politically sensitive topic of the Holocaust.

There seems then to be something about the abstraction that arises from being seen to discuss literary characters rather than oneself that permits meaningful—and morally and politically useful—dialogue about difficult topics. The lay-reading approach that we see in Oprah's Book Club generates a double perspective—something that is always useful in critical thought—with the participants benefiting from the abstraction of the discussion of literary characters, while nevertheless contextualizing by personalizing their own claims. Indeed, in addition to the solidarity that seems to emerge from these kinds of discussion—which in itself suggests that politically useful empathy requires only recognition rather than understanding or agreement as in the Nussbaum model—the discussion also seems to generate contingency. It emerges not only from the apparently instinctive "I" statements that precede the moral judgments of such discussants, but also from the act of reading and discussing with others. An unidentified audience member notes that her reading of the text led her to listen and talk to others in a new way. "I have to say I read the book because I'm German. I was born in Germany. My parents are German; my relatives are all German. And that was the first time something really, really, made me think about what my family did, what my relatives did, what my grandparents did. . . . And now I'm very, very interested and I've started asking my father questions." The lay approach to reading—which we might characterize as having a certain humility before the text—promotes exactly this sort of questioning. The professional and decidedly "knowing" approach of Nussbaum, Rorty, Spivak, and Conway seems to promote not listening and questioning, but telling and asserting, the sort of thing that draws Valentine Cunningham's ire in his *Reading After Theory*.

The theoretical claim that reading certain novels will make us better citizens of a liberal democratic society seems to flounder on a problematic account of textual interpretation, one in which the text seems to be doing all the work. It is an approach that obscures the real origin of the moral and political claims under discussion: those of the critic. The textual approach that we see in Oprah's Book Club—that which has drawn the scorn of certain professional writers and critics—seems to stand as an important corrective to this claim, for it suggests that the conversation about the texts is equally—if indeed not more—important than the reading itself. The way that readers speak about the texts has, in itself, important consequences for the way in which this conversation, and with it the likelihood of important moral and political values, develops. Nevertheless, to regard the "Oprah approach" as a cure-all for the problems posed by the professional approach to reading and moral values would be something of a mistake. The response to *The Reader* was by no means as universally constructive as the earlier examples suggest. The sexual relationship between the fifteen-year-old Michael and the thirty-six-year-old Hanna drew a great deal of potentially problematic comment.

As Winfrey herself noted, "all of my friends with sons, and particularly a friend with a son who is the same age, were really upset with me about choosing this selection because they . . . felt it was abuse." Indeed, Winfrey read out a letter from a Chester and Joy Goode, public schoolteachers, who declared:

> We watch your show with regularity. We must, however, tell you that your choice for your book club this time, *The Reader*, that discusses sex between a fifteen year old and an adult is reckless. In a day and time when people are questioning morals and young people are struggling to find the answers and love in a time when people like Mary Kay LeTourneau have disgraced the relationship between adults and children, you have chosen a book that not only romanticizes immoral choices but will feed it in a frenzy to the American people. We are so very disappointed.

Where public schoolteachers lie on the lay–professional reading spectrum is not exactly clear, though here they choose the professional mode of address: adopting the objective voice ("immoral choices") and condemning the book for its depiction of an allegedly abusive relationship. Although Winfrey herself tried to mitigate such a claim—"You can love the book without loving the relationship"—this tendency to project one's own moral values onto the texts uncritically as if they were absolutes is a major stumbling block to the development of the values beneficial to liberal democracy. For the book to be morally and politically useful, it seems that it must be capable of disorienting its readers: the sort of thing we see when Linda, having just declared that she would not mind if her teenage boys had a sexual relationship with somebody like Hanna, observed, "Yes, that statement does shock even me." We see the same thing when John, a middle-aged African American member of the Book Club, addresses the author, Bernard Schlink, directly. "One of the things I know about reading" he said, "is when something is unsettling, I have done a lot of thinking, and you have caused a lot of unsettling, Professor"; or indeed, when an unidentified reader responds "Absolutely" to Winfrey's question: "Did you come away from this book feeling differently about yourself, your life, this life, this time?" Texts, that is, must be able to exercise a dialectical impact on their readers.

A dialectical text, according to Stanley Fish, is one that forces its readers "into a rigorous scrutiny of everything they believe in and live by" (1). It is one that forces them to think differently about the world and the way that they live. Fish's work (especially his later work) suggests, however, that whether or not a text has a dialectical impact is—in part at least—a function of how it is read. The readers in Oprah's Book Club happily read themselves into the text, imagining themselves in the dilemmas depicted therein, especially with regard to the question that Hanna raises during her trial: "What would you have done?" Nevertheless, they also seem to recognize, unlike the public schoolteachers Chester and Joy Goode, that this world depicted in the text is a world that is somewhat different from their own. There is both familiarity—that which allows the readers to see themselves in the text—and unfamiliarity—that which generates contingency by making readers uncertain or uncomfortable in their literary surroundings. It is precisely this mix of familiarity and unfamiliarity, comfort and discomfort, that creates the sort of critical self-reflection that generates the potentially useful moral and political discussions that we see in Oprah's Book Club. However, for lay readers in particular, though by no means exclusively, the problematic tendency to conflate these literary and nonliterary worlds is always there: We see it in John's question to the author of *The Reader,* "How autobiographical is this?," and in Winfrey's seconding of it, "Yeah, that's all of our questions, really." Schlink's response is, however, instructive for the role of the academic or the intellectual in this exercise of trying to generate moral and political values that are useful to liberal-democracy.

"Well, Oprah, I mean—of course, in such a book, there go autobiographical elements, but I wrote a novel," declared Schlink in response to Winfrey's question. "That means it's not an autobiographical tale that I wrote." Indeed, he continues, "It's a book about my generation, so it's also a book about me, but not to specify what element is autobiographical and what isn't." In so doing, Schlink identifies his literary world as neither simple autobiography nor complete fiction; he portrays it as both a world that we know and one that we do not. As such, he cultivates the very familiarity, and unfamiliarity, that allows readers both to see themselves in the text and to see themselves potentially transfigured by it. His reluctance to specify and map out what it what makes the text both familiar and strange potentially disrupts the "knowing" responses of readers such as Joy and Chester Goode and, indeed, or Nussbaum, Rorty, and Spivak. In this we see, perhaps, a model for teaching our students how to use literature to think and talk about politics, recognizing, in Italo Calvino's words, "that no book that talks about a book says more than the book in question" (128–29).

Describing her motivations for choosing particular books, Oprah Winfrey declared: "I want books that can pull you into the story, take you different places and allow you to connect and expand your vision of other people in the world" (Pepper Sinkler 1). It is a motivation that is shared by the likes of Nussbaum, Rorty, and Spivak. Nevertheless, Oprah's Book Club suggests that the text is not enough; the way that people read and talk about texts has a direct impact on the likelihood that a particular novel is going to have positive effect on liberal democratic society. There appears to be a balance that must be struck between encouraging citizens to read and letting them read; between generating their interests in texts and standing back and allowing the texts to do their work on and through readers. Describing her approach as "Socratic," Martha Nussbaum declares: "The most important ingredient of a Socratic classroom is obviously the instructor" (*Cultivating* 42). Winfrey's work suggests otherwise. Instructors such as Nussbaum, Rorty, and Spivak seem anxious to insert themselves between the reader and the text, to mold and shape the outcome of the discussion. Winfrey's Book Club suggests that they should also learn to listen. It does not mean, however, that there is no role for the instructor. If they wish to use literature to generate the values of contingency and solidarity, then they can encourage this by facilitating the dialectical impact of texts: teaching their students to see that text as another world, both similar and different from their own. This will generate both the comfort and discomfort that is necessary for democratically productive conversations. Thus, perhaps, academics and intellectuals should see Oprah Winfrey not as a threat, but as a useful ally in a common and worthy cause.

I began this piece by confessing an embarrassment. I will end by confessing a hope. Both are related to Oprah's Book Club. The embarrassment was the possibility of being seen with a book that Oprah recommended. The hope is that perhaps one day my embarrassment will end: that Oprah, or at least her Book Club, will cease to be a target of intellectual snobbery such as my own. For, in stark contrast to the approach of literary intellectuals,

Oprah has not only gotten America reading, she has also gotten her talking, too. It is the combination that is most likely to produce the values beneficial to liberal democracy that are championed by Nussbaum, Rorty, and Spivak. Perhaps, it is time that she received our respect.

Notes

This work was completed with the assistance of a Faculty Summer Research Grant from The College of William and Mary. The author is grateful to Caroline Hanley, Kip Kantelo, and Christine Nemacheck for their critical input and comments.

    1. All references are to "Oprah's Book Club." *The Oprah Winfrey Show*. 31 Mar. 1999.

    2. For a discussion of these differences, see Stow 2000.

Works Cited

Aristotle. *Poetics*. New York: Penguin, 1997.

Arnold, Matthew. *Culture and Anarchy and Other Writings*. Cambridge: Cambridge UP, 1993.

Booth, Wayne C. *The Company We Keep: An Ethics of Fiction*. Berkeley: U of California P, 1990.

Braun, Stephen. "The Oprah Seal of Approval." *Los Angeles Times* final ed. 9 Mar. 1997: 8.

Calvino, Italo. *The Uses of Literature*. New York: Harcourt, 1986.

Conway, Martin. "Compassion and Moral Condemnation: An Analysis of *The Reader*." *Philosophy and Literature* 23 (1998): 284–301.

Cunningham, Valentine. *Reading After Theory*. Malden, MA: Blackwell, 2002.

Fish, Stanley. *Self-Consuming Artifacts. The Experience of Seventeenth-Century Literature*. Berkeley: U of California P, 1972.

Habermas, Jürgen. *The Structural Transformation of the Public Sphere. An Inquiry into a Category of Bourgeois Society*. Trans. Thomas Burger. Cambridge: MIT P, 1991.

Locke, John. *Two Treatises of Government*. Cambridge: Cambridge UP, 1988.

Mill, John Stuart. *On Liberty and Other Essays*. Oxford: Oxford UP, 1998.

Miller, David. "Deliberative Democracy and Social Choice." *Debating Deliberative Democracy*. Eds. James S. Fishkin and Peter Laslett. Oxford: Blackwell, 2003. 182–99.

Minzesheimer, Bob. "Oprah Feted at Book Awards." *Chicago Sun-Times* 18 Nov. 1999, final ed.: 47.

Nafisi, Azar. *Reading Lolita in Tehran. A Memoir in Books.* New York: Random House, 2003.

Nussbaum, Martha C. *Poetic Justice. The Literary Imagination and Public Life.* Boston: Beacon, 1995.

———. *Cultivating Humanity: A Classical Defense of Reform in Liberal Education.* Cambridge: Harvard UP, 1997.

———. "Exactly and Responsibly: A Defense of Ethical Criticism." *Philosophy and Literature* 22 (1998): 343–65.

"Oprah's Book Club." *Oprah. The Oprah Winfrey Show.* 31 Mar. 1999.

Posner, Richard A. "Against Ethical Criticism." *Philosophy and Literature* 22 (198): 366–93.

Rawls, John. *A Theory of Justice.* Cambridge: Harvard UP, 1971.

Rorty, Richard. *Consequences of Pragmatism.* Minneapolis: U of Minnesota P, 1982.

———. *Contingency, Irony, and Solidarity.* Cambridge: Cambridge UP, 1989.

———. Introduction. *Pale Fire.* By Vladimir Nabokov. New York: Knopf, 1992.

Rose, Jonathan. *The Intellectual Life of the British Working Classes.* New Haven: Yale UP, 2001.

Ruthven, K. K. *Critical Assumptions.* New York: Cambridge UP, 1979.

Schlink, Bernard. *The Reader.* Trans. Carol Brown Janeway. New York: Vintage, 1998.

Sinkler, Rebecca Pepper. "My Case of Oprah Envy; She's Got American Reading— And Critics Weeping." *Washington Post* 6 Apr. 1997, final ed.: C01.

Smith, Adam. *The Theory of Moral Sentiments.* Cambridge: Cambridge UP, 2002.

Spivak. Gayatri Chakravorty. *The Death of a Discipline.* New York: Columbia UP, 2003.

Stow, Simon. "An Unbecoming Virulence: The Politics of the Ethical Criticism Debate." *Philosophy and Literature* 24 (2000): 185–96.

14

EVERYTHING OLD IS NEW AGAIN

Oprah's Book Club Returns with the Classics

KATHLEEN ROONEY

> The book club is back and I am on a mission. My mission is to make this the biggest book club in the world and get people reading again. Not just reading, but reading great books!
>
> —Oprah Winfrey

> Winfrey's first selection arched some eyebrows in academe. The literati do not hold Steinbeck's *East of Eden* in particularly high esteem—an opinion that begs some thorny questions that have occupied literary critics and English professors for more than a decade: What is a "classic" anyway? Who gets to decide?
>
> —Mark Coomes

Having worked several summer vacations at Anderson's Book Shop in Chicago's western suburbs, I'm all too versed in the frantic drill of high school summer reading: June, July, and the better part of August laze humidly by as the small yet solid "classics" section toward the back of the store goes relatively untouched in favor of paperback beach books, travel guides, and magazines suitable for reading on a plane or in the family car. Then, T-minus-ten or so days before the scheduled start of classes, it hits: the inexorable tidal wave of kids, accompanied in many cases by harried parents, all urgently purchasing the time-honored texts that they should have started

Kathleen Rooney, excerpt from *Reading with Oprah: The Book Club that Changed America.* © 2005 by The University of Arkansas Press. Reprinted with the permission of the University of Arkansas Press, www.uapress.com.

reading weeks ago. It struck me as fitting, then, that Oprah Winfrey—in many ways one of the nation's most prominent, albeit self-styled, educators—chose Anderson's as the site of the segment in which she announced what amounted to her own massive summer reading assignment. On Monday, 16 June 2003, Winfrey herself appeared in the downtown Naperville store to hand-deliver crates of the mystery selection that had compelled her to bring her hugely influential Book Club back after a fourteen-month hiatus, a selection that would be revealed at the taping of the 18 June show to be John Steinbeck's *East of Eden*.

Personally, I was delighted with the almost novelistic circularity with which my own project had come back to where it started—the store with the anti-Oprah university press poster on the wall of the employee bathroom. The poster, I noticed, was still hanging during my July visit to the store to interview employees about their brush with massive fame. Thank goodness Winfrey didn't ask to use the restroom during her visit. And thank goodness the super-fandom and avid love of books of my former coworker Johanna Monteith inspired Winfrey to visit the store in the first place. "I'm just kind of possessed by her," Monteith explained. "I've watched her forever, and I just really like what she has to say. I joke with my family that I'm going to be her girlfriend some day, and I'm getting closer." This candid affinity for all things Oprah prompted Monteith to e-mail the producers of *The Oprah Winfrey Show* almost immediately upon Winfrey's February announcement of the Book Club's impending revival. After writing to them about Anderson's itself and the multiple specialty book clubs that operate through the store, as well as her own book group, Monteith received a message back expressing producerly interest. Meanwhile, Anderson's owner Tres Anderson received a call on 13 June informing him that "someone from the show" would be arriving the following Monday around noon. "Of course, we never dreamed it would be Oprah herself," said employee Carol Katsoulis. But, of course, it was and, just like that, Oprah's Book Club was back.

Although it was that simple for Anderson's to be thrust into the limelight, the cultural ramifications of Winfrey's revival of Oprah's Book Club are—as with everything else surrounding the club—complex indeed. For with this entirely new focus on the great books, Winfrey seems to be instating an entirely new—for her anyway—borderline-academic, close-reading approach to literature as a whole. Indeed, this more honest scholarly positioning of herself as a teacher of great novels was both foreshadowed and underscored by her eloquent remarks in a speech on 26 February 2003 at the annual meeting of the Association of American Publishers. Accepting an award honoring her for her unique contribution to American literary life, Winfrey declared, "Our society values, for some reason, swiftness of experience. I ask, can the slow art of reading—the slow, sensual art of reading—and its difficult pleasures survive?" (qtd. in M. Mills, screen 1). Winfrey's answer, obviously, is yes, it most certainly can, and, statistically speaking, there's no mistaking that Winfrey's still got what it takes to help see that it does.

In an article entitled "Ye Oprah Book Club Returneth" in the February 2003 issue of *Forbes*, Lisa DiCarlo speculated that Winfrey's impact on the sales of classics could be greater than that of Hollywood, pointing out that *Mrs. Dalloway*, published in 1925, jumped to number eleven on the *New York Times* best-seller list after Michael Cunningham's Pulitzer Prize-winning novel *The Hours* was made into a movie (DiCarlo, screen 2). Sure enough, she was right; Winfrey beat Hollywood hands down. Within twenty-four hours of her televised announcement, *East of Eden* rocketed from 2,356 to number two (second only to J. K. Rowling's *Harry Potter and the Order of the Phoenix*) on the amazon.com sales list (Coomes, screen 1). Meanwhile, Penguin, which usually sells about 40,000 to 50,000 copies of *Eden* a year, has shipped out more than 1.5 million since then (Sharma-Jensen, screen 1). The sixteen dollar trade paperback became the top-selling softcover book in the country in the early weeks of July 2003 (Gillin 1), prompting Susan Petersen Kennedy, president of Penguin Group USA—which owns exclusive rights to John Steinbeck's novels—to say, "When Oprah first broke the news that she was re-launching her Book Club with a focus on classics, we were ecstatic. Penguin Group is committed to writers and readers. We felt this program would be good for books in general and especially the classics. We are grateful to Oprah for her passion for books and her unwavering committement to literacy" (qtd. in "Oprah Revives Book Club with Steinbeck," screen 1). Moreover, fifty-one years after its original publication, *East of Eden* rose to the number one slot in the August 3 paperback fiction division of the *New York Times* best-seller list (Coomes, screen 3).

Thus, over the course of the summer months, any doubts as to whether Winfrey still possessed her alchemical ability to turn literary lead into gold— or as journalist Mark Coomes would have it, whether "a billionaire populist has the chops to upgrade the intellectual reputation of any old book she pleases—starting with John Steinbeck's oft-maligned 1952 novel" (screen 1)—were laid to rest. "First day sales of the Oprah edition of *East of Eden* were among the strongest of all Oprah's selections," Bill Nasshan, senior vice president of trade books at Borders Group, told several newspapers. "We expect the new book club choice will drive traffic to our stores and revive interest in the classics" (Gillin, screen 1). Nasshan is hardly alone in placing his renewed faith in Oprah's Midas touch. David Ebershoff, publishing director of the Random House classics imprint Modern Library, believes that regardless of whether or not Winfrey's classics book club results in sales as stratospheric as those of her previous selections, her new focus is still of enormous significance to the publishing industry and the books themselves. "Her bringing attention to the classics is going to have a deep impact on what America's reading," he explains. "I'm not just talking about the one book she's focusing on. If she's bringing attention to Hawthorne or Eudora Welty, more people are going to think about browsing the classics section and not just the front of the bookstore" (qtd. in M. Mills, screen 1). One could take Ebershoff's argument a step further and add that not only will Winfrey's new focus impact *which* classics Americans read, it will also impact *how* they read them, how they think about them—and, in turn, how cultural critics will think about their thinking about them.

Given the Book Club's track record as an almost accidental locus of anxiety in the ever-raging struggle between high and low culture, it should come as no surprise that the club's latest incarnation has been the target of many a skeptical potshot since its June 2003 renaissance. Rumblings from the groves of academe and in the op-ed pages of the nation's newspapers have attempted to call into question the wisdom and validity of Winfrey's turn from the literary present to the past. University of Louisville English professor Dale Billingsley has gone so far as to warn Winfrey, "I hope you know that you are stepping into the middle of what the '90s called the campus 'culture wars,' "(qtd. in Coomes, screen 2). Yet, when situated in a broader cultural and economic context, Winfrey's turn appears both very wise and very valid after all. As journalist Geeta Sharma-Jensen points out, "Even *sans* Oprah, the classics have been a nice, stable deal for publishing houses for years, akin to a CD in the investment market" (screen 1). William Murphy, a Random House senior editor of the paperback line of the Modern Library classics, agrees. "I think if you know what you're doing, and are committed to publishing the classics in a vigorous way, people will respond," he explains. "In these uncertain times, it *is* a stable market" (qtd. in Sharma-Jensen, screen 1). In fact, recent evidence seems to indicate that not only are the classics a stable market, they may even be a burgeoning one. According to Beth Gillin of the *Philadelphia Inquirer.*

Market leader Penguin Classics saw its sales rise 13 percent last year over 2001. Penguin is now face-lifting its entire 1,300-book library, slapping snazzy new covers on works of authors from Charles Dickens to Jack Kerouac. Publishers and retailers are pushing classics because they are cheap to produce—no need to pay an author, much less organize an expensive book tour—but also because they've recently discovered just how well these babies sell. Last year *Pride and Prejudice,* first published in 1813 and now available in at least 130 editions, sold 110,000 copies, according to Nielsen Book Scan, which began tracking sales at cash registers in 2001. In other words, Jane Austen outperformed perennial chart-topper Mary Higgins Clark, whose *Mount Vernon Love Story* sold 108,000 copies. (screen 1)

Thus, if Jane Austen can handily outperform Mary Higgins Clark, then Oprah Winfrey and John Steinbeck can certainly hold their own against, say, Kelly Ripa and Carole Matthews.

For what it's worth, Winfrey hardly stands alone in the field of contemporary recommenders of great books. Yet, as usual, she remains the only figure at whom critical stones are being thrown. Many a classic can be located at Great Books Online at www.bartleby.com and Project Gutenberg at www.gutenberg.net. Meanwhile, Representative Ike Skelton, a Democrat from Missouri and a senior member of the House Armed Services Committee, has compiled and posted a "National Security Book List" in June 2003 at www.house.gov/skelton (Gillin, screen 1). Here, readers can browse a list of books ranging from Sun Tzu's *The Art of War* to Edward Shepherd Creasy's *Fifteen Decisive Battles of the World: From Marathon to Waterloo,* all of which Skelton strongly recommends to anyone interested in national defense. Moreover, in May 2003, New Leaf Press released a book entitled *A Philistine's Journal—An Average Guy Tackles the Classics.* Thus, rounding out this army of self-appointed compilers of classical canons, we have author Wayne Turmel chronicling his adventures as a forty-year-old suburbanite who finally decides to read—in one year!—all the books he should have read in school. Bearing this motley classics-pushing crew in mind, one can't help wondering: Why take Winfrey to task for her own impulse to preach the power of great literature to the people?

Hearteningly for anyone with an interest in seeing an end to the knee-jerk categorization of each and every cultural enterprise beneath banners emblazoned either "high" or "low," the answer seems to be that far fewer people rushed to condemn Winfrey's efforts in 2003 than in 1996. Certainly, there was a smattering of the usual gripes against Oprah's Book Club and its selections such as those uttered on Slate.com by the snarky Christopher Suellentrop:

> If Oprah wanted to get pats on the back from literary types for introducing viewers to the American canon she chose a curious way to do it. Not only is Steinbeck the canonical American writer most likely to have his work dismissed by critics as sentimental (Oprah-like?) pap, but *East of Eden* just might be his most controversial book. In fact, Steinbeck has more reason to worry about his literary reputation being sullied—at least in the short run—by association with Oprah than Jonathan Franzen ever did. (screen 1)

For starters, garnering patronizing pats hardly seems to have been Winfrey's intention at all. If anything, she seems to have learned from the Franzen dust-up during Oprah's Book Club Part I that she needn't court the approval of those who will never accept the validity of her efforts regardless of how she frames them.

To her immense credit this time around, Winfrey actually acknowledges potential critical complaints with grace and intelligence. Suellentrop goes on in his drubbing of Winfrey's inaugural author to declare that "during last year's Steinbeck centennial, Harold Bloom decreed to the *New York Times* that the John Ford movie version [of *The Grapes of Wrath*] was the greater artistic accomplishment, and that Steinbeck didn't belong in the American canon (even though Bloom included *Grapes* in the 'canonical prophecy' section of his book *The Western Canon)*" (Suellentrop 1). In canny anticipation of just such an attack, Winfrey's Web site featured an extensive section entitled "Steinbeck Versus the Critics: Why Was *East of Eden* a Book Critics Loved to Hate?" Here, in this freely accessible public space, she encouraged her readers to discover the answer to the question, "Though it quickly made its way into the public's heart, what did the literary elite *really* have to say?" as well as to "get a glimpse of Steinbeck's thoughts on criticism and reviews—straight from the mouths of the critics!" Via the provision of such a format for candid extratextual deliberation and debate, Oprah's Book Club Part II exhibits marked improvement over the insularity, defensiveness, and self-imposed isolation of Part I.

In light of such progress, even Suellentrop must concede—albeit back-handedly—that "while [Steinbeck] has his flaws—to name only one, his characters are often closer to symbols than people, his women always monsters or saints—it's unfair to criticize him for not writing in the modern style of his superior contemporaries Hemingway, Faulkner, and Fitzgerald, or because his books are too easy to understand," adding that, "even if Steinbeck's critics are right that he is overrated, that he's a regional writer and a minor novelist, it's hard to question Oprah's selection of him as the writer to launch a book club on the American masters" (screen 2). Again, Winfrey seems to understand the importance of preparing herself for debate over Steinbeck's literary superiority or lack thereof. At the time of the announcement of the club's revival, she openly admitted that Steinbeck is "not like Shakespeare, or even Faulkner; it's reader friendly. I want to lead people down this path without them thinking they're back in school. When you read something that's good and juicy and it's called literature, then you're not closed to the idea of it" (qtd. in "Oprah Revives," screen 2). Here, then, is a woman who knows exactly what she's doing, and this time she's not going to stand quietly by while anyone tells her otherwise. In the end, even an extremely grudging Suellentrop has to accept Steinbeck's "power as a gateway drug—something you pass out to people to get them interested in the hard stuff. Oprah wants to create a few addicts. Good for her" (screen 2).

I've had to rely rather heavily on Suellentrop's complaints in order to flesh out the concerns behind the elite criticism of this latest manifestation of Oprah's Book Club because the majority of Winfrey's usual detractors—both in the media and in the academy—seem unable to find much to complain about. If anything, Winfrey's new and improved incarnation of the Book Club has provided not only the impetus for your average lay readers to engage with the classics, but also the impetus for your trained literary professionals—critics and columnists and seasoned academics—to reassess, reevaluate, and reexamine their own approaches to literature, the canon, and what exactly constitutes a classic in the first place. Regarding the periodic need for a radical change in perspective or direction, Rilke writes in his "Archaic Torso of Apollo": "You must change your life." And while Winfrey's no visionary poet, she is providing a much-needed catalyst for dramatic transformation: She is offering an opportunity for reading individuals everywhere to change their literary lives.

The responses of belletristic "professionals" to the Book Club this time around have remained far more in the realm of sincere curiosity than self-righteous condescension. In the weeks immediately following Winfrey's announcement of her new focus on the classics, Indiana University Southeast Dean of Education Gloria Murray observed, "It's a pretty ambitious undertaking. Can she create her own classics and sell a mass market on great literature? Even with her power, I don't know" (qtd. in Coomes, screen 1). Now that the sales figures have begun to roll in, the answer is clear; yes, Winfrey can sell a mass market on great literature, and she has. Commercial success aside, though, anecdotal evidence at least suggests that Winfrey's most recent version of the Book Club is achieving some measure of critical success, as well—at least to the extent that those who self-consciously count themselves among a specialist class of literary elites are discussing Winfrey's endeavor with a seriousness that is both uncharacteristic and refreshing.

In other words, many of Winfrey's erstwhile detractors now wonder with genuine interest which classics she will select and how the club itself will work. According to former Colorado congresswoman Pat Schroeder, current president of the Association of American Publishers, "No one's quite sure what she means by 'classics.' Does she mean things we would call backlist, the oldies but goodies like *To Kill a Mockingbird* or the Hemingway stories? Or does she mean the Greeks and the Romans and Shakespeare?" (qtd. in M. Mills, screen 2). Thus far, Winfrey's interest seems to lie with the former rather than the latter, but Oprah's Book Club Part II is still so incipient, one mustn't discount any possibilities. Speculating in the *Halifax Herald Limited*, critic Nicholas Wapshott writes, "By 'classics' she does not mean Pliny, Euripides, Aeschylus and the ancients, but the sort of books the BBC makes into starchy costume dramas which eventually turn up here on public television, introduced by Alistair Cooke. Which begs the question: which classics will America's first black billionaire recommend to the nation?" (screen 1). After tossing around a short list of possible classical Winfrey authors—including such heavyweights as Mark Twain, Louisa May Alcott, George Eliot, Marcel Proust, and the soon-to-be-selected Leo Tolstoy (but more on that later)—he goes on to suggest that, even though Winfrey has demonstrated "little time for white males" (Wapshott 1), she may be willing to look in their direction for her definition of what constitutes a classic. In the beginning, he was right. With her announcement of Alan Paton's novel of South African racism, struggle, and reconciliation, *Cry, the Beloved Country*, Winfrey put her record at two for two in terms of white male authors, though these picks were followed by *100 Years of Solitude* by Colombian-born Gabriel Garcia Marquez and *The Heart Is a Lonely Hunter* by Carson McCullers.

Critics as well as fans of Oprah's Book Club have good reason to pay close attention to the titles Winfrey selects over the coming months, for these books draw attention not only to Winfrey's opinion that more people should be reading the classics, but also to the entire concept of "classic," including what exactly it means and who gets to say so. For while the books Winfrey has selected so far are undeniably older, their status as "great books"—whatever you take that to mean—is hardly indisputable. Winfrey herself openly acknowledges the trickiness of this issue, saying, "There are some who would argue that [*East of Eden*] is not really a 'classic' . . . and I realized that that was a conversation that would come up over and over again. . . . I just want to read great books without it becoming controversial" ("Oprah Revives," screen 1). Once again, Winfrey has put herself in the position of straddling the high versus pop cultural divide. For even though Steinbeck's book was a best seller at the time of its 1952 publication, conventional wisdom holds that the novel's ponderous, unwieldy quality ranks it well below, say, *Of Mice and Men*. Thus, regardless of whether she intends to court or to avoid controversy, Winfrey's decision to call her latest recommendations great books "will soon show the world whether her clout extends beyond the cash register to the court of critical opinion. 'Never underestimate the power of Oprah,' says Purdue University professor John Duvall, editor of Modern Fiction Studies, an academic journal. 'I think she has the potential to broaden the horizon of what a classic means.'" At issue, then, "is the right of any group, no matter how learned, to decide which novels constitute the canon, the scholarly term for the small collection of works recognized as the acme of English prose" (Coomes, screen 2).

In his book *Highbrow/Lowbrow*, cultural critic Lawrence Levine points out that in the past, there has been a

> sense that culture is something created by the few for the few, threatened by the many, and imperiled by democracy; the conviction that culture cannot come from the young, the inexperienced, the untutored, the marginal; the belief that culture is finite and fixed, defined and measured, complex and difficult of access, recognizable only by those trained to recognize it, comprehensible only to those qualified to comprehend it. (252)

Not so, says Winfrey, and Levine likely would be glad to hear her say it. For her decision to present great books via mass market television to an audience of relatively untrained millions suggests a passionate conviction that culture—literary culture anyway—is in fact accessible to anyone, including the inexperienced and the marginal, as well as the conviction that, far from being fixed and immutable, culture is fluid and flexible, with the potential to reach—and to be reached by—virtually everyone.

Winfrey is far from alone in her desire to expand the audience for classic literature. According to Michael Millman, an editor at Penguin Classics,

"Publishers are constantly looking to expand their titles. . . . I think we are expanding the definition of the canon . . . and what we are doing with Penguin Classics is not only including the classics of literature, but also of philosophy and the social sciences'" (qtd. in Sharma-Jensen, screen 1). Thus, Winfrey is positioning herself squarely alongside contemporary critics of a more democratic mindset. By acknowledging that the decision to designate a work as "great" is an enormously subjective one—influenced by gender, economics, race, and countless other concerns not necessarily related to a particular work's inherent value—Winfrey stands poised to usher in a new era of critical, canonical honesty, candor, and dynamism. Even though she has not bothered to outline her official criteria of what constitutes a "classic"—nor is she likely to do so—we can arrive at an ostensive definition of what it is she looks for in a "great book." Indeed we can infer that her standards for the qualities a true classic must possess are fairly—well, classical. For on the most basic level, Winfrey tends—like Horace in his own classic, *The Art of Poetry*—to favor those works that take it on themselves to simultaneously delight and instruct.

As has been mentioned previously, *East of Eden*—along with the oeuvres of other social novelists such as Dos Passos, Dreiser, and Sinclair—has fallen out of favor in English departments across the nation. Even Steinbeck biographer Jay Parini has described the novel as "a magnificent failure," albeit "quite readable" ("Oprah Revives," screen 1). Thus, Winfrey is making a bold intellectual move by even suggesting that *East of Eden* is a "great" or "classic" book, for, in doing so, she makes the tacit assertion that readability and enjoyability (delight!), as well as appeal to the reader's moral imagination (instruction!), are components of great literature. All in all, Winfrey's selection of Steinbeck, Paton, Garcia Marquez, McCullers, and Tolstoy remains consistent with the values implied by her previous selections, and anyone concerned with the relevance and role of literature in contemporary culture should be pleased with this fact. The novels balance strong populist appeal with acknowledged literary quality. Winfrey should be commended for her decision to pick such little-read, but relatively well-regarded novels as *East of Eden* alongside such standard canonical fair as *Anna Karenina*, for this choice articulates a real desire on her part to encourage an active readership—and not merely the appearance of readership—in America.

In a thoughtful opinion piece that ran in the *Chicago Tribune* on 23 June 2003—mere days after Winfrey unveiled her new version of the Book Club with the announcement of *East of Eden*—Heidi Stevens addressed the groundless concerns of various high priests of high culture that Winfrey's selection of such a great novel (and, by extension, her future selection of others like it) would inevitably result in a sacrilegious desecration of the sacred cows of the Western canon. "The bottomline," she concludes, "is thousands of people have just been turned on to a classic piece of literature that will introduce them to a collection of characters and ideas they didn't know existed."

> Why does it matter who turned them on to it? Will that alter the plot and character development? Is it somehow more appropriate to read a book when a tenured professor you're paying to learn from tells you to, rather than a TV personality who enters millions of homes a day for free? Are we better off as a society if the classics are reserved for those who received a liberal arts education at a four-year university? Will the book become less poignant if the person sitting next to you at Jiffy Lube is reading it? (Stevens, screen 1)

Stevens adds that if Winfrey were planning to "dumb down" the classics, "that would be a different story." Yet, if anything, Winfrey's approach to said classics seems to be to smarten them up. Thus far, Winfrey has used Book Club Part II to encourage her readers—through all manner of prompts, hints, tips, study guides, and question-and-answer pages on the Web site as well as on the show—to approach the classics in a scholarly fashion.

In a moment, I'd like to analyze this landmark move toward serious scholarship of the classics in some detail. But first—and here's the big surprise, the suspenseful plot twist in the latest chapter of Oprah's Book Club—I'd like to point out that, yes, Winfrey has turned tens of thousands of eager readers onto various works of classic literature, but (brace yourself): *she herself is not referring to these works as "classics."* And although no one else, to my knowledge, has pointed this out—perhaps since they're all too busy either simply reading the books or deliberating about the nature of a true classic—the significance of Winfrey's choice of vocabulary cannot be overstated. Her decision not to refer to the books in question as "classics" even as virtually everyone else—publishers, editors, critics, and, of course, readers—applies the term with tremendous vigor seems immensely consequential. For the names and labels one chooses to apply to one's enterprises—cultural or otherwise—are never accidental or value-free, nor have they ever been. Describing critic Matthew Arnold's dominion over the creation of the nineteenth-century categories that sway our ways of thinking about art even now, Levine writes that:

"High," "low," "rude," "lesser," "higher," "lower," "beautiful," "modern," "legitimate," "vulgar," "popular," "true," "pure" . . . were applied to such nouns as "arts" or "culture" almost *ad infinitum.* Though plentiful, the adjectives were not random. They clustered around a congeries of values, a set of categories that defined and distinguished culture vertically, that created hierarchies which were to remain meaningful for much of this century. That they are categories which to this day we have difficulty defining with any precision does not negate their influence. (224)

Levine goes on to point out that, naturally, certain audiences reacted with hostility toward this implicit ascendancy of high culture, turning their backs on—if not thumbing their noses at—the classic works of art and letters that had been demarcated so clearly as beyond their ken. And, naturally, scholars and other self-appointed members of the cultural elite have been hasty to misunderstand this response, "labeling it simple Philistinism or anti-intellectualism" (Levine 240), when in reality the situation is far more complex. Thus, by refusing to resort to the handy—albeit loaded—label of "classic" in relation to her Book Club (although it's worth noting that the URL for the online version of the club reads, sneakily, http://www.oprah.com/obc_*classics*), Winfrey has decided to give her audience an opportunity to reclaim a culture that has long been presented as off-putting if not entirely off limits.

Lest Winfrey's avoidance of the term "classic" be attributed to mere happenstance or oversight, I feel compelled to emphasize that her decision is, in fact, a considered one. Originally, Winfrey intended to title her revived club "Traveling with the Classics," but as the time to relaunch the project drew near, she decided to pick up where she left off by calling it "Oprah's Book Club," exactly as she had before. Winfrey claimed that this choice was made in order to "avoid 'the self-imposed box' in which she found herself: the fewer expectations, the better. She will not make monthly picks, but three to five choices a year. She will focus on authors of the past, but doesn't rule out living ones" as evidenced by her selection of Garcia Marquez ("Oprah Revives," screen 1). Thus, Winfrey has alleviated much of the stress she had admitted to feeling regarding book selection prior to the Book Club's fourteen-month hiatus. For by turning to authors of the past while scrupulously avoiding the term "classic," Winfrey has given herself far more works to pick from; she may revisit her old favorites while still permitting herself to toss in the occasional book by, say, Toni Morrison as she sees fit. But more than merely allowing herself greater freedom of choice in terms of book selection, Winfrey's omission of the word "classic" from her latest literary project deflects many a potential complaint about her cultural authority or lack thereof.

For by stepping back and watching others struggle with the concept of what exactly constitutes a classic, Winfrey has given herself space to accomplish her project of promoting the active readership of great books in relative peace. For even as Winfrey declines to do so, others—in the press, in the academy, and in the public at large—have rushed to identify her selections so far as classics (or at least to debate whether or not they deserve that rare appellation). That *East of Eden, Cry, the Beloved Country, One Hundred Years of Solitude, The Heart Is a Lonely Hunter, Anna Karenina,* and all the as yet unnamed works she will select in the future are "great books," Winfrey will admit, and the idea that they are therefore "classics" is, of course, implicit. Yet Winfrey's decision to let other people make this leap in categorization is terribly clever. By encouraging others to do the hierarchical heavy lifting for her, she has delegated for major cultural work to be done, acting as its administrator and catalyst, while allowing it to play out within the culture as a whole.

Thanks to Oprah's Book Club Part II, the appropriate question is no longer, "Who does Oprah think she is?" but rather, "Who do we think we are?" She has pushed those among us who concern ourselves with such things to wonder: What do *we* consider the classics to be? Where does *our* authority come from? How do *we* decide what works are worthy of inclusion in the canon? Thus, with her simultaneous turn toward the classics but away from the term itself, Winfrey has managed to make the Book Club more inclusive than ever. Not only has she motivated her fans to pore eagerly over the words of great writers of the past, she has also compelled her critics and potential detractors to ponder how great these writers are in the first place. In short, Winfrey continues her quest to bring about cultural change and improvement while avoiding the accusations that assailed her before, among them that she pushed so-called middlebrow literature with a facile and condescending attitude under the pretense of unearned expertise. She has figured out how to prompt a healthy cultural exchange without situating herself too squarely in the middle of it and, as a result, she appears more savvy and less self-important than she did during Oprah's Book Club Part I.

Moreover, she appears less egotistical and authoritarian, not to mention less conservative and misogynistic, than such established literary experts as Harold Bloom, who declared ominously in 2003 that:

In the early 1950s and 1960s, it was understood that the great English romantic poets were Percy Bysshe Shelley, William Wordsworth,
Lord Byron, John Keats, William Blake, Samuel Taylor Coleridge.
But today they are Felicia Hemans, Charlotte Smith, Mary Tighe,
Laetitia Landon and others who just can't write. A fourth-rate play-
wright like Aphra Behn is being taught instead of Shakespeare in
many curriculums across the country. (Bloom, screen 1)

Unlike many critics within the academy, Winfrey has nothing to fear and
nothing to prove. She happily allows women and people of color into her
informal canon alongside writers of an Anglo-Saxon male persuasion without giving any particular group preferential treatment. By refusing to adhere
to the belief that there exists an inflexible, time-honored template to define
who can or cannot write—whose works are worth reading and whose are
fourth-rate—Winfrey has given herself the freedom to promote books she
considers truly great, regardless of who wrote them or when. Thus, the new
Book Club, with its catholic taste, its ability to look beyond the automatically accepted 'classics' of the Western canon, and its willingness to distribute
critical authority among all its participants, stands poised to accomplish all
the beneficial cultural work of the first, if not more, without leaving the bad
taste of questionable means and authority in the mouths of her critics.

In order to better understand how Winfrey has positioned this latest
incarnation of the Book Club to break down even more anachronistic hierarchical barriers, we must understand the new—and notably more scholarly—
protocols by which she has chosen to have the club operate. In keeping with
her stated mission of making Oprah's Book Club "the biggest book club in
the world," anyone with access to a computer may sign up to join Oprah's
Online Book Club, the sumptuously appointed Web supplement to the
Book Club. You can have a firsthand look of your own at her approach to the
classics at www.oprah.com. Having already been on the mailing list for Part
I, I joined the Web community surrounding Part II at the first possible
opportunity, going so far as to set up a somewhat ridiculously named Hot-
mail account for this express purpose. If you do sign up for updates yourself,
I strongly encourage you to consider doing the same, because, believe me,
once you join, you will soon be the proud recipient of a whole heck of a lot
of Oprah's Book Club-related e-mail. And I don't mean spam. I don't mean
junk mail or advertisements or exhortations to watch *Oprah* every single
weekday or anything of that nefarious sort. I mean step-by-step, section-by-

section study guides pertaining specifically, edifyingly, excitingly to the great books at hand.

Like a tech-savvy college professor making use of the class listserv, Winfrey has arranged to have online members of Oprah's Book Club receive what amount to strikingly syllabus-style assignments on a regular basis. All participants receive—as I did on 3 October 2003, for instance—periodic bulletins under the subject line "Start Reading the Next Book," whose breathless yet authoritative text advises, "so—if you haven't already—pick up a copy and start reading the first five chapters of book one. And check Oprah.com for reader discussions, study guides (coming soon!) and all kinds of features, insights and fascinating details about *Cry, the Beloved Country* and its author, Alan Paton—it's a journey that will sweep you away." Also included in such mailings are links to every extratextual resource imaginable. The series of messages and postings leading up to the 29 September 2003, screening of the segment on *East of Eden* included—but was hardly limited to—links to the 1952 best-seller list; links to Dr. Susan Shillinglaw, professor of English and director of the Center for Steinbeck Studies at San José State University (a Steinbeck scholar who served as an editor and contributing writer for coverage of the novel on the Web site); links to the elaborate real-life and fictional family trees of Steinbeck's own ancestors and the characters in the novel, respectively; links to the biblical story of Cain and Abel; and last, but hardly least, a concise, well-sourced explanation of the novel's main theme as centered on the Hebrew word *timshel*. This latter cites evidence from both *The New Jerusalem Bible* and "the authoritative Orthodox Jewish translation from *The Chumash: The Stone Edition,"* and arrives at the conclusion that, "like all of us, Cain had free will to decide between good and evil. In this semi-autobiographical work, Steinbeck does not envision a virginal Eden as our birthright. As much as we inherit Cain's curse, we also inherit his ability to redeem himself." Certainly, this analysis, with its emphasis on struggle, self-improvement, and redemption, can be seen as very Oprah, yet so, too, must it be viewed as an inarguably strong reading of the classic in question.

Just in case all this scholarship isn't enough to satisfy the most thorough readers—to say nothing of the toughest critics—that she's serious about getting the most out of the classics, Winfrey has decided to actually bring in a professional critic to field questions pertaining to each of the great books selected. Pulitzer Prize-winning critic Margo Jefferson, for instance, served as the gifted go-to girl for *East of Eden*. During her tenure as resident Steinbeck expert, Jefferson fielded such questions from Oprah's Book Club members as the historical, "What new meanings can be read into this book that weren't possible when it was published?," the sociological, "Why can't people just read for the sake of a story," and the multicultural, "What is the reason for Steinbeck's harsh description of nonwhite groups in the book?" Dr. Rita Barnard, who has a Ph.D. from Duke University, is associate professor of English and director of the Comparative Literature Program at the University of Pennsylvania in Philadelphia, filled the position of resident literary guide for *Cry, the Beloved Country*. *One Hundred Years of Solitude* and *The Heart Is a Lonely Hunter* received similar attention. Like an educator bringing in a guest lecturer, Winfrey has added even more scholarly clout to her project by inviting so-called experts to help explicate the meanings of the chosen texts. This can't be taken to mean that she feels herself inexpert on the subject of classic literature, or that she feels her readers are too, say, lowbrow to "get" the works on their own—it just means she knows that there are multiple ways to approach any text, and that the more voices brought into discussion on a particular book, the richer the insight and edification. As might be the case in a graduate school seminar-style literature class, everyone's invited to speak up, ask their questions, do their research, and offer their answers.

Thus, Oprah's Book Club Part II seems a deliberately far cry from Part I, when updates were fewer and farther between, and an even farther cry from your average small-potatoes, nontelevised neighborhood book club, which typically picks a book and asks only that you have it read by—and maybe bring some cookies or something to—the next meeting at whomever's house. (Although Oprah's Book Club online offers means of improvement to even the most humble of traditional book clubs, featuring links to assorted clubs from all over the nation, each with ideas of how to make get-togethers fancier and more ambitious.)

Still, as ostentatiously new and improved as Oprah's Book Club Part II is, it has not gone so far as to jettison the techniques that made Part I—whatever its weaknesses—such a phenomenally popular success. In other words, while Winfrey may have covered her intellectual bases more thoroughly, her approach to the classics is still indefatigably Oprah: effusive, inclusive, enthusiastic, hellbent on personal betterment, and fun, fun, fun. Even after a fourteen-month interruption, Winfrey's canny ability to market a particular read to her target audience proved undiminished. In the typical hyperbolic style she adopts whenever she speaks of her latest literary passion, Winfrey billed *East of Eden* as "the book that brought the book club back!" proclaiming, "I *love* this book! It's the perfect book for summer. It's a saga . . .

it's *so* good! You won't be able to turn the pages fast enough. I brought the book club back to share this jewel of a novel. I was turning every page thinking, 'Oh my *goodness!*' You just don't want it to end!" And if that weren't enough, her Web site gushed that the 602-pager "has it all! Sex, murder, suicide, infidelity, greed, blackmail, nasty manipulation: no subject is taboo." Having read the book myself on Winfrey's recommendation, I can verify that regardless of whether or not one considers the book a classic, it is undeniably a page-turner. And while I wouldn't go so far as to announce, as Winfrey did, that "*East of Eden* might be the best novel she had ever read" ("Oprah Heads 'East of Eden'," screen 1), I had a good time reading both it and the online supplemental material.

Clearly, Winfrey's proclivity for the generous use of superlative and drama abides. Her approach—by necessity designed to play well in the sweeping, stylized, superficial realm of the televisual—remains as flashy as ever. Her application of such techniques to the alleged classics will undoubtedly irk some of the same self-proclaimed "high" cultural detractors so eager to find fault with her club before. Yet how else could you compel thousands of people who may have ignored these books and others like them in high school and college to pay attention to them now? For by being her usual effusive self—and by promising plenty of literary sex, secrets, and scandal—Winfrey has proven that she is capable of achieving her stated goal of drawing thousands of readers to her club—a club, which, as has been previously stated, supplements its sometimes lurid sales pitches and subject matter with genuine scholarship.

Even as Oprah's Book Club Part II becomes more scholarly, the feel-good attitude toward active literacy that characterized Part I remains intact. During her announcement of the selection of *East of Eden*, for instance, Winfrey proclaimed, "John Steinbeck—wherever he is in the spirit world—is very happy today!" And while this statement may be taken quite rightly as more than a bit presumptuous, extravagant, and perhaps even improvident, the woman has a point. According to Thomas Steinbeck (who appeared, along with Jane Seymour and Kelsey Grammer, on the California road-trip segment featuring his father's book):

> John kept his Nobel Prize for literature in the closet and used his Pulitzer for a paperweight. But having . . . *East of Eden* designated, "the book that brought Oprah's Book Club back" would have delighted him. "My father would have been very much tickled." His father was known for his interest in working people rather than the

literati. "He would have loved that this incredibly savvy black woman who has broken ceiling after ceiling has put him on top of the best-seller list." (Donahue, screen 1)

Thus, it is, as University of Louisville English professor Matthew Biberman says, "very hard to say Oprah is wrong. She seems to be reinventing the notion of a classic" (qtd. in Coomes, screen 3). More than that, she seems to be reinventing the way in which we should interact with the classics based on the principle that they can delight and entertain us, in addition to educating us and exercising our moral imaginations.

In case all these innovations and additions to the club weren't enough, on Memorial Day weekend 2004, Winfrey took her great books project farther into uncharted territory by announcing not only that Leo Tolstoy's *Anna Karenina* would be the summer selection, but also that—like, presumably, the majority of club members—she herself had never read the 838-page Russian classic. Announcing her selection of the 126-year-old saga of the aristocratic Anna's adulterous affair, Winfrey declared, "I've never, ever chosen a novel that I had not personally read" (Wyatt, screen 1), adding on her Web site that "This book has been on my 'must read' list for years, but I was scared of it. Let's not be scared of it. I'm going to team up with all of you, and we'll read it together. It's one of the greatest love stories of all time . . . one of the greatest books of all time." (Oprah.com, Oprah's books login screen). Thus, while Winfrey's approach to literature in this second incarnation of the club certainly has been more thorough and scholarly than it ever was in Oprah's Book Club Part I, her tactic for Tolstoy has emerged as the most refreshingly experimental and egalitarian one so far.

I have suggested throughout this chapter that Winfrey's position in the current version of the club is an almost professorial one, yet, with this summer selection, one has to ask: What traditional teacher or academic professional would admit to, let alone proudly trumpet, his or her having not yet read the assigned reading? With her resolution to soldier through this sprawling Russian saga along with her readers—with her vow to "finish every page" of *Anna Karenina* and to send "e-mails all summer long to keep you posted on how I'm doing and hopefully give you encouragement, because I believe we can do this. We can read the real literature of the world" (Blais, screen 1)—Winfrey has proven yet again that there exists more than one appropriate way to deal with literature; she has set out to further the sense of community that is one of the secrets to the Book Club's success by joining the community herself, as an almost-equal.

In doing so, Winfrey has exhibited a shrewd understanding of how to manage and master one of the most fundamental pedagogical issues of higher education: the sometimes daunting balance of power between teacher and student. In my own Teaching Freshmen Writing class in graduate school—and, I'm sure, in many such classes across the nation—this delicate equilibrium was boiled down to a cheesy but apt saying about the need to know when to be "a guide on the side" as opposed to "a sage on the stage." Winfrey has certainly been both a guide and a sage at various points in her book-recommending career, but it seems a particular stroke of book-clubbing genius for her to have realized the benefits of presenting herself as both a model and a colleague in order to persuade hundreds of thousands of Americans to haul their way eagerly through what amounts to a highly atypical beach read.

As a result of Winfrey's careful positioning of herself as both the challenger, establishing the instructions and keeping the project productive, and one of the challenged, faithfully adhering to her own reading schedule, Winfrey has persuaded hundreds of thousands of readers to pick up their own copies of *Anna Karenina* and "train for reading greatness" as the Web site would have it. Realizing the importance of having all her readers on the same literal and proverbial page—as well as the value of dealing with the clearest available translation of a work not originally written in English—Winfrey explicitly selected the PEN/Book-of-the-Month Club Translation Prize-winning edition by the husband-and-wife team of Richard Pevear and Larissa Volokhonsky, intoning, "First of all, get this edition. You see the one with the little flowers on the cover, and it'll have the little banner? Look for the Oprah's Book Club little sticker there because there's lots of different editions. This is an award-winning translation, so you're really going to get scared if it's not translated well, OK?" (Wyatt screen 1). Subsequent to Winfrey's announcement, the Pevear and Volokhonsky translation rocketed to the top of Amazon.com's best-seller list, as well as Barnes & Noble's online list. Additionally, Penguin returned to press twice to print 900,000 copies since being notified secretly of the pending selection on 5 May, compared with about 60,000 copies since the book's original U.S. release in 2001 (Wyatt, screen 2). Also thanks to Winfrey's ringing endorsement, the edition, bearing the label "Oprah's Book Club Summer Selection," has shot to the top of *USA Today's* best-seller list, as well as the lists of *Publishers Weekly* and *The New York Times* (Colford, screen 1).

According to Tolstoy's obituary in *The New York Times*, *Anna Karenina* "provoked discussion throughout the whole civilized world" (Blais, screen 1).

Now, it can again. For as extraordinary as Winfrey's having managed to get this enormously intimidating brick of a book to fly off the shelves and into the hands of eager readers inarguably is, even more extraordinary is the way in which she encouraged them to discuss it. As has been the case with previously selected great books, Winfrey has made use of both her Web site and regular e-mail updates to provide copious supplementary material, including a historical overview of Tolstoy's own tumultuous turns of fortune within Russian society and quotations from the novel itself. In addition, owing to her self-imposed status as a fellow first-time reader, Winfrey has been able to use these electronic outlets to disseminate an impressive variety of resources to help her readers maintain their motivation throughout the novel's eight parts. Her initial announcement, for instance, came accompanied by a wealth of read-along-with-Winfrey materials at Oprah.com, including a reading calendar and character guide that can be printed out in bookmark form. And an e-mail entitled "From Oprah 'Anna Karenina' Part One," contained an informative letter from Winfrey to Book Clubbers (complete with the encouraging send-off: "I'm headed outdoors right now to sit under the trees and see what further rules will be broken. Which ideals will stand—family and honor, or the heat of the heart? Let's keep reading, y'all!"), as well as an invitation to "Take the Quiz" for Part One "to know how well you're doing," plus "10 questions guaranteed to spark your discussion."

Not only has *Anna Karenina* provided more of a sense of camaraderie with Winfrey herself than ever before, it has also allowed room for criticism as well as praise of the book itself, as well as of the reading experience in general. "Send Us Your Video Journal!" the Oprah's On-line Book Club Web site exclaims, continuing:

> Oprah sends you her thoughts over e-mail, now she wants to see what you think of *Anna Karenina*! Whether you're reading our big summer selection solo or with your book club, produce a video diary of your reading experience! Let us know the good and the bad—but most of all, have fun! Tell us how you're going to make it past the finish line with Oprah!" (oprah.com)

Winfrey should be praised for this unprecedented invitation to express readerly dissatisfaction and frustration alongside satisfaction and gratification, for, by permitting a more complex range of reader responses to her project, she promotes a more sophisticated model of reading itself. Clearly, you're still expected to arrive at the conclusion that Winfrey does in her Part

One letter, that "19th century Russia can be mastered" (and why not?), but you're permitted to consider the occasional unpleasant aspects of reading as well as the excitement and joy of the activity. All in all, while Winfrey has taken the opportunity with *Anna Karenina* to do "something she's never done before—she's reading the book with you!" (oprah.com), she has nevertheless remained indefatigably 'Oprah,' downplaying the difficulty of the work involved in tackling such a novel, while still conveying the sense that "cross[ing] the finish line by September" is a significant and worthwhile accomplishment.

Among the few complaints that may be legitimately leveled against the latest embodiment of Oprah's Book Club is the concern that Winfrey is once again commodifying the books in question, surrounding them with commercial trappings and complementary products. Oprah's Book Club Boutique is among the online club's most prominent features, and, unlike the materials pertaining directly to the books, one needn't be an official member to shop there; no special log-in screen bars one from browsing the logo-embroidered ball caps, bucket hats, and T-shirts. Before getting too terribly annoyed, though, one must bear in mind that this setup scarcely differs from the way books are commodifed virtually everywhere else as well. You'd be hard-pressed to walk into your average bookstore—even a venerable independent one—without being assailed by chocolate bars and specialty coffees, booklights and magnifiers, and all manner of other assorted, vaguely literary accessories. So if buying a pastel pink canvas beach tote emblazoned with the official insignia of the Book Club helps Winfrey's readers keep sand off their Steinbeck, fine. The point is, they're buying—and reading—the Steinbeck. As Cathy Davidson points out, "Americans still do not read many books in the course of a year and certainly cannot be accused of consuming books as frequently (or as programmatically) as they do, say, tubes of toothpaste or television shows" (17). Thus, if anything, Winfrey's doing more than her fair share to help even up those numbers. Plus all profits from the boutique go to Winfrey's Angel Network charity, which is more than can be said for the profits at, say, amazon.com.

Even though the complaint about the commodification of literature by Oprah's Book Club turns out to be a fairly minor one, it reminds us again of the issue of consumption as it relates to literature—which has less to with the fact that books are obviously a commodity and more to do with the complicated issue of who owns/reads which books and why. Nicholas Latimer, director of publicity at Knopf, explains that, "In this here-today, gone-tomorrow era of immediate gratification via the Internet, what a luxury to own a copy of a bonafide classic, to hold it in your hands, turn the pages, realize all the work that went into its production, and enjoy the actual experience of reading for pleasure—all at a relatively inexpensive price" (qtd. in Sharma-Jensen, screen 1).

Publishers have long understood the benefits of producing various editions of the classics aimed at various audiences. This means that:

> Readers can therefore find Herman Melville or Charles Dickens or Fyodor Doestoyevsky or F. Scott Fitzgerald or Dante Alghieri at many price points: in upscale hardcover editions costing $30 and more, nice-looking paperbacks between $7 and $14, or even simple Barnes & Noble editions for around $5. (The retailer's recent edition of Charles Dickens' *Great Expectations* was priced at $4.95.) (Sharma-Jensen, screen 1)

To her credit, then, via Oprah's Book Club with its inclusive invitation for everyone at every level of the socioeconomic spectrum to obtain and read the selection at hand, Winfrey keeps her readers—the more affluent ones, anyway—from becoming an army of Gatsbys, acquiring beautiful, costly libraries full of elegant books that remain dusty, unopened, their pages uncut.

Historically speaking, though, not all readers have been considered as valuable as others. Observing this trend, Davidson wonders, "Do books really decrease in value as they become more accessible? Books have always been available to the wealthy but did not suffer thereby—witness the common aristocratic valuing of a good library. Why, then, are books somehow diminished when they come more and more into the hands of middle-class or even poor citizens?" (16). Winfrey would answer that they shouldn't be. For while participants are encouraged to purchase the official Oprah's Book Club editions of selected titles, they are in no way required to do so. A less moneyed member would never be disinvited from the club, or kicked off the e-mail list, or even remotely looked down upon if her copy of a particular classic happened to come from a used-book store or library. As far as Oprah's Book Club is concerned, it doesn't matter what your books cost, where they come from, or how they look—the point is, and always has been, above all simply to read them, and read them club members do, with tremendous aplomb.

Over the course of the years I have spent working on this project, my opinions of, and approaches to, Oprah's Book Club have evolved and changed. So, for that matter, have Winfrey's. As Winfrey has taken the club in a more scholarly direction, many of her critics—myself among them—have come to take the institution more seriously as the embodiment of an inclusive pro-literacy sentiment that bodes well for the culture at large. If I've managed to convince you of nothing else, I hope I've helped you see that Oprah's Book Club has always stood for far more than just itself, in the sense that Winfrey, by entering into the highbrow versus lowbrow fray, managed to take what had been a relatively cold war and make it hot again. For the dueling camps of taste seem to have been at a standstill of sorts, characterized by a lingering animosity and a pervasive knowledge of who exactly was on which side and why. Via Oprah's Book Club as it existed from 1996 to 2002, and especially as it exists in its current incarnation, Winfrey has provided everyone concerned with literary culture—and culture in general—with an opportunity to look closely at the construction of taste, thereby exploring what we value, what we disparage, and how we differentiate between the two.

In a *Boston Globe* piece lamenting the National Book Foundation's decision in 2003 to give its annual Medal for Distinguished Contribution to American Letters to Stephen King, Harold Bloom declared, "Our society and our literature and our culture are being dumbed down, and the causes are very complex. I'm 73 years old. In a lifetime of teaching English, I've seen the study of literature debased. There's very little authentic study of the humanities remaining" (Bloom, screen 1). Clearly, there's a lot to take issue with in this rather egregious denouncement of Stephen King as the recipient of an award Winfrey herself earned in 1999. For now, I just want to point out that Winfrey has done more than virtually anyone else, Bloom included, to remedy the problem of declining readership in America. Not only has Winfrey not contributed to any sort of cultural 'dumbing down,' she has also actively cultivated a widespread literary 'smarting up.' By encouraging America's discussion of the humanities to become more polyvocal and inclusive, as well as more intense and authentic, she has shown us that there are many ways, not just one, to approach the great texts of our time and times past.

Thus, rather than merely signifying another temporary intensification of hostilities in America's ongoing battle of the brows, Oprah's Book Club Parts I and II prove that "evidence of what appears to be a growing cultural eclecticism and flexibility is everywhere at hand" (Levine 243). Readers from all backgrounds have been given a new source of literary recommendations, literary experts have been given the chance to reconsider the literary canon itself, and both have been given the impetus to realize that active debate and discussion about issues of taste are vastly superior to passive closed-mindedness and the thoughtless acceptance of handed down hierarchical categories.

For even if you were among those who hated the club in its original incarnation (and it certainly possessed its share of frustrating characteristics), or if you continue to hate Oprah's Book Club as it exists now (and it still possesses its share of annoyances, although they are far less serious) you absolutely cannot deny Winfrey's power as an arbiter of taste, and as a champion of the quiet, personal, contemplative pleasures of reading in a culture that at times seems determined to speed past or even erase such pleasures altogether. As Davidson observes, "aesthetic criteria, as book historians frequently note, change radically form one period to another and one century's bestseller—Jean-Jacques Rousseau's *Julie, ou la nouvelle Heloise*, Susanna Rownson's *Charlotte Temple*, or T. S. Arthur's *Ten Nights in a Barroom*—can be unread or even unreadable in another era" (3). Thus, we may never know how Winfrey's picks, contemporary or classic, will bear up under the weight of time, nor can we say for sure how much it matters whether or not they do. All we can be sure of is that the selections of Winfrey's institution have indelibly altered the literary landscape of our present moment, promoting not only literature, but also a healthy discussion of the role literature and its attendant, value-laden categories and hierarchies play in shaping this landscape.

Regardless of whether people still read *White Oleander* or *East of Eden* a hundred years hence, Winfrey has secured her place as a major cultural, literary figure in the here and now. She has provided us all with a working example of the fluidity of culture—a near-perfect illustration of what Larry Levine means when he declares that "culture is a process, not a fixed condition; it is the product of unremitting interaction between the past and the present" (249). Oprah's Book Club has long represented, and continues to represent, an opportunity for everyone—even, and perhaps especially, nonparticipants—to understand the reductivity, damage, and general silliness wrought upon culture of all kinds by rigid, anachronistic hierarchies of taste. The inalterable fact remains that the influence of Oprah's Book Club as an emblem of culture as a dynamic process stands to extend long after Winfrey herself, and all the rest of us, have read our last.

Works Cited

Blais, Jacqueline. "Oprah's the Toast of Book Publishers." *USA Today* 11 Feb. 1999: 4D.

Bloom, Harold. "Dumbing Down American Readers." http://www.boston.com/news/globe/editorial_opinion/oped/articles. Published 24 Sept. 2003.

Colford, Paul. "Tolstoy top seller, thanks to Oprah." http://www.nydailynews.com/business/story/201661p-174030c.html. Published and accessed 11 June 2004.

Coomes, Mark. "Literary Eyes Focus on Oprah's Version of 'Classics.'" *Olympian* 24 August 2003. 26 Oct. 2003.

Davidson, Cathy, ed. *Reading in America: Literature and Social History.* Baltimore: Johns Hopkins UP, 1989.

DiCarlo, Lisa. "Ye Oprah Book Club Returneth." Forbes.com 27 Feb. 2003. 26 Oct. 2003 http://www.forbes.com/2003/02/27/cx_ld_0227bookclub.html.

Donahue, Deirdre. "Steinbeck on Oprah? He Would be 'Tickled.'" *USA Today* 26 June 2003. 26 June 2003 http://www.usatoday.com.

Gillin, Beth. "The Incredible Bulk: This Summer's Books Have Heft. And Reading Lists Abound with Oprah Hooked on Classics This Time Around." *Philadelphia Inquirer* 7 July 2003. 15 July 2003 http://www.philly.com/mld/inquirer.

Levine, Lawrence W. *Highbrow/Lowbrow: The Emergence of Cultural Hierarchy in America.* Cambridge: Harvard UP, 1988.

Mills, Marja. "Oprah's Book Club to Take Classic Spin: Selections Could Mean Millions for Publishers, Lead to Rediscovery of High School, College Reading." *Akron Beacon Journal* 17 Mar. 2003. 26 June 2003.

"Oprah Heads 'East of Eden.'" AP online 18 June 2003. 18 June 2003 http://www.ap.org.

Oprah Web site. "Login screen." http://www.oprah.com.

"Oprah Revives Book Club With Steinbeck." *Associated Press* 17 June 2003. 17 June 2003 http://www.ap.org.

Sharma-Jensen, Geeta. "Publishers Find New Money in Old Classics." *Milwaukee Journal Sentinel* 31 Aug. 2003 http://www.jsonline.com.

Stevens, Heidi. "When Oprah Talks, People Listen." *Chicago Tribune* 23 June 2003. 23 June 2003 http://www.chicagotribune.com.

Suellentrop, Christopher. "John Steinbeck: Should He Be Afraid of Oprah?" *Slate* magazine 26 June 2003. 26 Oct. 2003 http://www.slate.com.

Wapshott, Nicholas. "Oprah Winfrey Goes Literary: Oprah Embraces Classics in New Club." *The Halifax Herald Limited* 16 Mar. 2003. 26 June 2003 http://www.hearld.ns.ca.

Wyatt, Edward. "Tolstoy's Translators Experience Oprah's Effect." *New York Times* 7 June 2004: E1.

AFTERWORD

Oprah, James Frey, and the Problem of the Literary

JAIME HARKER

Since the inception of Oprah's Book Club, critics have found it an ambiguous, if not sinister, intrusion into a pristine literary sphere (Farr 26). Such criticisms have dogged all such mergers of literature and the mass market. Janice Radway and Joan Shelley Rubin have detailed numerous educational ventures in the first half of the twentieth century, notably the Book-of-the-Month Club, that show marked similarities to Oprah's Book Club. Early twentieth-century critics feared that the Book-of-the-Month Club would undermine the authority of the individual reader for the standardized uniformity of market capitalism. Popular culture has long been feminized in this cultural critique; women artists at the turn of the century were seen as the personification of an effeminate, inferior mass culture (Douglas 6–7), and middlebrow literary ventures were similarly gendered (Radway 829).

As the chapters in this collection demonstrate, the foundation of Oprah's claim to cultural authority is even more complicated than that of the first middlebrow pioneers, who were originally trained as teachers (Rubin 26–27). Oprah's authority came, first and foremost, from her media celebrity (as Kelley Lewis's chapter maintains). She may read voraciously for pleasure, but she didn't build her career through literature or education.

Nevertheless, when Oprah began the Book Club, she guided approximately fourteen million Americans and became, immediately, the most influential literary critic in the world. Wu argues that Oprah's "*literary* authority" embodies Foucault's notion of the author function, one she bestows on the authors she chooses. Most scholars and critics, however, have refused to grant her *literary* authority, viewing literature and "the Oprah affect" as mutually exclusive modes, with competing bases for authority.

Read collectively, *The Oprah Affect* should set the stage for future complications of this opposition between "Oprahfication" and "literature." For while many essays embrace the "therapeutic" aspects of the Book Club (like Douglas, Perry, Farr, Hall, and Stow) and others critique it (like Lewis, Rodriguez, and Quirk), the distinction between the literary and the therapeutic is hardly absolute. Many contributors consider books, or readers, that challenge Oprah's reading practices. Racism, pedophilia, ambiguity, difficulty—all emerge as "problems" that Oprah's Book Club must solve. And though Oprah often disavowed a formalistic, literary influence in the first incarnation of her Book Club, many of her selections were traditionally "literary"—including Toni Morrison, Bernhard Schlink, Isabel Allende, Andre Dubus III, Joyce Carol Oates, and (notoriously) Jonathan Franzen. The tension around literary value comes through in selections that are most sympathetically described as "eclectic." In addition, as the Chapters in *The Oprah Affect* suggest, the reading practices of Oprah's Book Club are much more varied than most critics have allowed.

Like "Oprahfication," the "literary" is a hybrid conglomeration of contradictory impulses. Kevin Quirk notes that self-proclaimed anti-Oprah literary snobs like Jonathan Franzen often view literature as therapeutic in the best sense. Indeed, for the last thirty years, literary critics have argued convincingly that the "literary" is multiple, contested, and culturally contingent. By investigating the hybrid interplay of Oprahfication and the literary, scholars may begin to raise other questions: Why can't an aesthetic of identification and emotion be considered literary? How do different modes of the literary compete? What are the literary elements of the therapeutic—in other words, how is emotional authenticity *performed?*

These are questions that Oprah has avoided in the Book Club. Lewis noted that Oprah emphasizes identification, not form. Oprah's success has come from her embrace of emotional transparency and authenticity. Tensions over these terms, however, have erupted continually over the lives of the Book Club, beginning (at least) with *Paradise* and culminating, in the first Book Club, with Franzen. His discomfort with performing emotional authenticity on the show brought the "literary" and the "therapeutic" into visible conflict. I don't think it's an accident that shortly after this incident, and the media frenzy that followed, Oprah suspended the Book Club. Rather than fight this larger cultural battle, she cashed in her chips and went home.

Oprah, then, has tried to disavow her role as literary critic, first by suspending the Book Club, and then by reinventing it (a process that is ongoing). Kathleen Rooney suggests that the first reinvention, the classics, was intended to mute the highbrow critics; as Oprah herself said, "I just want to read great books without it becoming controversial" (254). And it seemed to work. "Far fewer people," Rooney writes, rushed to condemn Winfrey's efforts in 2003 than in 1996 (248–49) because her advocacy for classics made it difficult for "Winfrey's usual detractors—both in the media and in the academy . . . to find much to complain about" (250, 253 251).

Rooney finds an innately democratic impulse in this move—a "conviction that, far from being fixed and immutable, culture is fluid and flexible, with the potential to reach—and to be reached by—virtually everyone" (255). I am less optimistic; the "classics" Book Club implicitly accepts the fixity of cultural hierarchies in her embrace of the term "classic." By shifting focus, she, like her critics, accepts the distinction of the literary and the therapeutic; she simply brings forward the "literary" in her "classics" book club. Indeed, Rooney concedes that Oprah "has not bothered to outline her official criteria of what constitutes a 'classic'—nor is she likely to do so" (256). The move to the classics was a retreat, an attempt to avoid the controversy of literary debates without claiming her own right to mediate or influence them. But it dodges the central question that critics like Cecilia Konchar Farr have identified as central to the Book Club: a gendered middlebrow aesthetic tradition, grounded in identification and affect, that has shadowed and contested the more "masculine" literary traditions of high school and college curricula.

This implicit aesthetic marked much of the first incarnation, but, in the second, she tries to cover all the bases. While the term "classics" enmeshed the Book Club in an implied cultural hierarchy, the actual selections of the classics Book Club mixed "obvious" selections like Faulkner and Tolstoy with writers like Ernest Gaines and Pearl S. Buck, whose relationship to the canon is more complicated. By dodging the central question—why can't an aesthetic of identification and emotion be considered literary?—Oprah missed the opportunity to make a case for her own cultural intervention.

The selection of *The Good Earth* exemplifies these unresolved issues. On the surface, Buck appeared to be a very safe selection. She was the first American woman to receive the Nobel Prize, and the only one before Toni Morrison. Her books are still in print, and a biography of Buck, written by a full professor at the University of Pennsylvania, was released within the last ten years. Surely, Oprah may have reasoned, this selection was beyond reproach.

Of course, it was not. Pearl Buck has been patronized by critics ever since she first received the Nobel Prize in 1937, and she is rarely included in the list of great modernists from American literature. Critics tend to find her a jingoistic, simplistic "women's novelist," and even Peter Conn's biography has not made Buck a legitimate modern American writer in any of the competing canons of the period. Asian American critics dismiss her writing about China as inauthentic, Orientalist stereotype. As a cultural outsider, they argue, Buck served up images that confirm common, and mistaken, cultural impressions of China. Modernist critics dismiss her as a commodified sentimentalist, and twentieth-century feminist critics tend to favor more dramatic linguistic and cultural radicals.

For these very reasons, Oprah's selection was more prescient, and timely, than she knew. Pearl Buck first came to fame through the Book-of-the-Month Club, her generation's version of the Oprah Book Club, and she wrote for women's magazines, appealing to women reader's emotions and preexisting predilections. Buck was also famous for her political activism; she denounced racism and imperialism as un-American, and saw literature as a legitimate means of activism. She used her 1937 Nobel Prize address to make a case for the vernacular literary traditions of China, an early argument for multiculturalism.[1]

Though much of Oprah's Web site information on *The Good Earth* makes reference to these interesting aspects of Buck's career, much of the apparatus, both in the study questions and in the questions put to expert Peter Conn, focused on cultural stereotypes of China—Conn fielded numerous questions about foot-binding, for example. The cover featured a Chinese courtesan, despite the fact that a 1930s version of this cover outraged Pearl Buck because it emphasized sexual difference instead of common humanity.

Buck might have been an interesting case study for engaging the questions of gender and literary authority that have dogged Oprah's Book Club. Indeed, Buck might have become one of Oprah's literary foremothers, a link in an unbroken chain of women's reading and writing. Instead, Buck became just one more random shot in a scattershot of haphazard "authoritative" texts. The "classics" Book Club, then, provided no resolution to Oprah's issues with literary authority.

It shouldn't have come as a surprise when Oprah moved back to more familiar ground in the third incarnation of the Book Club—back to the "emotional honesty" of affect. Her cultural influence has been predicated on this link. Books that produce this quintessential middlebrow experience for her predominantly women readers became, once again, her primary focus and interest.

What was somewhat surprising—and, as it turned out, ill-fated—was Oprah's selection of James Frey's *A Million Little Pieces*. In the aftermath of the Frey scandal, it may be difficult to remember what an edgy choice the book was. *A Million Little Pieces* has random capitalizations of nouns within sentences, a prodigious amount of profanity, and graphic descriptions of feces, vomit, blood, and gore. It also questions the principles of Alcoholics Anonymous and, by implication, the self-help principles that have fueled the success of Oprah's talk show. Frey insists that going to therapy, submitting to a "higher power," naming alcoholism as a disease, and identifying genetic and environmental "causes" for substance abuse are simply sniveling excuses for a weak, effeminate character. His own mottos—"hold on" and "FTB-SITTTD," for "Fuck The Bullshit, It's Time to Throw Down," which he tattooed on his arms—challenge the very core of what Oprah does on her show every day.

Of course, in other ways James Frey conforms to Oprah's persona and worldview perfectly. His writes about his own experience brutally, and he never hesitates to place himself in a negative light. His willingness to write about himself this way—throwing up "chunks of flesh" every morning, beating up queers, breaking his parents' hearts—matches the other kinds of emotional nakedness that Oprah's talk show—and Book Club—values. His success story also provides the necessary balm to the edgier parts of his story. During the episode, she revealed that often while reading the book, she had to stop and say, "He's okay; he's still alive." Frey's embrace of his role as "Oprah's Book Club writer," his declaration that it was an honor to be chosen, was an additional incentive for Oprah.

Indeed, despite Frey's rejection of self-help, he must have seemed to Oprah a convert of sorts to her feminized, therapeutic literary values. Frey adopts an aggressively masculine voice in his memoir, but he talks about all of his angst in enormous detail, unlike the laconic masculine heroes of film. And when it comes to women, he is as romantic—even sappy—as they come. His love affair with Lilly, the "hooker with a heart of gold," is particularly romanticized. He is constantly rhapsodizing about her beauty, and staring at her publicly (101–102). Lilly guides him to his first breakthrough in rehab: tears and an embrace of "broken-ness."

In fact, in scenes with beautiful girls, Frey acts much like a romance hero, tough and gruff but willing to be redeemed through the love of a good woman. In the larger tradition of women's writing, particularly in the nine-teenth century, women writers hoped that their feminine values would trans-form the larger society, embracing both men and women in the larger, Christian, and superior "women's culture" (Tompkins 144). Frey seemed to have been similarly transformed over the course of his memoir. James Frey must have seemed a perfect choice for Oprah's revived focus on the therapeu-tic value of the reading experience.

As we all know by now, of course, he wasn't. It is impossible, after the scandal, to approach *A Million Little Pieces* without prejudice and decide whether Oprah and her staff should have known. Certainly, she was not the only one taken in. What struck me, however, was how self-consciously, even pretentiously, literary the tone of Frey's novel is. The resonances are legion—the "mean street" image of naturalists like Frank Norris and Stephen Crane; hard-boiled detective fiction by Dashiell Hammett and Raymond Chandler; Williams Burroughs's *Naked Lunch*, and other shocking memoirs of/creative nonfiction about drug addiction, like Hunter S. Thompson's *Fear and Loathing in Las Vegas*, Jerry Stahl's *Permanent Midnight*, and Jim Carrol's *The Basketball Diaries;* Jay McInerney's *Bright Lights, Big City*; even his contem-porary memorist/competitors like Dave Eggers and David Foster Wallace.

The conventions of each of these literary traditions help explain many of the liberties Frey takes with his story. *A Million Little Pieces* is a casebook on how the therapeutic is performed. One can see self-conscious literary ges-tures all through the text. The dramatic beginning, when Frey wakes up and doesn't know where he is, has precedents. Jay McInerney's *Bright Lights, Big City* begins with the title, "It's Six A.M. Do You Know Where You Are?" A later subheading in *Naked Lunch* is titled "*What Are You Doing Here? Who Are You?*" And since "I don't know what I am doing there nor who I am," the narrator "decide[s] to play it cool and maybe I will get the orientation before the Owner shows. . . . So instead of yelling "Where Am I?" cool it and look around and you will find out approximately" (199). Frey's own awakening ("I wake to the drone of an airplane engine and the feeling of something warm dripping down my chin. I lift my hand to feel my face. My front four teeth are gone, I have a hole in my cheek, my nose is broken and my eyes are swollen nearly shut. I open them and I look around and I'm in the back of a plane and there's no one near me. I look at my clothes and my clothes are covered with a colorful mixture of spit, snot, urine, vomit and blood" [1]) is much more dramatic, but just as predetermined.

Frey's bravado about police officers runs through the text:

These were Small-Town Cops, fat stupid Assholes with mustaches and beer guts and guns and badges. I knew them and they knew me. In the years I had spent in that Town, I had openly taunted them. . . . I laughed and told them to get the fuck out of my face. . . . The car ride down to the Station was bullshit. I sang the National Anthem at the top of my lungs, and in between renditions, asked the Cops when we were stopping for pie. (233)

In Frey's actual encounters with the police (which were infrequent), he appears to have been much more polite, even cowed ("A Million Little Lies" 4). But suspicion of "pigs" is a common theme in much of this literary tradition. William Burroughs embeds a critique of the police in *Naked Lunch:*

And always cops: smooth college-trained state cops, practiced, apologetic patter, electronic eyes weigh your car and luggage, clothes and face; snarling big city dicks, soft-spoken country sheriffs with something black and menacing in old eyes color of a faded grey flannel shirt. (12)

Hard-boiled detectives harbor similar doubts about police corruption and competence; their police officers are always fat, jovial, and treacherous.

Frey's descriptions of fights and almost-fights are straightforward, tinged with macho bravado. In one representative encounter, Frey stands up to the counselor:

Lincoln steps forward, I lean against the back of the bed. He looms over me, puts on his fighting face.
You're going to clean them whether you want to or not and you're going to do it right now and you're not going to say another word about it. You understand me?
I push myself off the bed and I stand and I stare him in the eye.
You gonna force me?
I stare him in the eye.
You gonna try to force me?
I stare him in the eye.
Come on, Lincoln. What are you gonna do?
We stare at each other, breathe slow, clench our jaws, wait for a jump.
I know what is going to happen and that gives me the advantage. I

know that if he touches me he'll lose his job. I know the job is too important to him to risk for me. I know he's gotten soft after years of sobriety and I know that at this point, the black clothes and the boots and the haircut are little more than a costume. I know nothing is going to happen and that he has taken this so far is humorous to me. I laugh in his face. (97–98)

Frey combines aggressive bravado with ironic humor because he knows he is tougher and smarter, and therefore more manly. In a similar scene in Dashiell Hammet's *Red Harvest*, the Continental Op describes a fight:

Jerry had another try at me. The girl spoiled it by heaving the corpse at him. The dead yellow head banged into his knees. I jumped for him while he was off-balance.

The jump took me out of the path of Thaler's bullet. It also tumbled me and Jerry out into the hall, all tangled up together.

Jerry wasn't tough to handle, but I had to work quick. Ther was Thaler behind me. I socked Jerry twice, kicked him, butted him at least once, and was hunting for a place to bite when he went limp under me. I poked him again where his chin should have been—just to make sure he wasn't faking—and went away on hands and knees, down the hall a bit, out of line with the door. . . .

I grinned at Thaler and said. "Well, this is nice," before I saw that Rolff had another gun, centered on my chubby middle. That wasn't so nice. But my gun was reasonably level in my hand. I didn't have much worse than an even break. (105–106)

The straightforward style, the competence, even the grinning at the bested foe—all of Frey's stylistic choices with violence resonate back to the hard-boiled detectives.

Even Frey's more graphic descriptions of pain and dreams about using invoke the fantastic dream sequences of *Naked Lunch*. In one user's dream, Frey writes:

Roaring pit bulls straining chains. A dead grass yard. Rats scurry across the floor they bit sleeping faces. An empty House no furniture nothing. It is empty but for empty People. The ghosts of the rock. There is smoke in the air mixed with gas and formaldehyde. I am screaming. (219)

Contrast this fragmentary style with William Burroughs:

white flash . . . mangled insect screams . . .
I woke up with the taste of metal in my mouth back from the dead
trailing the colorless death smell
afterbirth of a withered grey monkey
phantom twinges of amputation . . . (212)

In the context of fragmentary hallucinations and paranoid fantasies, Frey's extended, graphic description of the dentist makes more sense. One selection should suffice to give the flavor of the section:

The drill is back on and it is working through the fragment of my left front tooth. It is moving through a thinner, more fragile section of bone, so it works quickly. It shoots the grit, makes the hole, penetrates. At the point of penetration, a current shoots through my body that is not pain, or even close to pain, but something infinitely greater.

Everything goes white and I cannot breathe. I clench my eyes and I bite down on my existing teeth and I think my jaw might be breaking and I squeeze my hands I dig my fingers through the hard rubber surface of the tennis balls and my fingernails crack and my fingernails break and my fingernails start to bleed and I curl my toes and they fucking hurt and I flex the muscles in my legs and they fucking hurt and my torso tightens and my stomach muscles feel as if they're going to collapse and my ribs feel as if they're caving in on themselves and it fucking hurts and my balls are shrinking and the shrinking fucking hurts and my dick is hard because my blood hurts and my blood wants to escape and is seeking exit through my dick and my dick fucking hurts and my arms are straining against the thick blue nylon straps and the thick blue nylon straps are cutting my flesh and it fucking hurts and my face is on fire and the veins in my neck want to explode and my brain is white and it is melting and it fucking hurts. There is a drill in my mouth. My brain is white and it feels as if it's fucking melting. I cannot breathe. Agony. (69)

The repetition of phrases and sentences; the graphic description of bodily functions; the Hemingwayesque lack of subordination; even the hackneyed metaphor of "white" for "pain"—all combine to construct a dream sequence that gestures toward Burroughs, a metaphoric passage about addiction.

The naturalist tradition values the underside of American cities as more real and authentic than more prosperous, middle-class locales. Hard-boiled detective fiction featured succinct tough guys, loners who can slip in and out of any cultural moment, whose ability to see past lies and hypocrisy to the truth is rivaled only by their ability to take a punch. Addiction memoirs emphasize the degradations of drug abuse in shocking detail; the protagonists of these tales always leave a safe middle-class existence for the degradations of flophouses, prostitution, and family betrayal. McInerney's tale of drugs in the big city takes the reader through the protagonist's own experience, as if in real time; McInerney even uses "you" instead of "I" to encourage readers to identify themselves with the protagonist. All these features of plot, characterization, and even language animate Frey's text—so much so that Harold Bloom's argument about the "anxiety of influence" seems particularly germane.

Frey, in other words, filters his own experience through these preexisting structures of feeling; what seems authentic is utterly dependent on the kinds of traditions commonly used to describe such experiences. And the structures of feeling are explicitly, even aggressively, masculine. Through his performance, he could become a man so hard-boiled that even the shadowy Mafia boss is frightened of him, so tough that he survives four root canals without Novocain, so stoic that only he, of all his recovery friends, survives. As a suburban literary geek from Ohio, being a "bad guy" who can throw down with anyone fulfilled Frey's biggest fantasy. *Men*—his literary forebears taught him—face the world as it is, and stoically "hold on."

Frey's embrace of manhood, of course, is as sentimental as the implicitly feminine therapeutic tradition he rejects in treatment. It is Frey's "melodrama of beset manhood," to use Nina Baym's still-relevant phrase, that defines *A Million Little Pieces* and the literary tradition he so explicitly honors—or rips off. Because of his literary influences, success, survival, and manhood are so inextricably linked that women appear as temptations, or nags, or muses, but never as heroes. Frey doesn't seem to realize that masculinity is as potently addictive as the Twelve Steps. He can't resist over-the-top masculine performances. For example, in a deeply ironic passage, Frey denounces those who falsify the truth of addiction:

> An Addict is an Addict. It doesn't matter whether the Addict is white, black, yellow or green, rich or poor or somewhere in the middle, the most famous Person on the Planet or the most unknown. It doesn't matter whether the addiction is drugs, alcohol,

crime, sex, shopping, food, gambling, television, or the fucking Flinstones. The life of the Addict is always the same. There is no excitement, no glamour, no fun. There are no good times, there is no joy, there is no happiness. There is no future and no escape. There is only an obsession. An all-encompassing, fully enveloping, completely overwhelming obsession. To make light of it, brag about it, or revel in the mock glory of it is not in any way, shape or form related to its truth, and that is all that matters, the truth. That this man is standing in front of me and everyone else in this room lying to us is heresy. The truth is all that matters. This is fucking heresy. (178)

Frey is clearly protesting too much here, since he dramatizes his own life just as shamelessly as the rock star he parodies. He was a well-to-do frat boy who struggled with alcohol and cocaine, but chasing "the rock" in crack houses with whores and hard-core addicts seemed more "real" than getting shit-faced at a kegger. As Trysh Travis devastatingly frames the choice, "Why be just a run-of-the-mill jackass when you can make yourself into a monster?" He thus creates a male melodrama of addiction.

Melodrama, of course, is usually associated with women writers, and has been one of the most common epithets used to dismiss the selections of Oprah's Book Club. But as Nina Baym and many other feminist critics have noted, the literary tradition tends to see masculine posturing as "authentic" and feminine posturing as "sentimental." A women's middlebrow tradition, which Oprah's Book Club exemplifies, is the necessary correlative to critics' too willing acceptance of male melodrama as "realistic" and "gritty."

This raises, again, the question of why Oprah chose a book so aggressively masculine that it often seems to verge on camp. I believe that Oprah, like her critics, accepts the binary of "literary" and "therapeutic" without questioning the significant overlap between them. Oprah seemed to believe that his portrayal of himself as a "bad guy," as he described himself somewhat proudly in his first appearance on Oprah, made his narrative true in some fundamental way. Both parts of the binary come under question with the Frey incident. If the "therapeutic" is "literary," as Frey's aestheticization of his life suggests, this casts doubt on the power of emotional nakedness to confer truth in a transparent, unmediated way. If, on the other hand, the "literary" isn't a separate, accepted field of unchanging literary value, then Oprah's foray into the "classics" looks a bit silly, and her claims for the transformative power of literature are harder to justify.

There is, of course, another option for Oprah. She could articulate her Book Club as part of an ongoing middlebrow women's tradition, a legitimate, if contested, mode of the literary that incorporates what we call the therapeutic. So far, Oprah hasn't ever addressed these questions about gender and the literary/therapeutic dyad head on. Even her shellacking of Frey in his reappearance didn't get at these larger issues of the (feminine) therapeutic and the (masculine) literary. It instead focused on truth and lies, not the multiple ways that both masculinity and the therapeutic are performed.

These implicit tensions continue to haunt Oprah's Book Club. Since the Frey scandal, Oprah has chosen memoirs, novels, and self-help books. All of them, however, have been written by men. *Middlesex*, of course, complicates the very notion of gender, but Cormac McCarthy's writing is as self-consciously, even stereotypically, masculine as James Frey's memoir—even though his masculine melodrama is much more deftly performed. Oprah still seems to be trying to avoid controversy. Until Oprah can articulate these issues of literature and emotion in reading, especially in terms of gender, the Book Club will continue to be a problem. Exposing James Frey on her show must have been satisfying, but it did not solve the larger dilemma that the Book Club has become for her. Oprah—and Oprah scholars—must, I believe, interrogate the multiple valences of the literary directly to continue the complex work of Oprah's Book Club.

Note

1. For more information on Pearl Buck's career, see Jaime Harker's "Modernists Passing the Buck: 'Orientals,' Middlebrows, and *The Good Earth*." *Precursors and Aftermaths* (1.1) Spring 2000: 5–26.

Works Cited

Baym, Nina. "Melodramas of Best Manhood: How Theories of American Fiction Exclude Women Authors." *Locating American Studies: The Evolution of a Discipline*. Ed. Lucy Maddox. Baltimore and London: Johns Hopkins UP, 1999.

Burroughs, William S. *Naked Lunch*. New York: Grove, 1959.

Douglas, Ann. *Terrible Honesty: Mongrel Manhattan in the 1920s*. New York: Farrar, 1995.

Frey, James. *A Million Little Pieces*. New York: Anchor Books, 2003.

Hammett, Dashiell. *Red Harvest.* New York: Vintage, 1929.

McInerney, Jay. *Bright Lights, Big City.* New York: Vintage, 1984.

"A Million Little Lies: Exposing James Frey's Fiction Addiction." *The Smoking Gun.* http://www.thesmokinggun.com/jamesfrey/0104061jamesfrey1.html

Radway, Janice. "On the Gender of the Middlebrow Consumer." *Southern Atlantic Quarterly* 93.4 (Fall 1994): 820–45.

Rooney, Kathleen. *Reading with Oprah: The Book Club That Changed America.* Little Rock: U of Arkansas P, 2005.

Rubin, Joan Shelley. *The Making of Middlebrow Culture.* Chapel Hill: U of North Carolina P, 1992.

Tompkins, Jane. *Sensational Designs: The Cultural Work of American Fiction 1790–1960.* Oxford: Oxford UP, 1985.

Travis, Trysh. "James Frey: Feelings as Facts." *The Chronicle of Higher Education: The Chronicle Review* 52.22 (3 February 2006): B5.

CONTRIBUTORS

TIMOTHY AUBRY is an Assistant Professor in the English department at Baruch College. His articles have appeared in *Modern Fiction Studies,* the *Iowa Journal of Cultural Studies,* and *Critical Matrix.* He is now working on a manuscript devoted to middle-class reading cultures in the United States.

KIMBERLY CHABOT DAVIS is Assistant Professor of English at Bridgewater State College, where she teaches 20th-century American literature and film. Her first book, *Postmodern Texts and Emotional Audiences,* was published in 2007. She has also published articles in *LIT, Modern Fiction Studies, Twentieth Century Literature, South Atlantic Review, JPCS: Journal for the Psychoanalysis of Culture and Society,* and *The International Journal of Cultural Studies.* This essay is drawn from her new book project, Beyond the White Negro: Cross-Racial Empathy, White Audiences, and Contemporary African-American Culture.

KATE DOUGLAS is a Lecturer in the Department of English and Cultural Studies at Flinders University, South Australia. She researches and teaches primarily in the areas of contemporary fiction and non-fiction, and is particularly interested in the social and political utility of contemporary literature. Her current project is an investigation of the myriad ways in which we read or witness representations of trauma in contemporary life narrative texts.

CECILIA KONCHAR FARR is professor of English and Women's Studies at the College of St. Catherine. She teaches, studies, and writes about modernism, American literature, feminist theory, reception theory, and contemporary

U.S. culture. Her study of Oprah's Book Club, *Reading Oprah: How Oprah's Book Club Changed the Way America Reads*, was published by SUNY in 2004.

MARK HALL is Associate Professor of Rhetoric, Composition & Literacy Studies at California State University, Chico. He directs the University Writing Center and writes about popular culture, literacy, and writing pedagogy. His essay "The 'Oprahfication' of Literacy: Reading 'Oprah's Book Club'" appears in *College English* 65.6, July 2003. *American Icons: An Encyclopedia of the People, Places, and Things That Have Shaped Our Culture* includes his entry on Oprah Winfrey.

JAIME HARKER is an Assistant Professor in the English department at the University of Mississippi. She is the author of *America the Middlebrow: Women's Novels, Progressivism, and Middlebrow Authorship Between the Wars* (University of Massachusetts Press, 2008).

KELLEY PENFIELD LEWIS is a PhD candidate at Dalhousie University in Halifax, Nova Scotia. Her interest in Oprah fits within her ongoing work on cultural capital and reader reception. Her Master's thesis looked at how the 2001 Jonathan Franzen scandal with Oprah's Book Club spoke to the historical dialogue between middlebrow reading practices and the gatekeepers of "Highbrow Literature." Kelley's current doctoral research is on the *Paris Review* Interviews and the role of the author in mid-century America, and is generously supported by a Canada Graduate Scholarship and a Killam Fellowship.

KATHRYN LOFTON (A.B., University of Chicago, M.A. and Ph.D., University of North Carolina) is an assistant professor in the Department of Religious Studies and the Program in American Studies at Indiana University, Bloomington. A specialist in nineteenth- and twentieth-century American religious history, she has published articles in *Church History, Religion and American Culture, Religious Studies Review*, and the *Journal of Popular Culture* on the evangelical preacher as an American type, the fundamentals of theological modernism, masculinity in religious research, and the ritual practices of Oprah Winfrey's multimedia empire. She is currently working on her first monograph, *The Modernity in Mr. Shaw: Fundamentalisms and Modernisms in American Culture*. She is also co-editor, with Laurie Maffly-Kipp, of *Women's Work: An Anthology of African-American Women's Historical Writings, 1832–1920* (Oxford University Press, forthcoming).

MICHAEL A. PERRY is currently a Ph.D. Candidate at Arizona State University. His current doctoral research focuses on blues music and African American literature and continues his interest in the intersections of academic and popular cultures: Toni Morrison's participation with Oprah Winfrey's Book Club has proven fertile ground to explore the potential such an intersection brings.

ANA PATRICIA RODRÍGUEZ is Associate Professor of U.S.Latina/o and Central American Literatures in the Department of Spanish and Portuguese at the Universityof Maryland, College Park. Her research focuses on U.S.Latina/o and Central American literary and cultural production, popular culture, and transnational cultural studies. Her forthcoming book, *Dividing the Isthmus: Central American Transnational Literatures and Cultures*, examines metaphors and narrative geographies of economic, symbolic, and human excess in Central American isthmian and diasporic texts.

KATHLEEN ROONEY is a founding editor of Rose Metal Press, and the author of *Reading With Oprah* (University of Arkansas, second edition 2008). Her book of poetic collaborations with Elisa Gabbert, *That Tiny Insane Voluptuousness*, is available from Otoliths Books, and her first collection of poetry, *Oneiromance* (an epithalamion), won the 2007 Gatewood Prize from Switchback Books. She lives in Chicago with her husband, the writer Martin Seay, and works as a Senate Aide.

KEVIN QUIRK received his PhD in American Studies from the University of Iowa and is Visiting Assistant Professor of English and American Studies at DePaul University in Chicago. His research interests include contemporary American fiction, literary reception and the history of reading. His current research investigates the literary texts claimed by the American counterculture in the sixties.

SIMON STOW is the author of *Republic of Readers: The Literary Turn in Political Thought and Analysis* (State University of New York Press, 2007). He is an Associate Professor in the Department of Government at the College of William and Mary.

JULIETTE WELLS, an assistant professor of English at Manhattanville College, is a co-editor of *The Brontës in the World of the Arts* (Ashgate, 2008). She has published articles on chick lit and women's literary history; George Eliot and amateurism; Jane Austen and the arts; and Jasper Fforde's reworking of *Jane Eyre*. She is currently working on several projects related to Austen's presence in contemporary popular culture.

VIRGINIA WELLS was the popular-materials specialist at Chantilly Regional Library in Fairfax County, Virginia, from its opening in 1995 until her retirement in 2008. She received her MLS from Columbia and has been an active member of book clubs for several decades.

YUNG-HSING WU is an Assistant Professor of English at the University of Louisiana at Lafayette, where she teaches critical theory and ethnic and women's literatures. Her work has appeared in *Modern Fiction Studies*, the journal of the *National Women's Studies Association*, *PMLA*, and *Profession*. She is working on an essay titled "Oprah and Faulkner (with Toni Morrison, too)."

Oprah's Book Club List

2008
A New Earth By Eckhart Tolle

2007
The Measure of a Man by Sidney Poitier
The Road by Cormac McCarthy
Middlesex by Jeffery Eugenides
Love in the Time of Cholera by Gabriel Garcia Marquez
The Pillars of the Earth by Ken Follett

2006
Night by Elie Wiesel

2005
A Million Little Pieces by James Frey
As I Lay Dying by William Faulkner
The Sound and the Fury by William Faulkner
A Light in August by William Faulkner

2004
One Hundred Years of Solitude by Gabriel Garcia Marquez
The Heart is a Lonely Hunter by Carson McCullers
Anna Karenina by Leo Tolstoy
The Good Earth by Pearl S. Buck

2003
East of Eden by John Steinbeck
Cry, The Beloved Country by Alan Paton

2002
Sula by Toni Morrison
Fall on Your Knees by Ann-Marie McDonald

2001
A Fine Balance by Rohinton Mistry
The Corrections by Jonathan Franzen
Cane River by Lailita Tademy
Stolen Lives: Twenty Years in Desert Jail by Malika Oufkir
Icy Sparks by Gwyn Hyman Rubio
We Were the Mulvaneys by Joyce Carol Oates

2000
House of Sand and Fog by Andre Dubus III
Drowning Ruth by Christina Schwarz
Open House by Elizabeth Berg
The Poisonwood Bible by Barbara Kingsolver
While I Was Gone by Sue Miller
The Bluest Eye by Toni Morrison
Black Roads by Twani O'Dell
Daughter of Fortune by Isabel Allende
Gap Greek by Robert Morgan

1999
A Map of the World by Jane Hamilton
Vinegar Hill by A. Manette Ansay
River, Cross My Heart by Breena Clarke
Tara Road by Maeve Binchy
Mother of Pearl by Melina Haynes
White Oleander by Janet Fitch
The Pilot's Wife by Anita Shreve
The Reader by Bernhard Schlink
Jewel by Bret Lott

1998
Where the Heart Is by Billie Letts
Midwives by Chris Bohjalian
What Looks Like Crazy on an Ordinary Day by Pearl Cleage
I Know This Much is True by Wally Lamb
Breath, Eyes, Memory by Edwidge Danticat
Black and Blue by Anna Quindlen
Here on Earth by Alice Hoffman
Paradise by Toni Morrison

1997
The Meanest Thing to Say by Bill Cosby
The Treasure Hunt by Bill Cosby
The Best Way to Play by Bill Cosby
Ellen Foster by Kaye Gibbons
A Virtuous Woman by Kaye Gibbons
A Lesson Before Dying by Ernest Gaines
Songs In Ordinary Time by Marry McGary Morris
The Heart of a Woman by Maya Angelou
The Rapture of Canaan by Sheri Reynolds
Stones from the River by Ursula Hegi
She's Come Undone by Wally Lamb

1996
The Book of Ruth by Jane Hamilton
Song of Solomon by Toni Morrison
The Deep End of the Ocean by Jacquelyn Mitchard

INDEX